걸프 사태

언론 보도 및 분석

걸프 사태

언론 보도 및 분석

한국학술정보

| 머리말

걸프 전쟁은 미국의 주도하에 34개국 연합군 병력이 수행한 전쟁으로, 1990년 8월 이라크의 쿠웨이트 침공 및 합병에 반대하며 발발했다. 미국은 초기부터 파병 외교에 나섰고, 1990년 9월 서울 등에 고위 관리를 파견하며 한국의 동참을 요청했다. 88올림픽 이후 동구권 국교 수립과 유엔 가입 추진 등 적극적인 외교 활동을 펼치는 당시 한국에 있어 이는 미국과 국제사회의 지지를 얻기 위해서라도 피할 수 없는 일이었다. 결국 정부는 91년 1월부터 약 3개월에 걸쳐 국군의료지원단과 공군수송단을 사우디아라비아 및 아랍 에미리트 연합 등에 파병하였고, 군·민간 의료 활동, 병력 수송 임무를 수행했다. 동시에 당시 걸프 지역 8개국에 살던 5천여 명의 교민에게 방독면 등 물자를 제공하고, 특별기 파견 등으로 비상시 대피할 수 있도록 지원했다. 비록 전쟁 부담금과 유가 상승 등 어려움도 있었지만, 걸프전 파병과 군사 외교를 통해 한국은 유엔 가입에 박차를 가할 수 있었고 미국 등 선진 우방국, 아랍권 국가 등과 밀접한 외교 관계를 유지하며 여러 국익을 창출할 수 있었다.

본 총서는 외교부에서 작성하여 30여 년간 유지한 걸프 사태 관련 자료를 담고 있다. 미국을 비롯한 여러 국가와의 군사 외교 과정, 일일 보고 자료와 기타 정부의 대응 및 조치, 재외동포 철수와 보호, 의료지원단과 수송단 파견 및 지원 과정, 유엔을 포함해 세계 각국에서 수집한 관련 동향 자료, 주변국 지원과 전후복구사업 참여 등 총 48권으로 구성되었다. 전체 분량은 약 2만 4천여 쪽에 이른다.

2024년 3월

한국학술정보(주)

| 일러두기

· 본 총서에 실린 자료는 2022년 4월과 2023년 4월에 각각 공개한 외교문서 4,827권, 76만 여 쪽 가운데 일부를 발췌한 것이다.

· 각 권의 제목과 순서는 공개된 원본을 최대한 반영하였으나, 주제에 따라 일부는 적절히 변경하였다.

· 원본 자료는 A4 판형에 맞게 축소하거나 원본 비율을 유지한 채 A4 페이지 안에 삽입 하였다. 또한 현재 시점에선 공개되지 않아 '공란'이란 표기만 있는 페이지 역시 그대로 실었다.

· 외교부가 공개한 문서 각 권의 첫 페이지에는 '정리 보존 문서 목록'이란 이름으로 기록물 종류, 일자, 명칭, 간단한 내용 등의 정보가 수록되어 있으며, 이를 기준으로 0001번부터 번호가 매겨져 있다. 이는 삭제하지 않고 총서에 그대로 수록하였다.

· 보고서 내용에 관한 더 자세한 정보가 필요하다면, 외교부가 온라인상에 제공하는 『대한 민국 외교사료요약집』 1991년과 1992년 자료를 참조할 수 있다.

| 차례

정 리 보 존 문 서 목 록

기록물종류	일반공문서철	등록번호	2021010221	등록일자	2021-01-28
분류번호	721.1	국가코드	XF	보존기간	영구
명 칭	걸프사태 : 자료 및 언론보도, 1990-91. 전3권				
생 산 과	북미1과/중동1과	생산년도	1990~1991	담당그룹	
권 차 명	V.1 자료, 1990-91.3월				
내용목차					

0001

90 - 35

主要國際問題分析

이라크의 쿠웨이트 侵攻 : 脫冷戰時代의 地域紛爭

1990 . 9 . 5

外 務 部
外交安保研究院

主 要 國 際 問 題 分 析

이라크의 쿠웨이트 侵攻 : 脫冷戰時代의 地域紛爭

一 內   容 一

0003

이라크의 쿠웨이트 侵攻 : 脫冷戰時代의 地域紛爭

이라크의 쿠웨이트 侵攻과 合倂 등 훗세인 이라크 大統領의 覇權 追求로 빚어진 페르샤灣 危機는 脫冷戰時期의 地域紛爭의 중요한 前例가 될 가능성을 내포하고 있음. 國際經濟安定의 중요변수가 되는 에너지 供給의 확보를 위하여 美國과 西方國들은 이라크의 무조건 철수 등 강경한 經濟的·軍事的·外交的 대응을 하고 있고, 이에 대한 UN과 周邊 아랍國들의 支持로 이라크는 軍事的 劣勢와 國際的 孤立에 직면하고 있음. 美·英 등 이라크에 대한 制裁를 주도하고 있는 西方國들의 軍事的 挑戰 가능성과 더불어 이라크는 이라크·쿠웨이트 殘留 外國人들을 인질로 억류함으로써 兩側은 현재 첨예한 對峙狀態에 있음.

최근 美國은 蘇聯의 同意를 얻어 UN 安保理에서 經濟制裁에 이어 軍事力 使用에 있어서 國際的인 正當性을 확보함으로써 軍事行動의 가능성을 높이고 있음.

그러나 한편 이러한 美·이라크의 軍事對立을 協商으로 타개하기 위하여 드케야르 UN 事務總長이 개인자격으로 仲裁에 나서고, 훗세인 이라크 大統領이 이를 환영함으로써 協商氣運이 상승되고 있음. 軍事的 對決은 이라크에 있어 자살행위로 인식되고 있으며, 美國 역시 상당한 희생을 감수해야 할 것인 바, 美國이 승리할 경우에도 아랍圈과 國內外 輿論의 비판이 고조될 가능성이 있어 二重的인 負擔이 될 것임. 물론 協商이 훗세인의 제거라는 궁극적인 목표에 미치지 못할 가능성이 있으나, 中東地域에서 美國이 長期的 利益을 추구함에 있어서 軍事的 勝利보다는 協商에 의한 이라크軍의 쿠웨이트 撤收가 페르샤만 地域에서의 美軍 駐屯을 가능케 할 것이고, 美國의 影響力 堅持에 도움이 될 것임.

페르샤만 危機로 폭등세를 보이고 있는 國際油價는 戰爭에 의해 페르샤만 産油施設이 대규모로 파괴되는 경우를 제외하고는 危機 終熄 後에 배럴당 20-25 달러 선으로 복귀할 것으로 예상되고, 國際經濟 특히 先進工業國에 대한 經濟的 충격은 심각하지 않을 것임. 그러나 韓國과 같은 原油 依存度 및 對外輸出 依存度가 높은 國家에서는 상당한 景氣沈滯 要因으로 작용할 수 있음. 따라서 90年代 中盤부터 예상되는 高油價 時代에 대비한 에너지 정책을 시급히 시행하여야 할 필요성이 대두되고 있음.

페르샤灣 事態 이후에도 中東情勢는 資源(원유, 물), 領土問題와 理念對立 및 政治改革 등의 問題로 계속 不安定할 것으로 전망됨. 이번 事態를 게기로 中東各國은 安保能力을 제고할 것이고, 이에 따른 軍備增大는 地域不安을 더욱 조장할 수 있음. 이라크 견제를 위해 시리아·이란 등이 美國과의 關係를 改善할 가능성이 높아지고, 이와 관련하여 레바논에서의 인질 석방문제가 진전될 可能性이 있음. 한편, 美國과 다수 아랍國家들과의 關係改善은 美國에 큰 부담요인으로 작용하여, 美國은 팔레스타인 문제해결을 위한 協商을 적극 추진할 것으로 보임.

- 2 -

0005

페르샤만 事態를 계기로 脫冷戰時代의 國際秩序는 美·蘇 兩國體制에서 억제되었던 地域紛爭의 增大傾向을 보일 것으로 예상됨. 이에 따라 地域紛爭 管理는 그 중요성에 따라 國際化, 多國化 努力의 양상을 띠게 되고, 美·蘇의 共同參與와 UN의 役割 增大 등이 예상됨. 그러나 蘇聯의 國力衰退와 改革의 信賴度를 構築하기 위한 노력에 비추어, 蘇聯의 적극 介入은 예상되지 않으므로 당분간 美國의 主導下에 危機管理가 행해질 것으로 보임. 따라서 脫冷戰時代에서 美國의 影響力은 감소되기 보다는 오히려 확대될 가능성이 있음.

韓國은 地域紛爭 管理의 國際化 傾向에 대비하여 對UN 外交를 강화하고, UN 單獨加入도 고려해야 할 것임. 美國의 世界的 役割 지속으로 빚어질 防衛分擔 增大 요구에 적절한 對應이 필요할 것이고, 이와 관련하여 韓國의 軍事 現代化를 강력하게 추진하여야 할 經濟的 二重負擔에 직면할 것으로 보임. 한편 地域安保管理를 위한 地域集團安保體制 構築 必要性이 증대됨에 따라 東北亞 6者會談의 當爲性에 대한 關聯國家間 認識도 提高될 것이므로 이의 실현을 위한 外交的 努力이 필요할 것임.

- 3 -

1. 이라크의 쿠웨이트 侵攻 : 훗세인 大統領의 覇權 追求

가. 이라크는 기습적인 武力攻擊을 단행하여(1990. 8. 2) 쿠웨이트 王政을 붕괴시키고, 쿠웨이트 合倂을 선언하였음(8. 8). 또한, 이라크는 사우디 국경에 군대를 배치하여, 사우디 王政 진복을 위한 聖戰을 선포(8. 10)함으로써 地域紛爭의 확대가 우려되고 있음. 이에 따라 美國과 西方同盟國들이 多國籍軍을 페르샤만에 派兵하였으며, 國際油價가 폭등하여 국제적인 政治·經濟 危機를 야기시키고 있음.

나. 이라크의 對쿠웨이트 侵攻 名分은 쿠웨이트가 OPEC 産油쿼터를 위반하여 過剩生産함으로써 國際油價를 하락시키고, 이란· 이라크戰 동안 이라크의 原油를 도굴하여 이라크의 經濟難을 가중(이라크는 이로 인한 손실을 24억 달러라고 주장)시켰다는 것임.

다. 그러나 이라크의 쿠웨이트 侵攻은 國內外 情勢를 감안하여 볼 때, 훗세인 이라크 大統領의 政治·經濟·領土的 野慾에 따른 복합적 요인에 기인하고 있으며, 그의 政治的 野望이 主要 要因인 것으로 보임.

(1) 훗세인 이라크 大統領은 國內的으로 자신의 政治權力을 공고히 하고, 나아가서 아랍圈의 盟主로 부상하려는 의도를 갖고 있음.
  · 최근 이라크의 國內事情은 이란과의 長期戰爭으로 빚어진

- 4 -

0007

經濟難과 低油價로 인한 收入 감소, 戰爭으로 비대해진 軍部의 축소문제 및 훗세인의 終身制 大統領 체탈 등으로 야기된 國內의 政治的 불만을 타개하여야 할 입장임.

- 한편 최근 共産圈의 改革과 政治變化는 中東政治에서 아랍圈의 獨裁 및 王政에 대한 批判으로 나타나고 있으며, 政治改革의 필요성이 아랍人들 사이에서 대두되고 있음. 또한 冷戰終熄과 蘇聯의 改革으로 强硬아랍國들은 蘇聯이라는 강력한 支持 勢力을 잃게 되었고, 蘇聯의 유태人 移民 허용과 東歐의 이스라엘 承認 등은 아랍圈의 무기력함을 노정시켰음.

- 이와 같은 對內外的인 威脅要因의 증대와 國民들의 불만을 쿠웨이트 侵攻으로 전환시킴으로써 훗세인은 자신의 權力을 강화하고, 나아가서 아랍人들의 좌절감을 이용하여 汎아랍主義에 소극적이고 親美性向이 짙은 保守 王國들을 위협함으로써 아랍圈의 指導者로 부상하려는 것임.

(2) 經濟的 側面에서 이라크는 이란과의 戰爭으로 누적된 負償 問題와 油價下落으로 인한 原油 收入(年 150억 달러) 감소로 經濟建設에 곤란을 겪고 있음. 이에 따라 이라크는 쿠웨이트를 合倂하여 世界 原油 保有量의 1/5을 관할하게 되는 産油大國으로 부상하고, 향후 國際油價 動向에 결정적인 影響力을 행사하여, 美國과 西歐에 대항할 수 있는 아랍圈의 經濟·政治 大國으로 등장하려는 의도를 가짐.

- 5 -

0008

(3) 이라크의 쿠웨이트에 대한 領土 野慾은 지난 27년간의 領土 紛爭으로 나타나고 있음. 이라크는 쿠웨이트에 대한 領土權을 주장하여 쿠웨이트 獨立(1961)을 2년동안이나 인정하지 않았고, UN 加入과 아랍聯盟 加入을 반대하였음. 이라크는 현재까지 쿠웨이트와의 國境條約을 批准하지 않고 있으며, 페르샤만에 위치한 부비얀島와 와르바島의 반환을 계속 요구해 왔음. 특히 쿠웨이트의 풍부한 石油資源은 이라크의 領土權 主張을 강화하는 요인이 되었음. 또한, 이라크의 쿠웨이트 合倂은 과거 西歐의 植民主義 統治遺産을 청산하고, 아랍圈 統一과 社會主義로의 變革을 도모하는 이라크의 公式統治 理念인 바트 理念에 입각한 革命輸出 努力의 一環으로 볼 수 있음.

라. 이라크의 쿠웨이트 侵攻은 經濟問題에서 빚어진 侵攻이라기 보다는 覇權指向을 위한 事前에 준비된 軍事作戰으로 보이는 바, 그 理由는 다음과 같음.

(1) 이라크는 經濟問題를 外交的 努力으로 해결하려 하지 않았음. 이라크는 7월초부터 OPEC 쿼터위반을 이유로 쿠웨이트와 UAE를 공개적으로 비난하였고, 그후 이집트와 사우디의 仲裁로 개시된 이라크·쿠웨이트간 懸案問題를 해결하려는 협상에서도 非妥協的인 태도를 견지하면서 쿠웨이트 國境에 軍隊를 배치해 왔음.

(2) 이라크는 經濟難이 심각한 상황에서 原油輸出代金의 70%를 軍事部門에 사용하여 왔음.

- 6 -

0009

(3) 이라크 經濟가 극심한 危機에 직면하고 있었다고 볼 수도 없음.

- 이라크의 쿠웨이트·사우디에 대한 債務總額은 정확하게 계산할 수 없으나, 8년간의 戰爭中 매년 150억 달러의 지원을 받았고, 그 가운데 4분의 3은 사우디가 제공한 액수임(쿠웨이트 借款은 대부분 이라크의 原油販賣를 代行한 것임).

- 이와 같은 債務는 이란에 대한 保護資金의 성격을 띠고 있는 것으로, 利子도 없고 期限도 없는 長期 借款 形式으로 中東의 관례로 보아 대부분 갚지 않아도 무방한 것으로 알려지고 있음.

- 또한 사우디의 경우에는 貸與를 贈與로 바꾸었고, 쿠웨이트 支援의 경우에는 個人 資金支援의 경우에만 채무 성격을 띠고 있음.

(4) 이라크는 周邊 아랍國들의 介入을 배제하기 위하여 外交的인 事前 布石을 시도하였음.

- 이라크는 5월부터 라프산자니 이란 大統領에게 親書를 보내 領土問題 등에 이라크의 양보를 提議하는 등 宥和策을 모색하였고, 사우디에 대한 不可侵條約(1989. 3)을 제의하였음.

- 또한 아랍國과 아랍人들의 支持를 획득하기 위하여 이라크는 反美·反이스라엘 態度를 강화하여, 이집트· 요르단 등 아랍國들의 지지를 확보하였음.

- 7 -

0010

- 暫定 敵對國인 시리아의 경우에도, 이라크는 蘇聯의 支援 減少와 레바논 派兵으로 시리아의 軍事行動에 한계가 있을 것으로 판단하였을 것임.

(5) 최근 아랍 産油國들 가운데 페르샤만 保守王國들이 非産油 國에 대한 經濟支援을 삭감하고, 汎아랍主義 運動에 소극적인 태도를 보이자, 이에 대한 아랍人들의 비난이 증대됨. 훗세인 大統領은 이를 政治的으로 이용함.

- 훗세인 大統領은 아랍 産油量 14mbd에서 1달러씩을 떼어내 아랍地域 發展基金으로 이용할 것을 제의하여 非産油 아랍國들의 支持를 받았음.

- 한편 쿠웨이트는 原油産業을 國際化하여 高油價 政策 보다는 市場擴大가 OPEC의 戰略이 되어야 한다는 입장을 취하고 있으며, 사실상 쿠웨이트는 原油收入을 外國投資에 돌려 OPEC國家 가운데 政府豫算의 油價 依存度가 가장 낮음.

- 이러한 배경하에 이라크는 쿠웨이트의 油價政策이 美國과 西歐 帝國主義의 目的에 이용되고 있다고 주장하여, 쿠웨이트에 대한 攻擊을 對美·西方 공격으로 연계시켜 아랍人들의 支持를 얻는데 이용하고 있음.

(6) 이라크는 쿠웨이트의 不可侵條約締結 提案을 2개 島嶼返還을 구실로 거절하였음. 뿐만 아니라 쿠웨이트가 뺄리야티 이란 外相을 쿠웨이트에 초청(1989. 7)하여 이란과의 和解를 추구

- 8 -

0011

하는 등의 행동을 취하자, 이를 이라크의 影響力에 도전하는 것으로 인식함.

(7) 또한 美·蘇의 經濟·軍事力 약화로 中東地域에서 勢力空白이 야기되자, 훗세인은 이를 이용하여 페르샤만 地域 霸權 政策을 追求함.

---

2. 美國과 西方의 强硬對應 : 脫冷戰時代의 國際秩序 確立

가. 美國은 이라크의 侵攻 事態에 원상회복이라는 확고한 의지와 일관된 자세로 經濟的, 軍事的, 外交的 압력을 가하고 있음.

나. 美國은 이라크의 즉각적이고 무조건적인 撤收, 原狀回復(알사바 王政의 회복), 사우디 防衛 및 美國人 保護를 목표로 友邦國의 協調와 UN을 통한 國際的 支持를 추구하고 있음.
美國은 UN의 經濟制裁 措置, 外國人 人質 釋放 要求 등 UN 決議案을 실행하기 위한 多國籍軍의 최소한의 武力使用을 허용 받는 등 外交的 努力에 성공하고 있으며, 동시에 脫冷戰時代의 美·蘇協力을 실현시키고 있음(UN 決議案 內容은 附錄 참조).

다. 또한 美國은 親美 아랍國들을 설득하여 사우디·UAE, 카타르에 대한 軍事基地 使用權을 얻어냄. 한편 이집트의 주도 아래 아랍 聯盟 12個國은 아랍聯合軍의 페르샤만 派兵을 결정·파병하였 으며, GCC(걸프만 協力會議) 5個國도 공동 대응하기로 결의 하였음.

- 9 -

0012

라. 美國은 原狀回復이라는 원칙에 입각, 이라크의 무조건 撤收를
주장하며 經濟制裁를 통한 「枯死作戰」을 수행하고, 美軍의
增強으로 사우디 防禦에서 軍事攻擊 態勢로 전환하는 등
對이라크 威脅을 증대시키고, 國際的인 協商努力은 이라크軍
撤收에 관한 사항에 국한시킨다는 強硬한 立場을 견지하고 있는
바, 그 理由는 다음과 같음.

(1) 이라크의 쿠웨이트 侵攻은 단순한 地域紛爭과 覇權鬪爭이라는
차원에 그치지 않고, 그 事態 處理 여하가 향후 脫冷戰時代
에서 야기될 수 있는 地域紛爭을 해결하고 예방한다는 점에서
紛爭解決의 중요한 前例가 될 수 있다는 것임. 따라서 美國은
美・蘇 데땅트로 紛爭 可能地域에서 勢力眞空狀態가 생기고
있음을 인식하고, 이에 따른 武力紛爭 可能性을 사전에
예방하려는 것임.

(2) 國際經濟體制 維持와 安定과 관련, 미국은 그 중요성이 증대
되고 있는 國際原油供給이 훗세인 이라크 大統領과 같은 獨裁
者의 影響力에 의해서 좌우되는 것을 방지하려 함. 1990년대
중반부터 페르샤만 沿岸 産油國들의 原油 增産能力에 世界
原油供給의 依存度가 더욱 높아질 것으로 예상되고 있어, 페르
샤만의 地域安定은 國際經濟 安定, 특히 美國과 美國의 同盟
國들의 經濟安定에 직접적인 영향을 미칠 수 있음.

(3) 美國은 이번 事態를 계기로 가능하면 훗세인과 같은 地域
不安定 要因을 제거하고 이라크의 軍事體制를 근본적으로 개조

- 10 -

0013

하여 地域勢力均衡에 대한 威脅要因을 제거하려 함. 美國은 이를 軍事力을 통하여 성취할 수도 있으나, 그것은 엄청난 政治·經濟的 損失은 물론 人的 희생을 수반할 것이므로 經濟 制裁 및 國際的 壓力을 통해 훗세인을 스스로 屈服시키든지 또는 이라크 國民과 軍部의 불만을 야기시켜 훗세인을 제거하는 등의 方法을 택할 가능성이 높음.

마. 과거 아랍圈을 지지해온 蘇聯은 당면한 國內經濟 問題解決에 美國과 西歐의 支援이 필수적이고, 이를 위한 對美·西歐 外交의 성과를 무산시키지 않기 위하여, 美國이 주도하고 있는 對이라크 强硬制裁 措置에 동조하고 있음. 사실 蘇聯은 이라크의 侵攻으로 빚어진 油價上昇으로 經濟的 利得을 보고 있기도 함. 그러나 蘇聯은 美國이 提案한 UN 憲章 42條(武力사용 허용)의 發動에 동의하였으나, UN 合同軍이 형성되지 않는 한, 蘇聯軍의 派遣을 회피하고 武力制裁 보다는 아랍圈의 自力으로 協商에 의한 해결을 강조하는 소극적인 자세로 이라크와의 전통적인 友好 關係에 있는 自國의 곤란한 입장을 극복하려 하고 있음. 그러나 蘇聯은 과거에도 페르샤만에서의 原油供給에 대한 美國의 戰略的 利害關係를 인정하여 왔으므로 이번 페르샤만 사태에서 美國의 主導權을 인정하여도 그 정치적 부담은 크지 않을 것임.

3. 아랍圈의 對應 : 地域 勢力均衡 維持

가. 아랍圈은 개전 초기 분열상을 보였으나, 이라크의 사우디 威脅과 사우디의 美國 및 多國籍軍에 대한 軍事基地 사용 허용 등 事態가 급진전하자, 地域內 勢力均衡에 의한 安定을 도모하고, 아랍형제국에 대한 武力侵攻을 응징하기 위하여, 이집트의 주도로 아랍 聯合軍 파견을 결정하였음.

나. 아랍聯盟은 이라크의 無條件 撤收와 原狀回復, 美軍 등 多國籍軍의 사우디 駐屯 支持 등으로 美國의 立場을 支持하고, 이집트, 시리아, 모로코 등이 地上軍을 派兵하였음.

다. 초기 이라크를 지지했던 요르단은 부쉬 美大統領과의 會談 이후 UN 制裁에 동의하고, 이란도 이에 동조함으로써 이라크 支持 勢力은 리비아, PLO 등 少數에 그치고 있음.

4. 이라크의 孤立 深化와 훗세인의 誤判

가. 이라크는 對쿠웨이트 侵攻直後 가중되는 美國과 西方側의 압력에도 불구하고 쿠웨이트를 合倂하고 國家動員令을 발동하여 사우디와의 國境에 軍事配置를 증강함으로써 일전불사의 決意를 보였음.

나. 이라크는 武力示威外에 사우디와의 對決을 聖戰으로 비유하여 아랍圈의 分裂을 유도하는 心理戰을 폈음. 홋세인은 協商條件으로 이스라엘의 占領地 撤收, 시리아軍의 레바논 撤收, 사우디에서의 美軍 撤收 및 對이라크 經濟制裁 解除 등을 제시하여 아랍圈의 支持를 얻어 外交的 孤立을 탈피하려 하였으나, 아랍聯盟의 아랍軍 派遣 決議로 인해 이라크의 孤立은 더욱 심화되었음.

다. 이라크는 國際的 孤立과 軍事的 劣勢에도 불구하고, 이라크·쿠웨이트에 체류중인 美·英 등 西方人들을 인질로 하여, 이들을 主要戰略施設에 분산시켜 美國의 攻擊에 대한 인간방패로 삼겠다는 威脅을 하고 있으나 이러한 措置는 오히려 國際輿論에 否定的인 影響을 주었음.

라. 홋세인 이라크 大統領의 정치적 야심은 아랍圈 統一과 社會主義로의 變革을 지향하는 바트 理念에 입각하고 있는 바, 이라크의 이러한 바트理念을 바탕으로 한 "革命輸出" 企圖는 다음과 같은 점에 비추어, 國際·地域情勢에 대한 잘못된 판단에 기인하고 있는 것으로 보임.

(1) 前述한 바와 같이 이라크의 쿠웨이트 侵攻은 脫冷戰時代의 國際秩序 構築에 否定的 影響을 미치는 중요한 前例가 되며, 美·蘇 등 西歐勢力의 經濟利益에 중요한 이해가 걸려 있다는 점을 간과함.

- 13 -

0016

(2) 아랍地域 政治에서 전통적인 相互牽制와 勢力均衡이 작용하고
　　있다는 점을 간과함.

　　・ 이집트는 아랍圈의 政治·文化 中心地이고 軍事的 强國
　　　　으로서 팔레스타인 문제를 포함한 地域政治에서 主導權을
　　　　견지하려는 입장을 취하고 있음.

　　・ 시리아는 蘇聯의 支援減少에도 불구하고 이라크의 軍事
　　　　威脅에 대항할 능력이 있고, 시리아軍의 레바논 撤收를
　　　　요구한 이라크의 主張은 시리아를 자극시켰음.

　　・ 사우디도 軍事·外交·經濟面에서 상당한 저력을 보유하고
　　　　있어 무기력한 상대는 아님.

　　・ 요컨대 이들 아랍國들은 周邊國의 國力增强에 민감하게 대응
　　　　하고 勢力 均衡을 통한 自國 安保를 위해서 이라크의
　　　　쿠웨이트 侵攻을 용인할 수 없는 입장임.

　　・ 또한 中東政治에서 아랍 指導者들이 이구동성으로 汎아랍
　　　　主義를 강조하고 있으나, 이는 다분히 國內政治用으로 이용
　　　　되어 왔고, 이번의 페르샤만 危機도 이라크의 國內 政治用
　　　　으로 이용되고 있는 측면이 있음.

(3) 현재 이라크의 쿠웨이트 侵攻으로 빚어진 地域紛爭이
　　다분히 長期的인 持久戰 양상으로 진행되고 있음을 감안할 때,
　　훗세인은 自國의 國力을 점검하는데 소홀하였음.

　　・ 이라크는 사실상의 內陸國으로 國家收入의 90-95%가 他國
　　　　領土를 통과하는 送油管에 의한 原油輸出에 의존하고

- 14 -

0017

있으며, 식량의 75%를 輸入에 의존하고 있음. 현재 食糧
備蓄量은 2-3개월분으로 추정되고 있음.

- 또한 戰後 國家建設에 필요한 물자의 대부분을 美國과
EC 등 先進國에 의존하고 있는 바, 이라크는 美國 및
西方國의 經濟 制裁에 극히 취약한 實情임.

- 따라서 이라크의 美國과 西方國을 상대로 한 長期戰
遂行은 사실상 불가능함.

(4) 훗세인은 執權初期 2년간을 제외하고는 계속적인 전쟁상태의
지속으로 말미암아 이라크 國民들과 軍人들의 政治的 支持를
더 이상 持續하기 어려운 실정에 직면하고 있음.

마. 이라크는 國際的 孤立을 타파하고 아랍圈의 支持를 얻기 위하여
美國과의 對決 보다는 이스라엘과의 戰爭을 선택할 가능성이
있고, 실제로 對이스라엘 戰爭을 사실상 공언하고 있음. 그러나
다음과 같은 점에서 이라크의 對이스라엘 侵攻은 현실적으로
어려움.

(1) 이스라엘은 이라크의 요르단 國境을 赤色線으로 경고하고
對이라크 전투준비 태세에 있음. 이스라엘과의 戰鬪는 地上
軍의 接戰이 거의 불가능하고 空軍力과 미사일 등의 現代戰
에서 이스라엘이 絶對的으로 優勢하므로 이라크의 막대한
피해가 예상 될 뿐 승산이 희박함.

(2) 한편 이라크가 主導하는 對이스라엘 戰爭에 아랍强國인
이집트, 시리아가 가담할 가능성도 적음. 이집트는 이스라엘

과의 平和條約 遵守에 더 큰 의미를 부여하고 있고, 또한
시리아가 레바논에서의 旣得權을 희생하면서 競爭國인
이라크를 支援할 가능성은 희박하기 때문임.

5. 協商·妥結 可能性 增大

가. 훗세인 이라크 大統領은 戰力의 절대적 劣勢와 世界輿論의 批判
으로 協商에 의한 妥結을 모색할 可能性이 크다고 判斷됨.

(1) 현재 이라크의 戰力은 美國과 多國籍軍에 비해 절대적인 劣勢에
있어, 戰爭挑發은 政治的 자살행위가 될 것임. 이라크軍은
제한된 正規戰 經驗을 가졌을 뿐이며, 俸給 支給 지연과 열악한
생활조건으로 기강과 사기가 저하되고 있음.

(2) 또한 이라크가 보유한 스커드 미사일 등 現代 武器도 정확성과
파괴력에서 뒤지고 있음.

(3) 化學武器 使用 威脅은 非武裝 民間人 密集地域에서는 효과가
있으나, 防禦裝備와 機動性을 갖춘 軍事作戰에는 효과가 적음.
또한 이라크의 化學武器 使用은 대량 보복능력이 없는 쿠르드
族이나 이란의 人海戰術에 선별적으로 사용되었을 뿐이며,
만일 이라크가 美軍을 상대로 化學武器를 사용할 경우에는
심각한 報復에 직면하게 될 것임.

(4) 對決이 長期化될 경우 美國에게 不利한 점도 없지 않으나,
이라크에게는 치명적일 可能性이 높음.

- 16 -

0019

나. 美國은 軍事力 增強과 對이라크 威脅으로 이라크의 쿠웨이트 撤收를 겨냥하고 있으며, 사우디 侵攻이나 人質에 대한 피해가 자행되지 않는 한. 美國이 戰爭을 挑發할 可能性은 높지 않음. 그러나 美國의 對이라크 戰略目標에 대해서는 强·穩 兩論으로 분열된 意見이 나타나고 있음.

(1) 强硬論은 獨裁者에게 줄 수 있는 教訓은 패배시키는 것 뿐이라는 주장으로 軍事報復과 훗세인 제거를 주장하고 있음.

(2) 穩健論은 사우디 防衛公約을 준수하면서 지속적인 國際的 壓力으로 쿠웨이트 撤收를 유도할 수 있다는 것임.

다. 美國이 軍事的인 劣勢에 있는 이라크에 대한 軍事的 勝利를 추구 할 경우, 美國은 政治的으로 이중부담을 안게 될 것임. 戰爭에 따른 상당한 희생은 國內輿論과 11월 中間 選擧에서 부정적으로 반영될 것이고, 나아가서 아랍圈과 世界輿論의 비판을 면하기 어려울 것임. 또한 戰爭에 따른 油價暴騰은 世界經濟에 심각한 충격을 가져다 줄 것임.

라. 현재 드 케야르 UN 事務總長의 仲裁努力을 훗세인이 환영하고 있어 쿠웨이트 撤軍과 外國人 人質 석방에 대한 協商妥結 可能性이 높아지고 있음. 美國도 「先撤收 後協商」의 테두리 內에서 協商 妥結을 모색할 경우, 戰略的인 利點을 확보할 수 있을 것임. 美國은 中東地域에서 장기적인 美國의 戰略的 利益을 확보하기 위한 方案을 모색하여야 할 것인 바, 그것은 우선 훗세인의 쿠웨이트 撤軍을 誘導하고, 향후의 地域安定을

- 17 -

0020

위하여 사우디·UAE 등 페르샤만 지역에서의 美軍의 駐屯 또는 軍事基地 利用을 확보하는 것임.

마. 9月 9日 개최 예정인 美·蘇 頂上間의 헬싱키會談에서 美國은 「先撤收 後協商」立場을 견지하고 이에 대한 蘇聯의 協調를 요청할 것이나, 中東地域에서의 蘇聯의 影響力 增大를 憂慮하여, 蘇聯의 仲裁役割을 원하지는 않을 것임.

바. 協商은 이라크의 쿠웨이트 撤軍後에 본격화될 것으로 예측되는 바, 구체적인 協商內容은 이라크·쿠웨이트간의 國境條約과 不可侵條約, 이라크의 부비얀과 와르바島의 이용 문제, 이라크에 대한 債務蕩減 및 經濟支援 問題 등으로 될 것으로 보임.

| 6. 地域 情勢 展望 |

가. 페르샤만 危機에 따른 美國의 影響力 增大

(1) 協商에 의한 妥結은 地域紛爭 要因의 완전한 해소 보다는 잠정적인 消防措置로 끝날 것으로 보이나, 美國의 對中東 影響力은 제고될 것임. 이에 따라 美國은 과거 소원했던 시리아 및 이란과의 關係改善을 통해 이라크를 견제하고, 나아가서 레바논인질 석방에 극적인 타결을 이룰 수도 있을 것임. 또한 美國은 親美 아랍國에 대한 武器支援과 經濟協力 강화로 中東에서의 對蘇優位를 견지할 것임.

- 18 -

0021

(2) 아랍圈에 대한 美國의 影響力 强化는 逆說的으로 이스라엘 에게는 負擔要因으로 작용할 것임. 美國은 아랍國들의 압력 으로 팔레스타인 문제 해결을 위한 이스라엘의 양보를 촉구할 것임. 이와 관련 예상되는 代案의 하나로서 美國은 이스라엘 安保에 대한 美國의 책임과 보장 아래 非武裝 팔레스타인 獨立國 樹立을 추진할 수 있을 것임. 이번 事態를 계기로, 脫冷戰時代의 地域 問題解決에 대한 美國의 影響力은 더욱 제고되고 있음.

나. 中東 各國들의 對應과 立場

(1) 아랍 各國은 自國의 安保를 위한 措置에 특별한 관심을 갖게 되었으며, 이에 따라 아랍國家間 軍備競爭 可能性이 증대되고 있음. 특히 GCC 6개국은 集團安保를 위한 協力을 강화하고, 쿠웨이트도 이에 대해 과거보다는 적극적으로 참여할 것임. 페르샤만 危機 이전에도 世界 武器去來의 40%가 中東地域에서 이루어지고, 美·蘇·中·西歐國家들은 對中東 武器販賣로 상당한 經濟的 利得을 취하여 왔음. 美國은 이번 事態를 계기로 GCC 6個國과 이집트, 터키, 모로코 등에 武器販賣를 강화하여 自國의 影響力 增大와 더불어 아랍國들의 軍備競爭을 더욱 부채질하고 있음. 그러나 向後 中東地域 安定을 위하여 美·蘇와 아랍國들의 軍備 縮小 努力이 倍加되어야 할 것임.

(2) 이라크·시리아의 公式統治理念인 바트理念은 이번 事態를 계기로 아랍圈에서 퇴색될 것으로 보임. 왜냐하면 아랍圈의

- 19 -   0022

統一과 社會主義로의 變革을 추구하는 바트理念은 아랍
형제국을 顚覆하는 好戰的인 革命理念으로 간주되어, 아랍
各國에서 바트理念에 대한 牽制가 강화될 것이기 때문임.

(3) 이번 事態로 요르단은 政治的으로 취약한 입장에 처하게 될
것임. 政治·經濟的으로 이라크에 대한 依存度가 높기 때문에
이라크를 두둔하게 된 요르단은 부시 美大統領과의 會談 이후
UN 制裁에 동참하는 등 二重外交를 추진함. 이로써 요르단은
향후 兩側으로부터 모두 소외될 위협성을 안게 되었음. 앞으로
요르단은 사우디, 이집트 등 反이라크 勢力의 信賴를 잃게 될
뿐만 아니라, 훗세인 이라크 大統領의 불확실한 支援과 威脅에
직면하게 될 可能性이 있음. 즉 요르단은 과거 쿠웨이트와
같이 中立的이고 二重的인 對外關係를 추구하고 있으나, 이에
따른 危險負擔은 쿠웨이트 경우와 같이 상대적으로 높아질
可能性이 큼.

(4) 아라파트 PLO 議長의 이라크 支持 態度는 PLO에 대한 穩健
아랍國들의 支持 減少는 물론, 美國과의 對話再開 努力에
부정적으로 작용하여 外交的 孤立을 초래할 可能性이 높음.
이와 같은 孤立을 타개하기 위하여 앞으로 PLO가 對이스라엘
強硬政策을 追求할 可能性도 있음.

다. 地域 紛爭 展望

(1) 資源, 領土, 理念 및 政治改革 要求 등의 복잡 다양한 요인
들은 中東地域國家들의 紛爭要因으로 尙存하고 있고, 脫冷戰

- 20 -

0023

時代의 多極化 傾向은 美·蘇의 影響力 減少로 인식되어 地域 紛爭을 可視化시킬 가능성이 높음.

(2) 中東地域의 産油國과 非産油國間의 貧富의 隔差는 汎아랍主義라는 구호 아래 貧·富國家間의 對立으로 발전될 가능성이 높음.

　· 現存하는 아랍經濟協力機構들(ACC, GCC, AMU)의 經濟協力은 政治 不安定 등의 부자환경의 미비로 資源配分이나 投資의 移動에 있어 거의 무의미하며, 다만 勞動移動에 의한 經濟 利得 配分에 그치고 있음.

　· 유럽市場統合은 아랍 經濟 統合을 주장하는 불만 세력에 대한 자극 요인으로 作用할 것임.

　· 水資源은 인구폭발과 식량난 해결에 主要資源이 되고 있으나, 나일江, 요르단江, 유프라테스江의 이용을 위요한 隣接國家들 간의 異見도 갈등요인으로 등장할 可能性이 있음.

(3) 西歐 植民統治로부터 獨立하면서 임의로 획정된 新生아랍國들의 國境線과 전통적인 생활방식 및 地理的 特殊性(사막 등)으로 빚어진 領土問題는 앞으로 地域國家間에 심각한 紛爭 要因으로 작용할 가능성이 있음.

(4) 이란의 回教原理主義와 이라크·시리아의 바트理念 등은 保守王政들과의 政治的 對立·葛藤 要因으로 작용할 可能性이 큼.

- 21 -

0024

(5) 中東의 王政과 獨裁統治에 대한 아랍人들의 政治改革 要求는 최근 回敎主義者들의 政治得勢를 가져오고, 이들에 대한 아랍人들의 支持 增大는 좌절감에 따른 단순한 「항의투표」 (protest vote) 次元에 그칠 것 같지는 않음.

(6) 이와 같은 아랍國家들 간의 갈등과 軍備統制問題 등을 協議하기 위한 地域協力機構의 創設과 이들의 役割 증대가 요구될 것이나, 현재와 같은 아랍國間의 紛爭과 相互不信 등에 비추어 이러한 努力이 可視化되는데에는 상당한 時日과 共同 努力이 요구될 것임.

---

7. 國際油價와 OPEC 問題

가. 이라크의 쿠웨이트 侵攻이 國際油價의 폭등을 가져와 國際油價가 쿠웨이트 侵攻 이전의 배럴당 10달러선에서 31달러선까지 폭등하였고, 페르샤湾 事態 進展에 따라 큰 폭으로 변하고 있음. 이러한 의미에서 이라크는 쿠웨이트 侵攻으로 油價上昇을 소극적으로 기다리는 것보다 효과적으로 油價上昇에 성공했으나, 經濟制裁措置로 직접적인 利得을 보지 못하고 있음. 그러나 현재의 國際油價는 需要供給에 의해 合理的으로 형성되고 있다기 보다는 다분히 心理的이고 投機的인 側面에서 형성되고 있음.

- 22 -

0025

나. 현재 페르샤만 危機가 熱戰으로 확산되지 않고(확산될 가능성도 높지 않음), 軍事對峙와 協商이 지속된다면, 油價는 배럴당 20-25달러 線에서 安定될 것으로 보이며, 과거 世界原油의 수급 상황을 고려하면 지속적인 油價暴騰은 예상되지 않음.

(1) 쿠웨이트 事態 이전의 世界原油 供給量은 2.7mdb(日當 270만 배럴)이 공급과잉 상태에 있었고, 지난 몇해동안의 공급과잉으로 原油輸入國들의 비축량은 많음.

(2) 이번 危機와 經濟制裁로 말미암아 世界原油 供給에서 4.3mdb이 감소되고, OPEC의 減産 決定으로 세계원유 수요 64mdb(89년 기준)에 비해 2.1mdb의 부족이 예상되고 있음. 그러나 사우디, UAE 등 OPEC國의 증산과 非OPEC 産油國들의 증산은 供給不足分을 메꿀 수 있고, 西方先進國(OECD)들의 備蓄分(340억 배럴)은 98일간을 지탱할 수 있으므로 向後 2년간 이라크·쿠웨이트의 供給不足分을 대체할 능력이 있음.

(3) 또한 과거 油價暴騰은 中小産油業者들의 市場參與 增大와 原油 輸入國들의 에너지 보존과 代替 에너지 開發 등으로 油價 下落을 가져왔고 OPEC의 권한을 제한하는 要因으로 작용하였음.

다. 따라서 최근의 油價暴騰으로 世界經濟 전반의 인플레·景氣沈滯 등 심각한 經濟難이 야기될 可能性은 그리 크지 않음.

(1) 先進 工業國들은 에너지 절약과 대체 에너지 개발로 에너지 消費 構造를 조정하고 있으며, 油價가 배럴당 50달러 선으로

- 23 -

인상되는 경우에도 先進工業國들은 GNP의 1% 미만 만을 OPEC 收入으로 이전시키게 될 것임(과거 油價暴騰으로 OECD는 GNP의 2%를 이전).

(2) 한편 OPEC 産油國들은 財政赤字 등으로 油價收入을 빨리 지출할 것이므로 과거 石油波動과는 달리 西方經濟에 심각한 충격을 야기시킬 가능성은 적음.

(3) 현재의 經濟狀況을 볼 때, 인플레 요인은 있으나 과거보다 심각하지는 않음.

· 先進工業國들의 인플레는 4% 수준으로(과거 73년, 78년의 1/2) 緊縮財政政策을 취할 필요성이 적고, 국민들이 經濟問題의 심각성을 인식하고 있어 직접적인 충격폭이 크지는 않을 것으로 보임.

· 또한 經濟自由化 政策으로 인한 經濟의 탄력성 증대로 충격 흡수 능력이 높아지고 있음. 물론 油價上昇으로 經濟的 打擊을 받겠으나, 經濟의 規模에서 충격을 완화시킬 수 있을 것임.

라. 그러나 우리나라와 같이 對中東 에너지 依存度가 높고, 에너지 사용도가 높은 産業構造를 지닌 國家에서의 경제적 타격은 先進工業國에 비해서 더욱 심각하게 나타날 것으로 보임.

(1) 에너지 硏究院은 油價가 1달러 상승할 경우 GNP 성장율이 0.6%씩 떨어진다고 분석하고 있음.

(2) 또한 오일쇼크에 의한 先進國들의 景氣沈滯는 輸出 依存度가 높은 우리 經濟에 타격을 줄 것으로 예상됨.

- 24 -

0027

（3）한편 油價上昇에 따른 긍정적인 측면이 있다면, 中東 需要의 增大로 우리 經濟의 對中東 진출 기회가 확대될 수 있다는 것임.

（4）요컨대 1990년대 중반부터 예상되는 國際油價의 지속적인 상승 추세에 대비하여, 韓國은 合理的인 에너지 需給과 代替 에너지 開發 등 포괄적인 에너지 政策을 강구하여야 할 것임.

마. 向後 OPEC의 機能은 강화될 것이나, 가격문제로 인한 OPEC 國家間의 對立은 지속될 것임.

（1）세계 에너지 需要의 增大와 供給不足으로 빚어진 高油價 時代는 國際油價問題로 인한 會員國間의 대립상을 완화시킬 가능성도 있음.

（2）그러나 向後 國際油價決定에서 産油國들과 原油輸入國들간의 經濟的 相互依存性의 增大는 OPEC의 權限을 제약하는 요인으로 작용하고, 이에 따른 갈등이 심각한 國際紛爭으로 발전될 가능성도 배제할 수 없음.

---

8. 脫冷戰時代의 國際秩序와 危機管理

가. 地域紛爭 增大 傾向

脫冷戰의 전환기적인 國際情勢 하에서 美·蘇의 상대적 影響力 악화와 多極化 趨勢 등으로 美·蘇 兩極體制에서 억제되었던

- 25 -

0028

다양한 紛爭要因이 현재화되고, 이에 따라 地域紛爭 可能性도 增大될 것으로 전망됨.

나. 危機管理의 國際化·多國化

脫冷戰時代의 危機管理는 이번 쿠웨이트 事態와 같이 美·蘇의 協調 등 國際化·多國化 傾向을 띠게 되고, UN의 機能이 강화될 것으로 보임.

다. 美國의 主導的 役割 持續

脫冷戰時代의 地域紛爭 管理는 國際化·多國化 趨勢를 보이고 있으나, 蘇聯의 國力衰退와 改革에 따른 政治不安으로 당분간 美國의 主導 아래 이루어질 것으로 보임.

라. 脫冷戰時代의 集團 安保 傾向

地域紛爭에 대한 효과적인 對應을 위하여 冷戰時代의 유물인 地域安保體制가 다시 강화될 것으로 전망됨.

9. 我國의 立場과 考慮事項

가. 効果的인 外交能力 과시

현재까지 我國의 外交的 對應은 무리없이 진행되고 있음. 國際的으로 이라크에 대한 쿠웨이트 撤軍 要求, UN 制裁措置에의 참여, 多國籍軍에 대한 經濟支援 및 쿠웨이트 大使舘

- 26 -

0029

維持 등으로 美國과 西方友邦國 및 다수 아랍國들과 보조를 맞추어, 國際秩序의 基本原則을 준수하고 있음. 한편 現地 我國人들의 安全歸國을 도모하는 등 對이라크 外交에도 성공하고 있음.

나. 韓國 防衛 위한 二重負擔 增大

地域紛爭 管理에서 美國의 役割 持續으로 美國은 韓國에 대한 防衛分擔 등 危機管理에의 적극 참여를 요구할 것임. 韓國은 美國의 對韓 防衛公約을 강화시키기 위하여 적절한 防衛分擔을 수행하여야 할 것이고, 我國의 國軍 現代化를 지속적으로 추진하여야 할 것임.

다. 對UN 外交 强化

地域紛爭 管理의 國際化·多國化 傾向으로 UN의 重要性이 부각되고 있어 我國은 UN 單獨加入 등 對UN 外交를 적극 강화하여야 할 것임.

라. 東北亞 6者會談 實現 可能性 增大

脫冷戰時代에서 地域紛爭 管理를 위한 地域安保體制가 강화될 것으로 보이며, 이와 관련하여 東北亞地域에서도 東北亞地域 安定 등 地域잇슈를 논의할 必要性이 증대될 것으로 예상되는 바, 韓國은 盧大統領의 東北亞6者會談 構想의 具現을 위한 外交的 努力을 경주할 필요가 있을 것임.

1990. 9. 5.

作成 : 研究敎授 崔 宜 喆
討論 : 硏究部長 玄 熙 剛
       硏究敎授 朴 弘 圭

<附　錄>

決議案 660 號 : 이라크가　쿠웨이트를　侵攻한　2일　安保理는　美國과
쿠웨이트　要請으로　緊急會議를　개최，이라크軍의　즉각적이고
무조건적인　撤收를　요구하고　4個項　決議案　채택

決議案 661 號 : 6일　美國의　提議로　이라크에　대한　全面的　經濟制裁
措置　결의

決議案 662 號 : 9일　이라크가　쿠웨이트를　合併한　것과　관련，
「이라크가 쿠웨이트를 어떤 구실， 어떤 형태로 合併하든 그것은
전혀　法的　妥當性이　없으며，따라서　無效로　간주된다」고　만장
일치로　결의

決議案 664 號 : 이라크가　이라크와　쿠웨이트內에　잔류해　있던
外國人들에　대한　抑留方針을　밝힌　후　이들의　人質化를　우려해
安保理는　18일　外國人들의　자유로운　出國과　安全　및　健康의
보장을　요구하는　決議案을　18일　만장일치로　채택

決議案 665 號 : 이라크의　쿠웨이트　駐在　外國公館　강제　폐쇄가
임박함에　따라 25일　安保理는　이미　나온　UN 決議案의　즉각
실행과　필요한　경우　多國籍軍에 최소한의　武力使用을　허용하는
5個項의　決議案　채택

0032

초강대국과 유엔의 평화유지

커트 M. 캠프벨·토마스 G. 바이스

비효율성, 급진주의 그리고 허술한 재정관리에 대한 오랜기간의 비판이 제기된 이후 유엔은 제3세계의 분쟁에 대한 평화적 해결로 인하여 근래에 들어와서 긍정적인 평가를 받고 있다. 유엔의 평화유지정책은 1988년의 노벨평화상 수상을 계기로 전세계의 관심을 사로잡았으나 이는 최근의 갑작스러운 혁신에 의한 것이 아니다. 유엔의 평화유지 감독관이 최초로 파견된 것은 1948년 팔레스타인에서이다. 평화유지가 국제정치의 도구로서 이용되는 것은 시대에 따라서 부침(浮沈)을 보이고 있다. 그러나 1988-1989년에 아프가니스탄, 앙골라, 나미비아, 이란-이라크 국경지대 그리고 최근에는 중앙아메리카에서 유엔이 평화유지 활동을 펼치고 있으며, 다섯개의 활동이 중동과 아시아에서 계속되고 있다. 모든 제3세계의 분쟁지역에는 언제나 유엔 평화유지 활동이 가능할 것이다.

현재 진행되고 있고 미래에도 진행될 유엔 평화유지 정책에 관심을 갖는 이유는 지난 2년 동안 유엔의 평화유지 정책이 국제적 갈등관리에 일정한 기여를 하였기 때문이다. 평화유지는 일반적으로 두가지 기능을 수행한다. 1) 평화유지(정전「停戰」의 감독과 보고), 2) 적극적인 평화유지(법과 질서의 확립, 전쟁당사국의 분리, 그리고 비무장지대의 설정). 유엔평화유

0033

114 국제정세 1990. 9

지군은 일반적으로 소규모 국가들과 비동맹국가들의 군대로 구성된다. 안전보장이사회의 상임이사국의 경우에는 특별한 상황하에서만 군대를 파견할 수 있다. 경무장한 이들 중립국 군대는 전투를 중지하고 오직 방위를 목적으로 하는 경우에만 무력을 사용한다는 원칙하에서 전쟁당사국 사이에서 활동한다. 평화유지군의 영향력은 국제공동체의 도덕적 힘에 의존한다.

최근의 업적을 살펴보기 위해서는 역사적인 접근을 할 필요가 있다. 근래에 이르러 18회의 유엔 평화유지 활동이 있었으며, 그 활동은 세계의 중요한 전략적 지역에 미치지 않는 곳이 없다. 표는 현재 진행중인 10개의 평화유지 활동을 기록한 것이다.

아프가니스탄과 앙골라에서의 활동은 각각 소련군과 쿠바군의 철수를 감독하고 확인하기 위해서이다. 이란-이라크에서의 활동은 장기간의 전쟁을 치른 뒤의 휴전을 감독하기 위해서 시작되었다. 나미비아에서 군인과 시민은 휴전을 성공적으로 감독했으며, 군대를 특정지역에 한정시켰으며, 피난민의 무사복귀를 도왔으며, 1990년 4월 독립으로 나아가는 국민투표를 성공적으로 치루었다. 중앙아메리카에서의 비무장 감독관들은 해당지역 정부가 공약한 반란군에 대한 원조중단과 영토침입을 감독하였으며, 니카라과의 선거를 감독하기 위하여 유엔과 미국의 시민들과 협력하였다.

가장 최근에 이루어진 다섯가지 유엔 활동 가운데 세가지 활동은 오래전부터 계획되어 활동을 시작하였다. 사실상 그 업적은 사무국장과 스텝진의 줄기찬 노력에 돌려야 할 것이다. 평화유지 활동은 1949년 후반에 시작되었으나 한국(1950-1953), 수에즈침공 뒤의 시나이(1957), 그리고 콩고(1960-1964)에서는 초강대국과 유엔 활동국이 서로 달랐었기 때문에 유엔의 평화유지 기능의 발전에 대한 기대는 그다지 크지 못했다. 이미 1940년대의 이상주의는 냉전이라는 국제정세에서 선전전의 구렁텅이로 빠져들고 있었다. 그러므로 유엔의 평화유지 활동은 비효율적일 수밖에 없었다.

지난 몇해 동안의 유엔 평화유지 활동이 부활된 것은 소련의 '신사고' 정책과 밀접한 관계를 갖는다. 고르바초프의 유엔에 대한 호감과, 평화유지 활동에 대한 크레믈린의 주저함과 적대감이 사라지자 국제환경에는 많은 변화가 일어났다.

미국과 소련은 평화유지활동에 대한 통제와 군대의 구성 그리고 재정의

0034

문제에 있어서 사사건건 대립을 보였었다. 최근 소련의 변화된 자세는 이러한 갈등을 상당히 감소시켰다. 사실상 1987년 중반 이래로 안전보장이사회는 서로 대립되는 논쟁의 장이 아니라 유엔헌장이 의도했던 바대로 협조기구로서 작용하기 시작하였다.

최근들어 유엔에 대한 소련의 자세는 세가지 점에서 큰 변화를 보이고 있다. 첫째로 소련은 전통적으로 유엔의 광범위한 평화유지 활동에 참여하는 것을 꺼려 왔으나 근래에 들어와서는 자세가 바뀌고 있다. 1986년에 들어 남부 레바논에서의 평화유지 활동에(UNIFIL) 소요되는 비용을 부담한다는 발표를 한 뒤로 소련의 태도변화가 잘 나타나고 있다. 1986년 이전에는 소련이 비용을 부담하지 않는다는 전제하에서 UNIFIL의 활동을 인정하였다. 1987년부터는 연체금조로 2억달러의 경화를 지불하기 시작하였다.

소련의 두번째 변화는 사무총장과 유엔 사무국의 독립문제에 관한 소련의 입장변화이다. 과거 미국과 소련은 평화유지 활동과 국제외교에서의 활동자유에 관한 문제에 있어서 사무총장의 역할에 이견을 보였었다. 미국은 전통적으로 사무총장의 권한강화를 선호했으나, 소련은 안전보장이사회의 권한 강화를 선호하였다. 사무총장의 권한강화에 대한 소련의 승인은 국제외교에서의 사무총장의 활동을 강화하였을 뿐더러 하루하루의 활동에 대한 사무총장의 운영권이 강화되고 독립되었다.

세번째 변화는 평화유지 활동을 광범위하게 거의 보편적으로 수용하고 있다는 점이다. 아프가니스탄으로부터의 소련군 철수와 앙골라로부터의 쿠바군 철수에 대한 유엔군의 감독을 인정함으로써 소련은 국제분쟁 해결에 대한 변화된 시각을 보여주고 있다. 더욱이 새로운 제안이 지속적으로 크레믈린으로부터 나오고 있다. 미국은 페르시아만에서의 유엔 평화유지 해군의 창설에 반대 입장을 보여왔으나 소련이 이를 제안하는 것은 소련의 '신사고'를 실증하는 것이다. 소련은 정치적, 경제적 안전의 고려에서 유엔의 평화유지 활동을 지지하나, 그 목적에 있어서는 미국과 동일하다. 즉, 국제환경의 개선과 평화유지 정책을 국제적 갈등의 해결을 위한 테크닉으로서 사용한다는 목적에는 변함이 없다.

유엔의 활동에 대한 소련의 최근 자세는   환영한 만한 일이나,   최근

〈유엔의 평화유지 활동〉

기 간	활동내용
1948-현재	유엔정전감독기구(UNTSO, 예루살렘)
1949-현재	유엔인도-파키스탄감시단(UNMOGIP)
1956-1967	유엔비상군(UNEF 1, 수에즈운하)
1958	유엔레바논감시단(UNOGIL)
1960-1964	콩고에서의 유엔활동(ONUC)
1962-1963	신(新) 서기니아유엔안전군
1963-1964	유엔예멘감시활동(UNYOM)
1964-현재	사이프러스유엔평화유지군(UNFICYP)
1965-1966	유엔인도-파키스탄감시활동(UNIPOM)
1965-1966	도미니카공화국유엔사무총장활동(DOMREP)
1973-1979	제2유엔비상군(UNEF 2, 수에즈운하와 시나이반도)
1974-현재	유엔불간섭감시군(UNDOF, 골란고원)
1978-현재	레바논유엔군(UNIFIL)
1988-현재	아프가니스탄과 파키스탄의 유엔사무소(UNGOMAP)
1988-현재	이란-이라크유엔군사감시단(UNIIMOG)
1989-현재	유엔과도기원조단(UNTAG, 나미비아에서)
1989-현재	유엔앙골라검증단(UNAVEM)
1989-현재	중앙아메리카유엔감시단(ONUCA)

미국의 태도는 유엔의 한계를 더욱 드러낼 뿐이다. 소련의 적극적인 자세는 미국이 소극적이라는 인상만을 심어줄 뿐이다. 소련의 주도권으로 유엔은 무대의 중심으로 나아가고 있으나, 미국은 레이건의 일방주의와 유엔에 대한 질타의 유산에서 벗어나지 못하고 있다. 미국의 유엔에 대한 유보적인 자세가 모스크바가 평화유지방법으로서 서구적인 접근을 인정하기 시작한 때에 이루어졌다는 사실은 아이러니가 아닐 수 없다. 소련은 몇십년 동안이나 평화에 대한 서구의 접근을 신뢰하지 않았다. 수년간이나 모스크바에 지불독촉을 한 뒤에 미국은 어마어마한 재정적자를 짊어져야 했다.

총회에서 부시 대통령의 첫번째 연설은 고무적이지 못했으나, 부시행정부는 레이건 전임 대통령보다는 유엔의 활동에 대하여 더 긍정적이었다. 유엔이 미국의 이익에 반하는 정책을 취한다고 생각되지는 않았다. 미국은 유엔을 일방적으로 질타하지 않았으며, 레이건 행정부의 일방주의는 "선별적 다변주의"로 대체되었다. 1989년 11월초 미국과 소련은 총회의 결의사항을 공동으로 지지하였으며, 기자회견장에서 -유엔에서 최초로- 양국은 평화유지와 국제협력의 증진에 유엔이 좀더 적극적으로 활동해야 할 필요성을 피력하였다.

그럼에도 불구하고 부시 행정부는 소련의 주도권을 전적으로 인정하지 않았으며, 고르바초프가 1988년 12월 총회에서 독창적인 비젼을 제시하듯이 어떤 비젼을 제시하지는 않았다. 그대신 미국의 접근은 냉정하고 조심스럽다. 많은 사람들이 이러한 미국의 자세를 몰감정적이고 신뢰할 수 없다고 해석한다. 워싱턴은 지역분쟁 해결에서 활발해진 유엔의 활동에 어떻게 대처할 것인지 확신하지 못하는 것같다.

유엔이 창설된 뒤 처음 30년간 미국이 세계평화에 적극적이던 상황과 현재의 미국의 우유부단함과는 큰 차이점이 보인다. 미국의 소극적인 자세는 갈등해소 방법으로서의 유엔평화유지 활동이 미래의 갈등해결 방법으로서 발전하는데 일정한 한계를 노정시킬뿐만 아니라 국제평화와 안정보장을 위한 대안적 정체(Regime)로서 발달되는 데에도 한계를 보이게 된다.

다른 시각에서 본다면 소련의 주도에 의한 미소간의 협력증진은 제3세계에 불안감을 조장할 수도 있다. 예를 들면 나미비아와 앙골라 사태를 둘러싼 미소간의 막후외교는 초강대국의 연합에 대한 공포심을 불어 넣었다. 초강대국이 합의에 의하여 UNTAG 지원금을 감소시킨 것은 23년동안이나 게릴라 투쟁을 통하여 받은 피해보다도 훨씬 더 심각하였다. 더욱이 제3세계 국가들의 경우에는 소련의 유엔평화 활동을 의심의 눈초리로 바라보고 있다. 제3세계 국가들은 소련이 유엔평화 활동을 통하여 제3세계로부터 철수하고 이전의 동맹국을 헌신짝처럼 버리려는 의도를 갖고 있다고 생각하고 있다. 제3세계 국가들이 미소간의 평화유지 활동에 대하여 이와같은 시각을 견지한다는 것은 사태를 더욱 복잡하게 만들고 있는 요인이다.

0037

1988년과 1989년에 걸쳐서 유엔의 업적은 널리 인정을 받고 있으나 한계와 어려움이 없는 것은 아니었다. 최근 들어서 유엔이 완수한 네가지 활동은 평화유지자로서 유엔의 이미지를 크게 신장시켰으나, 그러한 사업을 위한 재정확보의 문제를 동시에 제기하였다. 특기할 만한 사실은 UN-TAG의 활동에서 보여지듯이 승인된 비용 안에서 임무를 수행하기 위하여 활동의 범위를 축소시켰다는 것이다. 과거 유엔은 다양한 방법을 동원하여 재정을 충당하였다. 가령 분쟁당사자에게 일정한 비용을 부담시킨다거나 모든 국가들로부터 모금을 하는 방법을 사용하였다. 분쟁당사국들은 재정적 부담을 감당할 만한 경우가 드물기 때문에 비효율적이었다. 사이프러스의 경우에는 자발적인 헌금에 의존하였으나 별다른 효과를 나타내지 못했다. 유엔회원국들에게 부담을 주는 경우에도 대부분의 회원들이 전액을 내지 않거나 일부만을 내는 경우가 잦았으며, 설사 내더라도 때늦게 내는 경우가 잦았다. 끝없는 재정유출과 부채만 짊어지게 된 꼴이 되었다.

유엔의 평화유지 정책이 계속된다면 앞으로 적자는 계속될 것이다. 1987년의 평화유지비가 2억달러에 그쳤다면 1990-1991년에는 20억달러에 육박할 것이다. 이러한 재정위기를 다양한 방법으로 극복하여야 할 것이다. 유엔회원국들과 초강대국들은 이미 현재의 재정적 부담을 해결하는데 한계를 보이고 있다.

물론 반대의견이 없는 것이 아니지만 생각해볼 수 있는 방법 중의 하나가 군대파견을 할당제로 운영하는 것이다. 현재의 형식은 중동사태때 정례화된 것으로서 1973년에 그 기원을 찾을 수 있다. 새로운 가이드라인은 평화유지에 대한 소련의 태도를 변화시키는데 기여하였다. 문제의 발단은 정규군을 사용하는 국가와 그보다는 더 비싸게 먹히는 의용군을 사용하는 국가의 차이에서 기인하였다. 현재의 형식은 모든 국가에게 동일한 비율의 부담을 지우는 것을 원칙으로 한다. 이러한 조치는 유엔의 활동에 소요되는 인력의 증가를 초래하였다. 사실상 이론적으로나 현실적으로나 군대는 유엔에 재정적으로 부담이 되지는 않았으나 소련의 제안인 여러가지 종류의 헌납의 문제는 유엔평화유지의 재정문제에 새로운 문제제기를 할 것으로 보인다.

할당된 의무이행을 위한 다른-선택사항들은 보급지원과 공급을 줄이는

0038

방법이다. 처음부터 미국은 유엔에 비용을 부과하지 않고서 분쟁지역으로 물자를 수송해 주었으며 최근들어 소련도 이에 가세하고 있다. 비용을 들이지 않고 물자보급과 수송을 할 수 있게 되면 전체경비를 절감할 수 있을 것이다. 초강대국들은 정보기술과 물자비축기술이 발달되었으므로 비용을 절감할 수 있게 되었다. 달리 생각해 볼 수 있는 영역은 공공재정(유니세프와 같은 기금마련), 사용자 세금, 그리고 특수기금 창설 등이다.

현재와 같은 자금사정으로서는 앞으로의 평화유지 정책은 신중을 기해서 실행하여야 할 것이다. 평화유지군을 전통적인 분쟁해결의 수단으로서 뿐만 아니라 마약단속, 테러리즘 규제, 시민전쟁 해결, 그리고 휴머니즘적인 사업의 지원 등의 활동에 사용하자는 제안도 있다. 이는 야심에 찬 계획이나 군대를 파견하는 당사국이 커다란 손실을 바라지 않으며 현재 유엔이 직면하고 있는 한계를 감안한다면 비현실적이라고 할 수 있다. 최근의 정치적 동향은 유엔의 평화유지 활동에 유리하게 작용하고 있다.

최근의 성공적인 활동과 유엔이 현재 맞이하고 있는 한계를 균형있게 조절하여야 한다. 유엔 평화유지가 맞게될 미래상을 설계하고, 다가올 기회와 도전을 현실적으로 심사숙고하고 냉정하게 판단하여야 할 것이다. 유엔의 미래 활동에 대한 개념, 강령, 그리고 활동의 잠재력에 대한 토론과 성찰이 요청된다.

또다른 하나의 대안은 1947년 이후 거의 거론되지 않은 군사참모위원회(Military Staff Committee ; MSC)의 부활이다. 소련은 이에 동의하나 다른 국가들이 동의하지 않고 있다. 유엔헌장의 한 조항에 의하면 MSC는 안전보장위원회의 5개국의 상임이사국들이 파견하는 고위장성들로 구성된다. 그러므로 군사참모위원회는 상임이사국들의 거부권에 따라 좌우되므로 군대파견국이나 재정후원국에게는 달갑지 않은 것이다. 그러나 MSC는 평화유지에 소요되는 군사문제에 대하여 국제안전-총서기장(Security-General)에게 조언을 해줄 수 있으며 비공식적으로 모든 관계 당사국들의 참가를 유도할 수 있다. 그러한 조치는 국제안전-총서기장의 요구사항에 대한 신뢰도를 높일 수 있다. 또한 이러한 과정은 MSC를 매개로 위싱턴과 모스크바간의 협력을 증진시키는 촉매제 역할도 할 수 있다.

유엔은 평화유지군이 공격군대가 아니라 자위군대라고 말하나 평화유지 개념의 확장은 유엔군의 무장문제에 대한 심각한 논쟁을 불러일으킬

것이다. 콩고와 레바논에서 유엔군이 사용한 무력은 경부기의 범주를 벗어난 것이다. "자위"의 개념도 "개인적 자위"에서 "집단적 자위"의 개념으로 바꿔었다. 1983년 베이루트에서 비유엔군지역인 미국과 프랑스의 인접지역에서 발생한 비극은 유엔평화유지군의 무절제한 무력사용이 본래의 효율성을 상실시키고 보복을 불러일으킨다는 교훈을 주었다.

그럼에도 불구하고 마약단속, 반테러리즘, 시민전쟁 등에 대한 미래의 활동은 차치하더라도 레바논과 나미비아에서 벌어지는 최근의 사태에 비추어 본다면 유엔평화유지군이 일정 규모의 무력을 사용하는 일은 불가피한 것으로 보인다. 가장 시급한 문제는 군대를 파견하는 국가가 있어야 하며, 자기방어를 위해서만 무력을 사용한다는 점에 동의하여야 한다는 점이다. 군대를 파견하는 국가들은 자국의 군대가 심한 피해를 입기를 바라지 않는다. 예를 든다면 유엔은 비살상무기(非殺傷武器 ; 경찰과 군대에서 이미 발달된)의 도입을 연구하고, 유엔의용예비군(이상적인 유엔 "의용군")의 창설을 고려해볼 만하다.

또다른 안은 이미 소련이 제안하였듯이 안전보장이사회의 상임이사국들이 군대를 파견하여 유엔평화유지군을 상설기구로 만드는 것이다. 과거 상임이사국들은 특별한 상황하에서만 군대를 파견하였다. 영국이 사이프러스에, 프랑스가 레바논에 군대를 파견하였다. 상임이사국들은 유엔비상군(UNEF 2)에 참가할 수 없다는 규정이 준수되고 있다.

많은 사람들이 아직까지 상임이사국들의 유엔군 참여를 의심의 눈초리로 보는데, 왜냐하면 그렇게 될 경우에는 정치화할 개연성이 상존하기 때문이다. 분쟁지역에 상주하는 것이 아니라 분쟁해결의 예비대 형식으로 참

0040

여한다면 그러한 의심은 어느정도 가셔질 수 있을 것이다. 그러한 예비적 성격의 참여는 국제적인 압력의 강도를 높이면서도 사태가 급박하지 않는 한 참여하지 않으므로 정치화될 위험성도 줄일 수 있다.

초강대국들의 개입은 이미 양자간의 협력이 효력을 발휘한 남아프리카나 동남아시아에서 사용될 수 있는 한 방법이다. 게다가 워싱턴과 모스크바는 해당지역의 집단에 의한 중개를 뒷받침해 줄 수 있다. 그들은 전문적인 군사기술도 평화유지에 소요되는 재정적 자산도 없지만 외교적 압력을 가하기 위해서는 유엔보다 더 효과적인 역할을 수행해 낼 수 있다. 캄보디아에서의 아세안, 니카라과에서의 중앙아메리카 대통령, 남아프리카에서의 국경지역(Frontline)국가들, 차드와 서부 사하라에서의 OAU 등의 사례를 들 수 있겠다. 유엔의 평화유지와 해당지역에서의 평화만들기의 적절한 조화의 필요성이 강하게 대두되고 있다.

마지막으로 전반적인 미·소협력의 증진과 구체적인 유엔의 사안에 대한 양국의 의견일치는 평화유지의 폭을 확장하는데 직접적으로 영향을 미칠 것이다. 초강대국간의 협력이 곧 연합을 결성할 것같지는 않지만 초강대국의 새로운 형태는 제3세계와 초강대국 사이의 새로운 관계를 촉발시킬 것으로 보인다. 이는 1972년의 '기본원칙에 대한 합의'에서 기원을 찾을 수 있다. 그러나 새로운 규정의 요구 —워싱턴에서보다 모스크바에서 더 강하게 제기하고 있다—는 일방적인 간섭은 배제하고 국제기구에 의존하기로 합의하고 있으며, 그러한 경향이 현재 진행되고 있다.

경쟁이 치열한 중동지역과 같은 곳에서는 초강대국들이나 다른 국가들이

0041

자제력에 의존하는 위와 같은 행위원칙을 준수한다고 보기가 어렵다. 그러나 초강대국들의 정치적 이해가 그렇게 첨예하게 대립되지 않는 곳에서는 그러한 행위규범은 유용하게 적용될 수 있을 것이다. 어떠한 행위규범이라도 유엔 평화유지 활동의 확장보다 선행한다.

유엔의 평화유지는 한계를 가지며 도전에 직면하고 있으나, 최근의 성공적인 임무수행으로 말미암아 국제분쟁의 해결을 위한 유용한 도구로서 널리 이용될 수 있는 가능성을 보여주었다. 소련의 "신사고"와 국제관계의 "탈이데올로기화"는 유엔이 활동하기 좋은 국제환경을 만들어 주고 있다. 많은 어려움에도 불구하고 평화유지 활동은 뜨거운 지지를 받고 있다. 많은 경우 평화유지 활동은 어떠한 개별적 상황에서도 훌륭하게 대응할 수 있도록 훈련받고 있다. 예산에 따른 활동범위의 설정은 많은 애로점을 노정하고 있다. 그리고 평화유지 활동이 늘어감에 따라 유엔의 재정적 어려움은 가중될 것이다. 유엔은 다양한 경로를 통하여 경비를 조달하여야 할 것이며 어려운 상황을 슬기롭게 처리하여야 할 것이다.

재정적인 어려움에도 불구하고 서부 사하라와 캄보디아에서는 유엔의 활동이 개시될 전망이 보이고 있다. 안전보장이사회는 서구에서의 최초의 활동을 인정했다. 비무장 감시군이 중앙아메리카에서 반란군에 대한 원조 중단 공약의 이행여부를 감독할 것이고, 일반시민들은 니카라과에서의 선거를 감독할 것이다. 그리고 평화유지군은 콘트라반군의 무기를 접수할 것이다. 다른 제3세계 국가들에서 유엔의 평화유지 활동에 대한 새로운 도전이 제기될 것이다. 초강대국들이 일정한 거리를 유지하려고 할 때 긴장이 증가될 것으로 보이며, 특히 무기 이전 문제에 합의가 이루어지지 않을 경우에는 사정이 더욱 심각해 질 것이다.

내일을 전망해 본다면 현재의 낙관주의를 건강한 현실주의로 처방하는 일이 요청된다. 미래에는 능력을 벗어나는 위임통치를 맡아서 해결책을 모색하는 무리를 함으로써 유엔의 중립성을 손상시키지 말아야 하며, 재정적 자원을 벗어나는 무리한 활동을 자제해야 할 것이다. 과거의 성공과 실패를 냉정하게 평가할 뿐만 아니라 전통적인 평화유지 정책을 창조적으로 발전시켜야 할 것이다. 유엔의 평화유지 활동은 국제평화와 안전유지를 위한 새로운 국제체제의 건설에 첫번째 초석으로 등장하였다.

0042

걸프만 사태

〈90, 10〉

사태 전망

(단기적 전망)

o 미국은 이라크의 쿠웨이트 무조건 철수등 목표를 중간선거 이전에
   달성하려고 노력하면서 군사적 압력 강화와 각종 봉쇄조치등 대이라크
   압박 전략을 가속화해 나가고 있음

o 반면, 이라크는 쿠웨이트 철군을 이스라엘 점령지역 반환 문제와 연계,
   금번 사태를 "대미 성전"으로 부각시켜 아랍 민족주의의 호응을 모색
   하고 아랍권내 반이라크 세력의 분열 도모와 쿠웨이트 합병 공고화를
   추진하면서, 장기적인 대항을 모색하고 있음

o 이러한 군사적 대치상황 가속화 과정에서, 미군등 다국적군의 배치가
   완료되고 시기적으로 미국 중간선거 직전인 10월 중하순경을 전후하여
   걸프만내 군사적 긴장이 상당히 고조될 것이며, 이라크측의 도발
   행위가 있을 경우 무력충돌의 가능성도 배제할 수 없음

0043

(장기적 전망)

o 그러나 미국이 무력사용을 선택하는데는 아래와 같은 몇가지 제약이
  있음
    - 인질을 포함한 인명손실
    - 유전 파괴등에 따를 세계 경제혼란
    - 이라크의 이스라엘 공격등 확전 가능성
    - 단기간내 해결 불가시 미국내 여론 악화 및 국제적 위신 손상등

o 따라서, 아래 고려에 기초하여 3-6개월동안 대이라크 경제제재 효과가
  실효적으로 나타나기를 기다리면서, 정치, 외교적 해결 노력을 계속할
  것임
    - 우방 및 관련국의 비용 분담으로 재정부담 경감
    - 사우디를 위시한 GCC 국가 및 온건 아랍국들과의 관계 심화로
      중동에서의 영향력 증대
    - 미국의 세계 경제상 상대적 영향력 강화
    - 미국 주도하에 세계 주요국가가 동참하는 새로운 국제질서 형성

o 결국, 이라크의 쿠웨이트 영구합병은 국제여론과 반대세력에 의해 실현
  불가능할 것이며 전쟁이 발발할 경우 궁극적으로 이라크가 패배할
  것임. 따라서 시간이 걸린다 할지라도 이라크의 패퇴에 의한 정치적
  해결 가능성이 더 높다고 볼수 있음.

0044

| 국제정치에 미치는 장기적 영향 |

가. 본쟁 관리의 국제화, 다국화

　　o 탈 냉전의 전환기적인 국제정세하에서 미, 소의 대립후퇴로 양극
　　　체제하에서 억제되었던 다양한 본쟁요인의 현재화로 지역분쟁(특히
　　　중강도 본쟁 : Mid-Intensity Conflict) 발생빈도 증대 가능성

　　o 이라크 사태는 지역분쟁 해결에 미, 소가 협조하고 다수의 국가들이
　　　이에 동참하므로서 탈 냉전시대 위기관리의 국제화, 다국화에 관한
　　　주요 선례 형성. 특히 UN 안보리가 강대국간 합의 도출에 성공하므로서
　　　향후 국제안보 문제에 UN의 역할증대도 기대

나. 미국의 주도적 역할 예상

　　o 미국은 금번 사태를 탈, 냉전시대 지역분쟁 관리의 시험대로 인식,
　　　사태의 원상회복을 통해 군사력 사용을 통한 국가이익 추구는 용납될
　　　수 없음을 국제관계의 기본 규법으로 확립코자 함

　　o 상기 국제화, 다국화 현상하에서 최근 소련이 국내사정으로 국제문제에
　　　관여할 여력이 감퇴하므로서 향후 국제정치에 당분간 미국의 주도권
　　　행사 예상. 아울러 금번 사태에 대응하는데 국제적 지지 뿐 아니라
　　　실제 관련국간 비용분담을 실현하므로서 향후 여타 지역분쟁 발생시
　　　선례로 작용 가능성

0045

다. 집단 안보체제 강화 경향

o 지역분쟁에 대한 효과적인 대응을 위하여 냉전시대의 유물인 지역
   안보체제가 다시 강화되는 추세도 있을 것으로 전망

o 걸프 사태의 경우, 이라크군의 철수로 사태가 종결된후라도 이라크의
   모험성과 군사적 능력(핵개발 가능성 포함)을 감안, 미국은 대이라크
   봉쇄전략의 필요성을 인식하고 있으며, 미국이 최근 거론한 중동
   안보 구조 구상도 미국이 참여하는 중동지역 집단안보 개념으로
   이해될 수 있을 것임

라. 중동지역 왕정체제 변화시기 단축 가능성

o 금번 걸프사태가 쿠웨이트 왕정 회복으로 결말이 난다하더라도 동
   지역내 왕정체제에 대한 개혁요구 움직임이 고조될 것으로 전망됨에
   비추어, 역내 왕정국가의 체제 변화시기는 지금까지 예상했던 것보다
   더 일찍 도래할 수 있을 것임

마. 중동국가 (GCC등)의 안보능력 제고노력 증진 예상

o GCC등을 위시한 중동제국은 향후 군사력 증진등 자국 안보능력 강화를
   위한 노력을 강화해 나갈 것이며, 미국등 서방국가와의 군사.안보
   협력관계가 가일층 증진될 것으로 전망됨

o 특히 왕정체제의 국가들은 군사력 현대화는 물론 자국의 안보 및
   체제 유지를 위하여도 타국과의 군사.안보 협력관계 증진을 모색해
   나가려 할 것임

0046

o 무력 충돌 가능성이 높아지고 있다는 의견이 일부언론에 보도되고 있는바,
   이에 대한 정부의 견해는?

   - 11월중에 있을 미국의 중간선거를 앞두고 부시 행정부가 그전에 가시적
      성과를 올리기 위한 대책 마련에 부심하고 있으며, 훗세인이 쿠웨이트
      병합을 고수할 경우 무력에 의한 해결이 불가피하다는 판단하에 그러한
      의견이 나오고 있는 것으로 보임. 그러나 미국으로서는 군사력 사용시
      예상되는 문제점 즉, 인질의 안전, 화학전 위협, 다국적군 참여 우방과의
      의견조정 문제, 군사력 사용후 중동내 對미 감정 악화등의 우려 때문에
      군사적 조치를 취하는데 여러가지 제약 요인이 있음

   - 이런 상태하에서 미국은 최후 수단으로 군사력 사용을 염두에 두고, 군사력
      사용시 부작용을 최소화 하는 방안을 고려할 수 있을것임. 미국은 이를 위해
      가능한 많은 나라의 다국적군 참여를 유도하고 특히 최근 지역 분쟁해결을
      위한 미.소간 협조 가능성에 착안, 유엔 안보리의 결의를 통해 군사력
      사용의 정당성을 확보하는 노력도 계속 경주할 것임

o 페만 사태가 탈냉전시대의 국제정세에 미치는 영향에 대한 정부의 평가는?

   - 탈냉전의 전환기적인 국제정세하에서 미.소의 대립후퇴로 양극체제하에서
      억제되었던 다양한 지역 분쟁요인이 현재화될 가능성은 오히려 증대될 수
      있다고도 봄

   - 이라크 사태는 지역분쟁 해결에 미.소가 협조하고 다수의 국가들이 이에
      동참하므로서 탈냉전시대의 위기관리의 국제화.다국화 경향 초래하고
      있으며 특히 UN 안보리가 강대국간 합의 도출에 성공하므로써 향후 국제
      안보 문제에 UN의 역할 증대가 기대되며, 아울러 잠재적 도발세력에 대한
      경종이 될 것임

0047

o 페르시아만 사태의 해결 전망은?

(현황)

- 미국을 위시한 다국적 연합세력은 이라크의 쿠웨이트 철군을 관철시키기 위하여
  경제.외교 및 군사적 압력을 강화하고 있으나, 이라크는 쿠웨이트 철수 절대
  불가를 천명하고 反美 아랍민족주의 선동 전략으로 맞섬으로써 긴장상태하의
  대치상황이 지속되고 있음

(해결 가능성)

- 미국은 안보리 결의의 완전 실현을 주장하는 반면 이라크는 쿠웨이트 포기
  절대 불가입장을 고수하고 있어서 양측이 조기에 정치적 타협을 도출할
  가능성은 희박함
- 한편 군사적 해결 가능성에 있어서는 미국이 자신의 결정으로 군사력을 사용할
  경우, 아랍권 국가들의 反美 감정 자극과 및 군사력 사용후 페르시아만 지역
  미군주둔 명분 약화 가능성등을 감안할때 이라크의 도발이 없는 상태에서
  선제 공격 감행은 어려움. 또한 이라크도 군사력, 특히 공군력의 절대적
  열세로 선제 무력사용은 어려운 사정임
- 그러나 이라크의 쿠웨이트 병합 영구화나 핵무기등 대량파괴 무기 개발로
  중동지역 세력 균형에 중대한 위협 초래될 경우, 이를 저지하기 위한
  미국의 군사력 사용 가능성을 배제할 수 없음

(사태의 장기화 가능성)

- 현재 진행중인 경제제재 조치가 차츰 효과를 보이고 있으나 훗세인이
  경제적 어려움 때문에 쉽게 굴복할 것으로 보이지는 않으며, 훗세인은
  쿠웨이트 병합을 굳혀 일단 목표를 달성하고 시간을 끌면서 반시오니즘,
  아랍 민족주의등을 조장, 현 대치상태를 미국대 아랍 민족주의간 대결
  구도로 전환시켜 자신의 입지를 강화시키려 할 것으로 예상됨
- 미국은 당장 군사력 사용에 의한 사태해결이 어려운 상황으로, 이라크에
  대해 정치.경제적 압력을 강화하는 한편, 세계적인 反이라크 단합을 공고히
  하여 단기적인 사태해결과 장기적인 중동안보구도 확립을 추구할 것으로 예상됨.

0048

90-45

主要國際問題分析

이라크의 쿠웨이트 侵攻(Ⅱ)
- 協商에 의한 妥結 摸索 -

90.11.28

外 務 部
外交安保硏究院

0049

主要國際問題分析

이라크의 쿠웨이트 侵攻(II)

- 協商에 의한 妥結 摸索 -

- 內　　　　容 -

1. 걸프灣 危機 : 對이라크 武力使用에 대한 國際的 合意 構築

2. 걸프灣 危機와 美國의 立場과 問題点

3. 이라크의 立場과 問題点

4. 反이라크 聯合國의 立場 : 美國의 强硬 立場에 同調

5. 관련 아랍國들의 立場 : 地域 勢力均衡 維持 努力

6. 平和的 解決을 위한 시나리오

7. 걸프灣 危機 後의 中東情勢 不安 持續

8. 脱冷戰時代의 安保와 韓國의 考慮事項

本 資料는 韓國外交政策 立案의 參考資料로 作成한
것으로서 外務部의 公式立場과는 無關한 것입니다.

0050

이라크의 쿠웨이트 侵攻(II)

- 協商에 의한 妥結 摸索

최근 걸프灣 危機는 美國의 主導下에 UN 安保理가 내년 1월 15일까지 이라크가 쿠웨이트에서 撤收하지 않을 경우, '모든 必要한 手段'을 취할 수 있다는 決議(678)를 通過시킴으로써 새로운 局面에 들어섰음.

이번 決議는 이라크에 대한 時限的 最後通牒을 意味함. 한편, 美國은 無力使用 등 對이라크 强硬政策에 대한 國內外의 輿論을 무마하고 훗세인 이라크 大統領에 대한 壓力을 더욱 加重시키기 위하여 이라크에 協商을 提議하였음.

이라크는 UN 安保理 決議에 강력히 抗議하면서도 美國과의 協商 提議를 受諾함으로써 政治的 妥結에 의한 危機 解決 可能性이 높아지고 있음. 사실상 美國으로서는 걸프灣과 中東地域에 대한 自國의 影響力을 堅持·强化하기 위하여 훗세인과의 協商을 필요로 하는 한편, 훗세인은 自身의 執權 延長과 아랍권의 指導者로서의 浮上을 위하여 協商에 의한 妥結을 바라고 있음.

協商을 통한 걸프灣 위기 해소는 훗세인의 體面을 살려 주면서 철군을 慫慂하는 方法으로써 이라크와 쿠웨이트간의 領土問題가 협상의 根據가 될 수 있음. 또한, 美國은 UN 및

-1-

관련 國際機構와의 연계하에 이라크의 化學武器, 核武器 開發
禁止 등에 관한 協商을 進行시킬 수 있을 것 임.

그러나, 이라크가 주장하는 바, 팔레스타인問題와의 연계
문제는 이스라엘과 관련 아랍국들의 參與가 필수적이기 때문
에, 이와 관련한 協商은 國際會議 摸索 등 기본적인 協商
틀에 대한 意見 交換 이상으로 發展될 可能性은 稀薄함.

이번 걸프灣 危機를 계기로 1990년대 中東 情勢는 이집트를
中心으로 하는 穩健國들의 現狀維持勢力과 이라크 등 強硬國
들의 現狀維持勢力間의 葛藤으로 兩分化 現狀을 빚으면서
地域 緊張狀態가 持續될 것으로 보임.

美國은 中東地域 安保體制 構築에 있어서 集團安保體制나
UN의 한계성으로 아랍 主要國들과의 雙務關係 發展에 依存할
可能性이 높음.

韓國은 걸프灣 위기와 관련된 아랍 戰線國에 대한 經濟支援
을 계기로 이집트, 시리아 등과의 關係改善을 위한 外交努力
을 竝行하여야 할 것임.

-2-

0052

1. 걸프灣 危機 : 對이라크 武力使用에 대한 國際的 合意 構築

가. UN 安保理는 全體會議를 열고 (11.29) 이라크가 내년 1월 15일까지 쿠웨이트에서 撤收하지 않을 경우 武力使用 등 '모든 必要한 手段'을 허용한다는 決議案(678호)을 贊成 12, 反對 2(쿠바와 예멘), 棄權 1(中國)로 通過시켰음.

나. 이와 같은 UN 安保理의 決定으로 걸프灣 危機는 새로운 局面에 접어 들고 있음. 美國은 기존 입장인 이라크의 無條件 撤收와 쿠웨이트의 正常 回復 등 對이라크 強硬政策에 대한 國際的 支持를 獲得하였음.

다. 美國은 UN 安保理 理事國 絶代多數의 支持를 얻어 냄으로써 國際的 團合을 誇示하였고, 이 UN 安保理의 決定은 美國 內 輿論의 分裂을 克服하는 데 肯定的인 效果를 가져올 것으로 期待됨.

라. 한편, 훗세인 이라크 大統領은 부시 美 大統領과의 조건 없는 頂上 會談을 提議하면서 UN 安保理 決議案(11.29)에 屈服하지 않겠다고 宣言함.

마. 이라크 政府는 UN의 '二重基準'을 非難하면서, 걸프灣 危機와 팔레스타인問題를 연계시킴으로써 中東問題의 包括的인 解決을 主張하고 있으나, 美國과 西歐 同盟國들은 이러한 提議를 단호히 拒否하고 있음.

-3-

0053

바. 최근, 훗세인 이라크 大統領은 人質釋放에 柔軟性을 보이고 있으나, 쿠웨이트 철군 不可라는 종래의 立場을 堅持하면서 美軍의 증파에 따른 軍事威脅에 對應하기 위하여 쿠웨이트 戰線에 25萬 兵力(기존 의 17만)을 追加로 增派함.

사. 이번 UN 安保理의 決議는 美·蘇·西歐 등 反이라크 聯合勢力의 단 호한 立場을 再確認하고 武力使用도 불사한다는 시한부 '最後通牒' 으로 看做되고 있음.

이에 대하여, 이라크는 UN 決議案은 '非合法的이고 無效'라는 論評 으로 강력히 反撥하고 있음.

아. 한편, 부시 美 大統領은 이라크의 철군에 관한 協商을 提議하고 이와 관련하여 팔레스타인問題 協商 可能性을 示唆함으로써 걸프灣 危機의 평화로운 妥結에 이라크의 協商 參與를 誘導하고 이라크는 美國의 협상 提議에 肯定的인 態度를 취함으로써 政治的 妥結 可能 性을 높히고 있음.

---

2. 걸프灣 危機와 美國의 立場과 問題点

가. 부시 美 大統領은 걸프만 危機에 대한 強硬政策으로 國內輿論의 分 裂을 招來하였고, 그 결과 大統領에 대한 美國民의 支持가 弱化됨. 부시 行政府의 20萬 大軍의 追加파병 決定에 대해 議會 指導者나

-4-

0054

中東 專門家들은 戰爭 가능성만 增大시킬 뿐이라고 主張하고 있음.

즉, 美國의 '無條件 撤收' 固守라는 强硬態度는 훗세인에게 代案
마련의 機會를 주지 않고 外交的인 協商 可能性을 排除하기 쉽다는
것임. 일부 美 行政府 官吏들도 부시 大統領의 對中東政策 決定에
있어서 中東 專門家의 참여가 거의 없고, 또한 行政府 내의 中東
專門家들의 意見을 구하는 努力도 부족하여 아랍文化와 思考方式에
대한 理解 缺如로 훗세인의 意圖를 오판할 可能性이 높다고 憂慮하
고 있음.

현재까지 부시 大統領과 補佐官들의 태도는 後退보다는 正面對決
로 이라크를 屈服시키겠다는 立場을 堅持해 왔음. 이에 따라, 부시
大統領에 대한 비판적인 輿論이 議會나 言論界에서 야기되었고,
지지율도 걸프만 위기가 시작된 8월의 80% 선에서 현재 50% 선으로
떨어짐.

나. 부시 행정부의 걸프灣 政策에 대한 의견 분열은 지난 上·下院
청문회(11.26 - 27)에서도 잘 나타나고 있음.

'愼重論(經濟封鎖論)'은 주로 民主黨係와 은퇴 장성들에 의해
대변되고 있는 바, 이들의 입장은 미군의 20만 增派는 조급한 결정
으로 戰爭 危險만 가중시킨다는 것임. 經濟制裁의 효과는 1년 내지
1년 6개월이 필요하고, 현재 진행되고 있는 美國의 '處罰性 抑制力
(punitive deterrence)'이 이라크에 심각한 經濟的 打擊을 주고

-5-

0055

있다는 것임. 또한, 時間의 遲延이 반드시 美國에 불리하지 않은 것으로 UN과 國際輿論의 糾合에 성공하고 있다는 것을 주장하고 있음.

현재 美國이 당면하고 있는 問題点은 부시 행정부의 걸프灣 危機와 관련된 國家利益의 규명이 불분명하고, 美國의 걸프灣 政策에 대한 토론이 缺如되어 있다는 主張이 분출되고 있다는 점임.

한편 '戰爭不可避論'의 입장은 經濟制裁의 효과를 단시일 내에 기대하기 어렵다는 것임. 또한 훗세인이 協商 提議에 동의할 경우, 長期間의 協商 과정에서 武力使用 可能性을 弱化시키고 경제제재 效果를 반감케하는 등 이라크의 意圖에 말려들 가능성이 높다는 것임. 아울러, 장기간에 걸친 協商으로 반이라크 聯合勢力의 결속이 약화되고 大規模 軍事力 駐屯에 따른 경제적 費用이 엄청난 負擔이 될 것으로 憂慮하고 있음. 전쟁의 경우, 美國은 이라크를 쿠웨이트에서 逐出하는 데 그치지 않고 이라크의 軍事力을 파괴하여 隣接 國家에 대한 威脅能力을 감소시키고, 걸프지역 安定을 꾀할 수 있다는 것으로, 부시 行政府의 對이라크 强硬政策과 戰略 목적을 지지하는 주장임.

다. 이번 美國이 주도한 UN 安保理의 武力使用 決議案에 의한 대이라크 시한부 最後通牒과 대이라크 協商 제의는 美國이 기존의 强硬策을 堅持하면서 愼重論의 의견을 收斂하려는 의도로 보임. 부시 美

-6-

大統領은 美國의 强硬政策이 협상 가능성을 배제하고 戰爭으로
몰아가고 있다는 國內外 非難에 대한 政治的 負擔을 줄이고, UN
經濟制裁의 효과를 관찰하면서 協商의 可能性을 타진하려는 것임.

그러나 美國은 현재의 對置狀態가 장기간(예 6개월 이상) 계속되
는 경우 분명한 威脅要因이 稀釋됨에 따른 政治·軍事政策에 대한
支持와 支援이 감소될 가능성, 駐屯軍 維持에 따른 비용 증대,
反이라크 聯合國의 結束 약화, 中東의 다른 지역에로의 분쟁 파급
효과 등 不安定한 要因들이 발생되어 이라크 膺懲에 대한 계기를
喪失하게 될 可能性을 우려하고 있음.

특히, 美國은 걸프灣 危機 이후 짧은 시간 내에 '安保'問題에
대한 아랍 指導層의 애매하고 모순된 立場을 이해하는 데 곤란을
겪고 있으며, 中東政治를 이해하는 政治的·心理的 부담을 안고
있음.

이와 같은 요인들은 美國의 걸프灣 危機 해결에 制約要因이 되고
있음.

라. 부시 美 大統領은 UN 安保理 결정 등 國際的 支持를 얻고 있어
'憲法'과 '戰爭權限法'에 따라 議會의 반대 壓力에도 불구하고, 필
요하다면 議會의 승인 없이 戰爭에 突入할 수 있을 것임. 美國은
二次大戰 後 공식적인 戰爭宣布 없이 地域紛爭에 介入해 왔으며,
'戰爭權限法'도 현실적으로 死文化되고 있음. 또한, 美國은 전쟁
등 國家危機時에 대통령을 지지하는 政治 傳統을 가지고 있음.

-7-

0057

3. 이라크의 立場과 問題点

가. 이라크는 和戰 兩面策으로 걸프灣 危機 解決을 摸索하고 있음. 홋세인 이라크 대통령은 '無條件 撤收'라는 미국과 국제적 壓力에 굴복을 거부하면서, 부시 美 대통령과 '條件없는 協商'을 제의하고 있음. 즉, 홋세인의 戰術은 필요시는 한판 승부를 거는 軍事力을 유지하면서 外交的 解決을 모색하는 것임.

나. 홋세인 이라크 대통령은 '無條件 撤收'는 이라크의 敗北를 意味하는 것으로 이라크의 쿠웨이트에서의 철수 뿐만 아니라 이라크의 軍事力減縮 압력으로 이어질 것이며, 美軍의 쿠웨이트 駐屯 가능성과 걸프灣 支配로 연결될 수 있다고 判斷하고 있음.

다. 이라크는 西歐 人質釋放問題와 걸프灣 危機의 政治的 解決 보장을 전제조건으로 協商을 摸索하고 있음. 이라크 政府는 초기에는 人質釋放 條件으로 미국의 이라크에 대한 軍事攻擊을 않겠다는 保障을 요구하였으나, 후에는 UN 安保理 常任理事國 또는 5개국 중 2개국의 外交的 解決 공약 천명을 내세우는 등 條件을 완화시켰음. 이러한, 이라크의 立場 變化는 人質問題로 國際的 孤立에서 脫皮하여 西歐와의 대화 기회를 갖고, 미·영·프랑스 등 국내의 反戰 무드를 고조시켜 反이라크 西歐 聯合의 分裂을 조장하여 미국 주도의 軍事 介入에 반대하는 支持勢力을 獲得하려는 데 있음.

-8-

0058

라. 이러한 人質外交는 시간을 버는 데 어느 정도 成功하였으나 對이라
크 制裁에 대한 國際的 合意를 무산시키는 데는 실패하였음. 이라
크측이 인정하고 있듯이 人質問題는 國際輿論에서 이라크의 立場을
不利하게 만들었고, 美國의 立場을 强化시켰음. 현재, 인질문제에
서 美·英·프랑스·蘇 등은 훗세인의 提議를 拒否함.

마. 또한, 이라크는 經濟的·軍事的 問題点을 안고 있음. UN의 經濟
制裁로 이라크는 매일 1억 달러의 經濟損失을 겪고 있고 주요 食糧
과 기름의 配給制를 강화하고 있음. 軍事的으로는 西歐製 주요
武器의 부품 부족으로 戰力損失이 예상되고, 戰線에 배치된 이라크
부대(약 43만)는 '이라크 革命守備隊' 등 정예부대가 아닌 가장
취약한 부대로 戰鬪 初期의 犧牲洋으로 간주되고 있어 士氣가 극히
저조함. 또한, 沙漠戰에서의 軍事配置와 이동이 노출되어 聯合軍의
우세한 軍事力과 制空權 掌握으로 막대한 被害가 예상되어 軍事的
勝利는 거의 기대할 수 없음.

西方 聯合軍은 反政府 쿠르드族에 대한 군사지원으로 이라크
內部的 負擔을 가중시킬 수 있는 代案을 갖고 잇어 훗세인의 危險
부담은 더욱 높음.

이와 같은 상황에서, 훗세인 이라크 대통령은 美國이 제안한
平和協商에서 체면이 損傷되지 않는 선에서 쿠웨이트 철군 등 걸프
灣 危機 해결과 美·이라크 雙務關係를 조정할 수 있는 契機 마련

-9-

0059

을 위하여 미국과의 協商에 응할 것으로 보임.

---

4. 反이라크 聯合國의 立場 : 美國의 强硬 立場에 同調

가. 蘇聯

(1) 蘇聯은 미국이 주도한 UN 安保理의 대이라크 武力使用 決議案을 공
동제출하고 미국의 강경 입장에 同調하고 있음. 소련이 전통적인
아랍 우방국인 이라크에 대한 强硬 立場을 취하고 있는 것은 고르
바초프의 新思考外交와 改革政策에 기인하고 있음.

(2) 소련의 新思考外交에 의한 對外政策, 특히 第3世界 政策은 미국과
西歐와의 관계에서 再調整·修正되고 있음. 소련의 對外政策의 변
화는 종래 미국과 동등한 地政學的·軍事的 同率에 의해서가 아니
라 근본적으로 美·西歐政策들을 수용하겠다는 묵시적 同意에 기인
하고 있음. 소련은 美·蘇 헬싱키 頂上會談(9.9)과 全유럽安保
協力會議(CSCE, 11.20-21)에서 美·西歐와의 結束을 다짐하였음.

(3) 소련의 對아랍關係는 과거에 비하여 重要性이 감소되었으며, 훗세
인에 대한 失望과 배신감으로 소련 내에서 이라크와의 親善友好
條約(1972)의 파기가 거론된 바 있음. 또한, 고르바초프는 國內

-10-

0060

改革에 따른 國內 意見對立으로 걸프灣 危機와 같은 地域紛爭에 대한 政策決定에 있어서 큰 제약을 받고 있음. 國內 保守·改革派間의 對外政策에 대한 意見對立은 있으나 공통점은 소련의 國際紛爭 介入을 回避하고, 對外政策은 국내의 여건을 고려하는 實用主義的 接近을 주장하고 있다는 것임. 고르바쵸프의 新思考는 이들 意見을 모두 受容하여 소련 능력에 벗어나는 國際紛爭에의 개입을 반대하고 安保는 軍縮, 協商과 協力으로 追求한다는 原則을 추구하고 있어 훗세인 이라크 대통령의 覇權 追求에 정면으로 對立되고 있음.

(4) 한편, 소련은 一方的인 미국 지지는 소련의 立場을 더욱 弱化시킬 것으로 인식, 마지막까지 政治協商에 의한 해결을 주장하고 있음. 그러나, 소련은 美·西歐와의 관계 중요성에 비추어 이라크가 讓步하지 않음으로써 결과되는 美·西歐의 對이라크 武力 膺懲에 反對하지 않을 것임.

(5) 소련은 UN을 통한 制裁나 협상 또는 소련의 직접 중재에 의해서 중동에 대한 影響力 行事를 추구하고 있으나, 최근 미국의 對이라크 直接協商 제의에 따라 蘇聯의 참여 폭은 줄어들 것임.

나. 西方 同盟國

(1) EC 諸國들은 걸프灣 危機에 EC의 團合을 과시하고 있으며 UN의 對

이라크 제재에 政治·經濟面에서 一致된 行動을 보이고 있음.

(2) 英國과 프랑스는 즉각적인 派兵으로 2次大戰時 同盟國으로서의 英·
프랑스의 위치를 강화하였고, 獨逸과 日本의 국제정치적 位置와 역
할에 대한 논의를 야기시킴. 獨逸과 日本의 세계적 役割은 당분간
財政的 支援에 제한될 것으로 보이는 바, 그 이유는 다음과 같음.

　　獨逸은 統一에 따른 政治·經濟的 費用과 憲法的인 制約으로
對外的인 軍事 役割에 제약이 따를 것임.

　　日本은 憲法과 自民黨의 위치 약화와 취약한 리더쉽으로 적극적
인 對外軍事支援에 한계가 있음. 현재 日本으로서는 財政的인 支援
외에 세계적인 역할 증대를 꾀할 國際政治的 與件이 미비되어 있어,
당분간은 國際的인 責任 擴大를 원하지 않을 것으로 보임.

(3) 걸프灣 危機는 EC의 군사적 역할에 대한 問題点을 노정시켰음. 즉,
EC는 政治的 決定을 실행하기 위한 軍事協力機構와 군사조직이
缺如되어 있어 기본적으로 脫冷戰時代의 安保的 對應策이 없다는
것임. 기존의 NATO는 유럽地域 외의 軍事介入을 금지하고 있고,
西部유럽同盟(WEU) 機構는 기능이 제한되어 있음. 이에 대해서,
美國과 英國은 NATO 기능과 역할을 擴大시키려는 의도를 갖고
있으나, 프랑스는 美國의 對유럽 영향력 확대를 우려하여 WEU의
强化를 摸索하고 있음. NATO와 WEU에 관한 문제는 유럽安保와 관련
되어 향후 美·西歐間에 조정되어야 할 課題임.

-12-

0062

(4) 미국은 걸프灣 危機에서 西歐의 支持가 절대적으로 重要하다는 인식에서, 또한 프랑스 등 EC는 미국의 獨自的 政策을 견제하려는 의도에서 UN의 決議를 推進해 왔음. 이번 UN 安保理의 武力使用 決議와 對이라크 協商 提議는 그동안 프랑스의 미국에 대한 獨走 우려를 일소하고 反이라크 西歐 結束을 다짐하는 계기가 되었음.

다. 中國

이번 UN 安保理 常任理事國 중 유일하게 棄權한 중국은 이라그의 侵攻과 쿠웨이트 合倂을 비난하고 무기를 포함한 對이라크 交易을 중지하는 등 UN의 決議를 支持하고 있으나 武力行事보다는 平和的 解決策을 强調하는 편임. 中國은 현재 中國이 당면하고 있는 다음과 같은 對內外的인 問題点과 관련 棄權한 것으로 보임.

(1) 中國의 對中東政策은 서구·소련의 '對中國包圍'를 견제하는 緩衝 地域으로 중요성을 지니고 있음. 최근 中國은 對中東進出에 적극적으로 노력해 왔으며 사우디와의 外交關係 수립과 이스라엘과의 非公式的 協力關係를 구축함으로써 自國의 影響力 擴大에 성괴를 거두고 있음. 그러나, 이라크의 쿠웨이트 侵攻으로 빚어진 걸프灣 危機는 中國의 국제적 역할과 第3世界 外交에 딜레마로 부각되고 있음.

-13-

0063

(2) 中國은 걸프灣 危機로 사우디 등 中東諸國의 對美·西歐 의존도가
심화되고, 外勢牽制勢力으로 간주되는 아랍연맹과 걸프協力協議會
(GCC) 등의 地域機構가 무력한 데 실망하고 있음. 또한, 中國은 아
랍국들간의 葛藤에 外部勢力의 개입으로 인한, 즉, 强大國의 中東
支配 결과를 憂慮하고 있음. 현재 中國은 第3世界 友好國들간의
분열로 中國이 第3世界 主導國으로 국제적 役割을 堪當할 能力이
不足하다는 것을 인식하게 됨. 즉, 獨立自主外交와 第3世界의 主導
的 役割을 추구하는 기존 外交路線과 관련, 중국은 國際的 制裁에
동참하여야 한다는 필요성에 따라 對中東地域 외교 행동 등에 制約
性을 안게 됨. 또한, 걸프灣 危機에 따라 빚어진 對中東 經濟關系
의 상실은 독자적인 役割 遂行에 制約要因으로 작용하고 있음.

(3) 中國이 당면한 外交的인 딜레마는 國內問題와도 연계되어 있는 바,
걸프灣 危機에서 中國이 國際的인 協力을 택할 것인가 또는 孤立
主義를 택할 것인가 하는 선택의 문제는 改革·保守派間의 葛藤을
심화시킬 가능성이 있음. 중국은 UN의 經濟制裁에 찬성하면서도
武力使用에 棄權함으로써 對中東外交와 國內政策 對立에서 빚어질
수 있는 否定的인 結果를 最少化하는 中立的인 태도를 견지할 것으
로 보임. 이러한 中國의 정책은 天安門事態 이후 疏遠해진 美國에
대한 門戶開放 등 經濟協力을 재개한다는 妥協의 소산일 수 있음.

-14-

0064

5. 관련 아랍국들의 立場 : 地域 勢力均衡 維持 努力

가. 걸프灣 危機로 아랍권은 親이라크勢力과 反이라크勢力으로 兩分化
되고 있음. 이집트, 시리아 등 이라크와의 主導權 競爭을 추구하는
强國들은 이라크의 弱化를 겨냥한 反이라크 聯合勢力에 가담하고
있으며, 이라크의 經濟·軍事支援에 의존하고 있는 예멘, 수단,
PLO 등 아랍 弱小國들은 이라크를 支持하고 있음. 한편, 여타 아랍
각국들은 걸프灣 危機 이후 장기적인 地域政勢에 불안감을 갖고 있
어 강력한 對이라크 制裁에 있어서 분명한 立場을 回避하는 中立的
인 立場으로 기울어지고 있음.

나. 이집트는 이번 事態를 아랍권에서의 主導的 役割을 構築할 수 있는
계기로 보고 '無條件 撤收'와 '쿠웨이트 正常回復'이라는 UN과
서구의 입장을 강력히 支持하고 있음. 그러나, 西歐와의 協力이라
는 인상을 회피하기 위하여 아랍聯盟의 決定의 명분으로 군대를
派遣하고 잇음. 이번 걸프灣 危機에서 西歐와의 協力으로 이집트는
서구와 사우디 등으로부터 負債蕩減, 經濟 및 軍事支援 등으로
利得을 보고 있고, 걸프灣 危機 後의 '安保體制' 構築에서 중심
국가로 浮上할 수 있는 입장에 서게 됨.

다. 시리아는 反이라크 同盟에서 이집트의 浮上에 비해서 시리아의
   역할에 대한 平價切下와 疎外感 등으로 美國과의 연계에 거리를
   두고 있음. 최근 美·시리아간의 頂上會談에서도 걸프灣 危機에
   대한 認識은 같이하면서도 對이라크 制裁와 地域問題 解決에
   인식의 차이가 있었음. 그러나, 美國과의 關係 改善으로 레바논
   事態와 골란高原 등 이스라엘과의 관계에서 美國의 協力이 필요
   한 이상, 反이라크 聯合에서 脫退하지는 않을 것으로 보임.

라. 이집트, 시리아, 모로코 등 아랍연맹군 派遣國家들도 무조건
   철수와 正常回復에 贊成하면서도 대이라크 軍事制裁에 있어서는
   美國과는 의견을 달리할 수 있음. 특히, 이라크軍 撤收와 관련
   되어 對이라크 군사제재나 美國의 繼續駐屯問題에서는 아랍圈의
   挑戰을 의식하여 美國과의 의견대립 요인으로 작용할 수 있음.

마. 이란은 이라크의 平和提案에 肯定的인 태도를 취하고 있으나
   이들 두 국가가 反西同盟關係로 發展될 가능성은 없고, 걸프灣
   危機에 대응하기 위한 獨自的인 行動을 취할 능력도 없음.
   이란은 이라크와 같이 西歐의 介入을 반대하고 팔레스타인 문제
   등 포괄적인 地域問題 解決을 주장하고 있으나, 傳統的인 양국
   간의 競爭關係로 이라크의 勢力이 弱化되는 것을 바라고 있음.
   그렇다고, 이 지역에서 美國의 支配를 招來하는 이라크의 崩壞도
   원하지 않고 있음. 이란은 美國과 서구의 제한된 軍事 및 經濟

-16-

0066

制裁로 이라크가 弱化되는 것을 바랄 것임. 또한, 이란 內政은 라프산자니 大統領이 主導하는 穩健派와 하메네이와 모타쉐미가 주도하는 强硬派의 權力鬪爭 狀態이기 때문에 겉프灣 危機에 介入할 가능성이 적음. 사실, 이라크는 겉프灣 危機로 빚어진 高油價로 經濟難을 겪고 있는 라프산자니 穩健政府를 도와준 결과를 초래하여 强硬派가 주장하는 外國軍 撤收를 위한 이라크 와의 연계 등 冒險的인 政策을 추구할 가능성은 희박함

바. 예멘, 수단, 리비아, PLO, 요르단 등은 이라크와의 政治·經濟· 軍事關係로 초기에 親이라크 立場을 堅持하였으나, 國際的 孤立 을 우려하고 아랍국들의 壓力으로 중립적인 平和的 解決을 주장 하고 있으나, 이들 국가들의 影響力은 겉프灣 危機 해결에 중요 한 變數가 되지 않을 것임.

사. 美國이 이라크와 協商을 제의하고 팔레스타인問題의 연계를 시사 함으로써 온건 아랍측과의 結束을 强化하고 親이라크國家의 反美 態度와 반온건 아랍국 태도를 다소 緩和시킬 수 있을 것임.

---

6. 平和的 解決을 위한 시나리오

가. 현재의 겉프灣 危機를 戰爭으로 解決할 경우, 이에 따른 費用은

-17-

0067

물론이고 장기적인 地域平和 構築에 생산적인 결과를 保障할 수 없다는 것이 一般的인 觀測임.

美國은 전쟁을 치룰 경우, 戰爭에 따른 많은 費用을 지불하면서도 地域安定과 自國의 影響力 構築에도 확신을 가질 수 없으며, 훗세인 이라크 大統領은 自身의 政治的 生命 뿐만 아니라 國家의 崩壞 危險性까지도 배제할 수 없을 것이기 때문임.

나. 이번 UN 安保理 決議(678)에 의한 武力使用 決議는 역설적으로 협상을 위한 突破口를 마련할 것으로 보임. 美國은 國際的 支持를 얻음으로써, 종래의 '讓步不可'가 '協商不可'라는 强硬立場에서 旋回할 수 있는 여유를 갖게 되었음. 한편, 훗세인 이라크 大統領은 막연한 시간끌기 작전에서 좀 더 現實的인 協商 代案을 제시할 부담감을 안게 되었음. 사실, 막대한 軍事力의 長期的인 대치상태는 좌절감으로 相互間의 忍耐를 減少시키고, 그 결과 軍事論理가 정책을 좌우하게 되어 戰爭 勃發 危險性을 높히게 될 것이기 때문임.

다. 協商 過程에서 美國은 '先撤收 後協商'이라는 기존 立場을 堅持할 것이고, 또한 이라크의 無條件 撤收 필요성은 국제적으로 正當化되고 있음. 그러나 문제는 撤軍과 관련하여 어떤 方法으로 훗세인의 채면을 살려주는가 하는 것임. 훗세인은 困境에 몰리면 戰爭을 選擇할 가능성이 있기 때문임.

-18-

라. 美國과 이라크와의 協商에서 주요 議題는 다음과 같은 事案이 될 수 있음.

(1) 이라크와 쿠웨이트간 未解決問題로 남아 있는 領土調整問題 논의

(2) UN이나 國際機構가 관련될 수 있는 이라크의 化學武器 生産과 核武器 開發問題 등이 地域安保와 관련되어 논의

(3) 팔레스타인問題는 이스라엘과 기타 아랍 관련국들의 參與가 필요한 것이기 때문에 구체적인 代案 마련보다는 中東 平和協商을 위한 국제회의 구성 등 平和的 解決을 위한 기본적인 구상 논의에 한정될 것임.

(4) 현재 상황에서 美國과 이라크 協商에서 이라크는 撤軍에 따른 영토문제와 팔레스타인問題 등 직접적인 結果를 期待하기는 어려울 것이나, 可視的인 代案이 보장된다면 撤軍을 斷行할 가능성이 있음.

이라크의 분명한 결과 없는 撤軍 조치가 훗세인의 沒落과 연계되어 곤란할 것이라는 우려는 證據가 稀薄함. 최근 이라크 國民과 아랍人들의 훗세인에 대한 支持는 훗세인 개인에 대한 支持보다는 차라리 고압적이고 도덕적으로 墮落한 西歐에 대한 抵抗이라는 象徵的인 要因이 크게 작용하고 있기 때문임. 또한, 현재의 걸프灣 危機를 계기로 이란의 위협을 牽制하기 위하여 취해진 이라크의 讓步는 훗세인의 執權 持續에 정치적 負擔이 되고 있지

-19-

0069

않음.

(5) 현실적으로 美·이라크 兩國은 自國의 利益 追求를 위하여 상호
협상을 필요로 하는 입장에 있음.

미국은 걸프灣과 중동지역에 미국의 영향력을 견지하기 위하여,
훗세인은 자신이 '汎아랍主義' 지도자로서 長期執權하기 위하여,
兩國은 상호 體面을 維持하는 협상으로 걸프灣 危機를 타개할
가능성이 높음.

---

7. 걸프灣 危機 後의 中東情勢 不安 持續

가. 걸프灣 危機를 계기로 90년대 中東地域政勢는 50년대와 비슷한
現狀維持勢力과 現狀打破勢力間의 대립으로 '汎아랍主義'가 다시
擡頭되고 西方과의 緊張關係가 持續될 것으로 전망됨.

나. 훗세인 이라크 大統領과 强硬 아랍국들은 '아랍統一'과 '富의
分配'라는 現狀打破 주장으로 現狀維持를 주장하는 産油富國과
穩健 아랍國들 등 親西方 아랍國들에 대한 挑戰이 예상되고, 이
에 따라 아랍圈은 이라크와 이집트를 두 축으로 兩分化될 가능성
이 높고, 또한, 이러한 아랍圈의 分裂相은 이스라엘과의 關係가
平和的으로 解決되지 않을 경우에 地域不安要因으로 작용할 것임.

다. 美國은 自國의 영향력 견지와 親美 아랍국들에 대한 支援을 위하

0070

-20-

어 地域安保體制를 강화할 것임. 그러나 美國 內의 介入 反對
輿論 增大와 親美 아랍國들(地域國들)의 확고한 支援 要求를
모두 滿足시킬 수 있는 雙務安保關係 構築에 역점을 두게 될 것
임. 美國은 地域集團安保體制와 UN 기능의 制約에 비추어 볼 때
集團安保 構築에는 消極的인 態度를 견지할 것임.

8. 脫冷戰時代의 安保와 韓國의 考慮事項

가 . 걸프灣 危機로 빚어진 國際紛爭 관리는 美國의 주도와 蘇聯·
英·프랑스 등의 지원 아래 수행되고 있어, 2次 世界大戰中의
西方 聯合勢力의 再結束이 나타나고 있음. 90년대 國際體制의
多極化 경향은 다분히 過渡期的인 성격을 띠고 있으며, 새로운
安保體制의 構築이 모색되고 있음. 이 과정에서 美國은 유일한
軍事强大國으로서 地域紛爭 管理者로서의 주도적 役割을 수행할
것임. 이러한 역할 수행에 있어서 日·西歐 등 同盟國들의 지원
을 필요로 할 것임. 또한, 美國은 만족할만한 새로운 國際的
安保體制가 구축될 때까지는 지역국들과의 雙務關係를 강화할 것
으로 보임.

나 . 현재, 蘇聯과 西歐 諸國들은 國內經濟問題와 西歐統合에 관련된
諸問題로 독자적이고 一貫된 對外政策을 추구할 可能性이 희박함.

中國·日本·獨逸 등도 당분간 地域紛爭 관리를 위한 國際的 役割 增大에 제약이 있음.

다. 韓國은 美國과의 安保關係를 계속 강화하고, 防衛分擔 增大와 國防力 現代化를 적절한 수준에서 調和시켜 나가야 할 것임.

라. 韓國은 걸프灣 危機로 빚어진 戰線國에 대한 經濟支援을 계기로 未修交國인 이집트, 시리아 등과의 外交關係 樹立 노력을 倍加하여야 할 것임.

마. 90년대 걸프地域의 不安定 持續으로 에너지 공급 확보 등 綜合的인 에너지政策을 樹立하여야 할 것임.

1990. 11. 28.

作成 : 研究教授   崔 宜 喆
討論 : 研究室長   金 國 振
       研究部長   南 洪 祐
       研究部長   玄 熙 剛
       研究教授   李 東 輝

0072

폐灣 軍事力 配置 現況

사우디 駐屯 多國籍 地上軍

美 육군	120,000
美 해병	45,000
美 소계	165,000* (57%)
사우디아라비아	38,000
이집트	30,000
시리아	15,000
쿠웨이트	7,000
폐灣 협력회의	7,000
모로코	1,500
아랍 소계	98,500 (34%)
영국	9,000
프랑스	5,000
유럽 소계	14,000 (5%)
파키스탄	5,000
방글라데시	6,000
세네갈	500
기타 이슬람 소계	11,500 (4%)
합 계	289,000 (100%)

이라크 軍

쿠웨이트 지역	430,000 (45%)
기타 지역	530,000 (55%)
합 계	960,000 (100%)

註: o 配置 兵力은 11월 이후 기준임.
   o 폐灣 協力會議의 반도방패군 구성국가는 오만, 아랍에미리트, 바레인, 카타르임.
   o 미국은 1991년 1월 말까지 20만을 추가배치할 예정이고, 이럴 경우 美軍이 總聯合軍의 70%선으로 美國과 이라크(또는 아랍권)와의 대결이라는 政治的 負擔을 안게 될 수 있음.
   * 기타 65,000명의 美軍 兵力이 艦上 혹은 隣接 國家에 전개중임.

-23-.

0073

90/2114

기 안 용 지

분류기호 문서번호	중근동 720-2969	(전화:)	시 행 상 특별취급	
보존기간	영구·준영구. 10. 5. 3. 1.	장 관 예		
수 신 처 보존기간				
시행일자	1990. 12. 12.			
보조 기관	국 장	협조기관	문 서 통 제	
	심의관			
	과 장			
기안책임자	김동억		발 송 인	

경 유 수 신 참 조	수신처 참조	발신명의	

제 목   걸프 정세 및 전망 분석자료 송부

    최근 걸프 정세에 관한 '걸프 정세 및 전망' 자료를

별첨 송부 하오니 업무에 참고 하시기 바랍니다.

    수신처 : 전 재외 공관장 (대사 주재지역 총영사관 제외)

0074

분류기호 문서번호	중근동 720- ~113 ( )	협 조 문 용 지	결	담당	과장	국장
시행일자	1990. 12. 12.		재			
수 신	수신처 참조	발 신	중동아프리카국장			(서명)
제 목	걸프 정세 및 전망 분석자료 송부					

당국에서 작성한 '걸프 정세 및 전망' 자료를 별첨

송부 하오니 업무에 참고 하시기 바랍니다.

첨 부 : 걸프정세 및 전망 1부. 끝.

수신처 : 장·차관실, 외교 안보 연구원장, 제 1, 2 차관보,

각 실·국 장.

0075

걸프 情勢 및 展望

1990. 12. 11.

外 務 部
中 東 아 프 리 카 局

目　　　次

0077

1. 狀 況

가. 유엔의 武力使用 決議 및 美國의 協商 提議

걸프事態는 11.29. 유엔 安保理가 이락에 대한 武力使用을 承認하고 사담후세인 이락 大統領이 이에 絶對 不服할 것임을 밝힘으로써 武力 對決의 危險이 성큼 다가오는듯 하였으나 ①이틀후 부쉬 大統領이 이락과의 直接 協商을 電擊的으로 제의하고 ②사담후세인 大統領이 이를 受諾한데 이어 ③12.6. 西方人質 全員을 釋放 決定 하므로써 平和的 解決의 曙光이 비치기 시작 하였음.

나. 外交的 努力의 展開

이와 함께 ①유엔安保理는 中東平和 國際會議 開催를 討議하고, ②一部穩健 아랍국가들은 쿠웨이트 領土의 割讓과 多國籍軍을 아랍군으로 代置하는 方案을 가지고 仲裁에 積極 나서고 있어 일단 武力衝突의 危險은 상당히 적어지고 相對的으로 平和的 解決의 可能性이 크게 높아진 것으로 보겠음.

다. 軍事的 動向

이에 앞서 11.8. 美國의 兵力 15萬名 增派 決定에 이어 이락은 25萬 兵力의 쿠웨이트 增派를 發表하므로써 이에 對應한바 있음. 또한 英國도 11.21. 1만4천명의 兵力 增派를 發表 하였음.

2. 分 析

가. 美國의 外交的 壓力

1) 걸프事態 發生 直後 美國은 美軍의 사우디 派兵에 즈음하여 ①美國人 人命 保護 ②이락軍의 쿠웨이트 撤軍 ③쿠웨이트 合法政府의 復歸와 ④걸프地域의 安保를 4大 政策目標로 設定하고 특히 人質釋放, 撤收 및 合法政府 復歸는 결코 協商의 對象이 될수 없다는 斷乎한 立場을 表明해 왔음.

1

0078

2) 이러한 立場을 貫徹하기 위해서는 이락에 대한 軍事的, 外交的 壓力을 極大化 할 必要가 있다는 判斷下에 安保理가 武力使用 承認 決議案을 採擇하도록 베이커 國務長官은 물론 부쉬 大統領까지 前面에 나서서, 득히 經濟 制裁 效果를 위해서는 좀더 시간이 必要하다는 立場에서 武力使用에 留保的 態度를 취했던 蘇聯, 佛蘭西, 中國等 安保理 常任 理事國 說得에 全力을 투구한 結果, 美國이 安保理 常任 理事國 議長職을 예멘에게 引繼하기 이틀前인 11.29. 同 決議案 採擇에 成功 하였음.

3) 美國이 武力使用 決議 採擇을 위해 큰 努力을 하게된 背景은 ①當初 1·2개월이면 效果가 나타날 것으로 보았던 經濟 制裁 措置가 豫想과는 달리 이락에 대해 決定的인 打擊을 주지 못하고 있다는 結論에 이르고 ②美軍을 包含한 多國籍軍의 配置만으로는 사담후세인으로 하여금 多國籍軍이 實際로 이락을 공격 하리라고 믿게 하기가 어렵다는 것이 西方側의 共通된 分析이었고 ③美國이 실제 軍事行動을 취해야 할경우, 國內外的 支持 基盤을 튼튼히 할 必要가 있다는 점이었음.

4) 美國이 武力使用 承認 決議案을 成立시킨 直後 다시 電擊的으로 이락과의 直接 對話를 提議한 것은 ①美行政府의 事態의 平和的 解決 意志를 부각시켜 美國內 反戰 輿論을 撫摩 하므로써 對話가 決裂되는 경우 武力使用이 不可避하다는 것을 美國民에게 說得할 必要가 있다는 考慮와 ②사담후세인 大統領에 대해 撤收할수 있는 名分을 주어 國內外的으로 體面을 維持하도록 할 必要가 있다는 考慮가 作用한 것으로 보임.

나. 이락의 心理戰
1) 이락이 美國의 協商 提議를 受諾한 背景으로는 ①安保理가 時限까지 정하여 武力使用을 承認 함으로써 美國의 戰爭 遂行 決意를 새로히 認識하게 되었다는 점 ②經濟 封鎖가 産業部門에는 아직 큰 打擊을 주지 못했지만 國民 生活에는 相當한 정도까지 打擊을 주고 있다는점 ③對美 協商을 지금까지 主張해 오던대로 팔레스타인 問題를 포함한 包括的인 中東平和 協商으로 이끌어 가도록 하여 時間을 벌어보자는 점을 들수 있을것임.

2

0079

2) 한편 종래 多國籍軍이 攻擊을 敢行하지 않는다는 保障을 하면, 크리스마스로 부터 3.15 까지 3개월에 걸쳐 人質을 釋放하겠다는 條件附 人質 釋放 立場을 바꾸어 이락이 西方人質을 크리스마스 以前 全員, 無條件 釋放할 것을 電擊 發表한 背景은,

① 유엔의 武力使用 承認 成立으로 나타난 美國의 一戰不辭의 결의로 보아 人間 防牌로서의 人質의 戰略的 價値가 크게 떨어져 人質의 繼續 抑留는 오히려 世界的 敵對感만 招來하고 있다는점

② 對美, 對西方 平和제스쳐로 美國內 反戰 輿論을 부추기고 多國籍軍의 結束을 弛緩시켜 戰爭 反對 움직임을 擴散시킬수 있다는점

③ 人質釋放이 12.4. 이락, 요르단, 예멘, PLO 頂上會談의 結果임을 부각시킴으로써 걸프事態를 아랍 內部에서 解決할 수 있다는 것을 對外에 誇示하고자 했던점

④ 또한 形式上 이락 議會가 사담후세인 大統領의 決定을 承認하도록 함으로써 이락 國民의 總意에 의한 決定이라는 점을 强調하여 對內的인 結束을 圖謀할 수 있다는점 등이 考慮되었을 것임.

다. 對이락 軍事的 壓力

1) 美國은 이락과의 協商 提議를 하는 한편, 12.4. 사우디 駐屯 美軍과 사우디 陸軍의 合同作戰으로 이락 國境 南部에서 大規模 訓練을 실시 하고 旣存의 防禦 姿勢에서 攻擊 態勢로 轉換 하였음을 發表 함으로써 ①이락에 대한 心理的 壓迫을 加重시키고 ②有事時 指揮體制 確立과 美軍의 沙漠戰 適應을 圖謀한 것으로 봄.

2) 한편 이락은 11.20. 쿠웨이트에 兵力 25만을 追加 派遣키로 決定하고 우선 7개 사단을 이동 配置하는 한편 豫備軍 15만명을 동원 하였음. 이로써 45만명의 이락군이 쿠웨이트에 배치된 것으로 추정됨.

3) 美軍을 包含한 多國籍軍의 兵力은 11.8. 美軍 약 15만명의 增派 發表와 11.22. 英國軍 1만4천명의 增派 發表等을 감안할때 兵力 配置가 완료 되는 1월 초순경까지는 약 55만 兵力이 될 것으로 일단 推定되나 안보리 決議가 採擇된 以後에는 總兵力 規模에 대한 報道, 특히 西方言論의 報道가 없어 과연 美側이 發表한대로 兵力 增派가 繼續되고 있는지 一抹의 疑問이 있음.

3

0080

3. 展望

가. 이락의 選擇

1) 쿠웨이트의 이락化 繼續 推進

가) 이락은 쿠웨이트 侵攻以後 4개월이상 推進해온 쿠웨이트의 이락化 政策을 加速化하여 쿠웨이트 王政이 復歸 되더라도 有效한 統治가 事實上 어렵게 되도록 繼續 努力할 것임.

나) 이락의 쿠웨이트 侵攻의 目的은 ①8년간의 이.이戰으로 인한 經濟的 逼迫에서 脫皮 ②原油 輸出을 위한 걸프만 港口 確保 ③7.25. 사담후세인 大統領의 終身制 改憲에 대한 國民의 비판을 外部로 돌리고 ④예멘, 요르단등과 提携하여 中東의 覇權을 確立 하는것 이었음으로 이 目的의 達成을 위해서는 쿠웨이트의 合併 내지는 隷屬化가 可能만 하다면 最善의 方策일 것임.

2) 領土 一部 割讓 妥協

가) 쿠웨이트 侵攻 名分중의 하나가 이락의 쿠웨이트 全國土에 대한 영유권 主張이었으나 侵攻의 重要한 目的이 經濟的, 戰略的인 것이었고 실제로 사담후세인 大統領이 8.12. 平和회담 條件으로 내세운것도 ①이락國境 루마일라 油田地帶의 領土 할양과 ②걸프만으로 나가는 戰略的 要衝地인 부비얀섬과 와르바 섬의 租借 要求였던점에 비추어 이러한 두가지 要求가 全部 充足될수 있다면 좋겠지만 部分的 으로라도 充足되어 體面만 維持될수 있다면 사담후세인 大統領은 유엔이 정한 明年 1.15. 에 臨迫해서 쿠웨이트로+부터 自進 撤收할 可能性이 있음.

나) 실제로 亡命 쿠웨이트 政府側과 사우디 國防長官等은 이락군이 撤收하는 境遇, 쿠웨이트 領土 一部 할양 問題도 協商 可能할 것임을 示唆한바 있었으며 그후 사우디의 公式 否認이 있기는 하였으나 割讓 可能性이 繼續 擧論되고 있는것이 事實임. 다만, 와르바섬 租借의 경우 軍事的, 經濟的 理由에서 이란은 이에 상당한 抵抗을 할 것으로 보임.

4

0081

3) 中東平和 國際 會議

　　　가)　이락이 쿠웨이트로 부터 撤軍하는것에 대한 諒解 事項으로
　　　　　쿠웨이트 問題를 包含한 中東問題의 包括的 解決을 위하여
　　　　　國際會議 開催를 主張할 可能性이 있음. 이는 아랍권의 呼應을
　　　　　받을수 있을 것이며 유엔 安保理에서도 美國을 除外한 蘇, 佛,
　　　　　中等 常任 理事國들이 이미 中東平和案 摸索을 위하여 適切한
　　　　　時期에 國際會議를 開催한다는 決議案 採擇에 원칙적으로 합의한
　　　　　것으로 알려지고 있어 쿠웨이트 問題를 包含한 中東平和 國際
　　　　　會議가 91년에 열릴 可能性도 큼.

　　　나)　사우디를 비롯한 걸프 沿岸 産油國들도 武力 解決 不辭 立場을
　　　　　表明하고는 있으나 內心으로는 걸프 地域에서 武力 衝突을
　　　　　바라지 않고 있어, 쿠웨이트로 부터 이락군이 撤收 한다면,
　　　　　쿠웨이트 문제를 이스라엘의 팔레스타인 占領 問題와 連繫시켜
　　　　　解決하자는 이락의 主張을 反對하지는 않을 것이므로 美國, 이락
　　　　　協商에서 이 問題가 擧論될 것이 確實視 됨.

　　　다)　美國은 지금까지 팔레스타인 問題와 쿠웨이트 撤軍이 別個의
　　　　　事案 이라는 立場을 固守하여 왔으나 사담후세인 大統領이 쿠웨이트
　　　　　撤軍의 前提로 이 問題를 들고 나올때 유엔 安保理 決議를
　　　　　理由로 이락의 條件없는 撤軍과 사바 王政 復歸를 主張하고
　　　　　있는 美國으로서도 이스라엘의 유엔 決議 不履行을 論議하게
　　　　　될 國際會議 開催를 拒絶할 수 없는 難處한 立場에 처하게 될
　　　　　것임.

　나. 美國의 選擇
　　1) 美軍 또는 아랍 平和 維持軍의 繼續 駐屯
　　　가)　美國은 이락이 쿠웨이트에서 撤收하고 쿠웨이트 王政만 復歸
　　　　　된다면 일단 一次的 目標는 達成할 수 있다고 보나, 걸프地域의
　　　　　安保를 保障한다는 窮極的인 目標는 이락의 軍事力을 弱化
　　　　　시키기 전에는 성취할수가 없으므로 이락의 쿠웨이트 領土
　　　　　할양의 代價로 美軍 또는 多國籍軍을 代置할 美國 影響下의
　　　　　아랍 平和軍을 域內에 常駐 시키고자 試圖할 可能性이 있음.

5

0082

나) 그러나 이경우 軍事 大國으로서의 이락의 位置는 弱化되지
않는다는 어려움이 있을것임.

2) 經濟 封鎖의 繼續
가) 美國은 어떠한 理由를 들어서라도 이락에 대한 經濟制裁 특히
武器, 戰略 物資에 대한 國際的인 禁輸措置를 斷行함으로써
이락의 軍事力 특히 核武器, 化學武器, 미사일 攻擊能力을
弱化 내지 除去 시키고자 할 可能性도 있음.

나) 이 경우 이락이 쿠웨이트에서 撤收하면 유엔 決議에 의한
經濟 封鎖는 더이상 妥當性을 喪失하게 되므로 다른 理由를
들어 리비아에 대한 禁輸措置와 유사한 措置를 施行해야 될
것임.

3) 武力 使用 可能性
가) 美國은 유엔이 정한 時限을 遵守하지 않았다는 理由로 이락
軍事力의 弱化라는 窮極的 目標를 達成하는 方法으로 武力
使用을 選擇할 可能性도 排除할수 없는바, ①目標를 가장
確實하게 達成할수 있고 ②人質釋放 및 駐쿠웨이트 美大使館員
撤收로 民間人 犧牲에 대한 負擔이 없어졌으며 ③大規模의
多國籍軍을 派兵하고 많은 나라에 軍費까지 分擔시킨 狀態에서
쉽게 撤收하기가 어렵다는점 등이 考慮될 것임.

나) 그러나 武力使用 경우 ①막대한 人命被害 ②이스라엘의 戰爭
介入으로 인한 擴戰 憂慮 ③美國과 世界 經濟에 미칠 影響
④名分없는 戰爭 主張이라는 批判的 輿論등을 역시 考慮하지
않을수 없을것임.

다) 디만 戰爭을 할 경우에는 奇襲的, 電擊的, 短期的인 大量
攻擊이 豫想됨.

6

0083

I. 主要 國際情勢 分析

1. 이라크. 쿠웨이트事態 分析(VI)

> ○ 폐湾事態는 1.9 美-이라크 外務長官会談이 決裂되고,
> 1.15 撤收 時限이 임박함에 따라 事態発生以後 戦争勃発 危
> 険이 가장 高潮되고 있는 바, 向後 最終幕後協商에 失敗여부
> 에 따라 和. 戦의 갈림이 보다 明確해 질 것임.
>
> ○ 한편, 폐湾 戦争 발발시, 両側 모두 막대한 人的. 物
> 的 被害가 豫想된다는 점에서, 戦争回避를 위한 幕後交渉이
> 活潑해 질 것으로 展望됨. 向後 交渉은 美-이라크 直接交渉보
> 다는 프랑스, EC 및 UN 事務総長을 통한 迂回的인 方法을 통
> 해 마지막까지 進行될 것으로 展望됨.
>
> ○ 向後 交渉의 요체는 이라크의 쿠웨이트 撤軍과 関聯,
> 후세인의 체면을 어떻게 세워주느냐 하는 것으로서, 팔레스타
> 인問題 解決 및 UN監視軍 派遣等 UN의 介入問題가 主要 争
> 点이 될 것으로 豫想됨.

—3—

가) 軍事的 対峙 現況

1) 多国籍軍 增派 現況

ㅇ 美国은 [부시] 美大統領이 지난 1 1 . 8 페湾 派遣 兵力
을 2 3 万에서 4 3 万으로 增派하겠다는 第2 段階 페湾 派兵計劃
을 發表한 以後 追加派兵을 계속하고 있는 바, 同 趨勢가 계
속될 경우 2 月中旬頃 美軍 및 多国籍軍은 6 3 万에 이를 것으
로 豫想됨.

ㅇ 其他 多国籍軍 兵力 現況

  - 사우디   3 8 , 0 0 0
  - 이집트   3 0 , 0 0 0
  - 시리아   1 5 , 0 0 0
  - 쿠웨이트   7 , 0 0 0
  - G C C   7 , 0 0 0
  - 모로코   1 , 5 0 0
  - 英 国   3 0 , 0 0 0
  - 프랑스   1 0 , 0 0 0
  - 파키스탄   5 , 0 0 0
  - 방글라데시   6 , 0 0 0
  - 세네갈   5 0 0

o 美 海軍은 페湾과 紅海上에 既配置된 3個의 航母戦団 (미드웨이, 사라토가, 케네디) 에 追加하여 지난 12.8 航母 '레인저'를 주축으로한 레인저 航母戦団(7 隻), 12.27 아메리카 航母戦団(7 隻) 과 루즈벨트 航母戦団(7 隻) 을 追加 派遣함으로써 美海軍이 現在 稼動中인 航母 12 隻中 半数가 中東地域에 集結하게 되었는 바, 戦争勃発時 대규모 航母航空隊를 利用, 主要 軍事施設을 爆撃할 수 있는 制空権을 強化함.

o NATO는 터어키의 요청에 따라 터어키와 이라크의 国境地域에 独逸, 이태리. 벨기에 所属 42台의 戦闘機를 派遣하였으며 現在 5,000餘名으로 구성된 NATO 機動打撃隊의 派遣을 検討中에 있는 바, NATO의 同 派兵措置는 이라크가 NATO 会員国인 터어키 攻撃時를 対備한 防禦目的인 동시에 対이라크 軍事圧力 加重이라는 政治的 意味도 큼.

o 한편 上記 NATO 飛行団 派遣은 危機状況에 対処키 위해 1960年 NATO 機動軍이 創設된 以来 最初로 投入되는 것이며 금번 페湾事態에 대한 NATO 次元의 첫번째 軍事介入임. 또한 独逸은 Alpha 戦闘機 18機를 派遣하였는 바, 이는 独逸 戦力이 最初로 海外에 派遣되는 것으로 주목됨.

o 美国은 駐쿠웨이트 美大使舘 要員을 全員 撤収시킨데

이어, 요르단 및 수단의 非必須 政府 雇傭員을 撤收시켰으며 12.26 페湾地域 国家와 親이라크 国家 居住 美国人의 1.15 以前 撤収를 勧告함. 또한 生.化学戦에 対備, 士兵들의 豫防 接種을 実施하는等 페湾의 軍事衝突 可能性에 対備하고 있음.

2) 이라크 戦力 現況

o 이라크는 総兵力 53万名, 탱크 4,000台, 大砲 2万 7千門, 裝甲車 2,500台를 쿠웨이트 및 이라크 南部地域에 既配置한데 더하여 10万名 規模의 8個 師団을 터어키 国境地域에 新規 配置하고 13万名 規模의 共和国 守備隊 5個 師団을 新規 編成, 이라크 南部地域에 追加配置 豫定임.

o 이라크는 쿠웨이트 占領以後 쿠웨이트内에 防禦陣地를 構築하고 地対地 미사일 試験発射를 実施하는等(12.26) 一戦不辞의 臨戦態勢를 誇示하고 있으며, 또한 이라크 指導層은 쿠웨이트 固守, 一戦不辞 言明等 一聯의 強硬姿勢를 계속 堅持하고 있음.

　- 12.22 [후세인], 스페인 T.V.와의 対談時 "이라크는 이스라엘이 対이라크 攻撃 加担与否에 관계없이 戦争 勃発時 이스라엘을 맨처음 攻撃할 것"이라고 警告
　- 1.6 [후세인], 軍創設 70周年 紀念式 演説에서

-6-

0087

"쿠웨이트는 이라크의 19번째 州로 영원히 남을 것이고 美国으로 代表되는 全体主義에 対抗해 폐湾에서 長期戦이 벌어질 것"이라고 警告

나. 外交的 解決 努力

1) 알제리 大統領의 仲裁 努力

ㅇ Chadli Ben Jedid 알제리 大統領은 12.11-18間 요르단, 이라크, 이란, 이집트, 시리아, 오만, 바레인, UAE, 카타르 等 中東 9個国을 巡訪한데 이어, 伊太利, 프랑스, 스페인, 모로코, 모리타니아를 12.21-23間 訪問, 폐湾事態 관련 当事国과의 幕後協商을 통한 平和的 解決을 試図함.

ㅇ 同 大統領은 事態 解決 方案으로서 1) 이라크軍의 쿠웨이트 撤収, 2) 아랍平和軍 配置, 3) 사우디. 이라크間 不可侵 合意와 中東平和会議 開催等을 提示한 것으로 알려짐. 한편, 上記 会談後 알제리 外務長官은 12.22. 記者会見時 이라크는 1) 世界 最強大国들과의 軍事的 対峙状況을 正確히 認識하고 있으며, 2) 폐湾事態를 平和的으로 解決코자 하는 意志를 갖고 있고, 3) 팔레스타인 問題解決에 대한 特別한 執着이 있다는 평가를 함.

-7-

0088

2) 프랑스의 独自外交 推進

ㅇ 1.7 [롤랑 뒤마] 仏外相은 페湾에서의 戦争 可能性이 漸次 高潮됨에 따라 프랑스는 美国의 路線을 追従하던 立場에서 벗어나, 美-이라크 会談이 失敗할 경우에 対備, 戦争을 막기 위한 独自外交를 펴 나갈 것이라고 밝힘.

ㅇ 한편 프랑스는 1.4 룩셈부르크에서 開催된 EC 外務長官会談에서 下記 7個項의 解決方案을 提議하였음. 反面 同 提案은 페湾事態와 팔레스타인 問題 連繫를 示唆하고 있어 [베이커] 美国務長官은 即刻 拒否立場을 밝힘. 또한 [미셀 모젤르] 仏 下院 外交委 委員長도 이라크를 방문, [후세인] 과 [아라파트] PLO議長과 長時間 会談을 가진 바 있음.

- 1.15前 이라크의 쿠웨이트 完全撤軍 発表
- 撤軍発表後, 西方의 対이라크 不侵 立場 表明
- 撤軍 実現後, 国際会議 開催, 包括的인 中東問題 論議
- 1.15前 이라크 外相을 招請, EC側과 会談周旋
- 事態解決을 위한 [부시] 大統領의 새로운 努力 支持 표명
- EC의 前職, 現職, 次期議長国(트로이카) 으로 하여금
  1.15前 유고(非同盟 議長国), 아랍諸国 및 UN事務
  総長等을 各各 接触케 하여, 이들로 하여금 EC와는

-8-

0089

別途의 事態解決方案을 摸索토록 誘導

- 長期的으로 CSCE 会議와 같은 形態의 中東安保方案 摸索

o [미테랑] 仏大統領은 1.9 [부시] 와의 電話会談後 記者 会見을 통해 프랑스의 西方体制内 結束과 参与의 基本原則을 천명함. 反面 事態解決의 主体를 UN으로 規定, 美国 主導의 事態解決 方式에 대한 留保를 表明하고 美国側이 中東問題의 包括的 解決을 위한 国際会議 開催를 受諾할 것을 促求하였으며, 페湾事態의 平和的 解決을 위한 独自的 努力 堅持 意志를 천명함.

3) 아랍4個国 頂上会談 開催

o [무바라크] 이집트 大統領, [아사드] 시리아 大統領 및 [베시르] 수단革命委 委員長은 아랍에 의한 페湾事態의 平和的 解決을 試図해 보려는 [가다피] 의 招請으로 리비아 무사라타 市에서 아랍4個国 頂上会談을 開催함. 同 会談結果, 共同声明 発表가 없었던 점에 비추어 4個国間 行動統一 導出에는 失敗 한 것으로 보이나, 派兵国인 이집트, 시리아의 指導者와 親이 라크 立場의 리비아와 수단의 指導者가 함께 모여 地域情勢에 関해 아랍国間 理解増進을 図謀한데 意義가 있는 것으로 評価 됨.

-9-

0090

4) 美. 이라크 外務長官会談

    o [부시]는 당초 [베이커]와 [아지즈] 両国 外相의 相互
交換訪問을 提議하였으나 이라크가 1.12을 会談日字로 提案하
자 이를 拒否, 両国 直接会談이 霧散된 以後, 1.3 美-이라
크 外相会談의 제네바 開催를 提議함. 이에 대해 이라크는
1.4 同 提議를 受諾, 1.9 両国 外相会談이 成事되기에 이
름.

    o 同 会談은 1.15 時限 以前 開催되는 마지막 회담으로
期待를 모았으나 両側이 既存 主張을 반복, 会談이 決裂된 바,
同 会談이 決裂된 것은 이라크의 쿠웨이트 撤収와 팔레스타인
問題의 연계에 관한 両側의 異見때문인 것으로 관측됨. 반면
両側이 장시간에 걸쳐 相互立場을 打診하는등 実質的인 会談을
가졌다는 점에서 平和的 解決의 여지는 남겨둔 것으로 評価됨.

다. 美 議会 動向

1) 民主党 및 共和党의 基本立場

    o 美議会는 当初 이라크의 쿠웨이트 侵攻(90.8.2)以後
10月末까지의 事態初期에는 [부시]의 페灣 政策을 적극 지지
해 오면서 上. 下院에서 行政府 政策에 대한 지지 決議案을 採
択하는等 行政府와 共同步調를 취해 옴.

-10-

0091

o 반면 [부시]의 폐湾 美軍增派 決定(90.11.8)以後 民主. 共和党間의 立場対立이 表面化 되어 民主党側에서는

- 戦争権限法 및 聯邦憲法 規定에 따라 開戦時 議会의 事前 承認 獲得을 요구하면서
    . 民主党 議員 45名, [부시] 대통령의 一方的 開戦防止를 위한 訴訟提起(90.11.20)
    . 民主党 議員総会, 議会의 事前承認 없이 이라크와 戦争 해서는 안된다는 내용의 決議案 採択(90.12.4)

- 관련 聴聞会(90.11.27-12.6)를 통해 経済制裁의 効果를 더 기다린후 武力使用 与否를 決定해야 한다는 輿論 造成에 注力함.

o 한편 共和党側에서는

- [부시] 大統領의 美軍增派 決定을 支持하면서
- UN 安保理의 対이라크 武力使用 承認 決議案과 類似한 決議案을 議会가 採択해야 한다고 主張하고 있음 (90.11.30 [돌] 上院議員)

2) 美 上. 下院 폐湾事態 審議 開始

o 議会가 폐湾事態에 대한 討議를 本格的으로 実施하게 된 背景은 첫째, 進歩的 性向의 民主党 議員 一部가 議会의 事前承認 없는 武力使用을 禁止하는 決議案을 이미 提出한 바 있고, 둘째, 금번 폐湾事態에 있어서 議会側이 意見表明을 위

-11-

0092

한 具体的 措置없이, 行政府側이 武力使用을 취할 경우, 戦争 宣布権이라는 議会의 固有権限은 有名無失해 짐으로써 代議政治의 民主主義 基本原則이 侵害되는 것을 議会가 傍観하는 結果가 될 뿐만 아니라 向後 War Powers에 대한 行政府와의 権限問題에 있어서 不利한 先例가 되기 때문임. 또한 議会를 掌握하고 있는 民主党側으로서는 페湾事態 政策과 같은 重要 国家政策 決定에 나름대로의 役割을 하지 못했다는 非難을 면치 못할 위험이 있기 때문인 것으로 観測됨.

ㅇ 1.3 開院한 美議会는 1.9 豫定된 [베이커] - [아지즈] 外相会談 以前에 페湾事態에 대한 討議를 自制한다는 民主党 指導部의 決定에 따라 上. 下院 공히 1.10부터 페湾事態에 대한 討議 및 関聯 決議案 審議를 開始함.

3) [부시], 戦争大権 要求

ㅇ [부시]는 1.8 当初 立場을 変更, 美政府가 이라크의 쿠웨이트 撤収를 実現시키기 위해 UN 決議案에 立脚, 필요한 모든 措置를 취할 수 있도록 支持하는 내용의 決議案을 採択해 주도록 議会에 要請함. 同 決議案은 事実上 対이라크 戦争 大権의 附与를 促求한 것으로 1.15 時限을 앞두고 美国의 決意를 誇示하려는 政治的 제스쳐로 분석되는데, 1.12 美議会가 票決豫定인 同 決議案은 民主党内 中道, 保守派 性向의 議員들의 支持를 얻어 通過될 경우 美国의 対이라크 軍事, 外交的 圧力을 보다 強化할 수 있을 것임.

-12-

라. 分析

(이라크의 戰略)

1) 和戰 両面 戰略

ㅇ 이라크는 쿠웨이트 侵攻以後 和戰 両面策을 基本的인
페湾 戰略으로 駆使하고 있음. 이라크로서는 1.15 以前 無
條件的 쿠웨이트 撤収라는 美国 및 UN 決議案에 대한 굴복은
[후세인] 政権 存立危機로 意識, 쿠웨이트 喪失, 이라크 軍事
力 萎縮 및 아랍圈内 指導的 位置 喪失로 이어진다는 점에서
最後瞬間까지 軍事対応 姿勢를 誇示하면서 最大限 有利한 結果
를 얻기 위해 [부시] 와의 條件없는 協商을 제의, 外交的 解
決을 모색하고 있음.

2) 遅延 戰略

ㅇ 이라크는 現 쿠웨이트 占領을 既定事実化, 占領 状態를
維持함으로써 有利한 立場에 있게된다고 判断하고 있음. [부
시] 가 提議한 両国 外務長官 相互 交換訪問이 이라크가
[베이커] 長官의 接受 日程을 1.12로 最大限 延期시켜 霧散
된 것도 UN의 撤収要求 決議 時限에 임박하게 함으로써 美国
의 対이라크 軍事行動을 最大限 遅延시키려는 이라크의 意図에
서 나온 것인 바, 이라크는 現 事態 遅延을 통해 下記 利得

—13—

을 취할 수 있음.

- 多国籍軍 駐屯費用 増大로 인한 西方의 経済的 負担 増加
- 反이라크 聯合前線의 結束力 弛緩
- 西方의 反戦 輿論 拡大
- 3月부터 中東地域 気温上昇 및 라마단 始作(3.17)으로 対이라크 攻撃 곤란

3) 팔레스타인 問題 連繋 戦略

ㅇ 이라크는 쿠웨이트 侵攻以後 現 페湾事態와 팔레스타인 問題의 連繋를 一貫되게 주장해 오고 있음. 이라크는 이스라엘이 UN 決議를 遵守하지 않고 있는데 대해 UN이 아무런 措置를 취하지 않으면서 이라크에 대해서는 이를 遵守토록 強要하고 武力使用까지 承認함은 二重的 基準 適用이라고 지적 하면서, 現 事態를 아랍対 시온主義, 아랍対 美国의 対決로 変質시켜 아랍圈의 支持를 獲得코자 함. [후세인]의 이스라엘 先制攻撃 警告 発言(1.6 創軍紀念式 演説)도 같은 脈絡에서 나온 것으로 分析됨.

4) 政治的 解決 摸索 戦略

ㅇ 이라크는 多国籍軍에 대한 이라크軍의 戦力이 劣勢하다는 認識은 가지면서도 認識下에 一戦不辞戦略, 遅延戦略, 팔

—14—

0095

레스타인문제 연계 戰略等을 통해 이라크에 유리한 協商環境을 조성한후, 美国의 対이라크 軍事行動直前 幕後協商을 통해 政治的 解決을 모색, 最小限의 撤軍 名分을 세우고 部分的 勝利를 獲得코자 하는 것으로 관측됨.

(美国의 戰略)

ㅇ [부시] 行政府는 対이라크 経済制裁 延長 및 軍事対峙 状態의 長期化는 駐屯軍 維持費用 增大, 反이라크 結束弛緩, 中東의 다른 地域으로의 紛争波及 効果等을 惹起할 뿐 아니라 時間이 経過할수록 이라크 응징의 名分이 弱化될 가능성이 있다는 憂慮에서 UN의 武力使用 決議案 通過以後, 이라크의 無條件的 쿠웨이트 撤收 및 一戦不辞 威脅의 圧力을 強化해 가고 있음.

ㅇ 또한 美国은 同 事態를 契機로 이라크의 軍事力을 弱化시켜 隣接国家에 대한 軍事威脅 素地를 除去시켜 폐湾의 軍事安定을 図謀함으로써 中東地域에 대한 西方圈의 長期的 利益을 確保코자 하며, 이러한 意図를 対이라크 協商 過程에서도 美国의 一戦不辞 意志를 強調, 伝達하는데 意味를 附与하고 있음.

- 1.5 [부시], 라디오 演説을 통해 이라크가 1.15

⋯⋯⋯   —15—

0096

以前 撤収않을시 悲惨한 結果를 맞게 될 것이라고 最後
通牒性 警告

- 1.8 [부시], 이라크의 쿠웨이트 撤収를 実現시키기
  위해 UN 決議案에 입각한 필요한 모든 措置를 취할
  수 있도록 支持하는 内容의 決議案 採択을 議会에 要請

- 1.9 [베이커], 1.12 以前 바그다드 駐在 美公館
  撤収 豫定 言及

- 1.9 [부시], 폐湾 戦争에 対備 戦争物資 動員令

ㅇ 한편 美国으로서는 '先撤収 後協商'이라는 立場을 固守
하고 있고 이라크의 無條件 撤収 필요성에 대해 国際的으로
正当性을 認定받고 있으나, 폐湾戦 勃発時 地域安定 및 美国
의 影響力 構築을 確信할 수 없을 뿐 아니라 莫大한 人的, 物
的 被害 및 油価引上等 世界経済에 대한 否定的 波及効果가
豫想됨에 따라 幕後交渉을 통해 마지막 外交的 解決을 試図할
것으로 보임. 특히 프랑스, EC, [케야르] UN事務総長等을 통한
迂回的인 이라크 協商 試図가 마지막 순간까지 継続될 것으로
展望되며, 協商進展의 関鍵은 撤軍과 관련하여 어떠한 방법으
로 [후세인]의 体面을 살려 주는가 하는 것임.

마. 展望

-16-

1) 平和的 解決 可能性

    ㅇ 1.9 [베이커] - [아지즈] 협상이 決裂되고, 1.15 時
限이 다가 옴에 따라 現 페湾事態는 軍事対決 危險이 事態発
生以後 가장 高潮되고 있음. 반면, 表面的으로는 軍事対決 危
險이 고조되고 있음과 더불어 兩側이 軍事対決의 政治的, 経済
的 費用負担과 戰爭에 의한 解決이 가져 올 莫大한 人的, 物的
被害에 대해서도 누구보다도 더 잘 認識하고 있을 것임에 비
추어 幕後交涉을 통한 妥協 摸索 努力이 強化될 것임.

    ㅇ 向後 協商의 焦点은 팔레스타인 問題의 解決方向에 맞
춰 질 것으로 観測되는 바, 이라크로서는 1) [후세인]의 政
權維持, 2) 와르바, 부비얀島 및 루마일라 油田地帯 確保, 3) 아
랍圈内 影響力 維持를 基本目標로 하고 있다고 볼때, [후세인]
支配体制 維持, 팔레스타인문제 解決을 위한 国際会議를 開催
하는 선에서 仲裁가 이뤄질 可能性이 가장 높은 것으로 観測
되며, 이라크는 有利한 協商与件 造成을 위해 最終時点까지
和戰両面 戰略을 계속 駆使해 나갈 것으로 전망됨.

    ㅇ 한편 이라크가 와르바, 부비얀島 및 루마일라 油田地帯
를 除外한 쿠웨이트 部分撤收를 斷行할 可能性도 豫想됨. 현
재 아랍圈 一角에서는 部分的 解決을 금번 事態의 窮極的 解
決 方案으로 受諾하려는 움직임이 있고, 同 方案에 대한 国際

0098

104 걸프 사태 언론 보도 및 분석

的 支持가 확산될 경우, 対이라크 공격 여부에 대한 論難이 더욱 심해질 것이며 현재와 같은 강도의 多国籍 封鎖 前線이 維持되기는 어려울 것으로 展望되는바, 이라크의 전격적 部分 撤収 단행으로 페湾事態의 장기화를 惹起할 可能性도 排除할 수 없음.

ㅇ 美国으로서는 [베이커] [아지즈] 会談 決裂以後 追加 会談 可能性을 排除하고 있으나 第3国을 통한 仲裁라는 迂回的인 方法으로 平和的 解決을 摸索할 것으로 관측됨. 특히 独自 路線을 宣言한 프랑스 및 EC, 케야르 UN事務総長, 사우디, 알제리등의 아랍圏 国家들을 통한 막판 仲裁努力이 加速化 될 것으로 展望됨. 특히 下記 発言等에 나타난 美国側 意図를 살펴볼때, 팔레스타인 問題에 대한 国際会議 開催等에 대한 美国側의 一步 譲歩를 통해 協商의 막힌 실마리가 풀릴 가능성도 배제할 수 없음.

- 이스라엘의 팔레스타인 占領 政策을 非難하는 UN安保理 決議案 採択에 拒否権을 行使하지 않은 事実
- 1. 5 [부시] 의 라디오연설시, 1. 15이 美軍의 武力 使用 時限은 아니라고 言及
- 1. 9 [베이커], UN 決議로 부터의 後退가 아니면, 政治的, 平和的 解決을 가져오는 어떠한 方案도 歓迎할 것이라고 언급

-18-

0099

ㅇ 한편 [케야르] UN事務総長은 1.12 바그다드를 訪問 [후세인]과 会談을 가질 예정인 바, [케야르]는 同 会談에서 UN 平和維持軍의 監視下에 페湾 駐屯 多国籍軍 및 이라크軍의 段階的 撤収를 提案할 것으로 観測되며 出発에 앞서 1.11 제네바에서 EC 外務長官들과 同 提案에 대한 意見調整을 할 예정인 바, 向後 仲裁努力은 프랑스, EC 및 UN을 중심으로 展開될 전망임.

2) 軍事対決 可能性

(戦争의 様相)

ㅇ 現 事態는 関係国의 仲裁 努力에도 불구, 両側이 合意点을 찾지 못하게 될 경우, 軍事対決에 의한 解決方案도 想定할 수 있으나 최근까지 이라크가 挑発的 軍事行動 自制, 協商을 통한 事態解決을 모색해 왔다는 점에서 이라크의 先制攻撃 可能性은 稀薄함. 美国의 戦略은 戦争의 否定的 効果를 最小化 하기 위해 막강한 空軍力을 為主로한 電撃的, 短期戦에 의한 軍事解決을 選好하고 있음.

ㅇ 反面 現 UN의 武力使用 決議가 쿠웨이트 解放에만 局限된 것인지, 이라크의 攻撃的 軍事力의 無力化에까지 拡大되

-19-

0100

는 것인지 不明確하다는 점에서 쿠웨이트 解放以後 아랍圈 大衆의 반발, 反이라크 聯合陣營內 龜裂도 豫想됨. 또한 이라크가 無力化 될 경우, 힘의 空白을 이용한 시리아, 이란의 이라크內 進入으로 現 事態가 더욱 複雜化 될 수 있는 可能性도 排除할 수 없음.

(攻擊時期)

ㅇ 최근 Calvin A.H.Waller 사우디 派遣 美軍 副司令官은 美軍의 裝備輸送 遲延으로 2月初까지는 攻擊準備가 어렵다고 발언했으며, [부시]는 1.6 라디오연설을 통해 1.15이 武力使用 時限은 아니라고 언급하고 있는 바, 軍事 解決을 試圖할 境遇, 最適 攻擊時期는 2月中旬頃으로 豫想되고 있음. 反面, 攻擊을 위한 必要條件은 이미 갖춘 상태이며, 12.27 [부시]도 軍事行動이 필요하다고 판단할 경우, 이를 미루지 않을 것임을 천명했으므로 和. 戰의 選擇은 美国側에 있으며 軍事的 側面만 考慮할 경우 1.15 以後 美国이 決定할 攻擊 最適時期는 다음과 같이 推定할 수 있음.

- 3月 以後 気温이 急上昇하고 모래폭풍이 시작
- 回教의 Rajab月에는 싸움이 죄악시 됨
- 이라크 空襲을 위해 달빛이 없는 밤, 上陸作戰을 위해 波高가 높은 것이 유리

−20−

- 3.17부터 回教 라마단이 始作
- 6.13-16 Haj (메카 巡禮)

3) 폐湾戦争이 油価 및 世界経済에 미치는 影響

(油田에 대한 豫想打撃)

o 戦争이 勃発할 경우 폐湾地域 油田에 대한 打撃의 정도
는 戦争의 規模와 持続期間에 따라 달라질 것이나, 一般的으
로 在來式 武器로 유전을 심각하게 損傷 또는 破壊한다는 것
은 어려운 것으로 알려지고 있고, 이라크軍의 油田攻撃能力에
대해서도 懐疑的인 視角이 支配的인 바, 폐湾地域 油田이 심
각하게 損傷될 가능성은 높지 않은 것으로 평가되고 있음.

- 사우디 油田中 戦争勃発時 破壊될 可能性이 있는 유
전은 全体의 10% 미만으로 평가되고 있음.
- 쿠웨이트 油田은 이라크軍이 이미 쿠웨이트 油田施
設의 相当部分을 심각하게 損傷하였으며, 기타 油田地域에
도 대부분 地雷를 假設하였으므로 戦争勃発時, 당분간 原
油生産이 不可能한 것으로 평가됨.
- 이라크 油田은 美国이 一部 精油施設을 除外한 이라
크內 油田을 軍事的 攻撃対象에서 除外하고 있으므로 전쟁

-21-

0102

이 短期間內에 終結될 경우 이라크內 油田이 破壞될 可能
性은 낮은 것으로 평가됨.

(原油生産 및 油価에 대한 影響)

o 原油生産

    - 이라크 및 쿠웨이트로부터의 原油輸入 中斷에 따른 世界
原油供給 不足量은 余他国의 增産으로 이미 充当하고 있으므로,
戰争勃発時에도 사우디 油田의 破壞程度가 輕微할 경우 세계
原油生産量에 미치는 영향은 微微할 것으로 평가됨.

    - 또한 戰争勃発時 美国은 1日 1百万배럴 以上의 戰略
備蓄原油를 放出할 것으로 기대되고 있고, 日本, 西独等 主要
西方国家들도 自国 保有 戰略備蓄原油를 放出할 것으로 豫想되
며, 사우디도 現 生産量보다 增産할 수 있는 能力을 갖추고
있어 原油供給은 큰 影響을 받지 않을 것으로 예상됨.

o 油 価

    - 戰争勃発 直後에는 心理的 要因에 의해 油価가 急速
히 引上될 것으로 豫想되며, 이러한 不安期를 거쳐 原油需
給에 큰 変動이 없을 경우에는 油価가 배럴当 25-35弗
水準을 維持할 것으로 전망됨.

-22-

0103

- 戰爭終結 및 破壞 油田施設의 復旧後에는 原油市場內의 心理的 反作用, 世界 経済成長 鈍化에 따른 需要減退, 過剰供給 発生 等으로 인해 油価가 急速히 引下될 수 있을 것으로 展望됨.

(世界経済에 대한 影響)

o 페湾에서의 戰爭이 世界経済에 미치는 영향은 주로 油価引上과 心理的 萎縮 効果를 통해 나타날 것이나, 영향의 정도는 戰爭의 규모, 期間 및 原油需給 変動状況等에 의해 決定될 것임.

o 戰爭勃発로 油価가 大幅 引上될 경우, 世界経済는 物価上昇, 利子率 上昇, 経済成長 後退 및 交易量 減少等으로 인해 큰 打撃을 받을 것이나, 그 打撃의 程度는 過去 1, 2次 石油危機보다 덜 심각할 것으로 전망하고 있음.

o 経済成長   •

- 油価가 배럴当 10弗 引上될 境遇, 先進国의 経済成長은 1% 減少되며, 物価는 0.5-1% 引上될 것으로 예상됨.

-. 先進国이 지난 10年間 生産量 対比 에너지 使用度(Energy Intensity)를 꾸준히 減少시켜 온 反面,

—23—

0104

開途国은 에너지 使用度가 오히려 계속 增加해 와, 현재 先進国에 2倍에 달하고 있으므로 油価引上에 대한 開途国의 経済成長率 減少 및 物価引上 効果는 先進国 보다 훨씬 심각할 것임(GNP 対比 에너지 輸入額 比重이 OECD 国은 1% 인데 비해 아시안 新興工業国은 3.2%임)

ㅇ 貿 易

- 油価引上은 世界経済成長 鈍化 및 消費.投資減少를 招來, 非石油産品 需要減少를 통한 世界交易量 減少라는 결과를 갖고 올 것임.

- 先進国의 경우 産油国에 대한 工産品 輸出増加를 통해 打撃을 일부 緩和할 수 있으나, 대부분의 開途国은 交易條件의 悪化, 先進国 市場에서의 原資材 輸入減退로 큰 打撃을 받을 것으로 예상됨.

ㅇ 金 融

- 油価引上에 따른 인플레이션 圧力을 緩和하기 위해 利子率 引上이 必要한 바, 이는 先進国과 開途国을 莫論하고, 経済成長을 鈍化시키는 결과를 초래함.

- 특히 世界金融市場에서의 利子率 引上은 過多한 外債 負担을 안고 있는 中南美, 東欧圏等의 開途国에 대한 打撃을 加重시킬 것으로 전망됨.

-24-

0105

攻擊 最適時期

● 만 월 　　　　　　　　◎ 그 믐
☆ 달빛이 最小가 되는 時期 　　* 초 승
~ 子正에서 04時間 쿠웨이트 해변에서 波高가 높은 時期（上陸作戰 適期）

1月

攻擊 最適期

| 1 | 2 | 3 | 4 | 5 | 6 | 7 | 8 | 9 | 10 | 11 | 12 | 13 | 14 | 15 | 16 | 17 | 18 | 19 | 20 | 21 | 22 | 23 | 24 | 25 | 26 | 27 | 28 | 29 | 30 | 31 |

◎　　　　☆ ☆ ☆ ☆ ☆ ☆ ☆ ☆ ☆　　　　　　*　　　　　●

Rajab 始作

2月

攻擊 最適期

| 1 | 2 | 3 | 4 | 5 | 6 | 7 | 8 | 9 | 10 | 11 | 12 | 13 | 14 | 15 | 16 | 17 | 18 | 19 | 20 | 21 | 22 | 23 | 24 | 25 | 26 | 27 | 28 |

◎　　☆ ☆ ☆ ☆ ☆ ☆ ☆ ☆　　　*　　　●

Rajab 終了

3月

→ 氣溫上昇, 모래暴風 始作

攻擊 最適期

| 1 | 2 | 3 | 4 | 5 | 6 | 7 | 8 | 9 | 10 | 11 | 12 | 13 | 14 | 15 | 16 | 17 | 18 | 19 | 20 | 21 | 22 | 23 | 24 | 25 | 26 | 27 | 28 | 29 | 30 | 31 |

◎　　☆ ☆ ☆ ☆ ☆ ☆ ☆ ☆　　　*　　　●

Ramadan 始作

0106

2. 中共 7中全会 結果 分析

° 90.12.25-30間 北京에서 開催된 中共 第13期 7中全会는 当初 豫想과는 달리 尚今 結果의 詳細한 內容에 관해서는 公式 発表가 없어 具体的인 內容은 正確히 把握되지 않고 있으나 우선 外国 言論 等을 통해 間接的으로 確認되고 있는 內容을 綜合, 同 会議結果의 윤곽을 아래 分析함.

° 同 7中全会는 다만 10年間 経済開発計劃과 第8次 5個年 計劃에 관해 具体的인 方向과 內容을 決定. 提示하지 않고 主로 基本的인 方針만을 採択, 막연한 原則만 提示했으며, 또 前総書記 [趙紫陽] 処理問題와 高位層 人事 問題에 대해서는 어떠한 発表도 하지 않고 있는 것은 이러한 問題들을 둘러싸고 그동안 暗鬪와 葛藤을 빚어온 保守. 改革派間 및 中央과 地方間에 금번 会議를 통해 表面的으로나마 일단 妥協을 追求한 것으로 보이나, 両派間의 異見이 完全 解消된 것은 아닌 것으로 보임.

° 主要 経済政策 方向이 91.3月 開催豫定인 全人代 第4次 会議에 建議하는 形式으로 採択된 것으로 보아 同会議前까지 各系派間의 異見調整 作業이 持続될 것으로 보이며, 各指導層 間의 論議如何에 따라 또 元老指導層의 去就 및 蘇聯等 東欧圈 変化等 外的要因 変化와 더불어 経済政策 方向도 상당히 달라지게 될 可能性도 排除할수 없으며, 具体的인 內容은 91.3月 全人代 開催以後에야 確定될 것으로 보임.

분류기호	중근동	협 조 문 용 지	결	담 당	과 장	국 장
문서번호	2655- 113	( )				
시행일자	1991. 1. 26.		재	청천	가7대	
						(서명)
수 신	외교안보연구원장	발 신		중동아프리카국장		
제 목	대 중동 중장기 정책 연구					

1. 중동은 아국 원유 수입의 약 70%, 건설 진출의 약 80%를

접하고, 전후 복구사업에 아국업체의 참여가 요망되는 경제적으로

큰 이해가 걸려 있는 지역일 뿐 아니라 앞으로 유엔등 국제무대에서

아랍권 내지 회교권의 지지가 긴요함을 감안할때 정치적으로도 큰

중요성이 있는 지역임니다.

2. 상기 중동의 중요성에 비추어 전후 중동의 세력

판도에 크게 변화 할것을 염두에 두고 아국의 대 중동 중장기 외교정책 수립이

긴요 할것으로 판단되어 표제를 귀원의 연구과제로 채택하여 주시고

그 결과를 가급적 조속한 시일내에 송부하여 주시기 바랍니다.

이와 관련된 주요공관의 전문사본을 별첨 송부 하오니 /계속...

0108

참고 하시기 바랍니다.

첨 부 : 주요 공관의 걸프사태 전망 및 분석 보고 전문 사본 **16**부.

끝.

예2 ~ 91. 12. 31 일반

걸프戰 關聯 韓國 政府의 追加 支援

1991. 2.

外　　務　　部

0110

目 次

0111

Ⅰ. 걸프戰 關聯 韓國 政府의 追加 支援 決定 公式 發表

1991. 1. 30. 18:15

1. 政府는 지난해 8.2. 걸프 事態가 發生한 이래 武力에 의한 侵略은 容認될 수 없다는 國際 正義와 國際法 原則에 따라 유엔 安保 이사회 決議를 支持하고 이의 履行을 위한 國際的 努力을 支援하여 왔음. 이러한 立場에서 政府는 지난해 9.24. 多國籍軍 및 周邊國 經濟 支援을 위해 2億2千万弗의 支援을 發表한 바 있으며 또한 지난 1.24. 사우디에 軍 醫療 支援團을 派遣한 바 있음.

2. 그러나 유엔을 비롯한 全世界 平和 愛好國들의 努力에도 불구하고 지난 1.17. 걸프 戰爭이 勃發하여 中東 地域은 물론 全世界의 平和 및 安定에도 큰 威脅이 되고 있으며, 더우기 이번 戰爭이 예상보다 오래 계속될 조짐이 나타남에 따라 多國籍軍은 이에 따른 막대한 戰費와 財政 需要에 직면하게 되었음.

3. 이에 따라 정부는 다음과 같은 추가 지원을 제공키로 결정하였음.

  ○ 追加 支援 規模는 2億8千万弗로함.

    - 이중 1億7千万弗 相當은 國防部 在庫 軍需物資 및 裝備 提供으로
      하고 나머지 1億1千万弗은 現金 및 輸送 支援으로 함.

      * 具體的 執行 用途 및 內譯은 韓.美 兩國間 協議를 거쳐 決定

    - 今番 追加 支援은 多國籍軍 특히 美國을 위한 것이며 周邊國 經濟
      支援은 不包含.

    - 我國의 總 支援 規模는 今番 追加 支援으로 昨年 約束額 2億2千万弗을
      包含, 總 5億弗이됨.

  ○ 上記 支援과는 別途로 국회의 동의를 받아 후방 수송 지원 복적을 위하여
    軍 輸送機(C-130) 5대를 派遣키로 원칙적으로 결정하였으며, 이를 위한
    기술적인 사항은 아국 國防部와 駐韓 美軍間에 협의 예정임.

Ⅱ. 걸프戰 關聯 多國籍軍에 대한 追加 支援 決定 說明 資料

91. 1. 30.

1. 追加 支援 決定 背景

○ 今番 걸프戰爭은 유엔 安保理의 決議에 立脚, 유엔 歷史上 最大의 會員國이
參與하고 있는 國際社會의 對이라크 膺懲戰인 바, 우리의 積極的 支援 및
參與는 우리의 國際 平和 維持 의지 과시등 國際的 位相 提高에 크게
기여

○ 걸프戰爭으로 인한 600億弗 정도의 막대한 戰費 및 軍需 物資 需要 增加에
따라 國際的으로 多國籍軍에 대한 追加 支援 必要性 增大

○ 日本 政府가 90億弗, 獨逸이 65億弗의 寄與金을 多國籍軍에 追加로 提供
하고 있고 國際的으로도 多國籍軍의 막대한 戰費를 國際社會가 分擔해야
된다는 與論이 일어나고 있음에 비추어, 我國으로서도 우리의 伸張된
國際的 地位等을 감안, 應分의 寄與를 할 필요가 있음.

-3-

0114

○ 多國籍軍 活動에 參與 및 支援에 대한 美國 및 世界의 耳目이 集中되어 있어 追加 支援時 國際社會에서 우리의 發言權等 立地 强化에 效果가 클 것으로 期待됨.

- 걸프 戰爭 終了後 各國의 支援에 대한 評價 效果 長期間 持續 豫想

* 美國內 與論은 걸프 戰爭에 대해 81%라는 壓倒的인 支持 表明

2. 考慮 事項

① 安保的 考慮事項

○ 이라크의 武力侵略을 단호히 응징하고자 하는 유연을 中心으로한 國際 社會의 努力을 적극 支援하므로써 韓半島의 有事時 國際社會의 共同 介入을 통한 平和 回復 期待 및 이라크에 대한 成功的인 膺懲時 韓半島 에서 武力 挑發 可能性 豫防 效果 期待

○ 韓.美 安保協力 關係 鞏固化

- 能動的이고 自發的인 支援을 통하여 我國이 信賴할 수 있는 友邦이라는 認識을 美國 朝野에 提高시키므로써 韓.美 安保協力 關係는 물론 全般的인 韓.美 友好關係 强化에 寄與

* 걸프戰 終了後 美國은 友邦國의 對美支援 實績을 통해 美國의 對友邦國 關係를 再評價하려는 움직임(현재 美國 議會 및 一般 與論은 日本, 獨逸을 "자기들이 필요할 때만 美國을 친구로 대하는 國家-fair weather ally-라고 批判)

- 4 -

0115

② 經濟 通商的 考慮 事項

ㅇ 걸프戰 終了後, 安定된 原油 供給 確保 및 戰後 復舊事業 參與 等 對中東
  經濟 進出 基盤 마련

ㅇ 걸프戰의 早速 終結을 위한 國際的인 努力을 支援하므로써 걸프事態가
  我國 經濟에 미치는 影響을 最小化 하는데 寄與
  - 事態가 長期化 되어 國際原油價가 上昇할 경우, 我國 經濟에 미치는
    影響 深大(原油價가 배럴당 10弗 上昇時 年33億弗 追加 負擔 發生)

③ 外交的 考慮 事項

ㅇ 6.25 事變時 유엔의 도움을 받은 國家로서 對이라크 共同制裁에
  관한 유엔 決議에 적극 참여해야 할 道義的 의무 履行

ㅇ 我國의 伸張된 國威에 副應하여 國際 平和 維持 努力에 一翼 담당
  - 我國의 支援이 微溫的일 경우, 經濟的 利益만 追求한다는 國際的
    非難 可能性 考慮
  - 追加 支援이 自發的인 것이므로 多國籍軍側이 어느정도 評價하는
    水準에서의 支援 必要

ㅇ 걸프戰 終了後 對中東 外交 기반 强化 布石의 일환

　　- 長期的인 觀點에서 사우디, 이집트, UAE 等 中東 友邦國들과의 關係
　　　增進을 위한 重要한 投資

　　　· 우리의 主要 原油 導入線이자 建設 輸出 市場이라는 점 및 其他
　　　　經濟的 活動 餘地等을 감안

　　- 戰後 樹立될 쿠웨이트, 이라크 兩國 政府와의 즉각적인 關係 强化
　　　基盤 마련

④ 支援 規模 關聯 考慮

　　ㅇ 우리의 自發的 支援으로서 伸張된 國力에 알맞는 우리의 성숙한 모습을
　　　國際的으로 과시

　　ㅇ 우리의 醫療支援團 派遣 等을 고려, 財政 支援 規模는 적정한 수준에서
　　　검토

添 附 : 1. 多國籍軍 派遣 現況
　　　　2. 各國의 支援 現況
　　　　　　가. 經濟 支援
　　　　　　나. 醫療 支援　　　　　끝.

多國籍軍 派遣 現況

91. 1. 30. 現在

國 家	軍事力 派遣 및 參戰	備 考
美 國	◦ 兵 力 ： 492,000 名 ◦ 탱 크 ： 2,000 臺 ◦ 航空機 ： 1,300 臺 ◦ 艦 艇 ： 60 隻 （航空母艦 7隻）	
GCC （6個國）	◦ 兵 力 ： 150,500 名 ◦ 탱 크 ： 800 臺 ◦ 航空機 ： 330 臺 ◦ 艦 艇 ： 36 隻	사우디, 쿠웨이트, 바레인, 오만, UAE, 카타르
英 國	◦ 兵 力 ： 35,000 名 ◦ 탱 크 ： 170 臺 ◦ 航空機 ： 72 臺 ◦ 艦 艇 ： 16 隻	

國 家	軍事力 派遣 및 參戰		備 考
프랑스	ㅇ 兵 力 :	10,000 名	
	ㅇ 탱 크 :	40 臺	
	ㅇ 航空機 :	40 臺	
	ㅇ 艦 艇 :	14 隻	
이집트	ㅇ 兵 力 :	35,000 名	
	ㅇ 탱 크 :	400 臺	
시리아	ㅇ 兵 力 :	19,000 名	
	ㅇ 탱 크 :	300 臺	
파키스탄	ㅇ 兵 力 :	7,000 名	6千名 追加派遣 豫定
터 키	ㅇ 兵 力 :	5,000 名	國境配置 約10万名
	ㅇ 艦 艇 :	2 隻	
방글라데시	ㅇ 兵 力 :	2,000 名	3千名 追加派遣 豫定

- 8 -

0119

國家	軍事力 派遣 및 參戰		備考
카나다	◊ 兵力 :	2,000 名	
	◊ 航空機 :	24 臺	
	◊ 艦艇 :	3 隻	
모로코	◊ 兵力 :	1,700 名	
세네갈	◊ 兵力 :	500 名	
니제르	◊ 兵力 :	480 名	
이태리	◊ 航空機 :	8 臺	
	◊ 艦艇 :	6 隻	
濠洲	◊ 艦艇 :	3 隻	
벨기에	◊ 艦艇 :	3 隻	
네덜란드	◊ 艦艇 :	3 隻	
스페인	◊ 艦艇 :	3 隻	
아르헨티나	◊ 兵力 :	100 名	
	◊ 艦艇 :	2 隻	

國　家	軍事力 派遣 및 參戰	備　考
그리스	○ 艦　艇 :　　1 隻	
포르투갈	○ 艦　艇 :　　1 隻	
노르웨이	○ 艦　艇 :　　1 隻	
체　코	○ 兵　力 :　　200 名	
總　計 (總 28個國)	○ 兵　力 : 760,480 名 ○ 탱　크 :　3,710 臺 ○ 航空機 :　1,774 臺 ○ 艦　艇 :　　154 隻	※ 蘇聯은 艦艇 2隻을 參戰 目的이 아니라 觀察 目的으로 派遣

걸프사태 : 자료 및 언론보도, 1990-91. 전3권 (V.1 자료, 1990-91.3월) 127

<添 附 2>

各國의 支援 現況

가. 經濟 支援

國　家	戰爭 勃發 前	戰爭 勃發 後
日　本	. 40億弗(20億弗 : 多國籍軍 支援, 20億弗 : 周邊國 支援)	. 90億弗(對美 現金 支援)
獨　逸	. 20.8億弗(33億 마르크)	. 10億弗(1億6千7百万弗의 이스라엘 支援額 및 1億1千4百 万弗의 英國軍 支援額 包含) . 55億弗(對美 支援)
E C	. 19.7億弗	
英　國	. EC 次元 共同 步調	
불란서	"	
이태리	. 1.45億弗(1次 算定額), "	
벨기에	. EC 次元 共同 步調	. 1億1千3百5拾万 BF
네델란드	"	. 1億8千万弗(戰前 支出 包含)
스페인	"	
폴투갈	"	
그리스	"	

- 11 -

0122

國　家	戰爭 勃發 前	戰爭 勃發 後
카나다	. 6千6百万弗	
노르웨이	. 2千1百万弗	
濠　洲	. 8百万弗(難民救護)	
G.C.C.國	. 사 우 디 : 60億弗 . 쿠웨이트 : 50億弗 . U.A.E. : 20億弗	. 사 우 디 : 135億弗 . 쿠웨이트 : 135億弗

0123

나. 醫療 支援

國 家	內 譯
美 國	. 사우디 담밤港에 病院船 2隻 派遣(1,000 病床) . 사우디 알바틴에 綜合 醫療團 運營 (專門醫 35 名, 350 病床)
英 國	. 野戰病院 派遣(醫師 200名, 400 病床) (有事時 對備 約 1,500名의 追加 軍 醫療陣 派遣 準備中)
濠 洲	. 2個 醫療團 派遣 檢討中
방글라데쉬	. 2個 醫務 中隊 300名 派遣
카 나 다	. 野戰病院 派遣(醫療陣 550名, 225 病床)
덴 마 크	. 軍 醫療陣 30-40名 英國軍에 配置
헝 가 리	. 自願 民間醫療陣 30-40名 英國軍에 配置
체 코	. 自願 醫療陣 150名 派遣
파 키 스 탄	. 1個 醫務 中隊 100名 派遣
오 스 트 리 아	. 野戰 앰블란스 1臺 派遣
필 리 핀	. 民間 醫療支援團 270名 派遣

0124

國　家	內　　　　譯
폴 란 드	. 病院船 1隻　派遣 準備中
뉴질랜드	. 民間 醫療陣 50名 , 바레인 駐屯 美 海軍 病院에 勤務 . 軍 醫療團 20名　追加 派遣 決定
싱 가 폴	. 醫療支援團 30名 , 英國軍 病院에 勤務
벨 기 에	. 民.軍 自願 醫療 支援團 50名 派遣 . 醫療 裝備 支援(野戰 寢臺 2,800個, 앰블란스 1臺, 負傷兵 護送用 航空機 2臺)

Ⅰ. 週間 國際情勢 分析

1. 걸프事態 分析(Ⅶ)

주간국제정되
(91. 1. 28.)

> o 1.17 8:50(韓国時間), 美国 主導 多国籍軍이 電擊的으로 이라크에 대한 大規模 空襲을 開始, Gulf 事態는 마침내 武力使用에 의한 解決追求의 새 局面으로 転換되었는바, 初期 多国籍軍에 의한 空中攻擊의 대대적 成功 報道에도 不拘, 이라크의 対応이 없어 일견 短期戰의 豫想이 拡散되었으나, 漸次 戰果에 대한 懐疑的 見解가 대두되면서 当初 優勢했던 短期的 解決 展望과 달리 戰爭 長期化의 憂慮도 함께 漸増하고 있음.
>
> o 금번 武力衝突事態 勃発의 背景은 地域勢力으로서의 이라크 [후세인]의 아랍圈 盟主에 대한 野心 実現과 이.이 戰으로 피폐된 経済破綻 解決 및 国内政治 解決을 위한 돌파구 모색의 一環으로 軍事力을 基盤으로한 現象打破 軍事冒険 試図가 冷戰体制 以後 蘇聯의 影響力 減少에 따른 多極化 現状下에서 美国의 国際的 単一指導力 確保 次元의 世界政策이 正面 衝突한데서 起因한 바, 向後 걸프 전쟁의 展開様相에 따라 戰後 美国이 中東地域의 平和体制 定着과 나아가 冷戰以後 世界秩序의 単一 指導勢力으로서의 主導權을 確固히 할 것인지의 向方이 判明될 것으로 보임.

-3-

0126

가. 戰況

1) 美国의 Desert Storm 作戦

ο 多国籍軍은 1.15 이라크 쿠웨이트 撤収時限이 経過하자 대규모 電子. 情報攪乱에 이어 1.17 마침내 ″사막의 폭풍″ 作戦을 開始, 이라크의 情報. 軍指揮 統制部, 核 및 化学武器 製造施設, 飛行場, 미사일 発射隊等을 目標로 敢行된 大規模 戦略的 空襲은 多国籍軍의 被害도 거의 없이 進行되어 外見上 매우 成功的으로 評価됨으로써 특히 매스컴이 主導한 輿論은 速戦速決의 展望을 내다 봤었음.

ο 그러나, 1.26 現在 1万6千餘回의 出撃에도 不拘, 이라크의 軍施設이 지하에 은닉되어 있어 多国籍軍의 대규모 空襲에 비해 이라크의 軍事施設의 被害 状況이 豫想과 달리 크지 못하다는 見解가 대두되고 이라크의 被害状況에 대한 正確한 評価가 不透明해지면서 短期戦의 기대는 後退하고 있음.

ο 이러한 状況 展開와 함께 戦争의 勝敗를 決定지을 地上戦 開始의 時期選択과 関聯, 被害를 最少化 하려는 美国의 意図에 따라 戦略空襲에서 戦術空襲으로 転換, 19日以後 空襲의 目標物을 쿠웨이트 西北部와 이라크 南部에 集結된 이라크의 地上軍 주력인 共和国守備隊와 쿠웨이트 後方 補給路, 軍需品 集結地, 바스라. 포港 等으로 점차 옮겨가는 同時에

—4—

0127

사우디內 병력을 쿠웨이트 接境으로 移動, 地上戰을 준비하고 있음.

o 현재까지 나타난 美国의 戰略은 초기의 戰略施設에 대한 攻擊에서 차츰 이라크 地上軍과 병참시설에 대한 戰術空襲을 충분히 시행, 이라크의 戰力을 초토화시켜 地上戰의 豫想 被害를 최소화하도록 한 다음 大規模 陸. 海. 空軍을 動員 決定的인 地上戰을 展開하여 쿠웨이트를 解放하려는 것으로 보임.

2) 이라크의 対応

o 多国籍軍의 奇襲的인 空襲 攻擊에 대해 죽은듯이 잠복해 있던 이라크는 多国籍軍의 空襲이 뜸한 사이에 간간히 이스라엘 및 사우디에 대해 스커드 미사일로 攻擊하고 쿠웨이트와 사우디 国境地帶의 油田 施設을 일부 破壞하고 있어 이라크 戰力의 被害 狀況에 疑問을 提起케 함으로써 多国籍軍의 短期戰 戰略에 制動을 걸고 있음.

o 1.26 現在 5차례에 걸친 이라크의 対이스라엘 미사일 攻擊은 이라크가 이미 公言했던 바대로 금번 戰争을 多国籍軍内 아랍권의 離脱을 図謀하고, 금번 事態를 아랍対 시오니즘의 対決 構図로 몰아 拡戰을 꾀하는 試図로 일응 解釈되나 尚今은 美国의 牽制와 이스라엘의 自制로 中東大戰으로의

—5—

拡大　機微는　보이지　않고　있음.

ㅇ　이라크의　基本戰略은　空襲　被害　狀況의　불가측성으로
선불리　예단키　어려우나,　短期戰의　불리함과　空軍力等　基本的
戰力의　劣勢를　意識,　軍事施設의　지하　내지　인근국　은닉을
통해　장기　地上戰으로　몰고가는　한편,　이스라엘을　끌어들여
戰爭을　수평적으로　拡散시키는　동시에,　最後　手段으로서　化学
武器,　油田施設　破壊等을　준비하고,　狀況에　따라서는　갑작스
런　先制　地上攻擊　等으로　対応할　素地도　있는　것으로　보임.

나.　아랍圏의　向後動向

ㅇ　걸프사태가　石油資源　確保의　経済利害의　側面과　함께
'인티파다'로　象徵되는　反시오니즘의　아랍　民族主義　意識이
팽배한　時点에　발생,　中東大戰으로의　拡散의　불씨를　안고　있
는　점에서,　短期的으로　隣近　아랍国　및　이스라엘의　향배는　戰
爭의　拡散与否를　決定하는　초미의　関心事가　되고　있고,　長期
的으로는　[부시]가　"전쟁이　끝나면　우리는　사담　후세인의　挫
折이　아랍인　전체의　좌절감으로　받아　들여지지　않도록　세련된
외교를　주도해야　한다"고　천명한데서　보여지듯이　戰後　이지역
의　窮極的　평화구도　構築의　関鍵이　되고　있음.

-6-

0129

1) 시리아

    o 걸프事態 이전 西方에 대한 테러와 폭압정치의 이미지로 代辯되던 시리아가 多國籍軍에 参与함에 따라, 老衰한 후원자인 蘇聯에 대체될 수 있는 西方과의 和解機会를 잡게 되었으나, 아랍세계의 反応을 考慮하여 美国과 이스라엘에 대한 両非論的 立場은 계속 堅持하고 있음.

    o 시리아의 前歷에 비추어 西方과의 一時的 聯合에 불과하며 시리아가 [후세인] 没落以後 汎아랍주의의 새로운 覇権을 試図할 可能性은 지난해末 레바논의 사실상 支配에 成功한 結果를 놓고 보더라도 今番 事態 이전보다 훨씬 커졌다고 볼 수 있음.

2) 사우디 및 GCC国家

    o [후세인] 没落 以後에 GCC를 모태로 보다 強化된 集団安保装置를 模索할 것으로 보이나 軍事的 脆弱性은 면치 못할 것이므로 美国 및 이집트와의 安保協力이 軍隊駐屯의 形態로 強化 될 것이나, 한편 解放된 쿠웨이트에서 豫想되는 進步的 改革과 함께 사우디内 이슬람 強硬論者들과 지방의 改革主義者의 反対에 直面할 것으로 보여 인근 아랍 貧困国의

-7-

0130

富의 再分配要求 增大와 함께 政治的 不安要素는 더욱 深化될 것으로 보임.

3) 이스라엘과 팔레스타인

　ㅇ 美国을 비롯한 多国籍軍의 対이라크 破壊 攻撃으로 向後 安保不安要因이 크게 緩和된 이스라엘은 이라크의 스커드 미사일에 의해 수차례 被襲되었으나 戦争의 새로운 拡散局面을 우려한 美国의 強力한 自制促求와 Patriot 요격미사일 支援, 経済援助 등으로 具体的 報復을 自制하고 있는데, 이스라엘의 自制는 今番 戦争이 美国의 勝利로 終結된후 새롭게 模索될 中東平和 論議에서 팔레스타인 問題의 譲歩를 받아내는 카드로 活用할 意図가 엿보이고 있음.

　ㅇ 美国은 PLO가 이라크를 支持하였음에도 불구하고 아랍国의 今番 戦争의 協力을 考慮하여 経済援助를 미끼로 提示하여, 이스라엘로 하여금 팔레스타인에게 定着地를 제공함으로써 아랍-이스라엘 紛争을 解決하도록 圧力을 넣게 될 것이나, 이스라엘의 이라크 報復攻撃의 継続自制와 이 문제에 대한 이스라엘의 強硬한 태도로 보아 実現 可能性은 크지 않은 것으로 보임.

-8-

0131

4) 요르단

　　ㅇ 이라크에 友好的인 中立을 취하고 있는 요르단으로서는 最悪의 假定은 이라크와 이스라엘間의 戦場化가 되는 것인데, [후세인] 国王은 이스라엘 空軍이 이라크 空襲에 대한 報復으로 領空을 通過할 경우 領空侵害에 대한 積極 対応意思를 表明하고 있어 분쟁에 말려 들 素地가 없지 않으나, 그 利得이 없음은 충분히 認知하고 있을 것임.

　　ㅇ 그러나, 国内的으로는 同 事態로 고양된 팔레스타인 多数派와 베두윈 少数派間의 騒擾가 예상되어 国内 不安定 加速化가 憂慮되고 있으므로 戦後 팔레스타인問題 解決이 失敗할 경우 UN経済制裁로 破綻状態에 빠진 経済的 困難에 더하여 現 王政体制의 没落과 함께 長期的으로 急進的 팔레스타인 또는 回教 原理主義 主導 政権이 得勢하게 될 政治危機에 逢着할 危険을 排除키 어려움.

5) 이 란

　　ㅇ 이란은 일응 対이라크 응징에 賛成하면서도 拡戦 및 戦争 長期化時 回教徒의 反美感情 拡散等을 西方側에 警告하면서 이스라엘 介入의 경우 事態가 悪化될 것을 憂慮하는 가

－9－

0132

운데, 表面上으로는 戰後 이라크의 領土保存 希望을 表明하고
있음.

ㅇ 그러나 이란이 現在로선 中立的 傍観立場을 취하고 있
으나, 이란의회 強硬論者의 이라크 支援 要求 主張 대두에
비추어 이란의 確実한 態度는 流動的이며, 戰後 새로운 新強
者로 아랍圈을 主導하려는 입장을 취할 수 있음.

6) 터 키

ㅇ 터키는 걸프사태 以後 이라크의 送油管을 폐쇄하는 한
편 美国 空軍의 인켈리치 基地使用을 은밀히 許可하는等 多国
籍軍에 적극 協力하고 있으면서도 이라크와의 直接 軍事衝突
은 피하면서 戰後의 利害関係 配分에는 積極 参与코자 할 것
으로 보임.

ㅇ 向後 미국의 터키 経済援助 増加와, 西方国의 EC 統
合에 있어서 터키 要求의 受容과 함께, 사이프러스 紛争 問
題도 美国의 親터키的 立場이 취해질 것으로 보이는 한편,
拡戰의 경우 이라크内 모술 油田에 대한 領土主張을 하고 나
설 가능성도 排除할 수 없는 상황임.

-10-

0133

다. 向後 걸프戰 展開 展望

1) 미국의 戰爭 主導 方向

o 미국은 이라크가 軍事的으로 完全히 壞滅될 경우 이
지역에서 인근 이란, 시리아등에 대한 牽制勢力이 없어지게 되
므로 이라크의 大量破壞 武器를 제거하고 在來式武器 施設에
타격을 가하면서도 군사력을 완전히 除去하지는 않는 것이 賢
明하며, 또 아랍圈의 輿論을 考慮할때 많은 아랍人의 殺傷은
바람직하지 않다는 점도 인식하고 있음.

o 따라서 미국은 이라크가 周边의 弱小国을 威脅할 수는
없지만 周边 最强国을 牽制할 수는 있는 範囲内의 힘을 保有
하도록 하며 그리고, 人命被害가 적고 빨리 끝내도록 하는
선에서 금번 戰爭이 終結되기를 希望하고 있음.

o 상금 상세한 戰況은 명확하지 않으나 美国의 可恐할
空爆에 비해 이라크의 被害는 아직은 致命的이 아닌 것으로
보이며 후세인은 이. 이戰의 경험과 국민의 团結을 最大限 活
用, 地下 참호시설등으로 戰力을 은닉, 전쟁의 成敗를 左右
할 地上戰으로 勝負를 걸려 할 것임.

o 미국은 速戰을 목표로 하나 초기의 戰略空襲이 효과가

-11-

0134

미흡함을 인식, 共和国守備隊를 비롯한 이라크 地上軍과 쿠웨이트 補給路, 軍需物資 集結地 등에 대한 戰術的 爆撃으로 転換, 많은 人命被害가 憂慮되는 地上戰 開始以前에 우선 空軍力에 의한 이라크 焦土化를 数週間 持続할 것으로 보여, 多数 軍事専門家들은 2月初項 地上作戰이 시작될 수 있을 것으로 보고 쿠웨이트 解放만을 위한 地上戰은 그 以後 5週-10週 정도 所要될 것으로 분석하고 있음.

2) 地上戰 遂行与件

ㅇ 전쟁의 持続期間과 관련된 軍事的 考慮事項으로서 우선 沙漠環境의 경우, 현재 이라크 및 쿠웨이트 지역은 이미 多国籍軍의 空襲에 막대한 지장을 준 바 있는 雨期가 3月末까지는 계속될 것이며 이후 高熱의 모래바람이 봄철내내 불게 되어 多国籍軍의 高度武器의 열취약성과 軍隊의 기동성 저하를 가져올 것임.

ㅇ 그밖에 이라크는 이. 이戰 経験에 의한 환경에 適応된 兵力과 스커드미사일 等 세련된 武器를 保有하고 있고 被害状況이 尚今 未確認되고 있는 空軍力이 온존해 있는 경우, 多国籍軍에게는 [후세인]의 노련한 沙漠戰 戦略과 油田破壊等의 火攻과 自殺 空中攻撃이 큰 負担이 될 것이며, 自然條件에 있어서도 向後 무더운 여름과, 3月의 라마단 期間, 6月의 回

-12-

0135

教 巡禮行事인 '하지' 期間等은 美国 및 多国籍軍에게 地上戰 遲延에 따른 不利함을 더욱 倍加시킬 것으로 보임.

3) 戰争 長期化 与否 展望

ㅇ 만약 周辺 아랍国家의 軍事的 弱化를 통해 国家存立을 維持해 오고 있는 이스라엘이 이라크의 化学武器等의 攻撃에 의해 걸프戰에 介入할 경우, 回教国 国民의 反美感情 拡散과 世界的 테러 攻撃의 発生과 함께 戰争의 垂直的 上昇으로 戰争 長期化의 可能性도 排除하기 어려우며 이 경우 美国은 많은 人命被害와 아랍圈의 반발로 인한 国内輿論의 沸騰과 経済的 負担을 안게 돼 난감한 立場에 처할 것임.

ㅇ 綜合的으로 向後 戰争期間을 決定할 重要変数는 곧 있을 쿠웨이트 해방을 위한 地上戰 展開 様相에 따라 크게 左右될 것이나 그 以外에도 첫째, 이스라엘 介入与否와 아랍제국의 反応, 둘째 美国의 作戰地域의 쿠웨이트 局限 여부, 셋째 이라크의 化学武器使用 및 油田爆破 敢行与否, 넷째 美国内 輿論의 향배에 의해 事態의 方向이 決定될 것임.

ㅇ 最近들어 미국 [부시] 大統領은 国内輿論 糾合을 위해 戰争의 数個月間 持続 可能性을 言及하고 있는 한편, 이라크 [후세인] 大統領 역시 전쟁 長期化를 이미 公言하고 있음에 비

-13-

0136

추어 비록 이스라엘의 不介入에 의한 中東大戰으로의 擴戰은 안되더라도 大量 人命殺傷을 招來할 核武器 및 化学武器 使用은 制限받을 것이므로 이라크의 地上軍事力이 意外로 長期間 頑強한 抵抗을 지속하는 경우 이. 이戰에서와 같이 전쟁의 長期 小康状態에 의한 事態長期化 可能性도 排除하기 어려움.

라. 걸프 事態가 미치는 影響

1) 新国際秩序 樹立에 미치는 影響

ㅇ 向後 戰争의 長期 持続与否는 戰争 遂行方法과 그 結果와 맞물려 상금의 冷戰以後의 世界 政治秩序와 全般的 後退 兆朕으로 代表되는 世界 経済의 未來를 左右할 것임.

(中東地域 情勢 変化)

ㅇ 短期戰을 봉한 美国의 쿠웨이트 回復이 成功하더라도 그 以後에 이스라엘의 安保 不安이 減少될 수는 있으나 아랍 民族主義 強化와 回教 原理主義 得勢로 中東 各国의 国内情勢 不安과 反美感情 拡散, 이라크内 수니派와 시아派 葛藤深化로 인한 政治的 混乱, 쿠르드族 自治運動 拡散으로 인한 인근국의 介入과 衝突 可能性 增大, 팔레스타인 問題 尚存, 힘의 空白을 틈탄 이란 시리아의 域内 主導権 掌握 試図의 可視化

—14—

0137

로 인한 이라크 分割企図等 問題가 尙存하여 美国은 中東秩序의 再編을 위한 安定된 勢力均衡과 平和体制 定着을 目標로 절제하여 破壞된 이라크를 維持시키고, 쿠웨이트에 多国籍軍이 暫定 駐屯하면서, 이스라엘 安保와 팔레스타인 権利를 相互 調整하게 될 것임.

ㅇ 이집트. 사우디아라비아는 금번 事態에서 公開的으로 美国側을 支持한 댓가로 自身들의 政治的 立地强化를 위해 팔레스타인 問題 解決을 主張할 것으로 보여 시리아와의 友好関係 再定立이란 새로운 状況과 함께 中東平和協商과 関聯한 美国側의 選択의 幅을 넓혀 줄 것으로 보이며, 周辺에 强硬国家의 消滅로 이란의 西方 接近 可能性도 엿보이는 等 中東地域의 秩序가 크게 再編될 것이나 從來의 不安要素들의 早期克服은 難望하여, 美国은 戰後의 最悪의 시나리오를 피하기 위해서는 戰争遂行과 더불어 새로운 平和 摸索 노력을 더욱 倍加하여야 할 것임.

(새로운 国際秩序의 再定立)

ㅇ 美国은 주저하는 유럽을 [부시] 의 새로운 世界秩序로 끌어들임으로써 冷戰以後 集団安保体制 維持의 確固한 先例構築과 함께 唯一한 Super Power로서 新秩序再編에 影響力을 確保하게 되며, 全世界的으로 侵略行為 抑制効果를 가져오

—15—

0138

고, [부시] 大統領의 政治的 리더쉽에 美国民의 信頼를 回復, 国内 問題解決의 전기를 마련할 것으로 보임.

ㅇ 그러나 戰争이 이라크의 意図대로 이스라엘 介入, 아랍圈의 이반, 世界的 테러 확산 등으로 長期化가 될 경우 反戰輿論과 経済的 負担으로 이중고를 겪게 될 美国은 새로운 国際政治 秩序 再編의 노정에서도 主導力이 弱化될 수도 있음.

ㅇ 한편 금번 事態로 美国과 英国, 프랑스, 이태리등 積極 支援国과의 関係는 보다 緊密해질 것이며 터키에 대한 援助와 EC統合에 대한 터키 要求 受容의 雰囲気가 이루어지고 있으나, 걸프지역에 대한 重大한 利害에도 不拘하고 消極的 支援에 머무른 독일과 日本과의 関係는 새롭게 調整될 可能性이 있고, 이들의 国際舞台에서의 積極的 立場이 萎縮될 수도 있으며, 事態 介入과 関聯된 西方諸国의 미묘한 立場 차이는 EC統合의 政治統合과 共同安保機構 摸索이라는 신항로에 큰 장애는 되지 않을 것이나 그 現実化에 새로운 복잡한 難題를 提起할 可能性도 있음.

ㅇ 금번 事態는 또한 最初로 中東地域에 대해서 美.蘇間의 意見一致를 보아 美.蘇関係를 強化하는 要因으로 作用, 美国의 対蘇援助와 닉슨-배닉법의 撤廃로 나타나고 있으나 걸프事態를 틈 탄 蘇聯의 리투아니아. 라트비아에 대한 武力介入

-16-

0139

으로 両国関係의 協調무드가 계속 順調로울지는 2월 頂上会談
開催 以後에 보다 明確해질 展望임.

(我国에 미치는 影響)

　o 금번 事態가 我国 対外関係에 미칠 影響은 첫째, 北
方政策에 대한 影響으로 我国의 올해 重要 推進 目標인 유엔
가입과 関聯, 유엔 安保理의 関心이 当分間 中東問題에 쏠리
게 될 것으로 보여 中東問題에 여념이 없는 美国이 対이라크
軍事 制裁에 比較的 消極的인 中国으로 하여금 美国과의 協調
를 離脱하는 것을 막기 위해서도 中国에 追加負担을 지우려
하지 않을 것이어서, 我国의 올해 유엔가입과 中国 修交 마
무리 目標에 약간의 負担이 될 전망임.

　o 둘째, 韓国이 軍医療支援団 形態로 多国籍軍에 加担하
고 있기 때문에 비록 人道的 支援의 次元에 지나지 않으나
事態의 推移에 따라 一部 아랍 民族主義를 刺戟할 可能性도
없지는 않으므로 70年代 以後 中東建設市場 進出로 다져온
아랍기반의 維持와 戦後 復旧事業等 我国의 参与 餘地를 고려
아랍圈과의 紐帯関係 持続과 均衡된 外交政策의 堅持가 보다
重要해질 것임.

　o 셋째, 戦争이 長期化될 경우는 美国의 追加的 걸프사

−17−

0140

태 지원금 要求가 豫想될 수도 있어 両国間 通商問題, 韓. 蘇関係 급진전에 따른 영향을 고려 韓. 美関係의 持続的 発展을 위해 세련된 対処가 重要함.

2) 世界 및 我国 経済에 대한 影響

o 戦争 発生直後 世界経済는 쿠웨이트 占領以来 지난 6個月間 이라크 쿠웨이트産 原油供給이 中断되었으나 産油国의 充分한 石油供給과 美国, 日本等의 戦略石油 備蓄分 放出, 短期戦 展望등으로 油価가 오히려 急落하였는 바, 楽観的인 展望대로 걸프戦이 短期戦으로 終結될 경우에는 不確実性이 除去되어 投資가 回復되어 오히려 世界経済의 沈滞局面 脱出에 순기능으로 作用할 수도 있다고 展望되고 있음.

o 1.20-21間 뉴욕에서 開催된 G7 財務長官会議는 걸프戦의 戦費調達問題와 戦争에 따른 国際金融市場 安定을 위한 方案이 論議되어 日本은 90億弗, 独逸은 매달 2억7千弗을 追加支援하기로 하고, 外換市場 介入等 緊密한 協調를 봉한 安定化를 協議하여 世界経済에 대한 影響의 最少化를 위한 노력을 講究하고 있으나 美国의 경우, 莫大한 戦費 支出과 함께 戦争에 使用되는 軍需物資가 [레이건] 집권기의 재고분 使用이고, 脱冷戦趨勢에 따른 추가 武器生産誘引도 없다는 점을 고려할 때, 군수산업의 景気扶養 効果도 크지 않을 것으

—18—

0141

로 보여 美国 経済의 沈滯局面은 쉽게 반전되지 않을 것임.

o 그러나 戰争의 短期的 勝利時 "越南戰 신드롬"을 벗어난 美国民의 자신감 回復을 통한 심리적 요인이 美国 経済 回復의 변수가 될 것으로 보여지나, 戰争이 長期化 되고 또한 사우디 및 기타 아랍圈의 油田과 精油施設의 상당한 破壞와 함께 戰争의 水平的 拡散이 되는 悲観的 假定下에서는 油價가 배럴당 50 - 60 弗線으로 上昇하고 経済主体들의 投資 마인드를 萎縮시켜 世界経済의 沈滯加速化 状況도 豫想할 수 있음.

o 我国은 現在로선 油價가 豫想보다 높지 않아 큰 打擊은 豫想되지 않으나, 확전과 油田被害가 없는 戰争의 持続의 경우에는 심리적 要因에 의한 油價의 小幅 上昇이 있을 수 있으며, 사우디 油田破壞 및 拡戰으로 치닫는 最悪의 경우 世界経済와 더불어 我国 経済도 克服하기 어려운 状況 到來의 可能性을 완전히 排除할 수는 없으므로 에너지 使用抑制 等 新에너지戰略의 持続的 遂行이 緊要한 것으로 보임. 그러나 全体的으로 我国의 올해 経済成長 目標가 배럴당 油價 25弗 水準을 상정한 것이어서 큰 変化가 없는한 올해 경제성장목표 7% 達成에는 異状이 없을 듯 하나, 中東地域 輸出 차질과 建設需要 中断, 戰争으로 인한 経済주체의 全体的인 萎縮을 고려해 危機克服 認識의 武装이 必要함.

−19−

0142

II. 主要 國際情勢 日誌

1. 政　治

(韓国関係)

1.20　ㅇ 駐韓 美大使 및 駐韓 美軍 司令官, [盧]大統領
　　　　에게 걸프戰에 관해 報告

1.21　ㅇ 이라크 滯留 韓国人 22名 連絡 杜絶
　　　　- 이란 国境으로 向한 것으로 推測

1.22　ㅇ 韓.美 年例 팀스피리트 合同 軍事作戰, 縮小된
　　　　規模로 今週부터 始作

　　　　ㅇ 蘇聯, 北韓에 武器供給 持続 示唆

　　　　ㅇ 韓国, 걸프사태이래 造船 受注 거의 全無

1.23　ㅇ 韓国言論, 対蘇 経協資金 30億弗이 한국 経済力에
　　　　비해 過度하다고 指摘

　　　　ㅇ 韓国 医療支援団, 사우디아라비아로 향발

91-08

主要國際問題分析

걸프戰爭 (Ⅲ) : 地上戰의 展開와 展望

91. 2. 28

外　務　部
外交安保研究院

主 要 國 際 問 題 分 析

걸프戰爭(III) : 地上戰의 展開와 展望

― 內　　　　　容 ―

1. 걸프戰爭 6週間의 戰況

2. 休戰을 위한 外交的 努力

3. 地上戰의 目標와 展望

4. 戰後處理 問題

本 資料는 韓國外交政策 立案의 參考資料로 作成한 것으로서 外務部의 公式立場과는 無關한 것입니다.

0145

걸프戰爭(Ⅲ) : 地上戰의 展開와 展望

걸프戰爭은 美國을 위시한 多國籍軍의 시나리오에 따라 戰略的
空襲, 戰術的 空襲, 地上戰의 3단계로 전개되어 왔으며, 多國籍軍은
이 過程에서 쿠웨이트 解放과 主權回復, 이라크 軍事力의 擊滅,
사담 후세인의 제거 등 애초에 設定한 戰爭目標를 충실히 수행하고
있음.

사담 후세인은 軍事的 敗退에도 불구하고 政治的 生存을 도모
하기 위하여 그의 權力基盤인 共和國守備隊를 撤收시키려고 협상을
시도하고 있으나, 多國籍軍을 主導하고 있는 美國은 이를 허용치
않고 퇴로를 차단, 섬멸전을 계획하고 있음. 地上戰의 目標인
쿠웨이트 占領·解放은 거의 달성하였으므로, 앞으로 速戰速決로
共和國守備隊의 擊滅과 12개의 유엔 決議案의 완전 이행 강요로
사담 후세인을 제거하려는 것으로 보임.

한편 戰後處理問題와 관련, 美國의 戰後 中東地域 政治秩序
構築의 基本方向은 베이커 長官이 밝히고 있는 4개원칙, 즉 中東
地域의 새로운 集團安保體制 構築, 軍縮會談을 통한 재무장의 감시
와 견제, 아랍권의 貧富隔差를 해소하기 위한 經濟協力 摸索,
그리고 이스라엘-팔레스타인, 이스라엘-아랍간의 紛爭解決 등이 될
것임.

1

0146

戰後 中東地域은 OPEC의 향방에 따르는 石油價格推移, 戰後 復舊
를 위한 방대한 규모의 건설수요, 生必品을 중점으로 한 輸出特需
및 戰爭被害 地域 再建을 위한 國際的 資金移動 등의 要因으로 世界
經濟에 큰 영향을 미칠 것으로 전망되는 바, 이는 戰後 中東地域
經濟秩序가 어떻게 再編될 것인가와 밀접히 연관되어 있음.

戰後 中東地域의 經濟秩序는 시리아, 이집트의 軍事力과 GCC
國家들의 經濟力이 交換되는 바탕하에서 형성될 地域國家間 協力
構造를, 역외국들이 재정적으로 支援하는 형태로 형성되어 갈 것으로
豫想됨.　　이 경우 美國은 自國의 經濟的 困難으로 大規模 財政
支援에 의존하기 보다는, 전후에도 일정기간 이 지역에 軍事力을
주둔시켜 전쟁기간 중 構築된 사우디, 쿠웨이트에 대한 영향력을
계속 유지함으로써, 中東版 Marshall Plan의 立案과 運營에 주도적
역할을 해 나갈 것으로 展望됨.

0147

2

가. 多國籍軍의 戰爭主導權 掌握
─────────────────────────────

(1) 지난 6주간의 걸프戰爭에서 多國籍軍은 시종일관 戰爭의 主導
     權을 掌握하여 왔음.

  ○ 多國籍軍은 開戰 즉시 制空權의 確保와 함께 戰略·戰術 目標
     에 대한 일방적이고 지속적인 공습으로 이라크의 戰力에 막대
     한 손실을 가함(약 30% 以上으로 추산됨).

  ○ 예정된 1단계 戰爭 시나리오에 따라 주요 戰略目標 공습을
     1∼2주 內에 완료함.
     (※ 美國 주도의 多國籍軍側의 戰爭 시나리오에 관해서는
     91.1.25 발간된 「主要國際問題分析」 91-03, " 걸프전쟁의 현황과
     전망(최초 1週)" 참조)
   - 國家 指揮·統制·通信(C³) 시설을 강타, 마비시키고,
   - 核·化生武器 生産 施設도 거의 파괴되고, 이라크는 이미
     單位部隊에 배치된 武器만을 보유하고 있는 것으로 보임.
   - 空軍力과 防空施設(미사일 기지)을 강타하여 制空權을 확보함.
     300여대의 舊式 戰鬪機는 발진 불능 狀態이고 SU-25, 미그-29와
     미라지 F-1등 新銳 戰鬪機와 戰爆機들은 이란으로 대피(150기)
     하거나 격추(200기) 당했음.
   - 또한 海軍力은 완전 除去된 것으로 확인되고 있음.

○ 2단계 시나리오인 戰術目標에 대한 집중 공습(총 공습의 80%)

　으로 이라크 地上軍의 戰力을 弱化시키는 데 성공함.

　- 前方에 배치된 地上軍의 指揮·統制·通信(C³)능력에 대한

　　지속적인 공습으로 地上軍의 상호 연락이 거의 불가능한

　　것으로 評價되고 있음.

　- 주요 補給施設과 補給路에 대한 攻擊을 계속하여 후방의

　　補給을 완전 차단함.

　- 탱크, 장갑차, 야포 등 地上軍 戰力에 심각한 피해를 주었음.

　　地上戰 開始 前까지 쿠웨이트 戰域에서 이라크 탱크의 40%,

　　야포 총수의 50%, 장갑차의 30%가 파괴된 것으로 보임.

(2) 2段階의 작전이 수행되는 가운데 終戰을 위한 協商이 제기되었으

　나, 이라크측이 유엔 安保理의 모든 決議案을 수락하지 않자,

　美國은 이라크의 戰力의 ⅓ 이상 파괴된 시점에서 地上戰

　준비가 완료된 것으로 판단하여 主導的으로 3段階의 地上作戰을

　전개함.

나. 多國籍軍의 戰爭目標 부각

(1) 걸프戰爭이 진행되는 과정에서 美國이 主導하는 多國籍軍의 戰爭

　目標들이 분명히 부각됨.

4

0149

o 이란은 外交的 仲裁努力을 통해 알제리, 에멘 등 이슬람국가
들의 仲裁要請을 받아들이는 등 中東의 回敎圈內에서 이란의
發言權을 强化시키고, 이란 回敎革命(1979.2) 以來 斷絶되어
온 美國과의 關係改善도 摸索하면서, 테헤란을 걸프戰爭 終結을
위한 外交的 努力의 중심지로 부각시킴.

(2) 이란의 平和案(7개항) 提議와 各國의 反應

o 라프산자니 이란 大統領은 1991. 2. 4 걸프戰의 終熄을 위해
후세인 이라크 大統領과 만날 用意가 있으며, 美國과도 接觸할
用意가 있음을 밝히는 등 이란이 仲裁에 나설 意思가 있음을
表明하였으며, 仲裁案으로서 '中東平和案'을 제의함.

o 이란이 제의한 '中東平和 7個案'(附錄-1)의 主要內容은 쿠웨
이트內 이라크軍과 사우디內 多國籍軍의 同時撤收, 이라크·
쿠웨이트 雙方間 賠償問題의 不提起, 팔레스타인 問題의 解決을
위한 國際的 保障 등임. 이러한 이란의 平和案은 이라크의
체면을 세워주기 위한 것일 뿐만 아니라, 多國籍軍이 아닌
이슬람국가들이 戰後 處理의 주된 役割을 擔當해야 된다는
見解를 表明한 것이라 하겠음.

o 이에 대해 美國은 冷淡한 反應을 보였으나 正面으로 拒否하지는
않았음. 美國은 이라크軍의 쿠웨이트 撤收以外에는 어떠한
休戰條件에도 반대한다는 强硬立場을 表明하였지만, 이란이
이라크 航空機를 抑留하고 있으며, 걸프戰爭 終熄을 위해
努力하고 있는 점을 讚揚하는 등 이란을 자극하지 않으려
노력함.

5   0150

○ 環境테러, 人質테러, 초토화(油井防火) 등을 통하여 西方側의
反戰 輿論을 자극하여 戰意를 약화시키고 多國籍軍의 分裂을
조장하려는 術策도 多國籍軍의 言論 統制 등으로 무위에
그쳤음은 물론 오히려 西方側의 對이라크 응징 輿論을 고조시킴.

(2) 사담 후세인은 多國籍軍의 지속적이고도, 대규모적인 軍事的
膺懲을 예측하지 못하고서 地上軍의 기동성 확보에 실패함으로써
임박한 地上戰에 대비하여 政治的 生存을 위한 協商을 모색하게 됨.

---

2. 休戰을 위한 外交的 努力

가. 이란의 仲裁努力과 이라크의 條件附 撤軍案

(1) 이란의 仲裁努力 摸索의 背景

○ 이란은 이번 걸프戰爭에 대해 中立을 宜言하였으나, 걸프事態
勃發 以後 이라크에 대한 食料品·醫藥品 등을 提供하고 이라크
空軍機의 이란 대피를 許容하는 등 親이라크적인 傾向을
보여줌.

○ 걸프戰 勃發 以後 이란은 國內的으로 일부 强硬 回教指導者
들의 對美 聖戰參加 要求를 무마하고, 中東地域에서의 發言權과
影響力을 增大시키며, 전후 中東地域에서 美國의 影響力 大幅
增大를 牽制하기 위하여 戰爭終結을 위한 外交的 仲裁努力을
모색하게 됨.

0151

6

○ 이란은 外交的 仲裁努力을 통해 알제리, 예멘 등 이슬람국가
  들의 仲裁要請을 받아들이는 등 中東의 回教圈內에서 이란의
  發言權을 強化시키고, 이란 回教革命(1979.2) 以來 斷絶되어
  온 美國과의 關係改善도 摸索하면서, 테헤란을 걸프戰爭 終結을
  위한 外交的 努力의 중심지로 부각시킴.

(2) 이란의 平和案(7개항) 提議와 各國의 反應

○ 라프산자니 이란 大統領은 1991. 2. 4 걸프戰의 終熄을 위해
  후세인 이라크 大統領과 만날 用意가 있으며, 美國과도 接觸할
  用意가 있음을 밝히는 등 이란이 仲裁에 나설 意思가 있음을
  表明하였으며, 仲裁案으로서 '中東平和案'을 제의함.

○ 이란이 제의한 '中東平和 7個案'(附錄-1)의 主要內容은 쿠웨
  이트內 이라크軍과 사우디內 多國籍軍의 同時撤收, 이라크 ·
  쿠웨이트 雙方間 賠償問題의 不提起, 팔레스타인 問題의 解決을
  위한 國際的 保障 등임.   이러한 이란의 平和案은 이라크의
  체면을 세워주기 위한 것일 뿐만 아니라, 多國籍軍이 아닌
  이슬람국가들이 戰後 處理의 주된 役割을 擔當해야 된다는
  見解를 表明한 것이라 하겠음.

○ 이에 대해 美國은 冷淡한 反應을 보였으나 正面으로 拒否하지는
  않았음. 美國은 이라크軍의 쿠웨이트 撤收以外에는 어떠한
  休戰條件에도 반대한다는 強硬立場을 表明하였지만, 이란이
  이라크 航空機를 抑留하고 있으며, 걸프戰爭 終熄을 위해
  努力하고 있는 점을 讚揚하는 등 이란을 자극하지 않으려
  노력함.

ㅇ 한편 케야르 유엔事務總長과 蘇聯은 이란의 提案을 歡迎한다는
意思를 表明하였으며, 이라크의 하마디副總理, 蘇聯의 벨로노
고프 外務次官 등을 비롯한 프랑스, 알제리, 에맨 등의 高位
官史들이 태헤란을 방문하여, 이 問題를 論議함으로써 걸프戰
終熄을 위한 外交的 努力이 활발해짐.

(3) 이라크의 條件附 撤軍案 提示와 美·蘇의 反應

ㅇ 이란의 平和案 提議에 대하여 별다른 반응을 보이지 않고 있던
이라크는 2月 15日 바그다드 라디오 방송을 통해 條件附 쿠웨이트
撤收에 관한 革命 評議會의 決定을 발표함. 10個項으로 된 撤收條件
(附錄-2)중 주요내용을 보면, ①地上, 公衆, 海上에서의
全面的, 包括的 停戰, ② 걸프事態 以後 취해진 UN의 모든
對이라크 制裁措置 및 決意 撤廢, ③停戰 1個月 以內에 多國籍
軍의 中東全域에서 撤收, ④이스라엘의 팔레스타인 및 모든
아랍점령지로부터의 撤收, ⑤이라크의 歷史的 領土, 領海權
보장 및 모든 外償蕩減 등임.

ㅇ 이라크가 조건부이기는 하지만 이같은 쿠웨이트 撤收意思를
公式的으로 表明한 背景에는 무엇보다도 開戰以來 多國籍軍의
계속적인 空襲으로 無力化되어 가는 이라크의 軍事力을 보호
하는려는 의도가 작용한 것임. 더욱이 그동안 이라크가 追求
했던 이스라엘의 介入誘導와 이로 인한 多國籍軍의 內部分裂
試圖가 成果를 거두지 못하였고, 최근 蘇聯을 비롯한 이란,

8

0153

中國, 非同盟會議 등의 仲裁努力이 모두 이라크의 쿠웨이트
撤收를 전제로 하고 있다는 점을 감안한 것이라고 볼 수 있음.

ㅇ 이에 대해 美國은 부시大統領의 聲明을 통해 이라크의 이같은
撤軍提議는 전혀 새로운 내용이 없는 " 잔인한 속임수"(cruel
hoax)에 불과하다고 비난하면서, 이라크의 쿠웨이트 撤收가
可視化될 때까지 戰爭은 계속될 것이라고 천명함(2.15). 또한
부시大統領은 이라크가 쿠웨이트에서 無條件 撤收해야 하고
中東地域의 다른 紛爭과 걸프事態가 連繫되어서는 안되며,
쿠웨이트政府가 原狀回復되어야 할 것을 주장함. 또한, 이라크軍과
國民들이 直接 나서서 후세인을 權座에서 退陣시킬 것을 촉구함.
英·프랑스 등 主要 多國籍軍 國家들도 이라크의 撤軍案을 多國籍
軍의 戰列을 와해시켜 地上戰 開始를 지연시켜 보려는 의도로
把握, 이를 거절하면서 이라크의 無條件 쿠웨이트 撤收를
주장함.

ㅇ 반면, 蘇聯은 이그나첸코 大統領室 代辯人의 發表(2.15)를
통해 고르바쵸프 大統領이 이같은 이라크의 撤軍案發表에
滿足과 希望을 표시한다는 지지 意思를 表明함. 이와 동시에
걸프事態를 논의하기 위한 아지즈 이라크 外務長官의 蘇聯
訪問(2.17)을 期待한다는 意思를 밝힘.

9

0154

나. 蘇聯의 外交的 努力과 美國의 最後通牒

(1) 蘇聯의 介入背景

    ㅇ 이라크의 쿠웨이트 侵攻(1990.8.2) 直後, 蘇聯은 이라크軍의
       쿠웨이트 즉각 撤收 및 쿠웨이트 合法政府의 原狀復歸를 요구
       (1990.8.3 美·蘇 외상공동성명)하고, 美國과의 協力下에
       UN안보리의 對이라크 制裁 決議案 積極 支持 등 UN主導下의
       걸프事態 解決努力을 지지해옴. 이와 동시에 蘇聯은 美國
       主導의 軍事行動에는 反對立場을 취하면서 수차에 걸친 中東,
       西歐地域에 대한 特使派遣 등을 통해 걸프事態의 平和的
       解決을 위한 外交的 努力을 경주해옴.

    ㅇ 걸프戰爭 勃發(1991.1.17)후 蘇聯은 戰爭 勃發의 책임을 이라크
       측에 전가하면서 戰爭擴大防止를 위한 國際的 努力을 촉구하는
       등 對美 協力關係를 維持해 옴. 그러나 걸프戰爭이 長期化의
       조짐을 보이게 되자, 蘇聯은 美國 등 多國籍軍側에 의한 이라크
       파멸 가능성을 우려하면서, 걸프戰의 軍事行動은 UN安保理의
       決議案들이 설정한 한도를 초과해서는 안된다는 立場을 表明
       함과 아울러, 여러 차례에 걸쳐 걸프戰 仲裁案을 提示하는 등
       戰爭의 早期 終熄을 위한 外交的 努力을 적극화 함.

    ㅇ 蘇聯이 美國의 戰爭遂行 目的에 憂慮를 表明하면서 戰爭의
       早期 終熄을 위한 外交的 努力을 적극화하게 된 데에는, 多國籍
       軍의 계속된 空襲으로 이라크의 軍事·經濟的 潛在力이 파괴될

10   0155

위기에 처했으며, 大規模 地上戰이 불가피해짐에 따라 걸프
戰爭의 擴散 및 長期化 조짐이 보이는 등의 戰況이 크게
작용함. 蘇聯으로서는 걸프戰의 長期化 趨勢가 經濟難 打開를
위한 西方側의 支援獲得에 결코 유익하지 못할 것으로 판단하고
있으며, 특히 이라크의 후세인 政權의 몰락으로 야기될 戰後
中東地域 內에서의 美國의 立地 大幅强化 및 蘇聯의 影響力
弱化를 우려하지 않을 수 없었음.

(2) 蘇聯의 外交的 努力

　○ 蘇聯의 걸프戰 解決 平和案(4個項) 提示(1991.2.18)

　　- 걸프戰 勃發 以後 蘇聯은 고르바초프大統領이 걸프事態의
　　　平和的 解決을 위해 조만간 重大決定을 發表할 것이라고 밝힌
　　　바 있음(1.29 이그나첸코 대통령실 대변인). 또한 蘇聯은 美·蘇
　　　外務長官의 共同聲明(1.29)을 통해 이라크가 쿠웨이트에서 撤收
　　　한다는 "分明한"(unequivocal) 約束을 하고 "可視的이며
　　　구체적인"(visible and concrete) 조치를 취한다면 戰爭은
　　　終結될 수 있으며, 美·蘇 兩國은 終戰後 아랍·이스라엘간
　　　平和와 中東地域의 安定을 위해 共同努力을 경주할 수 있음을
　　　分明히함.

　　- 그 후 蘇聯은 1월31일 蘇聯 共産黨中央委가 걸프戰의 休戰을
　　　촉구한 이래, 벨로노고프 外務次官의 이란방문, 프리마코프
　　　大統領 特使의 이라크派遣등을 통해 停戰努力을 加速化하는

11　　　　　　　　　　0156

한편, 이라크에 대해서 만약 쿠웨이트로부터 撤收하지 않을
경우, 중대한 결과가 초래될 것이라고 경고하기도 함.

- 조건부이기는 하지만 걸프事態 이후 처음으로 발표된 이라크의
撤軍提議가 蘇聯의 프리마코프 大統領特使가 바그다드를 방문
하여 전달한 蘇聯側 仲裁案을 考慮한 데 따른 것이라는 이라크
側의 報道(2.15) 以後, 蘇聯은 아지즈 이라크 外務長官의
모스크바 방문 이전에 大規模 地上戰의 개시 연기를 美國에
요구하는 등 積極的 仲裁努力을 모색함.

- 2.17-18간 이라크의 아지즈 外務長官이 蘇聯을 訪問, 고르바
초프大統領과 걸프戰 終熄에 관련된 問題를 協議한 자리에서
고르바초프는 이라크軍의 無條件 쿠웨이트 撤收, 이라크의
國家構造 및 國境維持, 후세인의 처벌 및 이라크에 대한
制裁反對, 팔레스타인問題 등 모든 中東問題協議 등을 내용으로
하는 4個案의 平和案(附錄-3)을 제의함.

- 이같이 후세인 이라크大統領의 체면을 살리려는 蘇聯의 平和案
에 대하여 美國은 이를 檢討·回信하겠다는 立場을 보이면
서도 英國과 함께 이라크의 無條件 쿠웨이트 撤收 以前에는
對이라크 地上戰 計劃에는 변함이 없음을 強調함.

○ 蘇·이라크간 平和案 合意(8個項)(2.22)
- 걸프戰 終熄을 위한 各國의 仲裁努力에도 불구하고 多國籍軍에
의한 大規模 地上攻擊이 臨迫한 가운데, 이라크의 조건부

12

0157

撤軍提議(2.15)와 蘇聯의 걸프戰 解決平和案(2.18)이 모두 美國
에 의해 거부당하게 되자, 이라크로서는 大規模 地上戰의
개시로 인한 이라크 國家存立에 대한 위기감 및 후세인 자신의
운명에 대해 不安을 느끼게 됨. 이에 사담 후세인은 아지즈 外務
長官을 다시 모스크바에 파견, 戰爭 終熄方案을 위하여 蘇聯과
撤軍問題를 論議하게 됨.

- 고르바초프 蘇聯 大統領과 아지즈 이라크 外務長官의 會談結果,
양국은 이라크군의 무조건 쿠웨이트 全面撤收, 休戰 다음날부터
撤軍開始, 兵力의 3분의2 撤軍 뒤 對이라크 經濟制裁 解除,
그리고 撤軍完了와 동시에 모든 유엔 決議案 無效化 등을 주요
내용으로 하는 8個項의 平和案(附錄-4)에 합의함(2.22).

- 同 平和案은 종전의 平和案(2.18일자) 보다 더욱 美國의 요구를
수용하는 것으로서 이라크측의 撤收를 조건으로 후세인의 政治
的 生命을 保障한다는 條項을 제외한 것이 주목됨. 이처럼 蘇聯의
대미 양보종용안을 대폭 수용한 이라크측의 撤軍 同意案은 美國이
강조해 온 이라크군의 무조건 쿠웨이트撤收를 전적으로 받아들이며,
지금까지 주장해 온 팔레스타인 문제의 연계주장을 전혀 언급하지
않은 점이 그 特徵이라 하겠음.

- 이라크가 이같이 蘇聯과의 協力을 통해 걸프戰爭의 解決을 推進
하게 된 데에는 臨迫한 美國의 地上戰 開始를 지연시키면서
이라크軍의 전열정비를 위한 시간을 확보하는 동시에, 蘇聯을
통해 美國側에 協商壓力을 가하면서 多國籍軍 參與 아랍圈과
美國을 이완시킬려는 의도에서 비롯된 것으로 보임.

13

○ 蘇聯의 修正 仲裁案(6個項)提示 (2. 23)

  - 美國은 蘇聯의 두번째 仲裁案인 8個項의 平和案(2. 22)이 ①美國
    의 주장과는 반대로 休戰을 撤收에 앞서 규정하고 있으며,
    ②이라크軍 3분의 2가 撤收된 후 유엔의 經濟制裁를 중지시키고
    撤收를 완료한 후에 모든 유엔安保理 決議의 효력을 정지시키도록 한점,
    ③撤收時限이 구체적으로 명시되어 있지 않다는 점, 그리고
    ④쿠웨이트 합법정부의 회복 및 쿠웨이트에 대한 이라크의 배상
    등에 대해 언급이 없는 점 등에 대해 불만을 표시하면서, 이를
    유엔이 決議한 無條件 撤軍이 아닌 이라크의 條件附 撤軍案으로
    파악함.

  - 蘇·이라크間에 合意된 平和案(8個項)에 대해 美國은 부시大統領의
    聲明(2. 22)을 통해 이라크의 쿠웨이트로부터 즉시 無條件 撤收를
    규정한 유엔決議案 660호 이외의 조건은 받아들일 수 없다고 밝히
    면서, 이라크가 워싱턴 시각으로 23일 정오(韓國時間 : 24일 새벽
    2시)까지 쿠웨이트로부터 卽刻的이고도 無條件的으로 撤軍할 것을
    촉구하였으며, 만약 이라크가 이를 거부할 경우 地上戰의 開始는
    불가피할 것이라는 最後通牒을 선언함.

  - 이에 美國이 정한 최후 通牒時限이 임박하자 蘇聯의 고르바초프
    大統領은 이라크의 同意를 얻어 전날의 8個項을 일부 修正한
    6個項의 平和案(附錄-5)을 새로 제의함. 이 6個項의 修正案에서
    는 蘇聯이 후세인의 체면용으로 붙인 "撤軍의 3분의 2가 이루어진
    시점에서 經濟制裁를 解除한다"는 條項이 삭제되었으며, 이라크軍의

14   0159

쿠웨이트로부터 21日間의 撤軍完了期限 明示 및 休戰後 72時間
內 戰爭捕虜를 釋放한다는 등 하루 전의 8個項보다 좀더 구체적인
休戰節次를 명기하고 있음.

- 蘇聯이 이같이 이라크의 最大限 讓步를 얻어내면서까지 地上戰
  開始를 막기 위한 外交的 仲裁努力을 시도한 것은 첫째, 과거
  蘇聯이 中東地域의 이라크, 시리아, 이집트, 예멘 등과 友好協力協定
  을 체결하고 막대한 量의 軍事武器를 販賣하는 등 긴밀한 관계를
  유지해 왔던 歷史的 關係를 무시할 수 없었으며, 둘째, 美國에
  대해 한정된 선에서의 終戰을 誘導, 후세인政權의 沒落을 방지함
  으로써 戰後 中東地域內에서의 美國의 影響力 擴大를 견제하는
  한편, 親후세인 아랍국가들의 지지를 획득하여 戰後 中東秩序
  再編過程에서 蘇聯의 입지를 확보하기 위한 것으로 볼 수 있음.

(3) 美國의 最後通牒과 地上戰 開始

ㅇ 걸프戰爭 勃發 以後 대규모 공습을 통해 이라크의 主要 軍事施設
  을 파괴하는 등 계획대로 전쟁을 수행해 나가고 있는 美國으로서는
  걸프전쟁을 미국의 의도대로 마무리 짓기 위해서는 大規模 地上戰
  의 개시가 불가피함을 인식, 이에 대한 준비를 해오던 중 소련이
  적극적인 중재노력을 시도하게 되자 딜레마에 처하게 됨.

ㅇ 만약 美國이 蘇聯의 平和案을 수락할 경우, 걸프戰爭이 終結되어
  이라크가 즉시 撤收하더라도 이라크의 軍事力을 보전하게 되어
  여전히 쿠웨이트 및 사우디 등에 위협적 존재로 남게 되며,

15

0160

후세인 대통령을 아랍圈의 英雄으로 만들 가능성이 커지게 됨.
또한 걸프사태 이후 수많은 전비의 부담과 병력을 파견한 美國
으로서는 대규모 지상전을 통해 전쟁의 승리를 자신하고 있는
현시점에서, 소련의 개입으로 戰後 中東地域에서의 美國의 影響力
擴大라는 정치적 목표가 견제당하는 것을 원치 않음.

o 따라서 미국은 이번 전쟁의 최초 목표였던 쿠웨이트 해방,
이라크 군사력의 파괴내지는 축소, 후세인의 제거 등 걸프
전쟁에 대한 美國의 立場을 분명히 하였으며, 사실상 이라크의
降伏을 요구하는 最後通牒을 선언함.

o 소련의 중재안에 대해 이라크가 이를 수락하는 등 지상전의
연기를 시도하게 되자, 美國은 이라크의 撤軍條件을 좀 더 구체화
하고 쿠웨이트주둔 이라크軍의 주요 군사 장비의 포기를 요구하는
9個項의 이라크 撤軍 條件(附錄-6)을 제시함으로써 이라크로
하여금 無條件 撤收 내지는 地上戰 開始 중 택일할 것을 요구함.
이에 대하여 이라크 후세인 대통령은 결사항전을 선포함으로써
걸프전쟁은 수많은 인적·물적 손실을 초래할지도 모르는
지상전으로 돌입하게 됨.

o 요컨대 이라크측과 多國籍軍側의 終戰을 위한 外交努力에서 명료
하게 드러난 이라크측과 多國籍軍측 입장간의 기본적인 差異는
① 終戰後의 사담 후세인의 입지, ② 이라크 軍事力을 재기
불능상태로 격멸하느냐, 아니면 전후지역 勢力均衡의 유지에

16   0161

필요한 만큼만 약화시키느냐의 문제, ③ 이라크에 대한 經濟
制裁·封鎖 措置를 終戰後 계속 유지하느냐의 문제, ④ 이라크에
대한 전쟁 배상금을 요구하는 문제 등에 집중되어 있음.

o 이와 같은 쟁점은 앞으로도 계속 논의될 것이나, 미국은
軍事的 壓勝을 바탕으로 사담 후세인의 완전 굴복시까지 양보
하지 않을 가능성이 큼.

3. 地上戰의 目標와 展望

(1) 多國籍軍은 精銳部隊인 美7軍團과 15機甲師團을 사우디·쿠웨
    이트 國境地域으로 移動配置하고 海兵師團을 쿠웨이트 해안으로
    이동하는 등 地上戰 준비를 2.15까지 완료하고 2.24 개시함.

(2) 美國 주도의 多國籍軍은 地上戰에서 다음과 같은 目標를 추구함.

    ① 쿠웨이트로 進擊하여 쿠웨이트 領土를 장악, 이라크로 부터
       해방시키고 쿠웨이트 領土內의 이라크 잔존 병력을 격멸함.

    ② 이라크 南部와 쿠웨이트 北部 隣接地域에 기갑, 기계화부대
       및 공수부대를 投入, 短期間內에 바스라에 이르는 地域에서
       포위망을 형성하여 이라크 최강의 精銳部隊인 共和國守備隊의
       퇴로를 차단, 이를 격멸함으로써 速戰速決을 거둠.

(3) 이와 같은 목표아래 多國籍軍은 이미 쿠웨이트·사우디 國境線에
    配置된 이라크군을 궤멸시키면서 쿠웨이트 市에 進入하여 이라크
    잔류병력의 소탕전만을 남기고 있으며, 쿠웨이트 北方 근처의
    共和國守備隊와의 大會戰을 서두르고 있음.

17

0162

(4) 美國은 애초에 설정하였던 戰爭目標와 관련하여 地上戰에서도
    이라크 地上軍의 탱크, 장갑차, 포병 등 攻勢作戰能力을 除去
    하는데 主眼點을 두고 있으므로 이를 충분히, 즉 이라크가
    더이상 軍事大國으로 再起하지 못할 정도로 충분히 擊滅한
    후에야 終戰協商에 임할 것임.

(5) 美國은 사담후세인을 권좌에서 물러나게 하거나 軍事的 擊滅을
    통하여 항복을 강요하고 12개의 유엔 決議案(附錄-7)의 이행을
    강행함으로써 그를 退陣시키려함.

(6) 그러나 美國을 위시한 多國籍軍은 이라크 武力의 충분한 擊滅
    이후에도 이라크 제2 都市인 바스라와 南部地域의 戰略的 要衝地
    (이라크의 유일한 海上 접근로)를 잠정적으로 점령하여 후세인의
    退陣이나 전후 처리에 유리한 協商카드로 활용할 가능성도 배제
    할 수 없음.

---

4. 戰後處理 問題

가. 戰後 中東地域秩序 再編 構想

(1) 현재 걸프전쟁의 종결과 관련한 전후 질서 구상의 두가지 시나
    리오가 대두되고 있음.

18

0163

o 첫번째 안은 전후 일정한 과도기 동안 美軍이 이 지역에 주둔
　하면서 미국의 국무장관이 제안한 이른바,「베이커 4개항의
　계획」을 실현하는 것을 내용으로 하는 미국, 영국 중심의 시나
　리오이고,

o 두번째 안은 프랑스 등 일부 유럽국가들에 의해서 제의되고
　있는바, 이는 유엔을 중심으로 同 地域에서의 平和維持軍 배치와
　함께 관련 국가들이 참여하는 國際會議를 통해 중동 전체 문제를
　다루는 시나리오 임.

(2) 그러나 후자의 유엔 中心案의 실현 가능성 여부는 현재로서
　　대단히 불투명한 것으로 보임. 그 理由는 무엇보다도 팔레
　　스타인 문제와 관련, 미국과 이스라엘은 국제회의를 통한 해결
　　방안을 원하지도 않고 있을 뿐 아니라, 그 효과에 대하여 기대를
　　걸고 있지 않기 때문임. 따라서 미국과 이스라엘이 참여하지
　　않는 국제회의는 무의미해질 것이며, 일부 유럽 國家들이 提議
　　하고 있는 유엔 중심의 中東秩序構想은 그 실현 가능성이
　　희박할 것으로 展望됨.

나. 美國의 戰後 中東地域 政治秩序 構想

(1) 따라서 현재 가장 實現 可能한 시나리오는 美國의 構想인 바,
　　美國은 戰後 中東秩序가 이 地域에서 새로이 부상하게 될 이란,
　　이집트, 시리아 등 주요 아랍國家間 적절한 勢力均衡에 의해
　　유지되어야 한다고 보고 있음. 또한 美國은 이라크에 대하여

19

0164

이라크의 過多한 軍事力 破壞 및 사담 후세인을 제거함으로써
이라크가 인접국을 위협할 정도로 强大國이 되는 것을 억제함과
동시에 인접국의 침공으로 이라크가 분할되는 등 약화되는 것도
막으려 할 것으로 보임.

(2) 이러한 美國이 主導하고 있는 戰後 中東 政治秩序 構築은 다음과
   같은 방향으로 전개될 것으로 보임.

   ○ 美國의 제임스 베이커 국무장관은 1991. 2. 6 美 下院 外交
      委員會에서 증언을 통하여 中東 政治秩序 構築과 관련, 4개항의
      원칙을 제시함.
      첫째, 걸프지역 국가들간의 새로운 集團安保體制 構築,
      둘째, 軍縮會談을 통한 재무장의 감시와 견제,
      세째, 아랍권의 富國과 貧國간의 격차를 해소하기 위한 경제
            협력 모색,
      넷째, 이스라엘- 팔레스타인, 이스라엘-아랍간의 분쟁해결을
            위한 외교적 노력 지속

   ○ 걸프戰爭 終熄後 새로운 中東地域 秩序와 관련, 이와 같은 베이커
      國務長官의 4개항의 原則을 보다 자세히 검토하면 다음과 같음.
      - 地域協力 均衡體制 構築
        美國은 걸프事態의 발생이 中東地域에서의 勢力均衡의 붕괴에
        기인하였음을 감안하여 終戰後 이 地域에서의 새로운 勢力均衡을
        構築하려 할 것임. 특히 걸프灣 地域에서 사우디 아라비아,
        이라크, 이란간의 勢力均衡을 바탕으로 地域安定을 꾀하고 美國

20

0165

자신이 이 地域에서 勢力均衡의 조정자 役割을 수행하려 할
것임. 또한 美國은 아랍圈의 전반적인 軍事均衡과 安定을
기하기 위하여 多國籍軍에 참여한 시리아, 이집트 등 아랍
연합국을 주축으로하는 集團安保體制 構築을 모색할 가능성이
있음.

- 地域軍縮

美國은 향후 中東地域에서의 軍事力 均衡 維持와 紛爭 勃發
가능성 억제 등 地域安定을 위한 地域軍縮을 추진할 것임.
이를 위하여 美國은 蘇聯과 西方國들의 在來式武器 輸出을
철저히 統制監視하고 특히 核, 化生 武器 등 대량살상무기의
제거와 이를 위한 國際的 檢證方法 등을 모색할 것임. 그러나
이러한 美國 主導의 軍備統制 努力에 이스라엘이 포함되지 않는
다면 그 효과를 기대할 수 없으므로 美國은 이스라엘에 대한
軍備統制 實現 方案도 마련할 것으로 보임.

- 貧富 隔差 解消

아랍圈 국가들간에 貧富隔差를 줄이기 위해 美國은 아랍貧國
支援을 위한 地域經濟 協力機構의 창설운영 지원 등 地域經濟
協力을 강화하는 한편, 産油富國에 취업하고 있는 아랍국민들
의 政治·社會的 지위향상을 보장하는 방안 등도 모색할 것으로
보임. 또한 많은 아랍圈 국가들은 人口爆發, 食糧難, 水資源
利用 및 富의 균등분배 등 심각한 經濟摩擦 要因을 안고 있으며
이러한 문제를 해결하기 위하여 地域國家들간의 相互協力이

21

0166

절실히 요구되고 있는 바, 美國은 걸프협력협의회(GCC), 아랍
협력협의회(ACC), 아랍-마그레브 동맹(AMU) 등의 기능 강화를
모색할 것으로 보임.

- 팔레스타인 問題 및 이스라엘-아랍 葛藤 解消
  中東平和의 관건은 팔레스타인 문제의 해결에 있는 바, 美國은
  이 문제의 원만한 해결이 없는한 軍縮統制와 國際테러의 規制
  등을 통한 이 地域에서의 진정한 平和構築이 어렵다는 점을 잘
  認識하고 있음. 따라서 美國은 이번 걸프戰爭을 계기로 관련

  당사국간에 아랍-이스라엘 紛爭을 근본적으로 해결하려는 새로운
  조정안을 중심으로 이에 따른 具體的 시도를 할 것으로 보임.
  팔레스타인 문제와 관련, 현재 이스라엘과 팔레스타인 양측이
  팽팽한 異見을 보이고 있는 바, 美國은 새로운 協商을 유도하기
  위하여 당사자간의 회담과 아울러 이를 보장하기 위한 國際會議
  의 개최도 병행하여 타결을 모색하려 할 가능성이 있음.
  그러나 팔레스타인 문제는 당사자 회담과 국제회의도 중요하지만
  아랍圈 전체의 政治·社會的 安定과도 밀접히 연계되어 있기
  때문에 美國은 장시간에 걸친 단계적 접근방법을 강구할 것으로
  보임.

(3) 이와 함께 베이커 장관은 이러한 戰後 中東秩序 確立을 위해
美國이 이라크의 재건을 支援할 것이며, 戰後 中東秩序 確立을
위하여 美軍의 中東地域 주둔 필요성을 강조하였음. 그러나 美國
은 中東地域에서 海·空軍 이외의 美 地上軍 주둔을 고려하지

22

0167

않고 있는 것으로 보이며, 이를 대치하여 GCC 지상군의 배치를
검토하고 있는 것으로 알려지고 있음.

(4) 결국 美國의 의도는 걸프전쟁 종결후 中東地域에 유럽형의 集團
安保體制를 構築하여 軍事安保的 安定을 기하는 한편, 經濟援助를
통한 아랍국가들의 반발을 吸收하면서 동시에 사우디, 이집트 및
온건 아랍국과 시리아 등 새로운 親美 국가 및 아랍연합국가를
규합하여 同地域에서 영향력을 강화하려는 것임. 또한 美國은
후세인 정권과 같은 反美的 强硬勢力을 철저히 응징하고 이라크와
쿠웨이트에 親美정권의 등장을 유도하고 있는 것으로 보임.

다. 戰後 中東地域의 經濟秩序 構想

(1) 戰後 經濟協力 構想

  ○ 미국을 중심으로 한 다국적군 참여국가들은 걸프전 후 중동질서
    재편 구상의 일부로서 중동지역 經濟 再建 및 開發問題를 논의
    하기 시작하였는 바, 그 理由는 다음과 같음.

    - 첫째, 금번 걸프전의 近因이 산유국, 비산유국간 또는 산유부국
      과 산유빈국간에 존재하는 극심한 빈부격차에 있었다는 인식의
      제고,

    - 둘째, 전후 미국을 위시한 다국적군 참여국가들이 중동질서를
      재편하기 위하여서는 전쟁기간 중 부각된 파괴자로서의 이미지를
      국제적인 개발 협력을 통하여 불식시켜야 한다는 政策的 必要性

23

0168

o 현재 공식적으로 언급된 것은 미국, EC 등 서방 다국적군 참여
  국가들의 중동판 마샬플랜 구상과 지역국가들의 전후협력 구상
  등이 있음.

  - 91.2. 6 美 상원 외교위 청문회에서 베이커 美 국무장관이 전후
    중동의 경제 재건을 위해서는 國際的 共同 努力의 필요성이
    있음을 강조하고, 90. 5 설립된 東歐開發銀行(EBRD)을 모델로 한
    中東復興開發銀行(MEBRD)의 설립을 주장함으로써 중동판 마샬
    플랜 구상을 밝힌 바 있으며, EC도 2. 19 개최된 EC 外相會談
    에서 전후 중동질서재편과 관련, 유사한 구상을 추구하기로
    하였음.

  - 또한 反이라크 연대를 결성하고 있는 이집트, 시리아 및 GCC
    국가등 8개 아랍국가들은 2. 16 카이로에서 외무장관회의를
    개최하고, 전후 중동지역에서의 평화유지를 위한 集團安保와
    經濟協力 방안을 논의하였음.

o 현재 상기 방안에 대한 구체적인 논의가 시작된 단계는 아니나,
  MEBRD의 경우 산유부국인 사우디, 쿠웨이트 등이 주로 出資
  하고 나머지는 일본, 독일 등 경제대국과 기타 다국적군 참여
  국가들이 출자하는 형태가 가능할 것임. 미국의 경우, 상존하는
  財政·貿易赤字의 압박으로 대규모 출연은 어려울 것이나 陸軍은
  철수하되 海·空軍은 이지역에 잔류한다는 구도하에서, 사우디,
  쿠웨이트 등 주요 出資國에 대해 이번 전쟁을 통하여 구축된
  정치·군사적 영향력을 사용함으로써 MEBRD 설립 및 운영에 있어
  주도적 역할 수행을 추구할 것으로 보임.

24

0169

- 8개 아랍국가의 전후 구상은 이집트 · 시리아의 군사력과 GCC
  회원국의 經濟援助를 상호 교환한다는 바탕위에서 걸프지역 평화를
  유지해 나아간다는 것으로 알려지고 있음.

- 현재 나타난 2가지 구상이 향후 어떻게 연계되어 구체적으로
  나타날 것인가는 예상하기 어려우나, 지역국가간의 集團安保 -
  經濟協力 구도에 대해 역외국가들이 MEBRD를 통한 재정적 기여
  로 밑받침해 나가는 형태가 될 것으로 전망해 볼 수 있을 것임.

(2) 戰後 中東地域의 經濟的 重要性

　　戰後 中東秩序 再編에 있어서의 經濟協力의 의미는 政治秩序
再編의 한 요소로서 뿐이 아니라, 세계경제에 있어서의 이 지역
중요성에 의해서도 판단될 수 있는 바, 분야별 중요성은 다음과
같음.

○ 石油

- 中東에 대한 세계 석유수출 依存度는 현재 40% 수준에 있으나
  2000년에는 60% 수준으로 상향될 것임. 특히, 1995년을 전후로
  중동 이외지역의 산유량 증가가 감속될 것으로 전망됨에 따라
  중동의 석유 공급원으로서의 중요성이 더욱 증대될 것인 바,
  현재 더 이상의 심각한 유전파괴없이 전쟁이 종식될 경우,
  유가는 15-20달러선에 머무를 것으로 예측되고 있으나, 중장기
  적으로 상승세가 될 것으로 전망됨.

25

- 이와 관련, 향후의 관심사는 多國籍軍 참여국가들이 기존의
  OPEC을 약화시키고, 생산국과 수입국이 공동 참여하는 새로운
  世界的 原油供給體系를 확립해 나갈 것인가로 귀결될 것임.
  새로운 국제원유 공급체계가 나타나지 않는 경우 향후의 원유
  공급은 상기한 장기수급구조 하에서의 중동지역의 중요성으로
  볼 때 OPEC내 세력분포 변화가 관건이 될 것임.
- 현 시점에서 볼 때, 이라크의 패퇴로 고유가정책을 주장해 오던
  OPEC내 강경국들의 입장 약화가 일반적으로 예상되나, 사우디,
  쿠웨이트 등 穩健國들이 아랍民族主義의 고양에 따라 고조될
  다국적군 참여 온건 아랍국에 대한 정치적 불만을 해소하고,
  막대한 戰費 및 戰後 復舊費를 조달하기 위한 방안으로 점차
  高油價 정책에 동조해 나갈 가능성도 배제할 수만은 없음.

o 建設

- 쿠웨이트 망명 정부에 의한 「쿠웨이트 國土再建 計劃」에 의하
  면 전후 쿠웨이트 복구는 3단계에 걸쳐 최장 12년이 소모될 것
  으로 예상됨. 현재 예상되는 복구액은 800억불 수준이나 地上戰
  의 결과에 따라 더욱 늘어날 수 있을 것임.
- 그러나 쿠웨이트 정부의 해외자산이 1,300억불을 상회함에 따라
  戰後 復舊費의 조달은 어려운 문제가 아닐 것으로 전망되고
  있으며, 이미 전후 복구 공사 참여와 관련 美國의 獨占的 位置
  에 대한 기타 다국적군 참여 국가의 불만이 고조되고 있는 실정
  임.

26

0171

- 다국적군의 공습에 따른 이라크의 피해는 이라크측 발표에 의하
  면 현재 2,000억불 수준에 이른 것으로 보도되고 있음.
  지상전 이후 피해 상황이 점검되어야 정확한 복구 규모가 나올
  것이나 이란-이라크 전쟁시 이미 발생한 600-1,000억불 상당의
  피해와 이번 걸프전의 피해로 이라크의 總復舊需要는 3,000억불
  수준에 육박할 것임.   그러나 걸프사태 발생 전인 1990. 8 현재
  650억의 외채를 지고 있고, 이번 전쟁의 패배로 약 1,000억불에
  이를 것으로 예상되는 戰爭賠償金 부담을 지게 될 이라크로서는
  MEBRD에 의한 무상원조 또는 서방국의 외채 탕감조치가 취해지지
  않을 경우 전후 복구비 조달이 어려울 것임.

○   輸出

- 전쟁으로 對중동 수출은 상당히 위축되어 있으나 전후 복구사업
  이 급진전되고, 終戰으로 세계 교역 여건이 정상화되면 중동지역
  은 특히 建設 機資材와 의류·식량 등 生必品 등을 중심으로 전후
  특수지역으로서 부각될 것임.   현재 중동 21개국은 2억 2,000만명
  의 인구를 가진 년간 1,500억불 상당의 수출 시장인 바, 전후
  중장기적으로도 시장 확대의 가능성은 큰 것으로 보임.

○   金融

- 中東開發銀行이 설립될 경우 대부분의 재원은 사우디, 쿠웨이트 등
  산유부국에서 출자될 것으로 예상되고 있음.   그러나 최근 사우디가
  전비 지출 부담 등으로 100억불의 차관을 도입하여야 한다는 실정을
  볼 때, 域外國家 즉 일본, 독일 등 다국적군 참여 국가 중 경제력을
  가진 국가들의 참여로 상당부분 이루어질 것으로 예상되고 있음.

27

0172

- 美國은 재정·무역적자의 상존으로 많은 출자를 기대하기는 어려울 것이나, 사우디, 쿠웨이트에 대한 政治·軍事的 影響力을 통해 MEBRD의 설립과 운영에 주도적 역할을 해 나갈 것으로 보임.

- 中東版 Marshall plan은 MEBRD을 통한 무상원조와 장기신용 제공으로 구성될 것이며, 이라크가 수혜대상으로 포함될 경우, 2차대전 이후의 Marshall plan에서 독일의 경우 (London Debt Agreement, 1953. 9)와 같이 이라크에 대한 채무경감조치가 필요해질 것임.

- 상기한 中東版 Marshall Plan 추진을 위한 각국의 출연금과 戰後 復舊를 위한 지역국가들의 자금 수요충족은 東歐圈의 改革·開放, 統獨 및 美,日 등의 금융 위축 등으로 이미 경색 현상을 보이고 있는 國際金融環境下에서는 용이한 일이 아닐 것임. 이에 따른 國際金利의 不安定性은 戰後 國際油價 安定과 戰後 特殊에도 불구하고 世界經濟의 불확실성을 높일 가능성이 있음.

                                        1991. 2. 28
                                作成 : 研究敎授 朴弘圭
                                      研究敎授 崔宜喆
                                      研究敎授 李東輝
                                      研究敎授 裵肯燦
                                討論 : 研究室長 金國振
                                      研究敎授 柳錫烈

28

0173

- 附 錄 -

1. 이란 라프산자니 大統領의 中東平和 7개안(2.5 쿠웨이트 인터내쇼날지 보도)

　① 이라크의 쿠웨이트 撤軍 呼訴收容

　② 多國籍軍에 平和呼訴

　③ 이라크軍 撤收와 동시에 多國籍軍 撤收後 回敎軍 配置

　④ 이라크·쿠웨이트간 異見解消를 위한 回敎委員會를 設置

　⑤ 前後復舊 回敎基金 設立

　⑥ 이라크·이란·GCC 6개국·터키·파키스탄간 不可侵協定締結

　⑦ 걸프지역 諸國家 포함 地域安保協力機構 設置

2. 이라크의 條件附 쿠웨이트 撤軍案 (2.15 바그다드 라디오 放送報道)

　① 지난해 8월 2일 이라크의 쿠웨이트 侵攻前·後 걸프 및 中東
　　地域에 派遣된 모든 軍隊와 함정·무기 등을 撤收할 것.

　② 軍隊와 武器 등의 撤收는 休戰後 1개월 以內에 실시되어야 하며
　　이후 걸프지역은 地域國家들이 스스로의 安保를 擔當하는 '外國
　　軍事基地 없는 地帶'로 宣布될 것.

　③ 이스라엘군은 팔레스타인 점령지구와 골란고원·레바논 등에서
　　撤收할 것.

　④ 걸프사태를 이유로 이스라엘에 提供된 모든 武器와 裝備 등이
　　撤收될 것.

29

0174

⑤ 쿠웨이트에 대한 이라크의 歷史的인 領土·領海權이 保障될 것.

⑥ 쿠웨이트에서 執權 알 사바 王家가 아닌 국민들의 진정한 民主的 權利行事로 民主主義 實現이 보장될 것.

⑦ 유엔의 對이라크 경제제재 및 결의 등이 철폐되고 各個國家 또는 集團的으로 이라크에 대해 취했던 各種措置들도 撤回할 것.

⑧ 多國籍軍에 가담한 國家들은 이라크가 입은 戰爭被害의 復舊에 배상금을 지급할 것.

⑨ 多國籍軍 國家들에 대한 이라크의 모든 負債를 전면 탕감할 것.

⑩ 요르단 등 외세의 侵略으로 被害를 본 國家들의 外債도 전면 탕감할 것.

3. 蘇聯의 걸프전 解決 平和案 (4개항, 2.17 獨逸 빌트지 報道內容)

① 이라크는 前提條件 없이 쿠웨이트에서 철수

② 蘇聯은 이라크의 國家構造 및 國境을 維持하는 것을 지지

③ 蘇聯은 후세인에 대한 刑罰的 措置 포함, 對이라크 제재에 반대

④ 팔레스타인問題를 비롯한 中東問題 協議 필요

4. 蘇·이라크간 합의 平和案 (8개항, 2.22)

① 이라크는 쿠웨이트로부터 無條件的인 全面撤收 準備가 되어있다.

② 撤收는 休戰 다음날부터 始作한다.

③ 撤收는 일정기간동안 完了한다.

④ 이라크軍 ⅔가 쿠웨이트로부터 撤收하면 對이라크 경제제재를 해제한다.

30

0175

⑤ 撤收가 完了되면 대이라크 제재를 규정한 유엔 안보리의 모든 決議案이 效力을 喪失한다.

⑥ 休戰 직후 모든 포로를 즉시 釋放한다.

⑦ 이라크군 撤收는 유엔 안보리가 委任하는, 戰爭에 직접 關聯이 없는 나라들이 감독한다.

⑧ 세부 項目들에 대한 作業을 계속, 22일 유엔안보리 開催前에 발표한다.

5. 蘇聯의 修正 終戰案 (6개항, 2.23)

① 이라크는 쿠웨이트로부터 無條件 撤收, 유엔 결의 660호에 따라 1990년 8월 1일 이전 위치로 復歸한다.

② 撤收는 종전 발표후 다음날부터 시작한다.

③ 撤收는 쿠웨이트市로부터 4일이내, 쿠웨이트 全域에서 총21일 이내에 完了한다.

④ 撤收가 完了되면 대이라크 制裁를 規定한 유엔의 모든 決意는 效力을 상실한다.

⑤ 休戰後 72시간내 모든 戰爭 포로를 즉시 釋放한다.

⑥ 이라크군 撤收는 유엔 안보리가 정한 감시단 또는 平和維持軍이 監督한다.

6. 美國의 이라크 撤軍 條件 (9개항, 2.22)

① 23일 正午內 撤收개시

② 撤收 시작 후 1주일내 完了

③ 48시간내 쿠웨이트 수도로부터 完全 撤收

④ 48시간내 國境 및 戰略據點의 방어시설 撤去

⑤ 48시간내 포로·民間人 釋放, 死亡軍人 遺骸 送還

⑥ 石油施設裝置 爆發物 제거, 지뢰·기뢰 부설 位置 資料提供

⑦ 多國籍軍에 의한 쿠웨이트 領空 統制, 이란 輸送機外 戰鬪機의
   비행중지

⑧ 쿠웨이트 破壞行爲 中止, 抑留 쿠웨이트인 全員 釋放

⑨ 이라크군의 安全撤收保障

7. UN安保理의 對이라크관계 결의

① 660호(90년 8월 2일) 이라크의 쿠웨이트 침공 비난 이라크군
   전병력 卽刻·無條件 撤收要求

② 661호(8월 6일) 對이라크 전면경제제재

③ 662호(8월 18일) 이라크에 의한 쿠웨이트 합병 무효 결정

④ 664호(8월 18일) 외국인 출국허가 요구

⑤ 665호(8월 25일) 海上에서 한정적 무기사용 용인

⑥ 666호(9월 13일) 對이라크 식품·의약품 공급 가이드라인 설정

⑦ 667호(9월 16일) 이라크군의 쿠웨이트 각국공관 난입 비난

⑧ 669호(9월 24일) 경제제재 감시위원회 권한 확대

⑨ 670호(9월 25일) 對이라크 공중봉쇄

⑩ 674호(10월 29일) 이라크 배상책임 확인 걸프전쟁에 의한 경제적
   손실에 대한 이라크의 배상책임을 확인

⑪ 677호(11월 28일) 인구 구성 변경에 대한 이라크 비난

⑫ 678호(11월 29일) 對이라크 전면 무력사용 용인 : 91년 1월 15일
   까지 이라크가 UN안보리의 모든 결의를 이행하지 않으면 쿠웨이트
   지원 가맹국에 평화회복을 위한 모든 수단을 사용할 수 있는 권한
   부여

32.

0177

91 - 12

主要國際問題分析

걸프 戰爭(Ⅳ) : 評價 － 多國籍軍의 勝利와 中東新秩序

91 . 3 . 27

外　務　部
外交安保研究院

91 - 12   91. 3. 27

主 要 國 際 問 題 分 析

걸프 戰爭(IV) : 評價- 多國籍軍의 勝利와 中東新秩序

— 內   容 —

1. 多國籍軍 勝利의 背景

2. 戰後 中東秩序 摸索

3. 結論 및 韓國의 考慮事項

本 資料는 韓國外交政策 立案의 參考資料로 作成한 것으로서 外務部의 公式立場과는 無關한 것입니다.

0179

걸프戰爭(Ⅳ) : 評價 - 多國籍軍의 勝利와 中東新秩序

걸프戰에서 多國籍軍의 일방적 승리로 美軍을 중심으로 한 多國籍軍은 戰術, 兵力 및 裝備 등에 있어서 그 우월함을 입증했으며, 특히 尖端電子武器의 위력과 재공권을 장악한 空軍의 활약 등이 多國籍軍의 승리에 크게 기여함. 美國은 걸프事態勃發以後 外交的 努力을 통해 多國籍軍의 結成, UN을 통한 對이라크 制裁, 同盟國들과의 戰爭費用의 공동 부담 등을 통해 각국의 지원과 협력을 획득, 이라크를 國際社會에서 고립시켰을 뿐만 아니라 美軍을 비롯한 多國籍軍의 행동을 정당화시키는데 성공함. 이와 더불어 美國은 戰爭의 확산에 따른 國際經濟危機에 대한 우려와 越南戰의 재판에 대한 우려를 불식시키기 위해 言論媒體를 통한 홍보선전에 주력함으로써 國內外 輿論의 지지를 확보해 나감.

걸프戰爭에 있어 美國의 이같은 주도적 역할 행사는 걸프戰爭의 戰後 處理 및 新中東秩序 모색에 있어 美國의 影響力과 發言權을 대폭 강화시켰으며, 政治·軍事的 側面에서 유일한 世界 超强大國으로서의 美國의 세계적 역할을 크게 부각시킴. 戰後 中東地域의 平和定着과 安定을 위해 美國은 걸프地域에서의 새로운 安保體制構築, 이스라엘-아랍國家間 紛爭의 해결, 地域 軍備統制 및 經濟協力 등을 추구해 나갈 것으로 보임. 이를 위해 美國은 1991. 3 베이커

1

0180

國務長官의 중동순방을 통해 이스라엘·아랍國家間의 關係正常化를 위한 協商 주선과 동시애 이스라엘·팔래스타인間의 對話 주선 등을 제시하는 등 적극적인 外交的 努力을 기울임.

그리하여 中東의 新秩序는 美國이 조정자로서의 역할을 맡는, 地域國家間 勢力均衡을 통한 地域平和의 구축이라는 양상을 띠개될 것이며, 이와 같은 世界秩序의 地域化 現象은 타지역에도 확산되어 나갈 것으로 보임. 따라서 韓國으로서는 이러한 中東新秩序가 東北亞地域에 미치는 파급효과 및 戰後 美國의 세계적 역할 증대 등을 고려하여 기존의 韓·美 友好協力關係를 더욱 증진시키며 韓半島 平和體制構築과 東北亞 新秩序 再編過程에 있어 주도적 역할을 모색하는 한편 戰後 國際經濟秩序의 改編애 따른 亞·太地域의 經濟共同體 構成 움직임 등에도 적극적으로 참여하는 것이 필요할 것임.

2

0181

가. 軍事的 優勢

(1) '91. 2. 28 부시대통령의 終戰宣言으로 多國籍軍의 일방적 승리로 끝난 걸프戰爭은 월남戰以後 최대규모의 地域戰爭으로 서, 美國의 尖端兵器가 그 위력을 발휘한 '尖端電子 軍事力의 勝利'라 하여도 과언이 아님.

(2) '사막의 폭풍'작전이라 명명된 걸프戰爭을 통해 美軍을 중심 으로 한 多國籍軍은 戰術·兵力 및 裝備 등에 있어 그 우월함을 입증함. 특히 戰爭勃發以後 5주간에 걸친 공습의 효과와 100 시간의 전격적인 地上戰을 통해 多國籍軍이 희생을 극소화하면 서 신속하게 全戰線에 걸쳐 압승을 거두게 된 데에는 과거 어느 戰爭보다도 美國式의 戰術·武器·訓鍊 등이 사막전 수행에 효과적이었던 점이 크게 작용함.

(3) 과거 越南戰의 경험을 바탕으로 美軍은 군사교리 및 훈련방법의 변화, 尖端技術을 이용한 무기의 지속적인 개발과 개량, 그리고 '低强度 戰爭戰略'을 추진하기 위한 무기의 경량화 등을 추진 해 왔으며, 이는 유럽에서 蘇聯의 在來式 軍事力의 위협에 대한 방어 뿐만 아니라 필요한 경우 地域紛爭에도 신속하고 효과적 으로 대응할 수 있는 軍事力 培養에 기여함.

3

0182

(4) 그.결과 美軍의 戰術的 優位, 그리고 신속한 배치 능력과 적진 깊숙히 타격을. 가할 수 있는 능력 등은 이번 걸프戰爭에서 이라크軍을 패배시키는데에 결정적으로 작용함. 특히 이라크군은 蘇聯製 武器 및 戰術로 무장해 있어 對蘇 중심이었던 美軍의 戰力이 공격에 효과적이었던 것으로 보임.

(5) 반면 이라크軍은 사담 후세인의 무능과 판단착오로 戰略과 戰術에서 多國籍軍에 적절히 대응하지 못하였으며 이는 테러리즘과 化學武器 등을 효과적으로 사용하지 못한데서 잘 나타나고 있음. 전투에 있어서도 이라크軍은 제공권의 상실과 이에 따른 共和國 守備隊의 戰力 궤멸 등으로 사기가 급격히 저하되어 多國籍軍에 완강히 저항하리라는 초기의 예상과는 달리 무참히 패배하게 됨.

(6) 多國籍軍의 軍事的 優勢는 병력의 수보다는 질적인 측면에서 이라크軍을 능가하고 있었으며 이는 실제 전투에서 각개 병사의 戰鬪能力에서 부각되었음. 多國籍軍의 군인들은 28개국의 상이한 군대로 이루어졌음에도 불구, 높은 사기 및 엄격한 규율을 유지하였으며, 걸프地域에 파견된 후 약 6개월간 주둔하는 동안 충분한 실전훈련, 풍부한 補給 및 支援 등으로 효율적으로 전투를 수행할 수 있었음.

(7) 또한 多國籍軍의 裝備들도 F-117A Stealth 폭격기로부터 토마호크 크루즈 미사일에 이르기까지 고도의 정확성과 정밀성을 지닌 尖端兵器들로서 전쟁초기에 이라크軍의 지휘·통제·통신

4

0183

체제를 무력화시켰으며, 이는 人工衛星과 컴퓨터를 이용한 情報·偵察·指揮·統制機能의 효과적 수행과 더불어 제공권의 장악에 크게 기여함. 또한 아파치 공격헬기나 M1-A1탱크 등은 地上戰에서 이라크軍의 주력인 共和國 守備隊를 포위·공격하는데 큰 역할을 수행함.

(8) 이같은 多國籍軍의 最新裝備는 최근 美軍이 채택한 바 있는 空軍과 地上軍의 統合戰術인 '空地戰'(Air-Land Battle) 개념의 적용으로 더욱 효과적이었음. 특히 多國籍 空軍은 5주간에 걸친 대규모 공습으로 戰略目標인 이라크의 空軍과 防空網에 큰 타격을 가했으며, 이라크軍의 補給路를 차단하고 地上軍 화력지원부대들을 궤멸시키는 등 이번 戰爭의 勝利에 결정적 역할을 담당함.

(9) 이처럼 兵力과 裝備, 그리고 戰術에서 우세를 보인 多國籍軍은 쿠웨이트해안에 대규모 상륙부대를 배치하고, 쿠웨이트남부 국경지역에 병력을 배치함으로써 이라크로 하여금 대규모 정면돌파에 대비하게끔 기만전술을 편다음, 主力部隊가 쿠웨이트를 우회하여 이라크국경선을 돌파하는 측면 공격으로 地上戰을 개시함으로써 이라크의 전투 중심을 파괴, 이라크軍을 효과적으로 와해시킴.

5

0184

나. 戰爭 外交의 效果的 遂行

(1) 美國은 이라크의 쿠웨이트侵攻으로 걸프事態가 勃發하자 사우디 방어의 명분으로 즉각적인 파병을 개시하였으며, 英·佛 등 西方 同盟國 뿐만 아니라 反이라크 聯合戰線을 펴고 있는 사우디·이집트·시리아 등 中東國家들을 포함한 多國籍軍을 형성, 이라크軍에 대치하는 한편 이들 多國籍軍 參加國과 戰費를 공동 부담하는 등 각국의 協力과 支援을 획득하는데 成功함.

(2) 또한 美國은 이라크를 國際社會의 平和와 安定을 위협하는 침략 자로서 규탄하는 全世界의 輿論을 바탕으로, UN을 통한 經濟 制裁 등 對이라크 制裁措置를 世界化시키는데 성공함으로써, 國際社會에서의 이라크의 孤立을 誘導해 나감.

(3) 이처럼 UN을 통한 美國의 外交的 成功은 美國의 對걸프政策 뿐만 아니라 多國籍軍의 武力 行使를 國際的으로 正當化시켰음. 또한 美國은 自國의 經濟事情惡化, 國防費削減 趨勢 등으로 엄청난 액수의 걸프戰爭의 戰費를 美國 혼자 부담하는 것이 어려운 상황에서 同盟國들과 共同負擔토록 하는데 성공하였음. 이를 위하여 美國은 雙務協商은 물론 美議會의 決議案 採擇 등 間接的인 外交的 壓力을 행사함으로써 과거 越南戰의 경우와는 다른 양상을 보여줌.

6

0185

(4) 美國은 脫冷戰時代의 美・蘇協力體制를 바탕으로 이라크의 전통적 우방국인 소련의 협력을 확보하는데 성공하여, 對이라크 制裁 등을 내용으로 하는 UN 決議案의 통과, 蘇聯의 對이라크 支援 中止 등을 가능하게 함. 이러한 현상은 과거 冷戰時代와는 달리 脫冷戰時代의 地域紛爭에 대한 美・蘇의 공동 대응이라는 새로운 양상을 보여준 것임.

(5) 이러한 美・蘇協力關係 유지노력은 美國의 戰爭外交 成功에 크게 기여하였음. 특히 中東地域에서 自國의 影響力 弱化를 우려한 蘇聯이 걸프戰爭勃發以後 地上戰의 개시를 막기 위해 이라크와 막후 협상을 통한 外交的 仲裁努力을 시도한데 대해, 美國이 이를 무시하지 않고 최대한 蘇聯의 의견을 존중했으며, 戰後 中東地域 問題解決에 蘇聯도 참여하는 國際會議 開催를 제안한 것은 이러한 戰爭外交의 일환이라고 볼 수 있음.

(6) 이번 걸프戰爭에서 이스라엘의 개입문제는 戰爭의 확산여부를 판가름하는 중대한 문제로서, 이스라엘이 이라크의 스커드 미사일공격에도 불구하고 계속 자제하는 모습을 보여준 대에는, 이스라엘의 전통적 후원국인 美國의 영향력이 크게 작용함.

(7) 美國은 이라크의 스커드 미사일을 요격할 수 있는 패트리어트 미사일을 이스라엘에 배치하는 한편, 이스라엘의 被害를 보상하기 위한 經濟的 支援을 약속하는 등 對이스라엘 外交를 적극 전개함. 이는 이스라엘의 이라크보복공격이 아랍聯合軍을 多國

7

0186

籍軍으로부터 이탈시키는 것은 물론 걸프戰爭을 中東戰爭으로
확산시켜 美國의 對걸프戰爭 수행에 차질이 생기는 것을 방지
하기 위한 것이었음.

(8) 한편, 美國은 獨逸, 日本 등이 自國內 輿論 및 國內法의 海外
派兵 제한으로 걸프戰爭에 직접 참여하지 않게 되자, 이들국가
들에게 그들의 경제력에 상응하는 國際的 役割을 수행할 것을
요구하고 걸프戰爭의 戰費 分擔과 多國籍軍 참여 中東地域國家
들에 대한 經濟援助 제공을 촉구함.

(9) 이러한 美國의 요구에 대해 獨逸, 日本 등은 수십억불의 財政的
支援을 부담함으로써 戰後 處理 및 復舊事業에의 참여와 自國의
對中東 發言權 强化를 기도함. 이같은 多國籍軍 形成 및 戰費
負擔 요구 등 美國의 對同盟國政策의 成功은 걸프戰爭의 승리에
결정적 배경이 되었으며, 앞으로의 地域紛爭에 대처하는데 있어
同盟國들의 支援을 통한 美國의 主導的 役割 遂行의 가능성을
엿볼 수 있게 하는 것이었음.

다. 世界輿論 支持確保

(1) 걸프事態가 발발하자 신속히 派兵을 단행한 美國은 戰爭의 효과
적 수행과 승리를 위하여 國內外 輿論의 支持 確保를 위하여
노력함.

8

0187

(2) 이러한 노력은 주로 言論媒體를 통하여 전개 되었으며, 國內外의 反戰輿論이 戰爭의 확산에 따른 國際經濟危機에 대한 우려와 越南戰의 再版에 대한 우려로 집약되자, 이를 무마하기 위한 홍보 선전에 주력함.

(3) 우선 美國은 걸프전쟁으로 인한 世界 油價의 급등가능성에 대비, 自國의 비축 석유를 國際市場에 무제한 공급하고 사우디 등 多國籍軍에 포함된 産油國들의 石油生産量을 증가시킴으로써 國際油價의 安定을 도모함.

(4) 또한 美國은 수차에 걸쳐 걸프戰爭이 越南戰化 되지 않을 것임을 自國民에게 다짐하고 戰爭에 의한 人命被害를 최소화할 것임을 약속하면서, 人命被害가 예상되는 地上戰 보다는 이라크의 군사력 파괴를 위한 공중공격에 치중함.

(5) 이처럼 美國은 言論媒體를 통하여 反戰 輿論을 무마시키는 한편, 사담 후세인의 非人間性과 非道德性을 부각시킴으로써 걸프전쟁에서의 勝利가 地域 平和는 물론 全世界의 平和와 福祉에 직결되어 있음을 강조함.

(6) 특히 지상전 개시 이후 多國籍軍은 戰況 報道를 엄격히 統制함으로써 輿論이 戰爭 遂行에 끼칠지도 모르는 악영향을 排除하고 이라크와의 宣傳戰에서 기선을 制壓하게 됨.

(7) 이러한 世界 輿論 支持 確保 努力으로 美國은 걸프전쟁을 '사담 후세인에 대한 全世界人의 응징' 이라는 性格으로 부각

9

0188

시키는데 成功하였으며, 쿠웨이트 奪還과 이라크 軍事力의 파괴
라는 戰爭目標의 달성과 더불어 신속히 終戰을 결정함으로써
걸프전쟁에 있어 美國이 주도하는 多國籍軍이 國際平和軍임을
부각시킴.

2. 戰後 中東秩序 摸索

가. 美國의 戰後 中東秩序 構想

(1) 美國의 베이커 국무장관은 1991.2.6. 美 下院 外交委員會에서
의 증언을 통해 戰後 걸프地域에서 美國의 당면 과제로서 걸프
地域의 새로운 安保體制構築, 이스라엘-아랍紛爭의 해결, 이지역
의 軍縮 및 武器販賣制限과 經濟協力 등을 제시함.

(2) 이러한 구상을 실현하기 위해 美國은 앞으로 걸프地域에서
사우디 아라비아, 이라크, 이란간의 勢力均衡을 바탕으로 한
地域安定의 구축과 이를 위한 美國의 조정자로서의 역할 수행,
후세인 정권과 같은 反美的 강경세력의 응징 및 이라크와 쿠웨
이트에 親美政權의 등장 유도, 戰後 中東秩序 확립을 위한 美軍
의 中東地域 주둔 등을 추구해 나갈 것으로 보임.

10

0189

(3) 또한 美國의 이같은 戰後 中東秩序構想과 관련, 中東地域의 經濟再建 및 開發問題의 해결을 위해 美國, EC등 西方 多國籍軍 참여국가들의 중동판 마샬플랜 구상을 통해 東歐開發銀行 (EBRD)을 모델로 한 中東復興開發銀行(MEBRD)의 설립이 제안 되고 있음.

(4) 이러한 美國의 戰後 구상에 관해 中東地域國家 및 西歐 同盟國 들과 협의하기 위해 배이커 국무장관은 1991. 3 中東地域을 순방하였으며, 부시 대통령은 1991. 3. 英의 매이저수상, 佛의 미태랑 대통령과의 頂上會談을 벌이는 등 美國은 외교적 노력을 적극적으로 추진함.

(5) 이와 더불어 美國은 多國籍軍의 대표로서 이라크와의 終戰協商 을 벌여, 이라크에 대한 美國의 의도를 그대로 관철시키는 한편, 아랍-이스라엘 紛爭의 핵심문제인 이스라엘-팔레스타인 문제의 해결을 위해 관계국간의 대화를 주선할 의사를 표명함으로써, 이 地域問題解決에 대한 美國의 역할과 영향력을 강화시켜 나감.

나. 걸프戰爭 終戰協商

(1) 美國은 1991.2.28 부시大統領의 연설을 통해 걸프전쟁의 終戰을 선언하면서, 이라크에 대해 다음과 같은 휴전조건, 즉 ①잔류 외국인을 포함한 모든 포로의 즉각 석방과 유해인도, ②억류된 모든 쿠웨이트 시민의 해방, ③쿠웨이트내 설치된 지뢰·기뢰

11

0190

위치에 관한 정보제공, ④12개 유엔결의안의 전면수용(쿠웨이트의 합병선언 철회 및 전쟁배상보상 등), ⑤전후문제를 협의할 이라크군 사령관을 선임, 48시간내 협의할 것 등을 요구함. 한편 후세인도 1991.2.28 이라크군에 대해 정전을 명령함으로써 걸프전쟁의 終戰協商이 시작됨.

(2) 한편, 유엔은 1991.3.1 안보리 회의애서 美國側이 제출한 걸프戰 終戰案을 바탕으로, ①걸프사태 관련, 유엔안보리의 12개 결의사항 준수, ②이라크의 쿠웨이트 합병에 관한 모든 법령 및 조치의 무효화, ③이라크가 억류하고 있는 모든 전쟁포로 및 쿠웨이트인 석방, ④적대행위 종식과 지뢰, 생화학무기 배치 지도 제출, ⑤이라크에 관한 경제제재 등 유엔안보리의 제재조치 해제 등을 주요 내용으로 하는 決議案을 채택, 이라크의 終戰條件 移行을 촉구함.

(3) 이같은 유엔의 결의는 多國籍軍의 승리를 공식적으로 인정함은 물론, 終戰에 관한 美國 등 多國籍軍側의 요구조건에 대해 이라크가 즉각 수용하도록 압력을 가하는 것이라 하겠음. 특히 이번 決議案에는 이라크가 휴전애 관한 조건들을 완전히 이행하지 않을 경우, 多國籍軍이 군사행동을 재개할 수 있는 권한을 갖는다는 내용이 포함되어 있어 이라크로서는 이를 받아들이지 않을 수 없게됨.

12

0191

(4) 그 결과 1991.3.3 이라크의 사프완에서 열린 多國籍軍 대표와 이라크 대표들간의 休戰會談에서 양측은 전쟁포로의 즉각 석방을 포함한 모든 합의에 도달함. 多國籍軍側은 전쟁포로의 즉각 석방, 매설 혹은 부설된 육·해상의 지뢰 및 기뢰위치 공개, 休戰協定 서명후 이라크 영토내 多國籍軍의 撤收 등을 이라크에 요구했으며, 이라크측은 이에 대해 별다른 이의 제기없이 이를 모두 수락함.

(5) 걸프전쟁 終戰協商과 관련, 美國 등 多國籍軍은 처음에는 사담 후세인의 전범재판에의 회부, 이라크에 대한 戰爭被害 補償金의 청구 등을 고려하였으나, 이러한 요구조건들이 현 이라크의 政治狀況 및 經濟能力을 고려할 때 적절하지 않음을 인식, 이 문제를 주요 요구조건으로 내세우지 않음.

다. 이스라엘-아랍問題

(1) 이스라엘이 점령하고 있는 요르단江 西岸 및 가자地區에 살고 팔래스타인들의 獨立國家 建設을 둘러싼 이스라엘과의 紛爭은 現在 中東問題중 가장 선결되어야 할·중요한 문제임. 이에 대해 美國은 이스라엘이 이웃 아랍국가들과 평화롭게 지내기를 원한다면 占領地를 반환해야 한다는 '平和와 占領地의 맞바꾸기 原則'(territory for peace)에 바탕을 둔 政策을 펴옴.

13

0192

(2) 1991.3 베이커의 中東 巡訪을 통해 美國은 아랍-이스라엘關係의 正常化를 위해 개별 아랍국가들과 이스라엘간의 平和定着 方案을 논의하면서, 동시에 팔레스타인과 이스라엘간의 對話를 주선하겠다는 '兩面協商'을 제의함. 그리고 팔레스타인들의 현 指導部인 PLO가 걸프戰爭중 이라크를 支援함으로써 美國은 앞으로의 協商에서 PLO는 제외한다는 立場을 밝힘. 그리하여 美國은 아랍국가들이 이스라엘의 生存權을 인정하는 대신 이스라엘은 팔레스타인 占領地區를 내놓게끔 이스라엘측의 讓步를 요구하는 방향으로 紛爭해결을 摸索함.

(3) 이스라엘은 팔레스타인 問題에 대하여 自國내의 팔레스타인들의 制限的 自治는 許容할 수 있지만, 이 地域을 返還할 수 없다는 見解를 表明해왔음. 이에 대해 팔레스타인들을 비롯한 아랍 國家들은 이스라엘의 占領地 返還을 전제조건으로 '팔레스타인 獨立國 創設'이라는 기본 立場을 고수해 왔으며, 1991. 3.10 베이커 國務長官과 아랍8개국 외상들의 회담에서도 이스라엘과의 協商을 통한 紛爭 解決 모색에는 찬성하지만, 이를 위해서는 이스라엘이 먼저 占領地를 返還할 것을 要求함.

(4) 1991. 3.12 베이커 美國務長官과 이스라엘의 샤미르총리간의 會談을 통해, 兩國은 中東問題의 解決을 위한 美國의 '兩面協商'을 추진하기로 基本的인 合意를 봄. 그러나 이스라엘이 팔레스타인 占領地區의 返還이 協商의 前提條件이 될 수 없다는

14

0193

종래의 立場을 고수함에 따라, 팔레스타인 問題의 實質的 解決
可能性은 크게 進展되지 못함. 그렇지만 베이커 國務長官의
中東巡訪을 통해 이스라엘과 아랍國家들간의 協商의 必要性을
부각시켰다는 점에서, 팔레스타인 問題를 包含한 이스라엘과
아랍國家들의 協商過程을 통한 關係改善의 可能性은 더욱 增大
될 것임.

라. 中東地域 平和協商

(1) 걸프戰爭의 戰後處理에 대한 각국의 입장은 이스라엘과 아랍
   국가간의 個別協商을 통한 문제해결 後 中東地域國家가 참가
   하는 다자간 회의의 개최를 고려하는 美國側 立場과, 中東國家
   및 걸프전쟁관련 국가들의 참여를 보장하는 國際會議를 통해
   中東問題의 論議 및 解決을 모색하자는 蘇聯 및 프랑스 등 EC의
   입장으로 크게 구별됨.

(2) 戰後 中東地域에서의 美國의 압도적 영향력 행사를 견제하고
   자국의 영향력을 유지하기 위한 소련의 제안에 대해, 현재 아랍
   국가들도 이에 동의하여 多者間 中東平和會談의 개최를 요구
   하고 있음. 이같은 아랍국가들의 태도는 현재 美國의 中東平和
   노력이 이스라엘에게 유리하게 전개될 것을 우려하고 걸프戰을
   통해 中東地域의 새로운 강자로 부상한 사우디, 시리아, 이집트
   등이 戰後 中東處理問題에 있어 發言權을 강화하기 위한 것으로
   볼 수 있음.

15   0194

(3) 베이커 國務長官의 中東地域 순방중 아랍국가들은 美國의 戰後
處理 4개원칙중 自國의 안보와 직결된 미국과의 軍事協力, 核·
化學 武器 擴散禁止, 지역내 국가간의 경제협력 등의 문제에는
긍정적 반응을 보인 반면, 이스라엘과의 관계에 대해서는 양보
할 수 없다는 태도를 보임.

(4) 이러한 아랍국가들의 선별적인 解決方式에 대하여 美國은 포괄
적 解決原則을 강조하고 있어, 이스라엘-아랍 문제의 해결 여부
가 美國의 新中東秩序 構築의 성공에 결정적으로 작용 할 것
으로 보임. 그리하여 美國은 이스라엘 및 아랍국가들과의 外交
的 접촉외에도 英·佛 등 西方同盟國 및 蘇聯과의 外交的 接觸
을 통해 이 문제의 해결을 위한 國際的 분위기 조성을 위해
계속 노력해 나갈 것으로 보임.

3. 結論 및 韓國의 考慮事項

가. 結論

(1) 걸프戰爭에서의 승리로 美國은 國內的으로는 과거 越南戰의
컴플렉스에서 탈피, 國民들에게 자신감을 갖게 함은 물론 부시
대통령의 인기가 급상승하게 되었으며, 國際的으로는 中東地域
에서의 發言權이 대폭 강화되고, UN을 비롯한 國際社會에 있어

16

0195

美國의 世界的 役割이 크게 부각되는 등 脫冷戰時代에 政治·軍事的 側面에서의 유일한 世界 超强大國으로서의 地位와 영향력을 확보하게 됨.

(2) 美國은 이번 걸프戰爭을 통해 中東國家들을 多國籍軍에 포함시킴으로써 美國의 對이스라엘 특수관계에 대한 아랍국가들의 오해를 불식시켰으며, 더우기 이스라엘로 하여금 아랍국가들과의 평화를 모색하게 하는데 크게 기여함.

(3) 이러한 美國의 對아랍, 對이스라엘 영향력과 발언권의 증대는 中東地域의 平和構築에 필요한 아랍-이스라엘問題 해결의 가능성을 보이게 하였으며, 이에 따른 이스라엘과 팔레스타인간의 문제해결, 地域國家間의 貧富隔差 해소, 地域安保協力體制 구축 등은 지역국가간의 쌍무관계 발전 및 다자관계의 형성과 더불어 새로운 中東秩序를 태동케 할 것임.

(4) 이러한 새로운 中東秩序構築過程에 있어서 美國은 유럽에서와 마찬가지로 地域平和는 地域勢力均衡에 의하여 모색되어져야 한다는 원칙아래 UN이라는 國際輿論을 바탕으로 이같은 勢力均衡의 조정자로서 개입할 것으로 보임.

(5) 이러한 中東에서의 新秩序構築은 世界秩序의 地域化 現象을 더욱 두드러지게 할 것이며, 冷戰以後時代의 國際政治秩序가 地域秩序를 바탕으로 한 世界平和의 구축이라는 美國의 구상에 따라 서서히 아시아에도 파급될 것임을 예견케 함.

17

0196

나. 韓國의 考慮事項

(1) 이번 걸프戰爭을 통해 과거 美國과 더불어 世界 超强大國의 하나였던 蘇聯이 유라시아대륙의 지역 강대국으로 전락한 반면, 美國은 유일한 世界的 超强大國으로 존속하게 됨. 따라서 韓半島 周邊 4强間의 역학관계를 볼 때 美國의 역할이 東北亞 秩序 再編에 있어서 어느 국가보다도 더욱 커다란 발언권과 영향력을 발휘하게 될 것으로 예상됨.

(2) 따라서 韓國은 韓美關係를 바탕으로 하는 北方政策推進이라는 기존정책을 일관성있게 추진하고, 對蘇·對中政策에 있어 對美 일변도로부터의 탈피라는 차원보다는 美國·日本과 더불어 中國·蘇聯과 협상할 수 있는 주요 지역세력으로 부상한다는 차원에서 東北亞 新秩序 構想에 임하여야 할 것임.

(3) 이러한 차원에서 볼 때, 東北亞에서의 韓國의 지역역할은 東北亞에서의 勢力均衡에 있어 주요한 역할을 담당해야 할 것임을 의미하는 바, 이 경우 韓國은 기존의 同盟關係와 對友邦關係가 갖는 중요성을 재음미할 필요가 있음.

(4) 더우기 아시아의 社會主義體制를 自由民主主義라는 世界秩序에 흡수한다는 차원에서 볼 때, 아시아의 自由民主主義 국가들도 유럽과 같이 나름대로의 政治·經濟共同體 구축이 우선 과제임을 인식하게 될 것이며, 韓國은 이에 적절한 대응방안을 마련하여야 할 것임..

18

0197

(5) 韓半島의 平和構築과 궁극적 통일이 '社會主義體制의 自由民主主義體制로의 吸收'라는 차원에서 이루어질 수 있다는 관점에서 볼 때, 北韓의 최근 對美·日 접근 등 활발히 전개되는 남방정책은 南北對話에 걸림돌이 되기 보다는 南北對話의 진전에 긍정적으로 작용할 수도 있을 것임.

(6) 世界秩序의 再編, 그리고 地域秩序의 태동이라는 世界史的 흐름을 외면할 수 없는 北韓은 나름대로의 지역역할을 모색하려 할 것이며, 이 경우 필요한 지역국가간의 대화와 협상을 위해서라도 韓國에 대한 기존의 革命戰略과 社會主義 統一政策을 포기하지 않을 수 없을 것임. 따라서 韓國은 北韓의 이러한 변화 가능성을 염두에 두고 南北韓 協商은 물론 예상되는 地域協商에서도 北韓과의 협력모색에 다각적인 노력을 경주해야 할 것임.

1991. 3. 27

作成 : 研究教授 朴 弘 圭
討論 : 研究室長 金 國 振
　　　　研究教授 李 東 輝
　　　　研究教授 裵 肯 燦

19·

0198

0001

주 영 대 사 관

영국(정) 723- 322   1991. 4. 2.

수신 : 장관

참조 : 아중동국장, 미주국장

제목 : 한국의 걸프사태 대처 관계 논문

91. 3.26-28간 캠브리지 대학에서 개최된 영국 한국학협회 (BAKS) 91년도 회의에
제출된 Dr Brian Bridges (Jati International)의 논문 "Korea and the Gulf
Crisis " 를 별첨 송부하니 참고바랍니다.

첨부 : 동 논문. 끝.

주 영 대 사

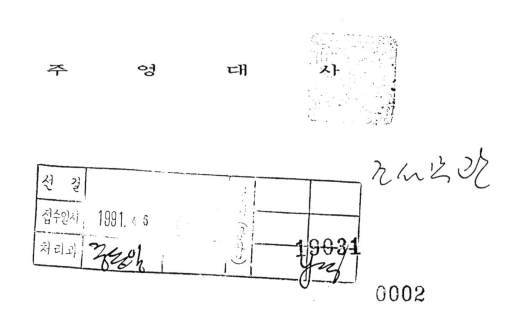

19031

0002

KOREA AND THE GULF CRISIS

by Brian Bridges
(Jati International)

Paper prepared for British Association of Korean Studies
Conference ,Cambridge, 26-28 March 1991.

Draft: not for quotation.

On 26 January 1991, two South Korean Air Force C-130 Hercules
transport planes landed at Dhahran airport in Saudi Arabia
carrying Colonel Choi Myong-ku and his military medical team
to join the multinational forces fighting in the Gulf. The
despatch of the 154-member medical team was the first occasion
for the South Korean military to serve in a war zone overseas
since the last of the South Korean 'Tiger Division' had been
withdrawn from South Vietnam in April 1973. The medical
corps's activities were limited ,however,by the speed of the
collapse of the Iraqi forces after the land war began in the
last week of February . Brief though it may have been, the
symbolism of the South Korean involvement was nonthelesss
important. The seven-month long Gulf crisis ,dating from the
Iraqi invasion of Kuwait in August 1990, also has a broader
significance for South Korea .This paper argues that it has
proved to be a dilemma, a diversion and a catalyst for South
Korea.

Serious South Korean contact and involvement in the Middle
East has been both recent and predominantly economic in
character.As South Korea began to industrialise in the 1960s
and 1970s , its burgeoning energy demands led to an increased
dependence on imported oil (the dependence ratio rose from
10% in 1964 to 75% by 1983) and, in particular, an increased
dependence on a few Middle Eastern countries (in 1978
Kuwait,Saudi Arabia and Iran supplied 96% of South Korea's oil
imports).The South Korean economy weathered the first oil
shock relatively easily, not least because of the post-shock
Middle Eastern construction boom, but it was hit harder by the
second oil shock and growth even went negative in 1980.
During the first half of the 1980s,therefore, the government
put greater emphasis on conservation and diversification ,both
in terms of other oil suppliers and of other energy sources,
but the Middle Eastern energy import and construction
activities remained important elements in the Korean economy's
development.Indeed, in the second half of the 1980s, the
dependence on Middle Eastern oil had started to creep up
again.

Politically,however,South Korea had taken a low profile in the
region, wary of radical Arab nationalism , broadly prepared to

0003

follow the Arab line on the Israeli-Palestinian issue after
the 1973-74 switch, and trying to continue to do business with
both sides during the lengthy Iran-Iraq war. As in other
Third World areas, diplomatic competition with North Korea was
a continuing feature. The North advanced notably in the 1950s
and 1960s, but in the 1970s South Korean companies' active
participation in construction and other activities led to
political contacts with even the more militant and generally
pro-North Arab governments (in the late 1980s this even
resulted in large-scale projects with countries such as
Libya). However,the Koreans have very few historical or
cultural connections with the Middle East.They feel very
little affinity either with Islam , which was formally
introduced into South Korea by Turkish troops during the
Korean War but even now has only about 20,000 adherents, or
with the Arabs in general.

Economic dimension:
The most immediate concerns for the South Korean government
after the Iraqi invasion of Kuwait on 2 August 1990 were the
safety of the Korean workers in the two countries and the
effects on the supply and price of oil imports.The four
largest Korean construction companies were involved in a total
of 17 projects ,valued at $2,510 million , and around 1300
Koreans were working in the two countries. The two countries
supplied around 12% of South Korea's import of crude oil (4.2%
from Iraq and 7.6% from Kuwait in the first half of 1990)'and
Kuwait supplied around one-fifth of imports of liquified
pretroleum gas (LPG), a key cooking fuel for families in the
smaller cities and rural areas.

As a result, government officials, while sympathizing with
Kuwait as a victim of aggression, were ,nontheless, extremely
cautious in commenting publicly ,even after the UN Security
Council resolution on economic sanctions. However, after
strong requests from UN Secretary-General Javier Perez de
Cuellar and visiting US Assistant Secretary of State Richard
Solomon, on August 9 the government announced a series of
economic sanctions which included an import embargo on Iraqi
and Kuwaiti crude oil and a total trade embargo, apart from
some medicines.This decision marked a victory for the Foreign
Ministry over the Economic Planning Board (EPB) , which had
initially opposed economic sanctions on the grounds that, even
if the domestic oil price were not raised immediately, the
psychological impact of the embargo would be inflationary.

The Gulf crisis, ironically, acted almost as a kiss of life
for the Energy and Resources Ministry, which not so long
before had appeared close to abolition due to bureaucratic
rivalries. Minister Lee Hee-il voluntarily forfeited his
summer holiday and a crisis management team was set up; the
Ministry took the lead in formulating the government's two-
part response. Firstly, to alleviate supply shortages and to
stabilise the domestic oil price , by drawing on the

0004

stockpiles of crude and petroleum products (39.8 million bbl. or the equivalent of 43 days' supply if all oil imports were to cease) and on the Petroleum Business Fund (then standing at 1.6 trillion won) to cushion spot-price oil purchasing.In addition, the Ministry decided to revive the national energy conservation campaigns that had flagged slightly in recent years. Secondly, for the medium-term, the Ministry decided to speed up work on the nuclear power plants already under construction, so as to reduce the relative dependence on oil, and to review and intensive the existing plans for oil exploration on the continental shelf.In early March 1991, in fact, the Ministry unveiled a revised long-term power plan for an additional 16 electricity power plants to be built by 2001,but none of them to be oil-fired.

Other ministries were concerned about the falling away in exports to the region (losses were estimated to be in the order of $500 million for the August-December 1990 period) and the uncollected payments for construction jobs undertaken in the two countries (about $1 billion outstanding).The government's response was to try to encourage exports to other regions and to arrange loan facilities for those companies which found themselves in financial difficulties. Consideration was also given to the evacuation of Korean nationals; some were evacuated, mostly from Kuwait to neighbouring countries, but about a hundred construction workers, including 23 from the Hyundai company working on the presidential palace in Baghdad , continued working in Iraq up until the eve of the fighting in January.

The government was successful in the short-term in finding alternative sources of oil supply, mainly through signing new, large contracts with Saudi Arabia,which agreed to supply more than double the amount that Iraq and Kuwait had previously supplied and whose share of Korean oil imports therefore rose in 1990 to 12% (in 1991 it is likely to reach around 25%).However, when oil prices jumped to $40 a barrel in the autumn of 1990, it was difficult to continue freezing all domestic oil prices; on November 24 the Energy Minister announced a 28% price increase in both kerosene and petrol.The Korean people were encouraged to practice austerity in energy consumption (thereby reinforcing an 'unofficial' campaign already underway against 'excessive consumption'). Although oil prices eased back towards the end of the year and after Operation Desert Storm began on 16 January 1991 actually dropped further (to around $ 16 a barrel), the government instituted a further set of emergency measures in mid-January .Neon signs and electronic advertisements were banned, street lighting was cut by half, TV broadcasts were cut down by two hours,and private passenger cars were forced to stay off the roads every tenth day.The effects were noticeable : in February private petrol consumption decreased by 12% compared with pre-war levels and electricity consumption dropped 3%. With the war over so quickly, these energy conservation gains

0005

may be only temporary; the test for the government will be whether , in the medium-term, it is able both to sustain this conservation mood and to consolidate the renewed enthusiasm for diversification of sources and types of energy supply.

The rapid end of the war not only has made more stable oil prices likely but also has raised prospects for Korean companies, particularly construction companies , of a new business surge as Kuwait is reconstructed. One government official even speculated that South Korean companies could expect to win 10% of the rehabilitation project contracts.However,since American companies seem to be getting the lion's share of the new work,Korean companies might well have to go into joint ventures and sub-contracting to maximise their orders.

Nevertheless, the new, more optimistic mood, like the bouts of 'panic' over the autumnal oil price rises , may actually be acting as a diversion from the consideration and remedying of more serious underlying problems within the South Korean economy. Although economic growth recorded a 9% figure in 1990, the trade and current account balances went into the red, to the tune of around $2 billion, for the first time since 1985; this year the growth rate will be down to 7% and the deficits will increase. Indecision and confusion has characterised economic policy-making over the past year , as ministers have been successively reshuffled and convoluted domestic political manoeuvering and dramatic diplomatic offensives have distracted President Roh Tae Woo . Protectionist sentiment has been rising in major markets, where South Korea no longer benefits from 'benign neglect', and the spluttering negotiations in the Uruguay Round of the General Agreement on Trade and Tariffs (GATT) will impact seriously on Korean trading practices. Rising demands for social equity and a better quality of life have exposed socio-economic tensions within Korea. Most serious ,however, has been the loss of international competitiveness as continued high wage rises and exchange rate changes coupled with the emergence of new, often Southeast Asian, competitors in traditional products hamper Korean export growth. South Korea,therefore, is an economy in transition; its relatively new emphasis on automation and skill training , overseas investment and,above all, investment into research and development to move it up the technological ladder will need to be sustained if it is to return to being successful.

Political fall-out:
Inter-ministerial wrangling had delayed the South Korean government's initial response to the Iraqi invasion in August, but,although not a member of the United Nations, it did decide to accede to the UN call for economic sanctions.However, calls from President George Bush at the end of August 1990 for greater commitments by those nations not yet actively participating in the multinational forces placed the South

0006

Korean government in a dilemma. US Treasury Secretary
Nicholas Brady visited Seoul in early September to
specifically ask South Korea for a $350 million contribution.
After considerable internal deliberation, the government
announced on September 24 a package of $220 million aid - $120
million to the multinational forces and $100 to help the
front-line states of Jordan,Turkey, and Egypt - and the
dispatch of a small medical team. Within the government,
concerns over the repercussions on the roughly 200 Koreans
still left in Iraq/Kuwait and on Korean companies' interests
were balanced against the desire to see oil price stability
ensured by an early resolution of the crisis and the need to
manage the burden-sharing relationship with the United
States.The financial package (when finally approved in January
1991, the number of states to receive aid had been widened,
but the dollar total remained the same) seems to have been
pitched at the level at which countries such as Taiwan were
also expected to contribute and it caused little controversy
domestically.The same could not be said about the plan to send
a medical team.

The main consideration behind the medical team plan seems to
have been to pre-empt calls from the US Congress and
government for South Korea either to contribute more
financially or to participate militarily. Discussion about the
composition of the team became protracted ,perhaps
deliberately so, as the South Korean government hoped that the
crisis might be settled by negotiation. Public opinion
certainly seemed ambivalent; an opinion poll by Chungang Ilbo
the day after the failure of the Baker-Aziz talks in January
1991 still showed 55% of the respondents not expecting war to
break out, only 30% in favour of using force to expel Iraq and
only 50% supporting the deployment of a medical team.However,
the UN deadline to Iraq concentrated the government's mind and
when legislation was finally drafted for the National
Assembly in January 1991 it became clear that a 154-man
military medical team would be sent; although in uniform, they
would be sent for humanitarian purposes.

Memories, but contradictory ones, of both the Korean and the
Vietnam wars were evoked by this decision. As Defence Ministry
officials argued, the dispatch of the medical team could be
seen as a way of repaying the UN forces for having shed blood
for the South Koreans during the Korean War;it would also help
in gaining broader international support should South Korea
again find itself subject to North Korean invasion in the
future. On the other hand, as Kim Dae-jung and the opposition
Party for Peace and Democracy (PPD) pointed out , South Korean
involvement in the Vietnam War began with the dispatch of
medical personnel in 1964 and escalated until over 4000 combat
troops had died before the final withdrawal in 1973.The fear
of escalating involvement and the concomitant of a heightened
role for the military once again was deep-seated and even some
members of the ruling Democratic Liberal Party (DLP),

0007

especially the faction lead by Kim Young-sam, were strongly
opposed to anything more than a medical team being sent. When
Defence Minister Lee Jong-koo suggested on 11 January that
South Korea would give careful consideration to any strong US
requests for combat troops to be sent, the adverse reactions
within the DLP and amongst other ministries forced him to
withdraw his remarks almost immediately.

The outbreak of fighting in mid-January posed further problems
for the South Korean government, which was aware of implicit
US hints that further help was needed. The National Assembly
quickly and overwhelmingly approved the dispatch of the
medical team, as the PPD dropped its opposition provided that
no combat troops were to be sent and only the small Democratic
Party voted against.On January 30, the government decided to
provide an additional $280 million to the multinational forces
and to send 5 C-130 transport planes to help ferry materials
and personnel to Saudi Arabia from neighbouring countries
(after National Assembly approval,the Air Force transport unit
left Seoul on 18 February for the United Arab Emirates, where
it was based).

The second dispatch was justified in terms of South Korea's
interests both in its relations with the United States and in
the post-Gulf War Middle Eastern order. Certainly,South
Korean-US relations had been strained over the past year by a
number of trade and market-opening disputes (compounded by
differences over the GATT Round negotiations) and by
disagreements over financial and operational burden-sharing in
the defence area.Some Americans had also noted the paucity of
the first Korean commitment to the US-led forces by comparison
with the $3 billion aid package agreed for the Soviet
Union.The predilection to equate the multinational forces with
the United States, a tendency found in other countries as
well,was a key factor behind the South Korean commitments
(and helped to explain the non-committal response to a request
made in mid-February by a visiting senior British Foreign
Office official for financial assistance).Foreign Minister Lee
Sang-ock described strengthening relations with the United
States as one of the primary diplomatic goals of 1991;the
second Gulf commitment was clearly envisaged as part of that
process.

The government, however, also felt - and this was an argument
accepted by the PPD as well - that South Korea could not
expect to have a voice , and a real commercial presence,in the
post-war reconstruction of Kuwait,Iraq and the surrounding
region unless it was prepared to stand up and be counted. Some
government officials argued, on the other hand, that South
Korea might suffer from adverseArab nationalist sentiment
because of its participation, but the majority Arab support
for the allied cause and the restraint of the Israelis
lessened these concerns.

0008

The Gulf crisis also heightened South Korean concerns in a number of other areas.The North Korean reaction was followed carefully. Despite its past military sales , including Scud missiles, to Iraq, North Korea did pass critical comment on the invasion of Kuwait. Yet it also criticised first the US involvement in the multinational forces and then the opening of the fighting in mid-January as being typical of aggressive American imperialism. North Korea, consequently, was scathing about South Korean efforts to contribute to the multinational forces and warned of the dangers of tension on the peninsula increasing as a result of the growth of warlike feelings in the South (President Roh was described as 'running amok like a cow on fire'). The South Korean government was worried that the North might take the opportunity of the United States being distracted by the Gulf crisis (and even reducing its forces on the peninsula) to cause trouble. As a result,the South Korean armed forces were put on full alert; North Korean troops too went on to the alert. Nevertheless, the South decided to continue with the joint South Korean-US 'Team Spirit' exercises in March, though much reduced in scale. The interruptions in the North-South dialogue,however,had little to do with the events in the distant Gulf.

The South Koreans were also worried about the course of the Japanese debate,much more intense and public than the South Korean one,about how to contribute to the Gulf crisis resolution. The Japanese government's plans , abortive though they ultimately were, to send Self-Defence Forces (SDF) to the Gulf under the UN Peace Cooperation Bill and,subsequently, to send SDF aircraft to transport refugees evoked memories of past Japanese military activities overseas and led to fears that it would be ' the starting point of the remilitarisation of Japan'(Foreign Minister Choi Ho-joong) ;moreover,if Japan did send the SDF then US pressure on South Korea to also send troops would also increase.In the end,however, the South Koreans were able to draw comfort from the fact that their country was one of only two countries in East Asia that were considered to be serious potential contributors to such a multinational endeavour and that they themselves had contributed men as well as money , unlike the Japanese who have continued to be criticised in the United States and elsewhere for giving money only, however large the amount.

A global player?:
The Gulf crisis , despite the economic and political difficulties it caused for South Korea,may ,nevertheless, act as a kind of catalyst towards what ministers have described as the fulfilment of responsibilities commensurate with its status in the international community. South Korea is not a member of the United Nations (and the UN Security Council might now be too concerned with Middle Eastern affairs to give priority to sorting out the admission problem), but South Korea did respond as if it were. In the 1982 Lebanon crisis South Korea had been asked to join the international peace-

0009

keeping forces but did not feel ready enough to participate.In
1988 South Korea felt unable to respond either with naval
forces or direct financial help to US requests for assistance
in the then Gulf crisis. In the 1990-91 Gulf crisis,
however,South Korea cautiously moved into action. Undoubtedly,
South Korea is now a much more mature economic and political
entity than nine or even three years ago. Concern about the US
relationship is still important, but the aspiration for a more
independent approach is clear. One Foreign Ministry official
said that the Gulf crisis had made the government 'realise the
limitations' of its diplomacy; now was the time to diversify
diplomatic activities and to develop independent capabilities.
Further steps can now be taken.

0010

주 영 대 사 관

영국 상무 764-356   1991. 4. 8

수신 : 장관 (사본 : 상공부장관)

참조 : 국제경제국장

제목 : 쿠웨이트 복구 사업 자료

1991.3.18 WESTMINSTER CONSULTANT 사와 영국 상무성 주관으로 당지

퀸 에리자베스 컨퍼런스 센터에서 개최된 쿠웨이트 복구사업 관련 세미나시

발표 자료를 별첨과 같이 송부하니 업무에 참고하시기 바랍니다.

첨부 : REBUILDING KUWAIT 사본. 끝.

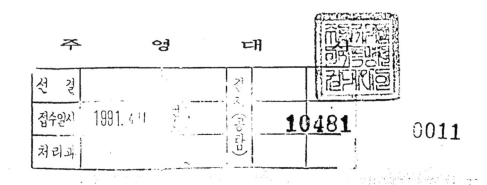

주	영	대	
선 결		경 유 (공 람)	
접수일시	1991. 4. 1		**10481**
처 리 과			

0011

REBUILDING KUWAIT: A BRIEFING FOR BRITISH BUSINESSMEN

Transcript of the Briefing held at the Queen Elizabeth Conference Centre, London SW1 on 18th March 1991

Organised by

Westminster Management Consultants Limited

in association with

The Department of Trade and Industry

and

The British Task Force for the Reconstruction of Kuwait

0012

TABLE OF CONTENTS

Page

1

0013

THE CHAIRMAN'S OPENING REMARKS

THE HON. DAVID DOUGLAS HOME (Executive Director of Morgan Grenfell & Co Ltd and Member of the Task Force): Ladies and gentlemen, welcome to this briefing conference today. During the day there will be an opportunity to ask questions after each speaker has finished. When you wish to ask a question, you will be given a microphone, without which you will not be able to be heard by the rest of the audience. In addition, all the proceedings today are being recorded and a transcript will be sent to you, we hope within a week or so.

For those of us who went on the recent visit to Kuwait, it was a fascinating but also a sombre and sobering experience. The people of Kuwait have been through a very traumatic period, and in human terms few of them escaped without any suffering. It will therefore take them some time to pick up the pieces of their very disrupted lives. No one in this country knows better how bad a time the people have had than His Excellency Mr Ghazi Al-Rayes, the Ambassador of Kuwait to the Court of St. James. Ever since the invasion of his country in August he has strongly but unemotionally defended the attitudes of his government, on television, on the radio, in public meetings and in private, and I am absolutely delighted that now, in much happier circumstances, I can invite him to address us today.

THE NEEDS OF KUWAIT

HIS EXCELLENCY MR GHAZI AL-RAYES (Kuwaiti Amassador): Thank you very much for giving me this chance to stand here today and talk to you. It is very frightening for me to see 1,200 distinguished people here today waiting for me to say something, which I have not prepared myself for. As you know, I am a very bad speaker, but I hope that this will not put you off. There are a lot of good speakers coming after me. For us it is Ramadan. We do not eat, we do not drink, we do not smoke, and I hope I speak just a little.

It is a very happy moment for me to see you all here anxious to rebuild Kuwait. To speak about Kuwait brings back very sad memories for me, as over the last seven months we have lost many lives which we cannot bring back. Buildings we can rebuild, anything destroyed we can bring back, but people we cannot, unfortunately, bring back.

We are very glad to see you in Kuwait, all of you. The opportunity will be there. It is not three months and finished. It will take us five to ten years to rebuild Kuwait and bring it back to where it was before. So please don't rush, thinking that the opportunity will disappear. It is not first come, first served. You are going into an open market. We would like you to compete on price, quality and time. It is not true that a big chunk will go to one country. All companies around the world who have the ability will get their share. So please be prepared, and you are welcome.

There is one thing now disturbing me. That is that some reporters are muddying the water and giving a very bad impression about Kuwait and how it is behaving. Kuwait is a democratic country. It will remain a democratic country. We do not like to see anybody mistreated in Kuwait. Of that I assure you. We have suffered and we do not like to see people suffer again.

What do we need? To be precise, we need everything. This is what I am going to tell you. We are in need of every service, because the country is completely destroyed. First, we must put out all the oil fires. The atmosphere there is unbelievable. The people do not notice that they are

2   0014

breathing and inhaling this smoke, but when they go out of Kuwait some of them call me from Bahrain saying they did not believe there was such clean air in Bahrain or anywhere else, although even there the atmosphere is polluted. So we need immediately to put out all the fires and then we need air filters so that everybody can feel that he is breathing clean air.

I have nothing to add, but if you have a question later, I shall be happy to answer it. Thank you very much for giving me this opportunity.

CHAIRMAN: Thank you, Your Excellency, for setting the scene for us this morning. We will try to keep questions as relevant as possible to the previous speaker. Does anybody have any questions relating to the policies of the government of Kuwait or anything which His Excellency might answer? I would take the privilege of the Chair to say that, having identified the question, I may ask you to ask it of a later speaker.

MR STEVE BACHE (Ron Bateham Productions): We have witnessed on British television the heroic struggle of the Kuwaiti people as the devastation took place in your country. Will there be an orchestrated effort to record the rebuilding of Kuwait?

CHAIRMAN: Do you mean by that an orchestrated effort on the government's part or do you want to know what the programme is? What are you referring to?

MR BACHE: I am meaning that there will be many separate companies out there rebuilding Kuwait. Will there be an orchestrated policy of recording on film or videotape the rebuilding of Kuwait for future generations? We have seen the destruction of the country. Are we now going to see the reconstruction of the country?

HIS EXCELLENCY MR GHAZI AL-RAYES: Yes, of course we are going to record this for coming generations to see, if that was your question.

MR BACHE: Yes, that was my question. I just wanted to know if it was government policy that these events will be recorded.

HIS EXCELLENCY MR GHAZI AL-RAYES: Yes.

CHAIRMAN: If there are no more questions of a general nature for His Excellency, could we move on now to the financial perspective of Kuwait, as seen through the eyes of Mr John Finigan, General Manager of the National Bank of Kuwait? Mr Finigan is more than qualified to speak to us this morning. He has worked both in the area and, more recently, in London on behalf of the National Bank. He has more qualifications than I dare to think, looking at his briefing, so I am sure he is the person to tell you how he sees it in Kuwait from a banking point of view.

THE FINANCIAL PERSPECTIVE

MR JOHN FINIGAN (General Manager, National Bank of Kuwait): It is a particular honour this morning to follow on immediately from His Excellency the Ambassador, Mr Ghazi Al-Rayes. As our Chairman today said, from the first moments following the shock of the invasion and throughout almost seven months of illegal occupation, the ambassador was a source of immense inspiration and leadership to all the Kuwaiti community and its friends. His dignity in the face

3   0015

of exemplary challenge set an example to us all. I am therefore delighted to have the opportunity publicly to pay tribute to the ambassador and to express the great sense of admiration felt by so many of us as a result of his exceptional leadership throughout this long drawn out crisis. One would also bid to the ambassador, as to all our Muslim friends here today "Mubarak alek al-hahar" at this the start of the fasting month of Ramadan.

There is great admiration for the ambassador, but I must also confess a great sense of admiration for our Chairman today and also for all his colleagues who are with us today, who comprised the delegation of six people who were fortunate enough to share a distinction in which I believe only our Prime Minister can join them, in that they have, since the liberation, been to Kuwait and seen what conditions are like on the ground. Certainly that admiration is tinged with more than a touch of envy at the fact that they have had the opportunity to see Kuwait at such an early stage. I, and I believe many of us, look forward to hearing more of their first-hand account to supplement the horrendous pictures that we see in the news media.

When invited to address this briefing today, the National Bank of Kuwait was asked to address specifically the financial perspective of the process of rehabilitation and refurbishment of Kuwait. That is obviously an extremely broad brief, and it will be one of the recurrent themes throughout all the presentations that we shall enjoy this morning. In the short time allotted, I shall merely endeavour to sketch a little of the background scenery, so that the key issues involved become a little clearer within the overall context of the briefing. One welcomes the opportunity for questions as, notwithstanding the many talents of the distinguished panel of experts assembled on the platform today, I have no doubt that the exchange of ideas, with the overwhelming response from attendees, will be one of the most valuable exercises that we conduct in this programme.

The format which we have worked out basically follows the one that we developed for NBK's most recently published annual report, which we entitled "Past, Present and Future", as being the most appropriate summary of the circumstances in which we found ourselves. So perhaps I may give a brief reprise of the past.

Kuwait is a very small country. It is virtually a city state, and immediately prior to the invasion had a population of about 1.7 million, of which approximately 700,000 comprised indigenous Kuwaitis. Kuwait has a long and proud history and culture, and its independent existence is traced back to the bronze age. By way of comparison with cities in the United Kingdom, the total population before the invasion would have been somewhat similar to that of the Merseyside conurbation - Liverpool and St. Helens. Oil was discovered shortly before the outbreak of the Second World War, and oil exports commenced in the late 1940s.

By the end of the last decade Kuwait had developed a highly advanced physical and communications infrastructure through the effective deployment of the revenue streams generated both from current oil revenues and investment income on the substantial capital surpluses which had been invested for the long-term benefit of the state and its people. Parallel with the development of such an advanced infrastructural base, there were advances in education, medicine and social welfare, and these combined to create a modern, sophisticated state with an extremely advanced and soundly based economy. By 1989, the last year for which complete records are available, total gross domestic product was equivalent to £13 million. Exports, almost entirely of oil and refined products, generated over £6 billion, which was offset by imports running at 50% of that level, so generating a positive trade balance of just over £3 billion. Official reserves have been built up over many years through both the state general reserves and the fund for future generations, so that they exceeded £50 billion.

That thumb-nail sketch of the past is intended to convey the fundamental picture of a small but highly developed and technologically advanced state, with a positive underlying economy backed by substantial public sector reserves. However, whilst the reserves of the state bear favourable comparison with those of the United Kingdom, the relative size of Kuwait in global economic terms can be fairly well appreciated by measuring its GDP against that of the United Kingdom. Kuwait's 1989 GDP of £13 billion was less than 3% of the United Kingdom GDP of £434 billion when measured in income terms.

Moving to the present, as His Excellency and our Chairman, David Douglas-Home, have highlighted, the cost in terms of human suffering of the dreadful aggression to which Kuwait was subjected from August last year will never be forgotten, but Kuwait and its people possess both the tenacity of purpose and the financial resource base to redress the physical damage and to work progressively towards restoring the physical infrastructure and the economy of the state towards new levels of equilibrium.

The long dark months while Kuwait remained under illegal occupation were not wasted by Kuwait or its friends. Throughout that traumatic period, a co-ordinated programme took shape so as to be able to proceed as soon as the country was freed. Today, less than three weeks after freedom was secured through the valiant auspices of the United Nations coalition armed forces, the first practical results which emerged from that planning process are already well under way. As His Excellency has stated, it is rather sad that there have been a number of ill-considered words of criticism, but it is worth remembering the tremendous uncertainty and also the dramatic speed with which the military campaign was pursued. We can rejoice at the quality of the planning and logistical processes of that campaign, at the vigour and gallantry with which it was pursued and, most of all, at the containment of casualties among the allied forces and the people of Kuwait. But the secrecy element was such that nobody could, with assurance, have predicted with accuracy when the campaign would conclude.

Prior to the commencement of the military operations for the liberation a three-fold programme had been established to restore all the essential services and infrastructure that were either looted or destroyed, or feared to have been damaged by the Iraqi forces. The three stages of this recovery programme comprise, first, the emergency relief, secondly, recovery and, thirdly, reconstruction. The first stage, emergency relief, is already well under way, so I will refer briefly to that in the context of the present.

The emergency relief programme is expected to cover a period of around three months - that is, until around the end of May. It embraces humanitarian assistance and the start-up of essential services. Kuwaiti teams covering the 14 key sectors of food, medical care, water, electricity, sanitation, communications, transport, ports, airports, public works, fire fighting, oil, gas and security had each drawn up detailed action programmes for their sectors. These were all best on a worst-case scenario - that is, all systems down and nothing functioning. Each sector's programme was specifically designed to be independent of existing infrastructural facilities. A critical list of goods and services was identified, and contracts for such services and procurement have either been signed or are under negotiation. This remains of course a very active process: the dynamism is certainly very strong.

This stage also includes damage assessment teams. For example, whilst mobile generators and tanker-supplied water are now being made available for critical facilities, desalination plants, which also provide electricity, are being assessed for damage and the repair needed for partial or complete start-up. In parallel with the emergency programme, a group of officially appointed

5

0017

strategists is reviewing Kuwait's economic and financial structure to determine appropriate policies and criteria during the recovery and reconstruction phases.

The government structure during this stage is operating as a crisis management unit under emergency legislation in the form of martial law, which was imposed by emiri decree on 27th February. Others in this forum to whom I have alluded have recently been in Kuwait and are therefore better personally qualified to report on the damage assessment programme. I would only pass on to you some reports which percolate back from my friends and colleagues in the bank, some of whom, being Kuwaitis, remained there throughout the occupation and others of whom have recently returned to Kuwait, together with the governor of the Central Bank of Kuwait and his team. As a consequence, they may have had an opportunity to see more of the country than could our friends in the British delegation the weekend before last.

The theme of much of the planning process prior to the return to Kuwait embraced two key facets: people planned for the worst but hoped for the best. It seems, as a result, that the theoretical approach has proved right on both counts. Reports so far indicate that, although there was widespread damage and looting, quite a substantial part of the non-oil infrastructural base remains intact. Damage, however, to the critical desalination plants is reported to be fairly severe, as is also the case with the electrical generating sector. Of the four major installations in Kuwait, Shuwaikh appears to be almost totally destroyed; both Doha East and Doha West power stations are fairly badly damaged but are believed to be capable of rehabilitation by cannabilising from other sources. But fortunately Al Zour, in the south of the country near the Saudi Arabian border, is almost intact and, according to our understanding, needs only the reconnection of power lines to be able to supply adequate generating capacity for most of the country. This is a function of the population base having now fallen to around 500,000, so over a million people have fled Kuwait or been forced to leave Kuwait since the dreadful invasion.

The reports from our colleagues indicate that the ports, specifically Shuaiba, the airport and the roads and bridges can soon be expected to be repaired. They advise, though, that telecommunications is the third sector which has suffered fairly badly. But, despite the well documented and quite shocking television footage, which shows wanton destruction of many prominent buildings, damage to the fabric of the majority of other buildings appears to be mainly less than had been feared and, of major significance, the hospitals appear to be coping well, even though estimates have been published that a total of US $2 billion would be required to meet the costs of re-equipping the 12 hospitals from which equipment was looted.

So much for the non-oil sector. In the oil and gas extraction, producing and exporting sectors the picture, alas, is far bleaker. As His Excellency the Ambassador has highlighted, the ecological damage from the shocking destruction and setting to the torch of the great majority of Kuwait's oil wells and production-gathering facilities leaves us all with great sadness. The long-term effects can only be guessed at.

The energy sector has therefore suffered immense devastation, and it is likely to be in this sector that the main thrust of the rehabilitation programme would expect to be concentrated. First, the infernos have to be overcome, and it is likely to be many months thereafter before the damage is alleviated and significant productive capacity restored. The situation in Kuwait is absolutely fluid, with each day revealing new developments of significance, but, as the next few weeks unfurl, the definitive damage assessment review should be completed.

In this first phase of emergency relief the contracts have been awarded both directly by the government and also through the United States Corps of Engineers, who have an overall 90-day contract to start the process. Despite the plethora of media speculation, the overall quantum of the contracts awarded has so far been modest - in the range of only $1 billion or about £540 million. The contracts have been awarded to contractors and exporters from a number of countries, including the United States, the United Kingdom, France, Sweden, Denmark, Germany, Austria, Italy, Turkey, Saudi Arabia and the United Arab Emirates, as well of course as Kuwait itself. The main specifications of these contracts are to clear and reconnect the roads and transportation, to restore water, sewerage and electrical systems, to reopen ports and the airport and to carry out emergency repairs to the buildings. As His Excellency also mentioned, environmental pollution is an immense concern.

Moving to the future, the second stage of the Kuwait emergency recovery programme is to be the actual recovery phase. The objective here is to bring the country back to a reasonable level of normal social and economic operation. The sectoral damage assessment inputs are to be used to identify and categorise urgent rehabilitation needs for essential public infrastructure and plant, without constraining the choices relevant to the subsequent third phase, the reconstruction phase. This recovery phase is expected to take up to two years and therefore is likely to run well into 1992. As His Excellency the Ambassador highlighted, there is no frantic rush: the planning process can now predominate.

The expected size and demographics of the population will be the most critical element in determining the level and the manner in which utilities will be restored. Most recent official indications, which emerged last week, of a total population target of 1 million persons are clearly of great significance to the pace of the second phase. Besides this demographic policy constraint, there will also be an economic efficiency constraint, and that is likely to be the dominant policy element of this phase. But in the earlier stages the critical activities, such as electricity and medical services, will again be expected to re-function with only modest staffing and necessarily constrained facilities.

As a banker, one would welcome the fact that a key issue of this recovery phase would be the restoration of the financial and banking sector, the restoration of the efficacy of the legal structure and private sector activity in general. It is likely that many private institutions will be in greater or lesser distress because of losses in assets or asset values, and much of the private sector rehabilitation process is likely to take place gradually within the parameters of co-ordinated public sector fiscal and monetary policies. These policy options will be defined during the first emergency relief phase. While they have short-term implications, they will clearly have long-term implications on the social and educational structure, and they are expected to include incentives to encourage management skills and excellence in educational priorities.

For British companies the five key sectors where expertise is likely to be required in the second phase, the recovery phase, are the energy sector, telecommunications, electric power and water, desalination and civil construction, although opportunities in civil construction may be fewer than had once been feared.

The third phase of the programme, again in the future, is that of reconstruction. This will be to implement the overall reconstruction programme based on national priorities. The government's role in managing the fiscal and monetary policy of the state will be critical for achieving the allocative effects of the restructuring actions to be initiated during the recovery phase. Most of the infrastructure is expected to be repaired, rehabilitated or replaced during this phase, after damage assessment and detailed designs and costing programmes have been completed. Education, training, organisation and management are expected to be the main thrust of this third phase, as life in Kuwait gradually moves back to the peaceful and prosperous course sought by all Kuwaitis and all other residents and friends of Kuwait.

I have run through the general overview of the recovery programme. What can we say now about the specifics of the programme and how can British businessmen secure tangible business opportunities in the face of intense competition from so many other nations? Those of us who are British can take great pride in the outstanding role which Great Britain has played throughout history in the defence of freedom. Our traditions were only heightened by the firm and resolute stance adopted by our government from the first moments of the invasion, the stand upon a matter of principle which achieved such glorious vindication only seven months later. All of us in this conference centre will have seen those moving advertisements placed by the government of Kuwait in the British press in the immediate aftermath of the invasion. All Kuwaitis now appreciate and will never forget that the Union Jack, and of course the Stars and Stripes, do indeed represent the true colours of friendship.

Kuwait's oft-repeated undertakings to ensure that future public sector contracts are awarded to those who participated in the United Nations coalition forces will prove of lasting benefit to the United Kingdom, which played such an immense part in the political processes and military operations which recovered freedom for Kuwait.

In the commercial field the United Kingdom's co-ordinated response, both official and private sector, has been simply overwhelming and without precedent. The co-ordination between public and private sector has been exemplary, as witnessed by the preparation and presentation by the Foreign Secretary to the Kuwaiti government in the form of the Crown Prince and Deputy Prime Minister in Taif of that splendid Department of Trade and Industry prospectus "Rebuilding Kuwait", which is included in the conference folders here today. That was of course presented well before the liberation of Kuwait had been achieved. The establishment of the City Kuwait Group, under the excellent leadership of Lord Limerick and of course David Douglas-Home, the untiring efforts of agencies such as COMET, the overwhelming response to the convening of this briefing today - you may be pleased to know that on Friday tickets were almost as scarce as for the rugby, so let us hope we have an equally successful day today - and the tangible initiatives such as the establishment by the two major British groups of the fully-equipped BRIT facility in Fahaheel, close to the headquarters of KPC, are all clear examples of the commitment at all levels by the United Kingdom authorities, contractors, authorities, exporters and their financiers and advisers to secure as large a role as can be attained by such a cohesive professional response.

The 64 million - or should it be billion - dollar question is what is to be the magnitude of the overall programme. There has been immense speculation as to the cost of the recovery programme. One would hesitate to be drawn within the range of figures, but now that people are able to assess the damage at first hand, it is likely to be nearer the more modest end of the range of speculation than the very aggressive numbers that have been presented.

Some expectations will, therefore, be dashed, in that the scale of the problem which we have to address is, thank God, more modest than at one stage had been feared. Nonetheless, there will still be great opportunities for British industry and British exporters, and in view of the great historic connections between Kuwait and the United Kingdom, there is no reason why the United Kingdom cannot play a disproportionately large role with Kuwait and its trade. Prior to the invasion Kuwait's import pattern had the United Kingdom standing third with 9.1% of imports, after Japan with 15% and the United States with 14%. Links between British exporters and contractors and both public and private sectors in Kuwait are very strong. Kuwaitis seek and welcome from British companies the five attributes of proven product, proven expertise, cost

8

0020

effective price structures, the ability to deliver on time and according to specification and a sound understanding of the business climate of the Middle East.

A lot has been written about Kuwait's financial capacity in the immediate aftermath of the invasion and at a time when the country faces the prospect of several more months, at the very least, without new energy sector export revenues on top of the period of seven months without such earnings throughout the occupation. This is not the most appropriate forum to debate the many financing options which would be open to the government in its overall liability management programme, but I believe we can say for our purposes that a country which at the time of the invasion possessed external reserves in excess of £50 billion continues to have more than adequate liquidity and sources of funding to meet all the financial commitments presently contemplated.

Kuwait following its liberation is not a newly emergent market. It is in fact a renaissance of an already tremendously advanced nation and market. The legal and regulatory structures are in place, although there are likely to be implementational difficulties in the early stages as a result of changes in personnel and the absence of records, computer systems and the like. The private sector, though, is already up and running very aggressively from a wide variety of centres, including Dubai, Damman, Bahrain and Cairo, as well as of course from London, whilst everyone is trying particularly hard to secure visas to re-enter Kuwait.

The regulatory framework for doing business and importing is precisely defined, as are the formal procedures for establishing the framework of bid, advance payment and performance bonds. I hesitate to mention that we even have a form of income tax levied upon foreign companies which carry on business in Kuwait. The regulations are not complex but involve the prerequisite of a Kuwaiti agent and the mandatory use of a Kuwaiti bank in the case of public sector contracts to interface with government departments for the provision of all bonding facilities necessary for public sector contracts.

In view of the immense interest evinced in the opportunities presented by the rehabilitation of Kuwait, we in NBK have rewritten the guide to doing business in Kuwait. It is intended to set out in full all the legal regulatory and practical issues which one needs successfully to do business in Kuwait, and a number of my friends and colleagues here today would be very happy to make copies available to you. They are wearing our NBK badges. As the only bank with both a domestic presence in Kuwait and an operating presence in the world's major financial centres, we shall be happy to provide any possible assistance to all the parties involved in or keen to become involved in the restoration of Kuwait.

Everyone connected with Kuwait has faced immense challenges over past months. There are still great challenges to be faced by all of us as we embark upon the immense task of the rehabilitation of Kuwait. But one feels confident that the unique combination of business, public sector and financial resources represented at this briefing can and will play a very important role in assisting Kuwait at this most critical time in the history of the state.

CHAIRMAN: Thank you very much, John. At this stage, sadly, we have to say good-bye to His Excellency the Ambassador. Your Excellency, we are most grateful to you for gracing us with your presence this morning and wish you very well in the reconstruction of your country.

We now have a little time to ask questions of Mr Finigan. I know that many of you are interested in the attitude of the Exports Credits Guarantee Department, but that is really something for the panel of speakers at the end, and we are fortunate to have on our panel representatives from ECGD in Cardiff and in London. So perhaps ECGD questions could be left till later in the morning. Are there any questions for Mr Finigan?

May I start off by asking you whether you can speculate as to the time when banks might be operational again in Kuwait. We understand that there is likely to be a newish currency, or a new look to the currency. Is it possible to tell us anything about that?

MR FINIGAN: Not, I am afraid, with any inside knowledge or any great expectations as to accuracy. We have received from our own colleagues reports on the status of some of our buildings. Obviously with over 50 entities in Kuwait it is a vast task. Some of the buildings still cannot be entered because of fears of booby traps or other horrors. Therefore, I am afraid that the only assurances we can give are that people are working flat out to achieve that aim. The governor of the Central Bank and a team returned to Kuwait last Wednesday with representatives not merely of NBK but also of all other Kuwaiti banks, but I am afraid I have no knowledge of what that programme would be. Again it is a function of the fact that we are still in the earliest days and that it is far better to address the issues in a systematic fashion than to be panicked into too rapid a restoration of services, which could lead only to complications if the level of service offered was inadequate for the demand.

As to a new currency, it certainly is the intention to replace the old dinar notes with new currency of like amount. The Central Bank was quoted as indicating that that may take place the week after next. It is likely to be a process which is not accomplished in one fell swoop, but the ergonomics and the logistics would dictate that that will take quite some time to be fully implemented. Meanwhile, Gresham's law will apply and the new currency will certainly be hoarded.

MR ALISTAIR DUNN (Clifford Chance): I understand from His Excellency that martial law is currently in force in Kuwait. Could you tell us, please, when civil law will be restored and which law will govern any contracts which are to be awarded?

MR FINIGAN: Martial law was passed by an emiri decree for a period of three months from 27th February and therefore can be expected to run until May. Certainly it would not be possible for me to speculate as to what the immediate extension would be after that, but those of us who know Kuwait well had always known of Kuwait's democratic status and the pride that all Kuwaitis feel in that. His Excellency the Ambassador highlighted Kuwait's democratic status in his address this morning, and therefore one would hope that at the earliest opportunity the restoration of the civil order would apply.

As I mentioned, Kuwait has a very well codified system of legislation and, in particular, a broad system of civil laws, most particularly Law 57 and Law 58 of, I believe, 1980. It is in the booklet "Doing business in Kuwait". Contracts, therefore, are covered by the civil code, which is a legislated form of law and which of course provides a very clear mechanism for understanding the various contractual rights and responsibilities and has been the basis upon which Kuwait has contracted, through public and private sector agencies, with the vast number of international companies which have over many, many years operated successfully in Kuwait. I hope that answers the question.

CHAIRMAN: Thank you very much, John. Perhaps we might now move on to our next speaker. Christian Adams has had long service in our diplomatic service and has been in a variety of overseas posts, particularly in south-east Asia. For the last two years he has been seconded to

10

0022

the Department of Trade and Industry. I have to say that, without the efforts of Christian and his team, we would not have made anything like the progress that we have made in registering the interests of British companies, getting the message across as to what needs to be done, liaising with our very embryonic staff in Kuwait and indeed coping with the logistics of getting to Kuwait and moving around there. None of that could have been done without the expertise of the Department of Trade and Industry, the Foreign Office, our embassy and indeed the armed forces. So it is a great tribute to Christian and his colleagues that he was able to get us there and back in one piece, so that we are in a position to say something to you this morning.

GOVERNMENT-INDUSTRY CO-OPERATION

MR CHRISTIAN ADAMS (Head of Projects and Export Policy Division, Department of Trade and Industry): First, thank you, Chairman, for those kind words.

It is a great pleasure to have the opportunity to talk to so many about this very important subject. Repairing damage to Kuwait has obviously presented a very particular challenge to government and industry. That is why I have entitled my talk "Government-industry co-operation", which so far it has been. The Americans had clearly given careful thought to reconstructing Kuwait well before the military offensive was launched, and of course in USACE, the US Corps of Engineers, they had a very effective vehicle to capture the commercial peace. We decided that we too had to create a structure which would integrate political, military and commercial objectives effectively.

The response from industry, and quite a few of them are up here on the panel, was magnificent. In no time, and well before the war started, we had an active steering group, a series of sub-groups representing the oil and gas, construction and consultancy, water and sewerage, power and telecommunications sectors, each with a chairman from my division in the DTI and an industry deputy or co-chairman, and recently - I know that David Douglas-Home will be talking about this - an invisibles sub-group has been set up. We concluded that the urgent requirement was for a database showing which companies had done work in Kuwait already, because they would clearly be in a favourable position once the company was liberated.

Meanwhile, on the diplomatic front the Prime Minister made clear to the Emir and the Crown Prince the United Kingdom's wish to play its full part in the rehabilitation work. We also needed a statement of capability and intent for the Kuwaitis, and in six and a half days, with the sub-groups, we produced this prospectus. It was a bold move, because we knew that, given the time that we had, we would leave certain worthy companies off the list. We inevitably did, and they were not at all pleased. But in general the document went down very well. I should add that if you think it is only in the private sector that there are jealousies and firms believing they have been left out, you would be wrong. The government is just as bad: we had complaints from our own colleagues as well.

The next step was to get the prospectus to the Kuwaitis. Working closely with the FCO, we sent a mission on 8th February to join the Foreign Secretary, Douglas Hurd, in Taif on his visit to the Kuwaiti government in exile. This mission of nine met the Crown Prince, who assured Britain of a substantial share and expressed the deep gratitude of himself and his people for Britain's military and political support in liberating Kuwait, not just in 1991 but in 1961. Lord Prior took the opportunity to present, on behalf of the businessmen on this mission, a proposal to provide skilled technicians and equipment once Kuwait was liberated. This contained the proposal for a ship, or ships, to float offshore. At this meeting in Taif the British mission also had the opportunity for a detailed two and a half hour discussion with Kuwaiti ministers. This proved very valuable in giving us some idea of Kuwaiti requirements and of how the Kuwait government would organise reconstruction. The British mission to Taif also had a wider benefit. It enabled the members of the team to get to know each other and help to bind the different companies and sectors together, and this has been vital to the British-Kuwait reconstruction effort.

These efforts, or the lack of them according to some, provoked widespread press interest. We were accused by some of being too late and by others of being too early and too mercenary. We were then, and remain today, robust about what we have done. Having helped Kuwait win the war, we had every reason to help them win the reconstruction as well. That we benefit commercially does not detract from this shared endeavour. I was very happy for us to meet in Kuwait on our recent visit General de la Billiere and a number of his colleagues, including Patrick Cordingley who led the Desert Rats. They were all extremely supportive of what we are doing. That is extremely encouraging, and very necessary as well.

Following the Taif visit we established a task force in Dammam, in the Eastern Province of Saudi Arabia, to work with the Kuwait Emergency Renewal Programme and report back to the sub-groups. As you may know, there was a flurry over the USACE pre-qualifications, but in fact Britain did put in a tremendous number - more than anybody else, 130 - and ten pre-qualified. In the end we won one of the seven awards - Shand for water and sewerage - but work will also come to us through the UK subsidiaries of US companies. For example, Brown & Root, who won the USACE contract for public building repair, are involving Howard Humphreys and Brown & Root Vickers in Britain. We were also by then beginning to win other contracts - Ruston mobile diesel generators worth £6 million, which we are trying to get there tomorrow, one of the reasons why I was late, and also 30 Land Rover ambulances and 50 Discoveries for the Kuwaiti Ministry of the Interior. You will hear later from Howard Lyons about the IHG contract for cleaning up the military hospital. Some of you will doubtless know of other contracts which I cannot talk about.

You will be interested above all in the situation on the ground now. A small mission, six businessmen and myself, visited Kuwait on 10th to 11th March. This was essentially a follow-up to the February mission to Taif. There we had heard what the Kuwaiti government in exile thought they would find when Kuwait was liberated. This was our chance to discuss with them what they had actually found. What we and they found was a Kuwait in an appalling mess. You would have been amused to see captains of industry, some of them here, later speakers, and myself stumbling in darkened hotels, gripping tightly a tarred and flickering candle as they made their weary way to shared bedrooms, apprehensive about no water and too much snoring.

The city we found had been seriously damaged and looted. Most shops were empty. Refurbishment work was clearly required on public buildings, hotels, leisure facilities, etc. The airport terminal, hangars and control tower were seriously damaged - by the Americans. But we should not exaggerate. The retreating Iraqi troops, surprised by the speed of the allied advance, could do only limited damage to the basic infrastructure. Roads and bridges were largely unscathed and of course enabled the Iraqis to escape. The hospitals which they were using are now operating adequately. Some more water and power will be restored soon; at the moment it is a very poor supply. There is therefore a limited need for new major project work.

You will be hearing in more detail from others about the main opportunities for reconstruction work and supply, but in oil and gas particularly there is a huge task, obviously after the oil well fires are put out, and Alan Cockshaw will be talking about that. Some of the power and

0024

12

desalination plants are seriously damaged - the Royal Engineers are working on part of that at the moment - and their distribution systems need careful checking and doubtless some repair, and Adrian White will have a word about that. The restoration of public buildings, hotels and leisure centres, including building equipment supply and furnishing are all major opportunities. I have mentioned the airport, and David Douglas-Home and Peter Berry will be talking about restocking shops, which were virtually all empty.

How do we tackle this major task? The British Task Force in Dammam will move this week - I have just had a telegram about it: they will be moving tomorrow - and will be housed in an office in the embassy grounds. Its membership is being adjusted to take account of the need for specifically targeted approaches, including an enormous requirement for general supplies and equipment. It will work closely with the British military forces in Kuwait in such areas as longer-term mine clearance, munitions disposal and public utilities. The members will be, on the oil and petrochemicals side, Hugh Shyvers of Matthew Hall, an AMEC subsidiary; on the consultancy side, Jack Knight of Mouchel; on water and sewerage, Gerry Bone of Biwater; on mine clearance and defence-related construction, also reporting to DESO, Peter Cross of British Aerospace; on civil construction, Mr Hocking of Costain; on procurement services, the Crown Agents; and on power and telecommunications, Andrew Nicholls of GEC Alsthom. Some of them of course are already in the team; others are new. On the invisibles side we expect an insurance representative to go for damage assessment for a short time.

We are establishing a land base for the use of the British Rehabilitation Implementation Team, know as BRIT, at Fahaheel near Shuhaiba Port. Adrian White and Alan Cockshaw will be describing that. The original ship proposal, as you see, has therefore come on land. Unfortunately there are mines on land as well, and we had a look at the site, a slightly nerve-racking experience. Later speakers will, as I say, tell you about this. The land base will be available to all, but at a fee.

Looking ahead to the next few weeks, it is most important that the UK exporting effort to Kuwait continues to be orchestrated through the structures I have described. These must not become bureaucratic. Companies obviously have to be free to pursue individual enterprise and the opportunities they see, and of course vital links need to be maintained all the time with Kuwaiti partners or others in the region. That will be vital in making successful business deals. Obviously neither the DTI nor this collaborative structure can win you the contract, but we will try to provide the vital support and information to help quality and competitiveness win.

In principle, you should use the DTI, the sub-group structure and the trade associations as your principal point of initial contact and rely on their immediate access to the Task Force on the ground in Kuwait. Do not attempt to ring the embassy direct. It has only one satellite telephone, and we need to use it.

I would like to point you to the DTI's Export Intelligence Service, the EIS. This is your best source of rapid information about export opportunities in Kuwait. If you are not familiar with the EIS, your local DTI regional office will tell you about it. Information available through the EIS includes supply inquiries, overseas agents seeking to represent British companies and invitations to tender. Details of opportunities in Kuwait are already starting to come through. Some 1,500 subscribers to the EIS are profiled for Kuwait, and in addition we ourselves in the DTI-Kuwait Reconstruction Co-ordination Team already have details of over 2,500 companies on our own database for Kuwait, and more are being added every day. So register your interest direct with the DTI as well.

A word on trade fairs and missions. These provide a good opportunity for companies to meet agents and potential customers. We are anxious to use the medium of trade fairs to promote British exports to Kuwait, and the DTI has agreed to fund a British pavilion at the Reconstruction Kuwait 91 trade fair, to be held in Bahrain in November, which seems a long way away. This is an international event and I hope that as many of you as possible can take space in our pavilion. You should contact Trevor Marsh of our Fairs and Promotions Branch, who is here today. In addition, we want to hold some all-British trade fairs in either Kuwait or a nearby country in the next few months. I should also mention that my own Secretary of State, Peter Lilley, intends to take a small business mission to Kuwait in late April. He would love to take all of you with him, but I don't think that will be possible.

There will be a full mission programme to the Gulf - that is the ordinary missions - in the next financial year, with 13 sponsored by the DTI. For details, you should contact your nearest DTI regional office.

A final word on travel. Kuwait currently has, as you will have heard, no police, no customs or normal transportation services. There are no taxis; there is very little power, water and food. There are numerous armed checkpoints. Fortunately most of these are manned by the Kuwait Army; those which are not are a little more formidable. The airport is open only for military use.

Against this backcloth, which some of you will have experienced in other post-war situations, transport is obviously very difficult indeed. Getting in there is difficult. RAF Hercules, which currently fly daily from Riyadh to Kuwait, can only be made available to those companies which have contracts from the Kuwaiti government or for whom the Kuwaiti government has specifically asked. The DTI/FCO are vetting all applications in consultation with our embassy in Kuwait, and I would particularly ask that companies do not pester the hard-pressed unit dealing with these applications unless they have a bona fide request. We will anyway be checking everything out with the Kuwaitis through the embassy, so it is a complete waste of your and our time to pretend that you have a contract or have been requested to visit Kuwait unless this is in fact clearly the case.

The other way into Kuwait is via Dammam in Eastern Province in Saudi Arabia, where it appears that you can drive in if you have a signed contract - or maybe if you have the right friends. There have, however, been delays at the Saudi Arabian border in some cases. I should add that no visas for Kuwait are currently being issued, only some permits.

I would like, in concluding, to thank the organisers, Westminster Management Consultants, for having the flair to organise this event. I would also like to urge you to take this opportunity to win the business, not least by forging your links with Kuwaiti companies and using the support structure we have assembled here in London to help you. As the Crown Prince reminded us, do not forget that you also have to be competitive. Kuwaiti goodwill will not be enough.

CHAIRMAN: Thank you very much, Christian, for that very realistic assessment of the situation. I would emphasise the difficulties of moving around and the bona fideness, if there is such a word, of those people are anxious to go. I am sure that everyone in this room is anxious to see for themselves, but that is not possible. Are there any questions for Christian?

MR STEVE HORNER (Air Thanet): We are based in Manston International Airport in Kent. Until last Saturday we were flying freighter aircraft from the Ministry of Defence from various RAF fields in Germany and the UK into the US Air Force base in Al Jubayl. In fact on one

14

0026

occasion one of our aircraft was seven nautical miles away from a Scud attack. We now have documentary evidence that an American commercial concern has been awarded an exclusive contract by the state department to ferry all air freight and sea freight into Kuwait. In fact certain British exporters whom we have talked to have been told that we cannot participate in this; they have to go through the Americans. This seems to us to be an incredible American intrusion, verging upon a stranglehold - a bottleneck - of British activity in the Gulf, and we wonder how we all can participate in rebuffing this attack. Perhaps the DTI could help us.

MR ADAMS: Thank you very much for telling us about that. We are working with the Ministry of Defence to try to make use of some of the space which you have on offer in terms of military chartered flights, because most of the aircraft going out are emptier than they are coming back at the moment. But I am very interested to hear about this arrangement with an American commercial flying organisation. If we could have a word afterwards, I should like to take down all the details. We are in touch all the time with the Americans. Obviously the line that we have taken with the American government is that we want to see fair shares. We also expect to work on a co-operative basis with a number of their companies, not least those which have major subsidiaries in Britain. But if there is an example of unfair practice, we shall certainly take it up with them.

MR BARRY GOULDBOURNE (Apex Transformers Ltd): We obviously lost the telephone lines and the telex links. What about the communications to many people in Kuwait, the postal service? Could you tell us whether the postal service is running or how long it will be before it is, because it is obviously very difficult at the moment to get in touch?

MR ADAMS: I don't think there is much of a postal service. That was certainly the impression we had. If there are communications which you wish to send, the best thing is to communicate by fax direct with the Task Force or through us at this end. But clearly there is a danger that if too many people fax the Task Force, it will be totally swamped, as happened around the time of the USACE contracts. I think the best thing is to talk first to the DTI unit, and we will try and feed your request through.

MR GOLDBOURNE: Could you tell us how long it is likely to be before the postal service is working?

MR ADAMS: I haven't the faintest idea. The same time as the banking system, it has been suggested.

MR J C M FORREST (Kenchington Little Plc): We are consulting engineers. This week's New Civil Engineer records emergency work being done by the Royal Engineers. I was formerly a member of a specialist team in the Royal Engineers Territorial Army and we had a number of specialist teams. Could I use this opportunity to ask whether the government has considered using members of the specialist teams in the Territorial Army as a basis for obtaining information at first hand by asking them to back up the regular Royal Engineer work in Kuwait, as a means of getting more positive information on the amount of work content in the country, which is clearly lacking at the moment? We have had an hour here, and I for one have no clear idea of just what is involved in Kuwait. I believe that we have in the country probably two or three hundred trained engineers who could back up the Royal Engineer commitment in Kuwait and get that information back to our government and our industry.

MR ADAMS: I think the answer to that question will come mainly from Alan Cockshaw and Adrian White when talking about the land base. We are obviously very aware of the major source

15

0027

of information that we have in the Royal Engineers, who are working on the spot, both on munitions clearance and on the power station and desalination plants. We had very useful discussions with them when we were there, and a lot of that information is being fed through to the sub-groups. I don't know whether you have been in touch with the sub-groups which I referred to earlier. Obviously if there is a source of trained personnel in this country who are keen and capable of working with the Royal Engineers, that is something we should look at actively. It is certainly our intention, when the land base is set up, to use that land base capability to work with the Royal Engineers, supplement what they are doing and in due course take over the work from them, because, as you know, there are political pressures to bring the troops home as soon as possible. The quicker it can, so to speak, be changed from the public to the private sector, the happier everybody will be.

MR JOLYON KAY (Gulf Consultancy): Does the DTI make available in any consistent way information about how to contact all the people who have been mentioned - their names, addresses, telephone numbers, fax numbers, etc. - especially as they are set up in Kuwait itself?

MR ADAMS: A question of that sort, asking about consistency in the DTI, could only come from an ex-member of the diplomatic service. The answer is yes.

MR HUGH RAYNER (S&H Housing Ltd): Can you tell me whether there will be any shortage of accommodation for the hoards, I hope, of construction workers that will be going out to Kuwait and can you tell me the policy in the short and the long term for providing accommodation for these people?

MR ADAMS: It would be much better, if you don't mind, if I left that to Adrian White and Alan Cockshaw, who are the experts on the land base and will explain the sort of people whom they are sending in this week and the type of requirement that they anticipate for the reconstruction.

CHAIRMAN: I am sorry to cut short questions to Christian Adams, and sadly I do not think Christian can be with us when it comes to the panel. However, Iain Millar, who is on the platform, will, I am sure, be able to answer questions which would have been addressed to Christian.

THE ROLE OF THE BRITISH TASK FORCE FOR THE RECONSTRUCTION OF KUWAIT

THE HON. DAVID DOUGLAS HOME (Director of Morgan Grenfell & Co Ltd and Member of the Task Force): You have already heard from previous speakers what the situation on the ground is. It is still one, I believe, of opportunity, but not so much as we anticipated when we were in Taif at the beginning of February. At that stage the Crown Prince was talking to us about the so-called zero option, the total destruction of Kuwait. There was talk today of the infrastructure being largely unscathed and indeed of the Al Zour power station being intact. It is, but the transmission lines are cut in 92 places, so that will take a little bit of time, but only one bridge is destroyed.

Before the outbreak of war, studies were already being undertaken by the government of Kuwait into what the demographic position of the country might be in the future and the structures that would be required to support alternative levels of population. The events of the last six months have brought these studies very rapidly to a head, and it is likely that the government will be looking for a pretty drastic reduction in the population, so that there will be a much higher proportion of pure Kuwaitis, as oppposed to non-Kuwaitis, who were considerably in the ascendancy before 1st August. There could indeed be a reduction in the population from over 2 million people to something below 1.4 million. It therefore follows that the infrastructure required to service the expected size of population will be considerably less than it was before. Indeed it may not be necessary to repair all the power stations, all the pumping stations or indeed all the hospitals, although we have already heard that the damage to the health system is not as bad as we had feared. Indeed, not all the 5-star hotels may be needed. Most of them have been pretty badly burnt, but as far as we could see, the hotels were more of a mess than badly structurally damaged. The Sheraton is probably the worst. But also how many bakeries will they need? How many hairdressers will they need? A whole re-think of these things is currently being done. I am not sure about the hairdressing side, but at least the rest are being considered at the moment.

Apart, therefore, from the oil and gas sector and security, the essential spend in the short term is likely to be considerably less than what we have seen even speculated on in this document, and I entirely agree with John Finigan that the resources of the government of Kuwait are well able to look after that in the coming months.

I think people still regard Kuwait's income as being largely that of oil. As John rightly pointed out, with external assets in excess of £50 billion, the income from them is considerable.

I do not, however, detract from the enormous problems that confront the government of Kuwait at the present time. The mess, as Christian said, in Kuwait City absolutely defies description. I would not advise you to walk along a beach: the amount of abandoned ordnance, tanks and guns that are scattered everywhere is such that the armies of the coalition are involved in an enormous task, for every tank, every wrecked car and every individual box of rubbish that you see could be booby-trapped.

As you know, the authorities have let some contracts for damage assessment and we must await their reports, which are due quite soon; it is very much a crash programme. The costs of putting the oil fires out, which are obviously a source of major speculation, will clearly be enormous. We went halfway into this pall of black smoke, and it will be a Herculean task. However, there was the good news last night that one fire had been put out, although it seems that most of the other fires are very much more difficult than that which they dealt with yesterday.

Again in this sector does the state really need a lot of export refineries? Does it needs its existing petro-chemical processing capability? The reasons that prompted construction of several petro-chemical plants over the past 20 years may not apply today. It may be that the government will think that it would be more efficient in terms of numbers, people and cost to export crude and import refined products. Again these questions need addressing. If we are to be ready to assist in what we now call the rehabilitation process, not the reconstruction process, it is, as Christian was saying, essential to be ready and to be ready quickly. Christian mentioned the requirement to talk to your Kuwait agents, those of you who have them. I would add that if you do not have a Kuwait agent, or if you cannot find him, because in some cases they are difficult to find, it is well worthwhile talking to friends or agents in neighbouring GCC countries. The Crown Prince told us both in Taif and again last week in Kuwait that they wished the private sector to take the prominent role in the rebuilding of their country.

May I mention now the financial side? I believe it is unlikely that Kuwait will have to borrow any significant amounts of money. Firstly, the structural damage is not as bad as we thought, and that is where a very considerable amount of money can be spent. If they have to borrow at all, I would not call it borrowing, I would call it bridging finance as far as the government is concerned. They have got a very considerable number of alternatives, should they decide that borrowing or bridging financing is necessary. Obviously there are the external assets and future oil flow. They could borrow oil from neighbouring countries. There will need to be a senior wrangler to work out the variety of combinations within this lot. It could be that, given their request that the private sector should participate more, they might ring-fence some of the projects and have private sector involvement on a project finance basis for some facilities that they might desire to have.

It is therefore with some of these possibilities in mind that the City of Kuwait sub-group which Christian touched on was set up following the visit to Taif, the reason that it followed on being really that finance and the financial services - here I include legal, accountancy and insurance - naturally come towards the end once the physical requirement has been identified. The group, which is set up under the chairmanship of Lord Limerick, the chairman of British Invisibles, who is in the audience today, will, I hope, be a conduit for merchant banks, legal, insurance, accountancy, training and other professions as to what is going on at the moment. As Christian mentioned, we cannot allow a vast array of people, even those of us with bowler hats and umbrellas, to go charging off and bother our Embassy. We do hope to have somebody on the ground who can act as financial counsellor as and when practical. Representatives on the group include the Committee for Middle East Trade, the Department of Trade and Industry and the Bank of England.

A last, brief word about the Committee for Middle East Trade and our involvement. We have throughout the past four months or so co-operated closely with the Department of Trade and Industry on this effort - indeed part of it arose out of discussions with the DTI, the Foreign Office and other representatives during one of our meetings in the autumn. We intend to take a full part in advising both Government and British companies about what we think they should be doing; but bear with us, because there are very few of us and it may take a bit of time to get some answers. We do, however, propose to - and will - support those missions, exhibitions and initiatives that we believe to be right. HMG knows to a degree that we can sometimes be a rather tiresome pressure group, which we certainly intend to be if any members of the audience can put a good idea to us that we can pick up and champion.

That is enough of the generalisations and the inevitable scene setting which a briefing like this should start with. During our second session we shall move on to the more detailed aspects as seen by sectors.

I have received an encouraging piece of news from Kuwait, which states that a separate report from a contact at a government office indicated that electric power may be restored by Wednesday, 20 March.

Our first speaker after the break is Peter Berry, who was looking in particular at the supply side, which has turned out to be extremely important. He has been Managing Director of the Crown Agents since 1988 and has had a great deal of experience of living and working overseas.

THE SUPPLIERS' EXPERIENCE

PETER BERRY (Managing Director of Crown Agents and Member of the Task Force): Many of you will no doubt be aware of the Crown Agents and our part in the initial phase of the emergency recovery programme, which was begun by the Kuwait government when it was in exile. For those of you who are not, I will begin by saying a few words about what sort of organisation the Crown Agents is and how we became involved, since over 2,000 suppliers have been in touch with us over the past five months and it is suppliers to whom I have been asked to address my remarks.

First, to avoid any misunderstandings, Crown Agents is a public sector corporation responsible ultimately, through the Overseas Development Administration, to the Secretary of State for Foreign Affairs. Our principal business - we are, I hasten to say, commercial - is procurement as an agent, to which we add both financial and technical assistance, although we have diversified in more recent years into a number of other related areas of expertise, relating to the supply business particularly, including shipping, inspection and logistic support. Almost without exception, our own clients are either other public sector bodies or governments throughout the world. The most important of them nowadays are the major aid donors of the United Kingdom, Japan, the European Commission, the World Bank, regional development banks and so on. Much of the work that many of you did with us on Kuwait could be applied elsewhere.

Our involvement in the Kuwait Government's Emergency Recovery Programme - or KERP, as it became known - began in early November, when on the advice of the World Bank the then head of the programme, Fauzi Al-Sultan, who is a director of the World Bank, approached our organisation with a view to assisting with the sourcing activities of the KERP team. The scope of our work rapidly expanded and we were asked latterly to look at the production of a comprehensive supply assessment in the primary sectors of health, food, water and emergency power generation. In addition, we researched the availability of supplies for other key areas of the Kuwaiti economy. The one exception was the oil and gas sector, which was handled separately and which will be dealt with later on. My comments today do not therefore apply in this area, although they may have some general relevance.

Our task in Washington before Christmas was governed by the UN deadline of 15 January. It was originally envisaged by the head of the KERP team that essential supplies would be ordered, shipped and in store at forward bases around the Gulf region by that date. In practice, as you know, there were management changes within the KERP and relatively few strategic purchase and logistic decisions were authorised before the KERP moved to Dammam in early February. Fortunately also, as we have heard, what the Kuwaitis were calling "the zero option", which they feared might be the outcome of a long war and fierce house-to-house fighting, has been far from the case. Therefore the exercise which Crown Agents and the KERP undertook and to which well over 1,000 British firms responded has been overtaken by events.

That is by no means to say that it was wasted. We produced a three-volume sourcing and availability report for KERP covering all the sectors I have mentioned, and we have internally updated it subsequently. We are very grateful to all the suppliers who responded to us. We are as sad as they are that more orders were not placed directly as a result, but I know that some received orders from the reconstructed KERP and for others the work should stand them in good stead now.

However, before suggesting where interested suppliers should go from here, it may be useful if I try to cover very briefly the experience of suppliers in Kuwait before 2 August last year. A brief glance at the trade figures for the period 1985-1990, as Mr Finigan noted, shows that UK exporters have consistently maintained a market share of around 10%, although the Japanese and Americans have generally been well ahead of both us and the Germans. The one marked trend in the figures over this period reveals a distinct decline in the Japanese position and a commensurate rise in the fortunes of American companies. I fully expect this trend to continue, given the relative inputs of these two countries in the recent conflict. The Crown Prince told us in Taif that of the initial contracts, something like 22% had been placed for British goods. This must be encouraging.

But you have not paid good money to hear what business was done in the past. You want to know about orders next week, next month and next year. I think, as we have been hearing, it is very much about looking slightly over the immediate hump into the medium term.

As you will know from our missions reports and from previous speakers, major damage assessment is incomplete. However, it is clear that the public sector is unlikely to be in the business of letting large civil engineering contracts. The job is rehabilitation in communications, power and water and refurbishment elsewhere.

I was personally particularly interested in the health sector. I should like to take that briefly as a wider case study for suppliers. As part of our exercise for KERP, Crown Agents sourced and priced some 6,000 items from 350 different British suppliers. Some of them the KERP purchased, but very largely from agents' stocks in Saudi Arabia and the Gulf. However, now that we have been into Kuwait City and had talks with the genuinely heroic team of doctors and technical supervisors who actually kept things going, it is apparent that they have managed to hide most of their supplies from the Iraqis and that, notwithstanding the looting of their hospital equipment and of their entire fleet of ambulances, they can operate adequately for the population they presently have, which has been put at about 500,000. They will consolidate their facilities in line with the returning population and in future they will cater for a maximum of 1.2 million people against the almost 2,000,000 they catered for before the war. On the bio-medical equipment side, they are very anxious to honour contracts which were in place prior to the invasion, and the day following our visit 10 days ago the director of supplies held a meeting with the four principal agents for drugs and equipment to see about the resumption of normal services.

Howard Lyons will speak to you about his military hospital contract, but in addressing suppliers, which is my slot in the programme, I do think there are wider lessons to be drawn from the Health Ministry story.

First, there are devoted teams who stayed in Kuwait and kept things going. Their voice is now extremely important.

Secondly, they will wish to buy short term needs quickly. As we have heard, you cannot readily put consumable stocks into Kuwait today, but I do hope that you are pressing them on to your stockists in Saudi Arabia and up and down the Gulf. That is where the short term needs are being very largely catered for.

Third is the desire to uphold previous contracts and relationships. This desire is strong, but if you were the previous supplier, do not be complacent, and if you were not, take heart. Change and upheaval in the market-place are the classic opportunities for a marketeer, and certainly some old suppliers are being abandoned and some new decision makers are emerging. Business will not suddenly be switched to Britain, but the goodwill is there and thus a greatly enhanced market opportunity.

Fourth, from my little case study and, in my judgment, absolutely crucial, is the role of the agent. I noted a meeting with agents almost immediately following our visit. All of you who know the Middle East will know the importance of the scope and nature of the agent, his contacts and connections. In pre-war Kuwait, rules applied to government supply tenders over 5,000 dinars, which, as Mr Finigan said, are very likely to remain unchanged post-war. These tended to restrict tenders by pre-qualified products and/or suppliers and frequently the tender notice in the gazette specified companies whose names it listed to purchase tender documents. Sometimes this was restricted to approved Kuwaiti bidders; sometimes - particularly on higher value contracts - a foreign company was mentioned; sometimes it was coupled with the name of its Kuwaiti agent. Pre-qualification was therefore vital, yet this was not the responsibility of the Central Tenders Board, but of the ultimate end user. Therefore you needed - in my judgment, you still need - to ensure that your products and services were - and remained - on the pre-qualification list of all significant potential government customers.

On performance, it was essential to comply with all the tender terms and conditions - and may I say, speaking from Crown Agents' general experience, that that is something on which British suppliers are generally rather weak - both technical and documentary, otherwise bids could be rejected on grounds of non-compliance.

The list goes on, but I think I have made my point. A good agent, to cover these matters with you, is absolutely essential. That said, most of the companies to whom I have spoken regarding Kuwaiti supply, rather than civil engineering, have said that contract conditions were not particularly onerous before the war and would normally back-to-back specific requirements, including funding, with their local agents.

On post-war contracts, GEC Alston, whom Christian Adams mentioned, have been kind enough to share with me details of their contract for the supply of emergency gas turbine generators. This was done directly between Ruston and the Ministry of Electricity and Water's own US office. Payment was by LC and delivery was, given the transport constraints, ex-works to very tight time constraints. The contract conditions, however, were regarded by GEC as quite normal. Other KERP purchases have been by LC, worked through the Kuwait government's American lawyers, but now that the government's funds have been unblocked, I am quite sure that financing will be done direct.

One thing that I might insert here is that details of other contracts let to UK suppliers seem rather difficult to run down, particularly as I understand that the lawyers of the Kuwait government have been insisting on confidentiality as a contract condition. If any of you have received contracts, either directly from KERP or indirectly from agents in the area, my colleagues in the DTI and in the UK Task Force would be pleased if you would share some of the detail with us to enable your colleagues in UK industry as a whole to perform more successfully in the market.

I have covered the public sector in some detail, because I have heard expressed from suppliers quite a number of doubts as to the rules of the road. However, the market which our mission identified last weekend and which David Douglas Home pointed out is probably far greater in the private sector than the public. Almost anything that can be moved from a house or shop has been moved; almost anything that is easily broken, like windows or shelves, has been broken. Clearly, the replacements will be purchased according to personal financial circumstances and over time, but again if you are in that business, you need to think of agents for stocks down the Gulf and ultimately in Kuwait itself.

I am quite clear that in the general supplies area, whether public sector or private, there will be a very large post-war market in Kuwait to replace sabotage and looting. The precise form in which it will be met is unclear, therefore Crown Agents will certainly continue to play its part in the Task Force and Chris Twyman, who has wide experience and is known to many of you, will be joining the Task Force team in Kuwait very shortly to help with that side of its efforts.

May I finish by looking at the longer term? I hope very much that Crown Agents will be able to return to its pre-war role in Kuwait of providing British experts to Kuwaiti ministries to supplement their technical expertise. I see a substantial role for us and also for other British institutions in the training of the reduced Kuwaiti population in skills that previously they purchased with immigrant labour. I was briefed to talk about supplies, but I do believe that expertise, training and technology transfer are absolutely inseparable from them, and this is the time to introduce that thought. I would urge you also to think of this in your business plan.

Mr Chairman, I must apologise to you and to the audience for being unable to stay for the panel discussion afterwards; I have a prior commitment. I will try to take some questions if you think there is time.

CHAIRMAN: Thank you very much, Peter. The answer is that there is time for one or two questions, but not many.

GORDON GRAY (Link 51 (Storage Products) Ltd): The ambassador told us earlier that we had to be competitive. You are now telling us that we can supply ex-stock from our distributors, for argument's sake, in Bahrain or Saudi. What is the position regarding re-exports from these countries into Kuwait and the withdrawal of any import duty that has already been paid? If this is still retained, we shall not be competitive.

PETER BERRY: I do not think I am qualified to answer that question in the detail that I think you want, namely, the withdrawal of import duties.

GORDON GRAY: I should like it answered today, because I am flying out this evening.

PETER BERRY: I do not think the government's structures in relation to the withdrawal of import duties and so on are, frankly, in place. You have heard of the literal, physical mess in Kuwait City. There are many other pressing pre-occupations. The fact is that there is also a pressing need for some of the supplies, and they have been bought from stocks up and down the Gulf. Therefore in the context of the emergency and people's need to have things, the requirements are presumably to be met duty paid.

CHAIRMAN: Thank you very much, Peter. Perhaps we might move on. Our next speaker is Alan Cockshaw, Chairman of AMEC, who has been looking particularly at the oil and gas side, but also heavily involved with Adrian White of Biwater in setting up the proposed camps. Without more ado, over to you, Alan.

THE CONTRACTORS' EXPERIENCE

ALAN COCKSHAW (Chairman of AMEC plc and Member of the Task Force): Thank you, Chairman, and good morning. When I look over here at these distinguished gentlemen on my right, I am reminded that just over a week ago, when trying to get into a somewhat seedy hotel in the back of nowhere in Kuwait City with no lights, power or water, the army very kindly lent us some gas lamps, and these great captains here were all trying to assemble these things on the floor. After about half an hour, we were all exhausted, because we had not had very much sleep, and we very quietly and discreetly said to the man, "Do you have any candles?" He did, so one after the other, with a candle in our hand, we climbed the stairs to a much deserved bed. Between us all we could not light a gas lamp, so training and development is fairly important.

I am very sorry that inevitably there will be a fair bit of repetition in this. It is also clear that it will be much more difficult to be definitive, but I hope that much of that will be cleared up subsequently in questions.

When my colleagues and I visited Taif at the beginning of February to meet with the Prime Minister and the government of Kuwait in exile, no one had any idea at all what the nature and extent of damage in Kuwait would be, and still less the date on which our Kuwaiti friends would be able to return home. You have already heard twice that they told us that they were considering the maximum range of options as to what they might find when they returned, down to what David mentioned, the zero option, the self-evident, almost total destruction of everything. It was difficult for us then - and it is even more difficult now - to come to terms with what the ambassador was saying about the scale of human suffering. We were - and are - not in a position to assess that.

What was, however, very clear from our discussions in Taif was that we had to put some people on the ground very quickly, close to the KERP team in Dammam. As you know, they were put on the ground within two or three days under Chris Wilton, the commercial counsellor from our embassy in Riyadh. That team was chosen to represent the sectors that we believed at the time to be the most important, but most of all from people who were physically in the area. That initiative was very well appreciated, particularly by Dr Shaheen, the head of KERP.

It was a considerable relief, therefore, just a week ago to fly into Kuwait City and see that in spite of the very considerable damage that had been occasioned, the worst fears of the Kuwaiti government - and indeed of all of us - had not arisen. The feared zero option had been avoided. Once more we were received, as in Taif, very royally by the Crown Prince, the Prime Minister and his ministers. It was surprisingly easy for us to pick up where we had left off, but this time to do so with access to a very considerable pool of knowledge that had been acquired by each of them since they returned to Kuwait. Our overview of the damage caused is therefore not simply that which we have seen with our own eyes in a relatively short time, but an aggregation of the detailed assessments given by the Prime Minister and the various members of his government to whom we spoke, Dr Shaheen, General Sir Peter de la Billiere and his principal officers and, finally, our marvellous ambassador, Michael Weston, and his team. I must say here and now what an absolutely fantastic job Michael Weston has done and how marvellous he was with the whole of our team when we were out there. A comprehensive picture, therefore, in a very short time that we could never have had by just looking at it ourselves.

There really is very little damage to roads and bridges in the general area of Kuwait City. Although we did not travel very far outside that area, the entire highway system seems to be operating more or less as normal, although a very significant clean-up is certainly required. As you have already heard, tanks, military hardware and cars are littered absolutely everywhere. We understand that one or two bridges have been damaged out on the road to Basra and into Saudi, but there is only a very short length of road which requires reconstruction. Overall the damage is minimal, although, not surprisingly, a bit of resurfacing is expected.

We understand there is very little major damage to the ports, although again, in the manner of the wanton dereliction that we have seen, cranes have been badly damaged and dropped inside the harbour; within the harbour most of the minesweeping is now virtually complete, courtesy of the Royal Navy.

Apparently there is no major damage to the water supply and sewage disposal system; but this cannot be properly checked out until power is restored and the pumping stations are brought back on stream. You have already heard about the power supply and distribution system, which has not been fundamentally damaged, but does require very extensive, detailed repairs. You heard of 90-odd breaks in the transmission system from one power station alone.

Overall therefore a lot of work is required to establish progressively the public utilities in the broadest sense. However, there is a considerable amount of damage to buildings. Whilst a number of the smaller ones, especially by the sea, have been destroyed, only a few major structures appear to have been damaged beyond repair. Elsewhere, in many of the major buildings, although the damage is very significant indeed, the structures appear to be reasonably secure, but, logically, detailed inspection will progressively determine the validity of that view. The hospitals, we understand, seem to have survived quite well. I am sure Howard will talk to you about them in far more detail.

The oil, gas and petro-chemical sector is an area that holds particular intertest for UK companies, my own especially, whether onshore or offshore. It is fair to say that it was impossible in the time available for us to get close enough to have a personal overview. However, the picture that we have been given by the Prime Minister and his team - and by the British army in particular - is that the damage is extensive and major reconstruction will be required, as the ambassador said earlier. The huge, black cloud that you see so often on television is there. Howard has a magnificent photograph taken on Tuesday, where you cannot see anything at all except a dull glow. The fires can be seen for miles. We were told that the fires were beginning to burn a little brighter, but I am sure that will be progressively the case anyway.

The decision was taken to relocate the Task Force from Dammam into Kuwait in offices within the British Embassy. Having done that, we shall be able to get much closer to the detail of what is required in each sector and feed that information back to the UK and all the businesses interested in becoming involved.

Overall, therefore, whilst the scale of reconstruction is, happily, nowhere near as large as was at first expected, it is nonetheless very considerable indeed, and there are good opportunities for British companies. However, everyone needs to remember that in the short term Kuwait is under military control. To travel anywhere, you must be under military escort, with no power or water, although, hopefully, that will begin to come on stream, as we have heard, this week. There are no customs, no immigration, no police, no shops, no banks, virtually no hotels, as I just mentioned, and security is - and must remain in the short term - paramount for everybody.

We were very impressed by the effectiveness and simplicity of the way in which the Kuwaiti government is now working without the normal communications systems. One must remember, they cannot pick up the telephone and check with people regularly. They have a Cabinet meeting at 8 o'clock every morning and as soon as it is over each minister goes off to monitor the progress in his own area of responsibility before reconvening at 8 o'clock each evening to overview progress. We were privileged to have a session with them immediately before one of those Cabinet meetings.

When we visited Taif in early February, we recognised that the most urgent need when hostilities ended was to have accommodation for British companies coming into the area, especially if the feared zero scenario had become a reality. That is why Adrian's idea of a flotel in the harbour was developed by the team and proposed formally to the Kuwaiti government. Since then, however, things have moved very much more quickly than any of us expected, and it became very obvious during our second visit that quicker and more economic options were available to us. We were advised of the presence of the old British army liaision camp at Fuhayhil, some 26 kilometers from Kuwait City, which we inspected. The Iraqis had looted and vandalised it unbelievably, but the buildings remain in excellent structural condition, and it was clear that the camp could be quickly re-established to serve the needs of British companies. Adrian will tell us about this in some detail. It was necessary to have some decisions made quickly, so Adrian and I immediately undertook to underwrite the cost of refurbishing the camp so that it would be available in the shortest time. Not only is it a good base to work from, but it can relate directly to the armed services and to the hard-pressed British Embassy team under Michael Weston. I understand that refurbishment is going quite well.

Once more the Prime Minister and members of the Cabinet restated how eager they were to see British companies win a good share of the work available. I have no doubt that we shall, provided that we all work hard and produce competitive proposals. The ambassador said earlier, "Time, cost and quality". It is important to remember those three ingredients measured together. Not only price, but time is very important in Kuwait just now. Being able to measure those three ingredients together is crucial.

It is, for example, becoming progressively clear that companies that have carried out work on some of the buildings that are now damaged have particularly good potential. We had a good illustration of that. In the conversation with one of the Ministers it became clear that Bovis had been responsible some years ago for the General Assembly building. Immediately after the meeting, Christian was able to go to the one satellite phone that was available anywhere and call to Frank Lamplough of Bovis to say that here was a special opportunity for his company if he could jump on to it straightaway - and he did. Those consultants, suppliers and contractors who have been responsible for buildings and installations in Kuwait over the years are in possession of information concerning those facilities, which at the moment the Kuwaitis do not have.

The 90-day programme to get the basic utilities back in service has only just started. We are in a period of assessing what needs to be done on a more permanent basis. We are trying to give a flavour of the areas where British industry can target most effectively in the later phases. Naturally, there will be an inclination for companies to want to rush out to Kuwait and present their credentials. I hope you will have gathered from what we have all said that in the short term, until the basic services are re-established, it is somewhere between difficult and impossible. It is very important therefore, in my view, to use the Task Force team, which next week will be on the ground in Kuwait and progressively in more instant touch with British industry.

Chris Walton, the commercial counsellor from Riyadh, as I am sure everyone knows, has done an excellent job in charge of the team in the first phase. We are very grateful to him for all is

25

0037

efforts. On 23 March, Laurie Walker will be arriving in Kuwait in a permanent posting from his current role in Ankara and will become a member off the Task Force then.

In summary, the overall amount of civil engineering work to do is negligible. Perhaps as Kuwait gets back on its feet, the amount of new building construction will be limited, but there is a very substantial amount of refurbishment in prospect. It is important to remind ourselves of the reducing number of people in the country in future.

In the oilfields the position is unclear, but our Task Force is addressing that issue urgently and will have a progressively more accurate picture over the next two or three weeks.

Clearly, those companies wanting to start from scratch will have a more difficult time, certainly in the construction industry, compared to those with a track record, but this is not necessarily true in the supply industry. In recent years, it must be said, British construction companies have had some difficulties in relation to contract conditions. We are hopeful that some improvement will be made in this important area.

Now that we are on the ground the quality of the information and the speed with which it is supplied will improve significantly. If we continue to support the Task Force and to focus all our efforts through it and press ahead with maximising the total UK involvement, each of us will benefit more significantly in the longer term. The more fragmented our approach is, the more difficult it will be for the government of Kuwait to respond to the hordes of people who are so anxious, even within the 90-day period, to get themselves established on the ground. It is especially difficult for the British ambassador and his team to deal with the many, many requests. It is opening up, and it will open up a good deal faster as the normal services come into operation. We should not panic about the orders placed in the first few weeks; the real volume of business is to follow.

CHAIRMAN: Thank you very much indeed, Alan. Again there is time for very quick questions, but he can stay until the end, so can we take most of them in the panel?

FRANCIS CUBITT (Hawker Siddeley Group): On wage rates. I understand that due to short supply and danger money premiums expatriate managers and technicians are being paid something like double pre-invasion rates for working out in Kuwait. For example, carpenters are said to be earning about £60,000 a year at the moment. This is understandable perhaps during the emergency period with mines about all over the place and so forth, but if it continues, it will not help our competitiveness in the long term. Could you comment on that, please?

ALAN COCKSHAW: I agree. It is very difficult in the short term. It is quite dangerous at the moment, not to overstate it. Mines are not cleared; there is still a fair amount of risk, and that is why everyone who goes there has to be under military escort. But progressively areas are being cleared, and it will return to a sense of normality. Therefore any wage rates that are appropriate now are not necessarily going to be the wage rates that will apply at the end of the three-month period. I do not think we should get too carried away with what the conditions are now. In three months' time we shall have a totally different picture.

CHAIRMAN: Thank you very much, Alan. We move on now to the consultancy side and we are lucky today to have Bill Pirie with us. Bill came to Taif on our visit to see the government in exile, representing the British Consultants Bureau, and he has been with Sir Alexander Gibb for longer than he cares to remember.

THE CONSULTANTS' EXPERIENCE

WILLIAM PIRIE (Chairman of the British Consultants Bureau and Member of the Task Force): Good morning, ladies and gentlemen. My brief is to talk to you about the consultants' experience in Kuwait, and I am going to do that for a short period. I shall tell you what we have been up to over the years there and about the recent consultant market in Kuwait. I will mention that, because we believe it is going to revert to what was happening just before August sooner rather than later. Then I will say what we have been up to as a sector since 2 August. Then, I am delighted to say, I am going to be able to sit down and you are going to see some pictures from Nigel Thompson, who is a director of Ove Arup. He returned from Kuwait last Friday and has some pictures to show you and will talk about today and tomorrow. Lastly, I am delighted to say that on the panel we have Bill Hyatt of W S Atkins, who handled Atkins's very considerable affairs in Kuwait from 1982 until 11 December 1990, so you will note that he is a hostage. He knows something about the market that I believe we can all benefit from.

I speak to you as chairman of the MENA Committee of the BCB, which probably none of you knows anything about. I had better explain what it is. The BCB is a trade association of professional firms, if that is not a contradiction in terms. It has about 250 members, drawn from enginers, architects, quantity surveyors and a rather stimulating bunch of others, who include most of the major banks and financial advisers, planners and other sophisticated experts. The BCB is set up to promote consultancy services abroad. It does this through a series of outward missions, inward visits, briefings to diplomats going abroad and so on and other meetings. It also has a good directory which has a wide distribution through our embassies around the world and other such places. The BCB is a focal point for discussions with the British Government and the consultancy sector, and that is probably why I am standing here today. It has a number of committees, some divided by discipline and some geographical. That is where the MENA bit comes in.

To revert to consultants in Kuwait, we have been there since 1950, when Harris, I think, was the first firm to start designing hospitals there. We have been there ever since, designing, planning and project managing large portions of the infrastructure of Kuwait and many of its buildings. I have to say that so far as members of the BCB are concerned the oil sector has been rather for the specialist firms and the oil work has been carried out by the majors, mostly American, but some of them British.

That activity has continued through the changing Kuwait market and on 2 August 1990 there were about 20 firms with ongoing contracts. Luckily, it was August, so a lot of our staff were away, but they did have a lot of hostages. We hope very much that those firms with current contracts may find them reinstated, because not only have they been through the trauma of having their staff stuck there in uncertain circumstances, but they have lost a hell of a lot of money.

Apart from those 20-odd firms, there were more who either had work in Kuwait or were bidding for projects in Kuwait or had associations with Kuwaiti firms. They, apart from anything else, held a lot of records of Kuwaiti projects. As has been heard, the damage, thank God, is not as bad as expected, but still those records will be useful. A number of the firms concerned have already been called back to Kuwait to advise the ministries concerned in reinstating damaged facilities.

I hope this explains to you that the consultancy sector probably has unparalleled knowledge of Kuwait and how its construction works. Perhaps most important of all, it has jolly good friends

27

0039

both in the public and private sectors of the Kuwait market. Initially, when Harris went in, this market was for international firms only. Then about 20 years ago the Kuwaiti professionals who had been trained abroad began to return and they formed some excellent Kuwaiti consultant companies. These firms grew and were very successful. Some had up to 300 staff in the mid-1980s and some were backed by very rich families. They had wonderful facilities, which were, frankly, the envy of some of us who did not have such backing. Those firms had generally run down to some extent by August 1990 - as the market went down in the Middle East, it affected them too - and their numbers were greatly reduced; nevertheless they were there, and a formidable force.

That force created a change in the bidding procedures for consultants in that it was absolutely essential in current bids to pre-qualify, which was quite a difficult process, and to pre-qualify also with good Kuwaiti joint venture partners. That was also a difficult process, because they had a buyer's market; the whole world was knocking at their doors, and they tended to form associations on a project-by-project basis.

Another reason to associate with Kuwaiti firms was that the Arab-funded projects abroad - which, as many of you know, were sometimes led by the Kuwait fund itself - were creating a continuing requirement for firms to associate with Arab companies on Arab-funded projects. That is fair enough: it was their money and they wanted to participate. It was a competitive market, difficult to get pre-selected, difficult to get the right joint venture and price was very important. Kuwait is not a rich place without being interested in the bottom line.

I refer to all this background because we are having indications from our members talking to Kuwaiti officials that they are going to try to reform the ministries sooner rather than later. We foresee the market returning on the consultancy side to what happened before. We also see preference being given to firms with good joint venture partners with Kuwaiti firms, which are probably pretty shattered at the moment but which will be favoured to try to re-establish their original capacity.

What have we been up to since 2 August? We had a MENA Committee meeting in December, at which time the hostages had just been let out. All the members of that committee are very experienced in working in the Middle East and most of them had good connections with Kuwait and were making their individual representations to Fauzi Al Sultan of KERP in Washington. Bechtel had just had its letter of intent reported to manage the oil sector, and at that time there was hot gossip that Parsons were going to do a similar exercise on the civil side. We realised, sitting round the table at the MENA Committee, that the firms represented there were much bigger than Parsons. Parsons is bigger than us individually, but combined we were stronger; also we had much more experience of the market. So we said we had got to work together, and we have started to do that ever since. That to a degree is evidenced by this talk being presented by three people from the consultancy sector.

We started a directory over Christmas of firms that were interested or involved in Kuwait, which served as part of the brief for John Major when he visited Taif on 3 January and referred to the construction industry for the first time. We have also been participating in Christian Adams's activities at the DTI by serving on his various sub-committees.

I visited the Kuwaiti government in Taif on 9 February with the British team that travelled with Douglas Hurd. Whilst the goodwill was warmly expressed, the right price was also added into the argument. How we are going to get into British hands the percentages that have been talked about is something we shall have to work hard at. The following week, Richard French of Atkins, who had been managing Atkins's affairs from Epsom with Bill Hyatt at the other end, joined the UK Task Force. I think it was his friendship with Ali Abdullah, the chief engineer of the Kuwaiti PWD, who was serving on KERP in Dammam at the time, that facilitated to a great extent the success of the communications with the KERP office, which, you will understand, was in a state of some excitement, because the war was going on and it was a very uncertain time for them. The reporting back that Richard has done to our members in BCB has catalysed the concerns of people to look after their interests and has given them an up-to-date, realistic view of what is going on in our sector.

Obviously, through the general government sectors there is a broader view, but the British consultants who are involved in Kuwait are very pleased to have somebody on the Task Force who can report to them and co-ordinate their interests going the other way.

Richard has been replaced now by Jack Knight, who is from Mushell. Mushell had 90 staff in Kuwait on 2 August, although, thank God, most of them were on leave; they nevertheless had 15 hostages. He is delighted that he is moving out to Kuwait tomorrow, because it has been rather frustrating the last couple of weeks with KERP in Kuwait and the Task Force in Dammam.

Rather like the DTI directory, we threw our first one together in a hell of a hurry and upset all sorts of people. We are now preparing a better directory of British consultants who have worked primarily in Kuwait, but in the adjacent states as well. It may be quite a useful document for a lot of people here. It will be available from the BCB by the end of the month.

I will just mention the US Corps of Engineers. Their initial programme is for the 90-day emergency programme. There was concern when an advertisement appeared in the Commerce Business Daily of 19 February asking for more wide-ranging services to be lodged with the Corps of Engineers. We have a feeling that this was a bit of a kite, because, as I said, we believe that the Kuwaiti ministries are going to re-establish themselves quickly and take their affairs into their own hands again. Nevertheless, if they find that they need an administrative arm, the US Corps of Engineer's call for pre-qualification for many firms - mainly consultants, but others too - may put it in a position to take on that management role. HMG should watch this with the US government.

I may have given the impression that consultants feel that the market will return to exactly what it was. That is probably true, but it does not mean to say that we are not looking at opportunities for design and construct packages if that is the way the Kuwaitis are going to move. A lot of our firms are not working for public sector clients any more. In Saudi Arabia, for instance, a number of firms are working with very large work loads to British Aerospace on the Al Manamah project. My own firm's biggest contract at the moment is for the Korean contractors Don Ar on the great man-made river in Libya, which one might say is a fairly orderly island in a rather unpredictable jamboreean sea. There has also been mentioned in the press Acer's combination with Trafalgar House and Kayser and Ove Arup with Laing on the health side; we are flexible and moving with today. With that, I am going to hand you over to Nigel Thompson for the picture show.

NIGEL THOMPSON (Director of Ove Arup): I was lucky enough to follow Christian and his team into Kuwait last Tuesday. Fortunately for me, I met them in Riyadh on Monday and Alan Cockshaw gave me some very good advice. He said, "For heaven's sake, buy a torch". That was enormously useful to us, because when they were there, although there was some black cloud, the wind was generally blowing it away from Kuwait, but when we arrived the wind had stopped and the cloud came right down. When we went to the embassy at midday, you could not see a yard in front of your face, it was that bad.

29

0041

I should also say that as consulting engineers, Ove Arup have been in Kuwait for more than 20 years. We have built over 60 kilometers of motorway, the Doha pass and very many buildings, some of which have been damaged.

(Copies of the following slides were not available in time for inclusion in this document)

Slide 1

This shows you the only way in at the moment, provided you have a contract. It is not easy. The excellent Hercules.

Slide 2

This is at the airport. We went round the airport and saw it in considerable detail. This is the communication tower. Inside it is horrific, but the structure is sound.

Slide 3

This is probably the most photographed plane, the British Airways plane that the Americans blew up. It is taken from the control tower.

Slide 4

Again the airport. This is as we arrived. The photographs are not very good, but that is because of the light. The sky was that colour. It sometimes rains, and it rained the sort of stuff that you spray over the apple trees in the winter.

Slide 5

Again you see the airport. Inside it was horrific, the fires, the looting and the devastation. There were two kinds of damage really, organised looting, which took place very early on. We even found it in the hospitals and universities. The professors from Iraq came down and organised the systematic removal of the computers, books and equipment. Even in the high voltage power distribution system the pylons were cut off at the base and transported back to Iraq. Later it was individual looting and vandalism on an horrific scale.

Slide 6

Inside the airport. Some of this has been cleaned up a bit. I only show that because of the sky. This was later and the cloud was lifting towards Kuwait, but you can see the black layer above the rest of the airport.

Slide 7

Again inside the airport. More shots inside. Although we say they are not major civil engineering contracts, which is true, in most large building contracts the structure, which in these cases is still sound, only represents 20% of the cost. The other 80% has been significantly damaged. That was all terminal 2. It is pretty significant damage, but the main part of the structure is not too bad, although I expect there one needs to remove the entire hangar.

Slide 8

These are more administrative buildings and a hotel at the airport next to terminal 1. It does not look bad, but inside it is unspeakable.

Slide 9

That is a medical building next to the hotel. You can see the cars there. They are looted, the whole lot. Terminal 1 is virtually totally destroyed, but it was not much of a building anyway.

Slide 10

This is the Sheraton. There are three blocks. The block on the left of the picture they were in the middle of refurbishing, so it did not have a lot of furniture in it. They took furniture from other parts to set light to it. They pulled everybody out and burnt it. The block on the right, the most recent one, again does not look too bad, but where it is very black, the floors are quite gutted. Then there are some holes where a tank fired at it and knocked holes through it. In that particular building there were signs where they had taken some of the residents hostage; all their belongings were still left.

Slide 11

That is another building, a typical street shop.

Slide 12

That is part of the Sheraton again. That is the coffee shop. That is a typical bedroom - you can see plumbing facilities and things, ripe for modernisation.

Slide 13

Another shot of the inside of an hotel. In the Sheraton and the Meridian the lifts have gone. These are the controls outside the lift. You can see that the telephone has melted.

Slide 14

That is part of the communications centre down town. Again the building does not look too bad, but it is inside where they have had all the fires.

Slide 15

That is the Meridien, again a rather bad shot. It was a brighter sky then. In the Meridien, which is quite well designed - there is a plug there - the fire has not gone all the way through the building; it did not go up through all the ducts and everything, because they were properly sealed. There is terrific damage on the bottom two floors. It needs a major amount of work and all the ebony etc. needs to be reinstated.

Slide 16

There it is again. My camera packed up, so I have no decent photographs of the inside.

Slide 17

That is the new port building. Where you see damage to the glass, that is usually because there has been a fire inside or a tank has fired at it. The possibilities for glazing and ceiling contracts are fantastic.

Slide 18

This is the Kuwaiti Institute of Scientific Research, a very high quality building, well constructed and well designed. Lots of computers inside there were plundered. Round the back there were terrible fires in all the laboratory areas. You can see on the righthand side where they had a tank and fired a few holes. They were not very good with their tanks; they were not very effective in knocking holes through things. You can see some of the damage. They are just shells.

Slide 19

This is part of the entrance to the Parliament building. With all the fires there have been in these buildings, the soot and the debris is horrendous. You all know, if you have had a fire, about getting the soot out of things and the smell. The cleaning up operation is huge. Inside the Parliament building they lit fires at either end. The main assembly hall is just horrific. There were some big circular columns supporting the roof, and the structure has been damaged to a degree because the columns were split by the heat back to the reinforcement. There is quite a bit of damage and an excellent job for Bovis, if it can get it. There are lots of those around.

I will mention briefly one or two things. I mentioned the two kinds of looting. Michael Weston, as Alan said, has given tremendous support. He and his team are working seven days a week from 6am until midnight and giving fantastic support in exceptionally difficult circumstances. When it was really black, at the end of the day your eyes hurt. One day it was dark all day long; it was very difficult. Going round, we had two soldiers in the car with us. There is no electricity, no water; the atmosphere is polluted and there are road blocks and a terrific amount of rubbish. There are no cars. The ones we had were those the military had managed to get working. There are cars all round the place with wheels and bits missing. There are no workshops anywhere, no supplies. There is a huge opportunity for repair, refurbishment, re-equipping and refurnishing, to design and construct buildings, industrial plants and workshops.

The US Corps of Engineers has a stranglehold on this position. They have already let a contract to Brown & Root and Karafi for damage assessment and, I understand, repair of all public buildings. How are those of us who have been responsible for designing the buildings going to get in there?

While we were there, we heard that Shand's contract - they were the one British contractor that had got 20% of the first stage - had been reduced by 75%. It has been reduced for two reasons. First, the American Corps of Engineers had overestimated the amount of work and, secondly, through the local ministry a local Kuwaiti contractor was going to be given a slice of the Shand work. That shows that we are already back to the old system of operation. To a certain extent I think that is an advantage, because every consultant and contractor among us who has been involved in Kuwait stands a chance of getting back in there.

Through Michael Weston we were able to see the Crown Prince two or three times and we saw all the ministers several times on separate occasions. I was able to put the point about those of us who has been responsible as project managers, construction managers or designers - or a combination - having the chance to do the damage assessment. The Saudi company that is doing the Seif palace are getting on now and repairing it. Once you start that, it is the best way to get on. The minister agreed that he would take it out of the hands of the Corps of Engineers. One of his buildings was going to be done by them, one that we had been involved with. So far, so good. I believe it is essential that BCB and EGCI get together and make a list of all the firms that had contracts, so that we can zero in on these different buildings. Provided that a genuine case can be made, we can get in there, but we need to do it now. We are stronger on the ground now than the Americans. All they have done is the work they did in Washington.

The idea of Adrian White and Alan Cockshaw for a Brit camp is excellent. When I told many of the ministers about it, they were very enthusiastic. Many of the buildings have been vandalised, and if we had a group of people there with mobile workshops, a project manager and people to handle the plumbing and some carpentry work, we would be in there. We need to have a sheet written in Arabic stating what we can do. Being there is the best way to get on.

On the health side, as has been said, the doctors have worked fantastically over the seven months. There will still be opportunities in health, but they will come later, particularly for training in this country or secondment of people.

There is another area where we could be helpful. Through the DTI, the BCB could offer to provide engineers, architects and quantity surveyors to be seconded to the Ministry of Public Works. If you go back to the 1960s, at that time the middle tier was largely British engineers. Latterly it has been run more by the Palestinians. There is a great opportunity for British firms for one of each of the consultants to be seconded there to work for a year. It would make British standards more user-friendly.

We met Wimpeys over there, who managed to get in through their Saudi contacts over the border, although it took them a very long time to get in. They were rather depressed. They are working as advisers with Karafi, who have some of the contracts for the American Corps of Engineers. Wimpey's view was that the American Corps of Engineers had such a strong hold that the only way forward was for British firms to have a US partner. I do not think that is necessary yet. Provided you have a genuine connection, you should follow that route first. Undoubtedly the opportunities are in the building materials side, in glazing, ceilings, M & E equipment, doors, light bulbs, paint, furniture and door knobs.

There are a lot of private sector clients there, who think they are terribly poor now, because they are going to have to spend all their money rebuilding their buildings. Many of them will look to us to come up with financial packages. What about the ECGD? Is there any chance of getting ECGD support? We need to have a clear line on this.

I was lucky enough to go to Twickenham on Saturday. To show you how hard the embassy works, it got a message through to me at Twickenham and I had to ring the British ambassador from the rugby football ground. The embassy works all the time. It made a request for the DTI to set up a special sub-group on building refurbishment.

Finally, a Kuwaiti said to me at the weekend that if Britain is not getting its share, there is a simple thing we could do: send Margaret Thatcher over there on a visit!

CHAIRMAN: Thank you very much indeed. Just before everybody goes -I see that some of you have to peel off for lunch - may I mention that AMEC and Biwater, who are represented by their Chairman, Adrian White, today, are also very much involved in the Brit camp that we have been talking about. Adrian, do you want to give telephone numbers or anything right now?

ADRIAN WHITE: The implementation of the camp, how to get there, what to do when you are there and what facilities are available I shall give in a five-minute slot which comes up in 10 minutes. If any of you have to go and you need to register that you wish to go to Kuwait yourself or with your staff, I ask you to fax - not telephone, because, like the DTI, they cannot handle 2,000 calls a day - your interest to 0306-885233. By the end of this week we will send you the complete Brit pack. It is very important that you try, where possible, to toe the Brit line, first, because your chance of getting paid during the next three months will be enhanced and, secondly, your chance of staying out of prison, either on the border or in Kuwait, and staying safe will be greatly enhanced, together with the facilities that we can make available, which are currently not available in Kuwait.

CHAIRMAN: One of our successes so far has been that of the International Hospitals Group, who have managed to secure a contract. Here to talk about it for us is Mr Howard Lyons, the managing director. Howard, welcome.

CASE STUDY OF A SUCCESSFUL CONTRACT TENDER: THE INTERNATIONAL HOSPITALS GROUP

HOWARD LYONS (Managing Director of the International Hospitals Group): Thank you very much. Good morning, ladies and gentlemen - or should I say "good afternoon" by now? It has been a long morning. I do not want to detain you much longer other than to tell a brief tale that warms my heart and, I hope, will warm yours, not by way of envy, but by encouragement: in these days of deep recession there are contracts that can be won very quickly and implemented, particularly in the opportunities presented in Kuwait at the moment.

By way of background, International Hospitals Group has been managing public and military hospitals in the Middle East since 1970. Since the mid-1970s we have been involved in recruitment, procurement, management consultancy and hospital management in the UK, Middle East, Far East and Africa. We currently employ approximately 4,000 health care professionals worldwide. From August onwards, like many of you, we were approached by a number of Kuwaitis in exile, who asked to represent our interests in the anticipated rebuilding of Kuwait following liberation. Nobody knew when it would be or what the situation would be like following the liberation, so, probably like many of you, we kept our options open. We could not find our own agent - I hope he is not in the audience this morning.

We kept our options open throughout that period. We have been associated with the British Health Care Consortium, but the contact that eventually came to us was only a week last Friday morning. It came direct from a senior government minister in the Kuwaiti government, who contacted us through the British ambassador. That was a week last Friday, and the Task Force was due to depart on the Saturday. The details were fairly sketchy, but we were told to get on a plane as quickly as possible. Two of us went out on the Saturday with the Task Force and arrived having slept at Riyadh airport overnight in transit because we did not have visas. On Sunday morning we were met by Michael Weston, the ambassador, who immediately took us off to a meeting with the Minister of Health and the team that had been responsible for maintaining health services throughout the occupation. They were keen to impress us, understandably, by the work they had done during that time. The minister seemed keen also to let them continue to hold the fort and to decide their own priorities for re-establishing health services. Generally speaking, there was no structural damage, but a lot of equipment had been stolen, as other speakers have said. There will be a need for a lot of re-equipping, but initially the Task Force appointed by the Minister of Health, representing the various Ministry of Health hospitals, is doing its own assessment of its equipment needs during the emergency phase and is also looking at its legal arrangements to see where equipment was under warranty and therefore in some way protected. After rushing out there at short notice, as you can imagine, we were a trifle disappointed to find that the Ministry of Health did not need any help at the moment, thank you.

In the afternoon, however, we got an invitation to go to the military hospital. Although from a humanitarian point of view it was discouraging, from a commercial point of view it was encouraging to see bags of dirt, linen and all kinds of refuse all round the hospital, which was obviously in need of a major clean-up operation. We realised then that perhaps we had arrived at the right place. We were well received at the hospital. It was evident from the first meeting that our name was known and that was why our company had been invited to go in at short notice. Nevertheless, there was still quite a bit of work to be done to assess their requirements and we agreed to return on the Monday to look at each department's needs in detail with a view to preparing a proposal.

As has already been mentioned, the next morning we had the opportunity to meet the Crown Prince and Members of the Cabinet. It was there confirmed that we were at the right place: that was where the lead had originated and therefore the urgent task to be undertaken had support from the very top.

We spent the rest of the day going round the departments in the hospital, taking photographs to enable us to brief people at home about the conditions there. Some of you may know that the military hospital took a long time to plan, build and commission. As someone said afterwards, it was nicely set up for the Iraqi invasion. They took over the hospital, which they used as one of the prime locations for treating their many casualties towards the end of the war. When we arrived the hospital had been used for treating a large number of Iraqi casualties. It was obvious that they had departed as quickly as possible once it was clear that Kuwait would be liberated by Allied troops. They had left theatres in the middle of operations, beds stained with blood and disgusting faecal material in various parts of the hospital, creating a health hazard and making it no place to treat patients at the moment. They had also marked rooms for removal of equipment or vandalism and so that the hospital had been quite severely damaged.

We assessed the needs during Monday and that evening, with the help of the only telephone line and fax into the country, communicated with our Head Office to prepare a proposal. In fact we were asked to prepare a contract in the form of a proposal contract for presentation on the Tuesday. We prepared a contract for 12 months, which involves the reinstatement of the hospital to restore it to its state before 2 August 1990. That involves a major clear up exercise, but also putting in staff to sort out all the support services, including catering, laundry, sterilisation, engineering and maintenance, biomedical equipment, stores and supplies.

We prepared that on Monday evening and took the proposal contract with us on Tuesday when we were met by a team of people in the hospital responsible for assessing their requirements. The proposals were well received and they went off to the appropriate Minister to gain his approval. The only time things went wrong was whilst we were waiting for the proposal's return, when the Army lost my baggage! But by the end of Tuesday I had a signed contract and jumped on to a New Zealand Hercules to get me back to Riyadh. I was then stuck there because I did not have a visa!

I arrived home on Thursday not only with a signed contract, which was obviously very valuable, but also a letter instructing the Kuwaiti Embassy here in London to make a mobilisation payment. I went to the Embassy on Friday and we received payment in Sterling. Our team went out on Saturday and hopefully will be there in the hospital now, although the contract officially starts tomorrow.

That is the history of the contract showing that there are days in God's providence when things work out well. Most of the time, obviously, it does not work out like that. My practical suggestions as to how you can secure business in Kuwait reflect my own experience and in no way represent a company or Task Force view. One or two tips are that if Michael Weston or Christian Adams contacts you on the telephone and asks you to get out to Kuwait tomorrow, make sure you are on the first plane. They will give you a good lead as to the prospects you are pursuing. Secondly have a broad idea of what you can offer, but wait to hear what the client wants, rather than trying to foist on him your solution before you know what his problems are. That may seem obvious, but there is a tendency when you are working so quickly to give a ready-made solution. Shape your response according to the client's needs, which is particularly true in the case of services.

Respond promptly, there and then. It was important that we were able to put a contract proposal together out there and bring it back to them the next day. It does not need to be too elaborate: they understand better than we do the difficulties in communicating with Head Office. Respond promptly there and then, because if you do not, there are the Americans, French and many others who will act promptly, given the opportunity. The response does not need to be detailed, but the need to mobilise quickly is important. It was important to our client for us to say that we would have people on site by the weekend. I said that we would be there next week, meaning the British week, but they obviously thought I meant the Muslim week and therefore we had to have people there on Saturday and Sunday. The contract, as I have said, starts on Tuesday and we had a week in which to fully mobilise. Mobilisation will be the next problem that we face.

In terms of agents I have to be careful what I say. You have had guidance from the National Bank of Kuwait and heard from other representatives on the Task Force and you have heard how we had quite a number of approaches. In the emergency phase, the first 90 days when martial law prevails, my advice would be to assume that you do not need an agent until either the client insists you have one, or your existing agent reappears. If you have no agent, or he has disappeared, be careful who you sign up with. See what the agent can do for you first. Remember that those who left Kuwait during the occupation may be at a considerable disadvantage with those who stayed. As you can imagine, there is some tension between those two sections of the community, which is likely to increase rather than diminish. The way things are going you will undoubtedly need an agent again eventually, so be careful not to give offence to anyone. I suggest that the potential client is the person who can give you the best guidance on that.

My final tip would be that you should be prepared to rough it when you go to Kuwait. You have already heard some of the tales about the hotels we stayed in, or sleeping on the floor of the Embassy. Most of all, do not pick up any strange objects. Kuwait is still a very dangerous place.

I hope that my tale stimulates optimism amongst the British community. The Kuwaitis I met were very pro-British and keen to have our help. There was a lovely sign up outside one of the burnt out hotels which said "Thank you very much Mrs Tatcher[sic]!" They obviously have a lot of respect for the British - and Mrs Thatcher in particular. They will not forget their friends easily.

Healthy competition notwithstanding, I trust that every business represented here today will benefit, whether directly or indirectly, from the opportunities presented by the enormous challenge of rebuilding Kuwait. Thank you.

CHAIRMAN: Thank you very much Howard, and again, our congratulations on moving so fast. I can only take two questions just now, but there will be a chance later.

RALPH WILLIAMS (The National Bank of Kuwait): On the subject of agencies - we receive many calls in the Bank from various companies inquiring about where their agents may be. It staggers me that many of the people who ring us have no real details about the agent. Please look through your records first and give us the full name if you are trying to trace someone. I should quickly say that we do not offer a tracing service, but if we can help, we do. May I also remind you that in the case of many of the old merchant families, the head of the family or in some cases their sons, were taken to Baghdad and may not have been released. I have friends, who represent several large UK companies, who are in that situation. If you cannot contact them, please be patient and keep trying.

I should like too welcome Bill back: we spent the same time there together. I am sure that he would second me in reminding the panel that the Fahaheel camp was called locally Tenco, after a famous book.

CHAIRMAN: Thank you. The gentleman just in front of you.

PAUL HARRIS (Able Staff): In supplying engineers to Kuwait, will any form of security clearance be needed. If we have to respond and act quickly, how soon can security passes be made available?

CHRISTIAN ADAMS: We have not come across this yet. So far we have only been sending small numbers. We shall look at that problem as it arises and let you know quickly. It would have to be done with the Foreign Office if there was a problem.

CHAIRMAN: I apologise for cutting short this particular part, but in about five minutes we shall be able to go into a full panel session. Perhaps I could ask Adrian White to go into more detail on his camp. Adrian, who will need little introduction, is Chairman of Biwater Limited, one of the moving forces in this team.

THE BRIT CAMP AND THE BRIT PACK

ADRIAN WHITE (Chairman, Biwater Limited): The food was not that bad, but there is a follow-up story on the gas cylinders. It was not that we, as engineers, were totally incompetent, because they informed us afterwards that the butane cylinders supplied had been shipped out, for safety, full of compressed air!

0049

37

The greatest need in Kuwait today is for the technician. That is the man with the screwdriver and with the spanner. To get him in is not too difficult, certainly up till the end of the 90 period. After that it will be more difficult when the requirement for visas and the permits just mentioned may be enforced. We have taken the initiative through and with the support of the DTI over four months ago as you know and we have had time to prepare. To get into Kuwait at present the only air access is by the RAF and they are to terminate that shortly - certainly within the next fortnight. Therefore things could become much more difficult. At the border they were moving at the rate of one foot a day. Things have moved on since then and now they are not moving at all. Yet when I spoke to the Ambassador this morning he said that it takes about 11 hours to get across the border. With the greatest respect, that may be the case for some Kuwaiti-inspired help, but the position at the border at the moment is pretty well deadlocked. Therefore if it is possible, and we are now on our knees to the Ministry of Defence, to give us additional help for air transport, not only for people but for goods, we need it and we need it today. Tremendous pressure has been applied to the Ministry of Defence by the armed forces in the field today and to the various Ministers this morning. Hopefully we shall have better news tomorrow morning.

There are 120 telephone lines working in Kuwait and they hope to have many more functioning by the end of this week.

There is no public transport because the bulk of it has had its wheels removed and taken to Iraq. There is no electricity or water and there is no food. The shops are shut. We are totally dependent, therefore, on yourselves taking with you that which is required. We were, even as a mission, forced to stay in the Embassy, though we did try a hotel. There are at the moment approximately 250,000 current residents in Kuwait and the only two commodities, bread and fuel, are available free to anyone in Kuwait by courtesy of the Kuwait Government.

You must be aware that martial law exists until the end of May. There is a dusk to dawn curfew and there are many road blocks. Therefore travelling on your own in Kuwait City at present is, I believe, out of the question. You need some form of armed guard and to date we have had British Army soldiers with us. That is essential because they also have wheels!

We are proposing to have available at the camp from tomorrow morning accommodation for 20 people and an RAF Hercules is taking in the bulk of the equipment and people then, with the help of Rustons' aircraft the furniture will go into the camp today. The camp was stripped bare by the Iraqis when they left. It was cleared by the Ordnance Section of the Army last Wednesday and the following day the Army Engineers went in to hook up a temporary supply for electricity and for water. A further team went in willingly over the weekend (because they said that they were fed up with making sand castles in the desert) to clear the camp. Therefore with the courtesy of the armed forces, whose help has been first class, the camp will be up and running tomorrow.

An Inmarsat telephone will be arriving tomorrow and that will have Telefax and Telex. As the Embassy themselves only enjoy one line through a similar facility this will be available at a premium, though not in terms of cost, which will be at net.

At the camp there will be food, transport and accommodation and on those days when the wind is blowing in that direction, there will be face-masks available for those in the camp during any smog periods. We have 40 radio units going in for mobile and hand use. This is for British industry, not for Biwater, AMEC, Rustons or BEI who are all mobilising to get people out there specifically. We ask you to move. A few of us have contracts because we are aware, having met the Ministers, that they require technicians. They did not know before they went in what was required, but they do know as they come across it.

0050

This has evoked a plea from the Ministers that we provide technicians and that they have a direct line to our camp - and therefore to British industry. If you are prepared to take a gamble and place somebody out there, we, as an accumulated group on behalf of British industry, will provide you with those facilities at a cost considerably less than a hotel in the days when Kuwait was quiet.

This requires some discipline on our part because Ministers are frightened to sign anything which commits them to something that could bite them afterwards. Each of us is very good for stating the requirement for returnable packing cases in the form of "accommodation (or food or air flights) will be extra for the services of our engineer". They do not want that. They want a composite rate which needs to be defined for one man/week. That is something to which we have bent our minds and have prepared one overall rate, whether for a fitter, welder, electrician, carpenter or any other standard tradesman. Hopefully since this rate will include accommodation, food, the flight and transport you will find it acceptable. A complete breakdown of the rate will be available in the Britpack which you are entitled to receive free by courtesy of British industry if you submit your application on the fax number 0306 (Dorking) 885233. We ask that unless you have somebody with exceptional skills outside the bracket I have outlined, you use that rate. Whether you do or do not, if you operate from the camp we shall ask you to adhere to sensible rules: not travelling at night, travelling wearing the Britcamp shirt (which will be provided out there and which has a union jack on the front shoulders and pocket), the name "Brit" should be on the vehicle and on your shirt (it can be unsafe to approach a series of road blocks and either be flippant or informally dressed and not recognised as British).

If you obtain a contract, we recommend that you use a Brit daywork sheet or material purchase order, with your name and the client's name on it. They are not buying from Brit, but from you. But because it is on this standard notepaper there will be instant recognition and also your chances of being paid will be improved, (although not necessarily guaranteed if your terms and conditions are not right). There will be standard terms and conditions which you may adopt and make available to the client.

Finally there are passes which every UK industry member is advised to wear. These have been printed for us in arabic by the Riyadh Embassy. Everyone should have a photograph taken at the camp and carry the pass wherever he or she goes. Britain stands for a lot in Kuwait. They are tremendously supportive and they want to place work with us. The most telling point was that the Ministers said "Because that which is British still works, we now want to go back to British standards".

Ladies and gentlemen, I urge you to take up this challenge and join us in Kuwait.

CHAIRMAN: Thank you Adrian. We shall now move into our panel discussion, for which we are joined by others (who have kindly consented to be here this morning and have so far been listening). You should have in your packs a briefing about them and I do not propose to go through them all individually. As before will you identify yourself and your firm when asking a question, but to give me some guidance can you say to whom the question is addressed. The first question will be one which we had to postpone earlier.

39

0051

PANEL DISCUSSION

Q: Good morning. I have two questions, one of which arises from the last speaker's contribution. Earlier in the presentation we were told that we would not be able to go out, or get into Kuwait, unless we had a contract. Adrian has just said that we should go out with a team of workers on "spec" to live in the camp and be called from there. Is that correct? Secondly, is the camp purely for the accommodation of management or is it also intended as a workers' camp or are alternative arrangements being made for that?

ADRIAN WHITE: You do not need a contract to get in, but certainly you can get in faster if you have one. If you liaise through the transport arrangements that we are trying to standardise that will avoid the RAF being pestered in ones and twos and enable us to fill the one Hercules flight a week which we have now arranged. This will only be for the next few weeks.

CHAIRMAN: The second point was whether the camp is purely for management or workers?

ADRIAN WHITE: No. The accommodation is in three bedroom bungalows very well laid out and spacious. We are replacing the facilities to their former state and there is a swimming pool and tennis courts (which I hope that they will not have time to use). We are expecting a business development manager, for instance, for each company to accompany his technicians and to act as front man, visiting the Ministries to obtain the daywork rate and material supply items.

It is our intention (and I apologise for omitting this) to bring in a roll on, roll off ship with the assistance, we hope, of the Ministry of Defence. They are sending out ships to Jubayel to bring back the tanks and transporter vehicles and we are asking them to divert one in about four weeks time to take in our goods to Shawaba port, Kuwait (which is very near the camp) where we shall also hope to have a workshop operating with the assistance of those hands-on engineers. There should hopefully, be some space available to you on that ship, which will then go on to Jubeyel empty, to help the Army.

CHRISTIAN ADAMS: That is a fair point - there is a certain amount of inconsistency in what we have both said. Let me add to my category of people who can come in those who have come to an arrangement with AMEC and Biwater at the Brit Camp. On the RAF Hercules I would like to add that it is not clear at the moment how long they will continue to fly, when they will fly and what sort of space will be available for us. We are working hard on the problem, but it is clearly related to the withdrawal of British troops and their timetable.

TED COOMBES (Scottish Power): What size will the camp be? How many people will it be able to accommodate and, if organisations like ours say that they can provide 50 people to help put the power lines up or get the power stations running, do you suggest we come to you and ask for places for them?

ADRIAN WHITE: That is correct. There will be 20 spaces available from tomorrow, if you are quick as that, and 200 available by the end of the month, or even sooner. We anticipate expanding that if the response from you is large enough. That means that the roll on, roll off ship will bring in additional accommodation. That further accommodation, beyond 200 people, would not be available for four weeks.

GRAHAM BARHAM (Natco (UK) Ltd): Good morning. I have a question for Alan Cockshaw. We have heard that a lot of equipment has been removed from Kuwait. Do you know what equipment has been removed, in general terms, from the oilfields?

ALAN COCKSHAW: No, we do not know in any detail what equipment has been removed from the oilfields. As far as we are concerned that has virtually been a no-go area. We hope that over the next week or so, now that we have people on the ground, that we shall begin to obtain that information.

RALPH WILLIAMS (The National Bank of Kuwait): Just to update you on the accommodation - while not wishing to detract from the speaker's offer, we have a team already in Kuwait. They are functioning and working out of the Holiday Inn, which is in operation, and they tell me that the Oasis, Plaza and the International Hotels are also operating. Admittedly they do not have all the accommodation that you would wish, but certainly they are there. (That was this morning's information from Kuwait.)

CHAIRMAN: Thank you very much. Of course in the camp we are talking about having quite a lot of almost permanent kit available. In addition, I do not know how well the swimming pool in the Plaza is working! Thank you, though, for bringing us up to date.

WILLIAM LAWRENCE (WH Associates, Epsom): Ramadan has started. Those who have experience that time in the Middle East know that the Arab's maximum working hours are limited to approximately two a day. How will that affect the run-in of the business in the next six to eight weeks?

CHAIRMAN: Although by tradition the working hours have not been as great as some others, certainly the way in which the Ministers were addressing the problems while we were there would lead us to believe that they will get through a considerable workload, even during Ramadan.

CHRISTIAN ADAMS: Can I add that the Ministers were not stopping for Fridays either - they were working a seven day week.

BOB GLASGOW (Droverim Ltd): It is essential, with the logistics involved, that if we take teams in early on we shall have to keep them to a minimum and bring more workers out as and when contracts are obtained. I would have thought that was the best way to go about it.

ALAN COCKSHAW: That must be true. Whilst the camp is being provided for the general use of British industry, it would be foolhardy for people to go in on a wing and a prayer with no idea of the business they were pursuing. That is what is intended. The purpose of the camp is to get something up and running quickly, bearing in mind the current conditions within Kuwait City itself and always remembering what Adrian said - that you need material, equipment and the ability to service that, which is not too easy from a hotel bedroom, even when those are available.

JERRY MARSHALL (Jerry Marshall Associates): Thinking of the longer term, there are many smaller engineering companies that feel they should be doing something about this opportunity, what would you suggest they do at this stage, bearing in mind that they are unlikely to be more involved for several months to come, particularly if they do not have any contacts in Kuwait? I think perhaps this question could be answered by Christian Adams.

CHRISTIAN ADAMS: Are you a member of the BCB?

JERRY MARSHALL: No.

CHRISTIAN ADAMS: What sort of engineering?

JERRY MARSHALL: I am a marketing consultant representing a variety of small engineering companies in sub-contract machining work, distribution, lifting equipment and a range of activities. I am asking this question on their behalf.

CHRISTIAN ADAMS: I think Alan should answer this one.

ALAN COCKSHAW: It has to be said that in the short term, identifying what needs to be done is the key issue. It is true that collectively we shall hopefully finish up having more people on the ground earlier than anyone else. It will rapidly emerge out of that how those people will be serviced. It is extremely important for people such as those companies you represent to keep the task force in the Embassy in Kuwait aware of the services you have available so that as and when the need for those services is demonstrated, they know exactly who to plug into.

CHAIRMAN: Iain Millar (from the DTI) would you like to comment?

IAIN MILLAR: Yes, I would. As you heard earlier, we are building up a data base within the

DTI. There are about 2,500 companies on that at present and they are going on at about 250 per day, although we shall step that up in the near future, hopefully to about 500 per day. Before I answer this gentleman's question specifically, could I make a point here. A large number of companies sending us information are sending it to us in their large brochure packs, which often run to one or two inches thick. The people working on the data base are temporary staff drafted in specifically to put names, addresses, fax numbers etc on to the computer. They are finding it extremely difficult to go through large packs and take out the relevant information. That is slowing us down a lot and if you could keep it to the basics when you send in information, we should be most grateful.

The aim of the data base is threefold. Firstly it is to allow Kuwaitis and others interested in the reconstruction of Kuwait to have a source of information on what Britain has to offer. Secondly it is a source of information to us on who we should target for specific information coming to us on opportunities - projects and otherwise. Thirdly, we hope at some stage to put out newsletters in terms of a general statement of what is happening in Kuwait and that data base will be used as a mail shot data base for newsletters. If you are on it, you are likely to get the information we send out.

The next thing you should be aware of is that across DTI there are a number of contact points. They can give you a fair amount of information, particularly if you are a small or medium sized company. I cannot go into all the types of information now, but perhaps I should say that one of the things that Kuwaiti Ministers said to us was that British companies should look very hard at joint venturing with Kuwaiti, Saudi, Egyptian and other "friendly Arab" consultants and contractors. We are assembling lists at present of contractors and consultants in these countries which we can let you have. That is one sort of information that we can give, but there is much more. Perhaps I could read out some of the numbers you might like to contact at DTI. First of all there are the teams for small, medium or large size projects. Each number is preceded by 071 and 215 the other numbers are as follows: 5381, 4887, 4433, 5268, 4585, 5159. And for more general inquiries, non project, I suggest you try the following numbers: 5491, 4388, 5081, 5221 and 4246.

PETER RICKELL (Maurice Baguley & Partners): This question will probably be directed to Mr Pirie. I have been lead to believe that the BCB are acting as a focal point for British consultancy as a whole. Is this correct, or are you acting only for your members?

WILLIAM PIRIE: No - that is correct. It started off as being for our members, but in consultation with the DTI it became apparent that we should be acting for the consultancy sector as a whole and we have received a number of applications from people who are not members to participate in our meetings. A meeting a week ago was attended by 90 people, again by courtesy of the DTI in their very good cinema, a number of which were not member firms. When it comes to participating and paying for people to be members of the Task Force on behalf of BCB, non-member firms are invited to pay a small premium because they are using BCB facilities without the normal membership charges.

CHAIRMAN: It is interesting to note that none of the questions so far have referred to the ECGD or, indeed, the requirement for it. Perhaps after the next question I could ask Ken Lockwood to touch on that.

PAUL PHILLIPS (Hewden Stuart Wolff Ltd): We are a major equipment hire and supply company. There has been a lot of talk about the need to get labour out there, but no mention of the availability of construction equipment to enable the workers to carry out the work required. Would you comment on that please?

CHRISTIAN ADAMS: The bulk of the plant in there at present, used by the British Army too, has been hired from the Saudis. That is expected to be the main source, in terms of lowest cost for plant, although we expect to be shipping out some of our own plant wherever there is a specialist industry or contracting requirement on the roll on, roll off ship.

MR RAYNER (S&H Housing Ltd): We registered with the DTI about two weeks ago, to be put on the opportunities list. Since then we have been getting calls from all over the United Kingdom from unemployed people wanting work. It is swamping our switchboard. Can you comment?

IAIN MILLAR: I cannot answer your specific question. We have had a number of companies who have expressed an interest in being contacted by others. Each of them was eventually swamped, but this was mainly in the manpower area where half a dozen companies where interested to know of people who would be prepared to work in Kuwait. Of the 2,000 calls we have been getting each day (the Wednesday before last the number peaked at 2,600 calls) a vast number have been from unskilled and skilled labour. These are the people we have been passing on to the manpower agencies. As far as I know, apart from well-known contractors, we have not passed people on to anyone else.

CHAIRMAN: Can we have some comment from the ECGD on the current thinking?

KEN LOCKWOOD: We have completed an urgent review of cover for Kuwait and have proposals currently being considered by the bodies we have to consult. I expect a decision very soon. The proposals include short and medium term cover, foreign risk cover and investment insurance. It is not clear at the moment what demand there will be for cover. In the past Kuwait has not been a major customer of the ECGD, mainly because of course it has been a cash market. We shall have to wait for the result of the assessment of the damage and the projects to be pursued, the Kuwaiti priorities and how they intend to finance them. I cannot, obviously, prejudge the decision of the bodies we have to consult, but I am fairly confident that we shall be able to provide whatever support is needed for British industry in the very near future.

0055

CHAIRMAN: Is it likely that we shall have to wait, particularly for private sector projects, until such time as we see bank records?

KEN LOCKWOOD: Yes. Private sector will obviously be a difficulty. We shall not have up to date information (to the extent to which there is such a thing) on the private sector in Kuwait. That is particularly a problem for my colleague, Dennis Kennedy from Cardiff (who is sitting next to me). Initially I guess that we shall be looking for security and probably ILC terms.

DENNIS KENNEDY: Yes. The availability of information in Kuwait has never really been comparable to that of other major markets. Prior to August we had exposures thereof on the short term side, totally some £150 million. A lot of that is the day to day necessities of life from food stuffs through to small plant machinery and even heavy electrical equipment. Most of that business will have been done with family firms or sole proprietorships and some of the difficulties in trying to assess the credit worthiness of such buyers has been mentioned earlier - whether people are alive or dead, and whether they are still in the country, whether the management of these firms was previously run by expatriates who are no longer there to provide expertise. All of those things are factors that will feature in our decisions and I expect that in the very short term we shall not be able to make realistic judgments of those vital factors and we shall therefore almost certainly be looking at secure terms on private buyers.

CHRIS GORDON-WILSON (Control Risks (Specialist Security Consultants) Ltd): We have heard a lot this morning about how strongly the US are involved in the emergency phase of the reconstruction. The UK actually has significantly greater levels of expertise in marine and land clearance of mines and explosive devices than our US brothers. This is true not only in the military sector but also in the private business sector. Can the Task Force and the DTI say what steps they are taking to stress and exploit these advantages?

IAIN MILLAR: At present we have recognised this by putting on data base a special list of ordnance clearing people and another of fire fighting specialists, which we are making available to those companies who need them. We believe that quite a number of the large companies will find when they go into Kuwait that they need ordnance people as part of their team. As the military begin to withdraw, the need for commercial expertise will grow. Therefore we are taking on to the database a list of commercial ordnance and fire fighting expertise in this country which we are passing on as necessary.

DAVID OWERS (Owers & Lumley, Architects): My question concerns physical planning in the future and takes up the point raised by His Excellency the Ambassador in his emphasis on the five to 10 year, medium term, in planning. It also refers to John Finigan's reference to a population of around 500,000 now and the various forecasts for rapid growth in the next two years or so. The British contribution to planning is unique since the 1950s. The lineage runs through the Minoprio and Spencley planning team, the Buchanan planning team, the contribution of the most recent consultant, Shankland Cox and of course (though not British) the important contribution by Samar Sheba. It is interesting to speculate on the extent to which the physical plan will now be contemplated in a way that takes account of the dangers as well as the possibilities for rapid population growth, leaving aside the nature of that population.

Whilst it is very interesting to hear of the short term crisis planning, which is important, what strategic thinking is taking place and in what areas? Particularly with the British Consultants Bureau, is there an interest and advantage being taken of the UK experience in this critical field for the medium term?

44

0056

CHAIRMAN: On three occasions we talked to His Excellency Dr Suleiman Al-Matawwa about the more medium term aspects and they may use this crisis as an excuse to do some rethinking. Within that context I hope that the excellent advice they have received over the past 40 years from the British will be continued. At this stage, in the short term, they will not be high priority people to be talking to. Many of Dr Suleiman Al-Matawwa's planners are in London and the intention is that they will be here for a bit longer. I hope that we shall therefore be contacting his people here. This sort of planning covers a wide range of subjects, such as higher education (which we touched on when we spoke to him in London). John, would you like to comment?

JOHN FINIGAN: I endorse the Chairman's summary. One saw only on Friday last the indication from Dr Al-Matawwa that the target population would be approximately 1,000,000. There are two relevant comments here: one notes carefully the coda you advance regarding the dangers of excessive growth, but Kuwait's circumstances are unique. This is restoration to the status quo ante, in many cases and therefore the infrastructure was in place for a City state of approximately 2,000,000 people. As the Chairman and other speakers today have said, Kuwait has this remarkable opportunity to re-base itself. Very little of the outcome from this terrible catastrophe in regional terms can be considered as positive, but Kuwait's ability to re-base its plans and to re-use the expertise it has traditionally drawn on is clearly there. I hope it does not sound too fulsome to repeat the final conclusion of the Time magazine article on Kuwait in December, before the war started "Is the war worth dying for?" - what was already a very good country has an opportunity for a renaissance, which could make it a great country.

CHAIRMAN: Would you like to take up this point, Nigel?

NIGEL THOMPSON: I would just add that we spoke to a number of Ministers about this point. To take the health side, they are rightly very proud of what they have achieved and during the past seven months they have worked harder than they have ever done before. They are conscious that in the past Britain has been involved with helping them with strategic planning. They are likely to come back for help, but at the moment they want to do it themselves, with a little bit of help from us, in all the sectors. The problems now are so great - for instance they are even having to argue about how to get water tankers through - so that the medium or long term plans will start in about three months time.

JOHN FINIGAN: My experience dates from the 1970s when, interestingly, Buchanan forecast a range of population growth, one stage of which was the 2,000,000 figure, which was close to being hit before the events in August. I was interested to the reference to Gazi Sultan in Washington. This is why I have made the point. He is an old colleague and friend. He was a member of the Kuwaiti counterpart team working with Buchanons based in Kuwait - and a very good member. He happens to be in Washington and, with the dangers that the work could be dominated from Washington, it is encouraging to hear that Dr Al-Matawwa's team will be visiting London. That is important because of the longstanding UK planning contribution. There is a need for strategic thinking and vision over the medium term, once there has been a recovery from the crisis situation.

CHAIRMAN: Thank you very much. We certainly intend to capitalise on it.

DAVID OWERS: Excuse me, it is not Gazi Sultan, but Fazi Sultan - a different cousin.

CHAIRMAN: We are beginning to run out of time, but let us have one from the back.

MELANIE DICKINSON (The Visa Shop Limited): So far as I am aware, no visas are being issued through the Kuwait Embassy in London. If companies are interested in sending their employees out to the Brit Camp, will they not need visas? Or is the alternative a Saudi transit visa? Also what provisions are being made for the reissue of visas after martial law has ceased?

ADRIAN WHITE: You would be very wise to obtain a Saudi visa. That is the main transit country. We do not anticipate requiring work permits or Kuwait visas, probably until the end of the 90 day period. Thereafter we are pretty sure that controls on both the borders and immigration, which is tightly limited now - certainly for any third country national employee for instance - will apply. You should watch the press carefully for that, but they certainly are not in a position to do so at present, because it is being controlled by the military under the martial law.

GRAHAM BARHAM (Natco UK Ltd): I think everybody here would agree that you have all done a superb job in positioning British industry for the Kuwaiti experience. Will a similar Task Force be set up for Iraq when that comes back into the fold? That potentially is a bigger market.

CHAIRMAN: That is obviously a popular question and it is one that I was going to touch on. This is something that has been debated in the Committee for Middle East Trade in the DTI. The present Task Force was a matter of priority that there was such an enormous amount of work to be done in a comparatively short time (although the DTI have been working on this now for a considerable number of months) and as soon as we have this system dampened down, we shall certainly be looking not only at Iraq, but at Iran and some of the other Gulf states which might have been over-run had the coalition forces not gone in there. The answer to your question is undoubtedly "yes". We shall hopefully be organising conferences and seminars, but as you can imagine the staff both of the Department and the Committee have been working overtime on this. This was a point well taken.

UNIDENTIFIED PANEL MEMBER: Yes, we have this very much in mind, but it depends on the nature of the Iraqi regime and there is one crucial point which will make a big difference between the two operations. Kuwait has money, but Iraq at the moment does not.

MICHAEL VALENTE (Aggreko Generators Ltd): We are a company that has an affiliate company in the US as well as companies throughout Europe and we have been looking at the Kuwait situation since late last year with some of our representatives visiting the Kuwait Embassy in Washington and also talking to the US armed forces. I am reassured today to see that we are also talking to the same people, the Dr Shanins and Chris Wiltons of this world. What is concerning is that Kuwait City still has no power, despite the fact that my company has 20-30 MW of power that could be rented out tomorrow. I would ask a pragmatic question to Adrian, Alan and Christian. What should we do from now on to get some work in Kuwait?

CHRISTIAN ADAMS: It has to be said that the priorities of supplying temporary generating power have been addressed. Adrian mentioned earlier that on a flight that went in only yesterday, a piece of Ruston equipment arrived there to do that very job.

ADRIAN WHITE: Over the past 48 hours we have worked very hard getting the Ruston generators in. This was on exactly the same basis - they had plant available. The Americans also had three 2.9 MW generators available that were delivered last May in Kuwait, but their industry feel it is not safe to travel or work in Kuwait, therefore they will not instal them and Rustons have been asked to do that job. This is the sort of opportunity that you can get, because we have the guts and the people on the ground. At the moment we have a one month lead and,

0058

with the blessing and help and support of the Ministry of Defence this afternoon or tomorrow, we can maintain that lead.

MR HESKETH (Toshiba International Europe Ltd): Ours is a UK company. I know that I am raising a sensitive point, but we have heard mention of the damage to Doha and Shuaiba and the fact that Al Zour remains relatively undamaged. The parent company provided the steam turbines for those stations which are damaged. We have also recently finished off fairly significant high voltage substation work at places such as Akmade, Unbadia and so on. Japanese participation in the refurbishment is a rather sensitive matter, but the reality is that there is possibility of UK participation and we have recently submitted detailed documents of all the equipment supplied on all the projects. Is there a point of contact for some exploratory discussions, bearing in mind that we have significant projects where we shared out the cake with a lot of UK and European manufacturers?

ADRIAN WHITE: I understand that your parent company installed a desalination plant to the power station?

MR HESKETH: Not in total - but the steam generators.

ADRIAN WHITE: The Minister for Electricity and Water, Dr Rugoba, whom we met last Tuesday or Wednesday was wondering where the hell you were, sir!

MR HESKETH: That is why I am here: I am trying to establish what is going on at the other side of the earth in Japan.

ADRIAN WHITE: They do require you on site - now!

CHAIRMAN: We are running out of time, but we can take two more questions. Hopefully members of the panel will be able to stay longer and can perhaps be asked questions individually.

MR MAHMUD (Mama & Company): There were almost 100,000, probably more, unskilled and semi-skilled foreign workers residing in Kuwait prior to the war. If British companies are to undertake major reconstruction work, will they need to recruit foreign workers? If so is the British Task force going to help in this in any way.

CHAIRMAN: The recruitment and training side is being dealt with by the sub-group from the City of London and I would suggest you get in touch through the British Invisibles with Lord Limerick who is address this very question. You are right that there will have to be an emphasis on shifts in training if there are to be fewer non-Kuwaitis proportionate to the population than there were before.

CHRISTIAN ADAMS: On construction we shall need third world nationals to help because they will be a lot cheaper for cleaning up. We shall need a camp associated with the Brit Camp to provide extra support at the labouring end.

CHAIRMAN: One last question from anybody?

JIM FELSTEAD (M East BAFF International Ltd): You mentioned a roll on, roll off vessel from the MOD going to Kuwait. When will that be available and what is the point of contact to book volume on that vessel?

ADRIAN WHITE: You can imagine that there are a considerable number of roll on, roll off vessels going out for the MOD. We have to choose one to suit the peak demand for UK industry. This is why it is vital that your response is not only urgent, but positive that you do anticipate sending out. The bulk of it will, I presume, be on spec - almost on a sale or return basis - but you will have to return it. We are aiming for four weeks time and the point of contact is the same fax number that you were given earlier.

CHAIRMAN: Ladies and gentlemen it has been a long morning. Thank you for your patience and attention. As I said earlier, I hope that some members of the panel can hang around so that you can ask individual questions and I apologise for being rather draconian in cutting some of you off. We wish you the best of luck in winning business in Kuwait.

END OF BRIEFING

© Westminster Management Consultants Limited
Westminster House
Victoria Road
Woking
Surrey GU22 7PL
(0483) 740730

THIS DOCUMENT MAY NOT BE REPRODUCED, COPIED OR STORED ELECTRONICALLY IN ANY WAY WITHOUT THE WRITTEN PERMISSION OF WESTMINSTER MANAGEMENT CONSULTANTS LIMITED. IT IS OUR POLICY ALWAYS TO PROSECUTE FOR BREACH OF COPYRIGHT, REGARDLESS OF THE SCALE OF THE OFFENCE.

주 영 대 사 관

영국(정) 723-517   1991. 5. 14.

수신 : 장 관

참조 : 중동아국장, 국제경제국장

제목 : 걸프관계 회의자료 송부

     91.5.9.-10. 양일간 당지 왕립국제문제연구소(RIIA) 주관으로 "BEYOND

THE CRISIS: THE GULF IN THE 1990S"라는 주제하에 개최된 걸프정세 관계회의

자료를 별첨 송부하오니 업무에 참고 바랍니다.

첨부 : (이하 각 1부)

1. Beyond the Crisis: The Gulf in the 1990s(Programmes).
2. Current and Future Issues in the Region, Fred Halliday.
3. Into the 1990s: An Islamic Perspective, Akbar Ahmed.
4. Marvin C. Feuerwerger.
5. The Conference on Security and Cooperation in the mediterranean
    and the Middle East(CSCM), Stefano Ronca.
6. Arab Regional Security: Between Mechanics and Politics,
    Yezid Sayigh.
7. Perspectives on the Future of the Region, Kamal Kharrazi.
8. Europe and the Gulf Region, Eberhard Rhein.
9. Oil Supply and Price, Silban Robinson.
10. How Much Influence will the US and its Allies have on
    Oil Policy, Peter Bild.
11. Post-War Economic Outlook in Saudi Arabia and the Gulf,
    Henry Azzam.
12. The Size and Distribution of Oil Wealth in the Region,
    George Joffe.

13. Financing Reconstruction in Kuwait and Iraq, Paul Barhen.
14. Rebuilding Kuwait & Socio-Economic Change after the Occupation, M. Al-Rumaihi.
15. Iraq: Priorities and Plans for Reconstruction, Jonathan Crusoe.
16. The Prospects of Political Change in Kuwait, A. Al-Khateeb.

끝.

주 영 대

0062

BEYOND THE CRISIS: THE GULF IN THE 1990s

A Two-day Conference
convened by

The Royal Institute of International Affairs
Chatham House, London

9 & 10 May 1991

THE ROYAL INSTITUTE OF INTERNATIONAL AFFAIRS GRATEFULLY
ACKNOWLEDGES THE GENEROUS SUPPORT OF THIS CONFERENCE BY
TEXACO AND BP

0063

SESSION SIX: PRIORITIES |ᵃᴰ PLANS FOR RECONSTRUCTION

Chair: **Dr Philip Robins**
Head, Middle East Programme, RIIA

11.20 Rebuilding Kuwait and Socio-Economic Change after the Invasion
Dr Mohamad Al-Rumaihi
Editor in Chief, 'Sawt Al-Kuwait' and 'New Arabia'

11.40 Discussion

11.55 Iraq: Economic Reconstruction Issues
Jonathan Crusoe
'Middle East Economic Digest'

12.15 Discussion

12.30 Iran: Current Economic Outlook and Investment Priorities for the Future
Dr Keith McLachlan
School of Oriental and African Studies, University of London

12.50 Discussion

13.10 LUNCH

SESSION SEVEN: POLITICAL DEVELOPMENTS IN THE REGION

Chair: **Edward Mortimer**
'Financial Times'

14.10 Prospects for Political Change in Kuwait
Dr Ahmed Khatib

14.30 Discussion

14.55 Prospect f Stability in Iraq
Dr Tim N■
Dept of Politics, Exeter University

15.15 Discussion

15.30 The Outlook for the Gulf Cooperation Council and its Member States
Liesl Graz
Correspondent, 'The Economist'

15.50 Discussion

16.05 TEA

SESSION EIGHT: THE GREAT DEBATE: THERE WILL NEVER BE STABILITY IN THE GULF

Chair: **Edward Mortimer**

16.25 For: **Roger Hardy**
Middle East Specialist, BBC World Service

16.40 Against: **The Hon David Gore-Booth, CMG**
Assistant Under-Secretary of State
Foreign & Commonwealth Office

16.55 Speeches from the Floor

17.30 END OF CONFERENCE AND DRINKS

0064

PROGRAMM

DAY 1: THURSDAY 9 MAY 1991

9.00   REGISTRATION AND COFFEE

SESSION ONE: THE POLITICO-STRATEGIC SITUATION: AN OVERVIEW

Chair: **Professor Laurence Martin**
Director, RIIA

9.30   Current and Future Issues for the Region
Professor Fred Halliday
International Relations Department, London School of Economics

10.00   An Islamic Perspective on the Region
Professor Akbar Ahmed
Visiting Professor, University of Cambridge

10.30   Panel Discussion

10.50   COFFEE

SESSION TWO: NEW SECURITY ARRANGEMENTS: THREE CONTRASTING VIEWS

Chair: **Professor Laurence Martin**

11.10   The Future Role of the United States
Dr Marvin Feuerwerger
Senior Strategic Fellow, Washington Institute for Near East Policy

11.30   Discussion

11.40   A CSCE for the Middle East: an Italian Perspective
Stefano Ronca
First Counsellor, Embassy of Italy

12.00   Discussion

12.10   Security in the Gulf: the Need for a Broader Definition
Dr Yezid Sayigh
MacArthur Scholar & Research Fellow
St Antony's College, Oxford

12.30   Discussion

12.40   Panel Discussion

13.00   LUNCH

SESSION THREE: PERSPECTIVES ON THE FUTURE OF THE REGION

Chair: **Sir John Moberly**
Consultant, Middle East Programme, RIIA

14.00   An Iranian Perspective
Ambassador Kharazi
Iranian Representative to the United Nations, New York

14.20   Discussion

14.30   A Saudi Perspective
Dr Abdulkarim Aldakheel
Riyadh University

14.50   Discussion

15.00   An EC View
Eberhard Rhein
DGI, Commission of the European Communities

15.20   Discussion

15.30   Panel Discussion

15.50   TEA

SESSION FOUR: THE POLITICS OF OIL

Chair: **John Grundon**
Regional Coordinator, Near East, Middle East & Indian Subcontinent, BP

16.10   The Politics of Oil in the Gulf
Paul Stevens
Dept of Economics, University of Surrey

16.30   Oil Supply and Prices: the Potential for Partnership with the West
Silvan Robinson
Chairman, Steering Committee, Energy & Environment Programme, RIIA

16.50   How much Influence will the US and its Allies have over Oil Policy?
Peter Bild
Chief News Editor, AFP-Extel News Ltd; Founding Editor, 'Energy Compass'

17.10   Panel Discussion

17.45   DRINKS

DAY 2: FRIDAY 10 May 1991

9.00   REGISTRATION AND COFFEE

SESSION FIVE: FUNDING FOR ECONOMIC RECONSTRUCTION

Chair: **Ms Noriko Hama**
Chief Representative, Europe
Mitsubishi Research Institute, London

9.30   The Gulf Economic Outlook in the Post-war Period
Dr Henry Azzam
Chief Economist, The National Commercial Bank, Jeddah

9.50   Discussion

10.00   The Size and Distribution of Oil Wealth in the Region: Economic Implications
George Joffe
Economist Intelligence Unit and SOAS, University of London

10.20   Discussion

10.30   Financing Reconstruction in Iraq & Kuwait
Paul Barker
Paul Barker Associates

10.50   Discussion

11.00   COFFEE

0065

REFRESHMENTS

Morning coffee, the buffet luncheon and afternoon tea and drinks will be served in the reception rooms on the ground floor.

LUNCH

Green badge holders: 9 May only
If you are wearing a green badge you will be eating at The East India Club in St James's Square, where a buffet lunch will be served in the Canadian Room. (Turn right outside Chatham House, The East India Club is situated on the corner of St James's Square and King Street)

All other badge holders:
A buffet lunch will be served at Chatham House in The Neill Malcolm and the Henry Price rooms.

MESSAGES

A message board is located at the doors outside the John Power Hall.

PROBLEMS

If you have any problems please see one of the conference staff in the front foyer of the building.

TELEPHONES

Two coin-operated telephones are on the lower ground floor beneath the central stairs. Please try to keep your conversations brief to allow others to make calls.

TOILETS

Toilets are located along the lower ground floor corridor.

CONFERENCE PAPERS

Some, but not all, speakers have undertaken to give us a written paper for distribution to participants after they have spoken. These will be put out for collection once we have copies or, at the latest, by the end of the day.

SECURITY

● Please wear your conference badge at all times while in Chatham House, and remember to keep your badge for day 2.

FUTURE CONFERENCES

22 May 1991

The Internationalisation of
Research & Development:
A British-Japanese Dialogue
Convened with the Japan External Trade Organisation (JETRO).
To be held at Chatham House.

30 May 1991

European Monetary Union
in a Turbulent World Economy
Convened with The Association for the Monetary Union of Europe. To be held at The Grosvenor House Hotel, London.

0066

Attendance

Faysal Abou-Zaki	Al-Iktissad Wal-Aamal
Andrew Ackroyd	RIIA
Mr Adefuye	Nigeria High Commission
Professor Akbar Ahmed	Selwyn College Cambridge
Motassim Al Maashouq	Saudi Aramco
Stuart Allen	Bank of England
F Al-Dalial	Embassy of the United Arab Emirates
Dr Mohamad Ghanim Al-Rumaihi	'Sawt Al-Kuwait'
Giti Amirani	St Antony's College Oxford
Andrew Apostole	Paul Barker Associates
H Amirsadeghi	H A International Associates
St John Armitage	
Dr James Arrowsmith	Texaco Inc
H Aryan	University of Newcastle
Quadar Assad	Girton College, Cambridge
Dr Henry Azzam	The National Commercial Bank, Jeddah
Yasmeen Bajwa	Pakistan Media Syndicate
Paul Barker	Paul Barker Associates
Andrew Barnard	Department of Energy
Robert Belgrave	Statoil UK Ltd
Peter Bild	'Energy Compass'
Olle Björk	Swedish Energy Administration
Ferhat Boratav	BBC Turkish Section
Pieter Bouwer	Embassy of South Africa
Susan Boyde	RIIA
David Bradshaw	'The Economist'
C D H Bryant	Midland Bank Plc
Nils A Butenschon	University of Oslo
Claire Carnel	RIIA
Julian Chisholm	British Petroleum Plc
S H Cho	Embassy of Korea
R Collins	British Aerospace Plc
Colonel R M Connaughton	Staff College, Camberley
Mark Cornelius	Cabinet Office
Ted Cox	BP International
Sir James Craig	The Middle East Association
Mike Cronin	Cabinet Office
Humphry Crum Ewing	STA Salmann Trust AG
Jonathan Crusoe	'Middle East Economic Digest'
Mark Curtis	RIIA
Elizabeth Dalton	School of Oriental and African Studies
Richard Dalton	RIIA
P Daneshvar	University of Southampton
Roland Danreuther	International Institute for Strategic Studies
Tapan Datta	American Express Bank Ltd
Peter David	'The Economist'
Heather Deegan	Staffordshire Polytechnic
B W Denning	Strategic Planning Society
Austin Earl	J P Morgan

0067

걸프사태 : 자료 및 언론보도, 1990-91. 전3권 (V.2 자료, 1991.4-5월) 271

Alan Eberst	BBC Monitoring Service
C F Elliott	Mobil Services Co Ltd
Cem Ergin	Embassy of Turkey
Mrs L D Fanous	Embassy of Quatar
Richard Fenny	Fluor Daniel International Ltd
R A Field	Department of Energy
P H Frankel	
Sir Michael Franklin	RIIA
S J Fraser	Foreign and Commonwealth Office
Dr Malcolm J Garratt	BP Exploration Operating Co Ltd
Carol Geldart	RIIA
Maurice Gent	'Yorkshire Post'
The Hon David Gore-Booth CMG	Foreign and Commonwealth Office
Seisaku Goto	Chubu Electric Power Co Inc
Liesl Graz	'The Economist'
Bernard Grelon	Berlioz & Co
Kevin Grire	ANZ-Grindlays Bank Ltd
Mr John Grundon	British Petroleum Plc
Anders Hagelberg	Embassy of Sweden
Professor Fred Halliday	London School of Economics
Noriko Hama	Mitsubishi Research Institute
G S Hand	Foreign and Commonwealth Office
John G Hanson	The British Council
Roger Hardy	BBC World Service
Desmond Harney	Middle East Consultants
Jack Hartshorn	
Hideyuki Hayashi	Toho Mutual Life Insurance Co
Dr John Hemery	University of Leeds
T Hirai	Osaka Gas Co Ltd
Major P R Hitchcock	DIOT RAF College, Cranwell
H Houshangi	Islamic Republic News Agency
Eleanor Hunter	RIIA
C N Hurst-Brown	Mercury Asset Management
Zuhair Ibrahim	Embassy of Lebanon
T Inoue	Nissho Iwai (UK) Ltd
Motoharu Iyama	Idemitsu International (Europe) Plc
Farhang Jahanpour	BBC Monitoring Service
Jennifer Jenkins	RIIA
Melanie Johnson	BBC Breakfast TV
Jeremy Jones	
Jill Kalawoun	RIIA
Nasser Kalawoun	
Kamran Karadaghi	'Al-Hayat'
Amina Khairy	'Sawt Al-Kuwait'
H E Ambassador Kharazi	Iranian Representative to the UN
Dr Ahmed Khatib	
Mehrdad Khonsari	
Dr John King	
Peter Knoedel	BP Oil International Ltd
Toru Kuroima	The Mainichi Newspapers
J D Larkman	Barclays Bank Plc

0068

H E Dr HongKoo Lee	Embassy of Korea
C Lorigan	American Express Europe Ltd
Hon Ivor Lucas CMG	
Brendan J Lyons	Embassy of Ireland
Dr Rory MacLeod	Baring International Investment
Alex Macleod	'Christian Science Monitor'
Jonathan Marcus	BBC World Service
Professor Laurence Martin	RIIA
Dina Matar	'Knight Ridder'
Professor Geoffrey Maynard	Investcorp
Bridget McCarthy	London School of Economics
Dr Keith McLachlan	University of London
Leslie McLoughlin	
Bernard Mills CBE	CAABU
K A Mitchell	
Corinne Mitford	BBC Arabic Service
Y Miura	Japan Oil Development Co Ltd
Sir John Moberly	RIIA
Philip Moon	House of Commons
Harvey Morris	'The Independent'
Gerry Morrissey	The Irish Export Board
Edward Mortimer	'Financial Times'
Baqer Mo'in	BBC World Service
Robert Murphy	J P Morgan
Steven Music	Petroleum Argus Ltd
Dr Fida Nasrallah	Centre for Lebanese Studies
Mr Nasser	Islamic Republic News Agency
Dr Tim Niblock	University of Exeter
Geoff Overs	BBC Stills Library
Oğuz Özge	Embassy of Turkey
Henry Pares	Inchcape Plc
David Parker	Shell International
J F E Paxton	Shell International Petroleum Co
Timothy Penn	'Knight Ridder Financial News'
Lesley Perry	RIIA
Dr Volker Perthes	Institute for Development and Peace
Somaini Pietro	Banco Popolare di Bergamo
Sir Michael Pike	Sun Int'l Exploration & Production Co
Sylvia Poelling	Economist Intelligence Unit
Rachid Rahmé	
Carol Reader	'Petroleum Review'
Camilla Reed	
The Lady Renwick	
Eberhard Rhein	Commission of the European Communities
Pida Ripley	RIIA
Barbara Allen Roberson	University of Warwick
Olin Robison	RIIA
Dr Philip Robins	RIIA
David Robinson	Texaco Ltd
Jim Rollo	RIIA
Signor Stefano Ronca	Embassy of Italy

0069

Christopher Rundle	Foreign and Commonwealth Office
Trevor Rutter	The British Council
Vicki Sabatini	Platt's Oilgram
Yoko Sagerman	NHK TV
Jaleh Salmanpour	
J Y Sanders	British Aerospace Plc
Catherine Savage	Nomura Research Institute
Annika Savill	'The Independent'
Dr Yezid Sayigh	St Antony's College, Oxford
Richard Schofield	University of Durham
Martin Scott	Lasmo International Ltd
Dr Paul Seaward	House of Commons
Valerie Seward	Wilton Park
HE Dr Mohamed Shaker	Embassy of Egypt
Greg Shapland	Cabinet Office
Y Shibutani	JETRO, London
Mr K Shimizu	Mitsubishi Corporation (UK) Ltd
E Spuhler	
Gillian Standford	'Yorkshire Post'
Paul Stevens	University of Surrey
Robert B Storey	Fluor Daniel International Ltd
Hiroko Sukuichi	NRI Nomura Research Institute
J Sunde	South African Dept of Foreign Affairs
Hideo Tahi	RIIA
Yasuhiko Tashiro	Idemitsu International (Europe) Plc
Teame Tewolde-Berhan	
R Thomsitt	Standard Chartered Bank
Daniel Thornton	Oxford Analytica
Christopher Tite	Stephenson Harwood
Pierre Tran	Reuters
Ali Usnan	'Daily Jang', Pakistan
Tsunehiko Wada	Idemitsu International (Europe) Plc
Anne Walker	RIIA
HE Mr B Walker	Foreign and Commonwealth Office
A S B Walkington	Texaco Ltd
M S Warwick	Shell International Petroleum Co
T M Whalley	Standard Chartered Bank
Dr Tony Wildig	Shell International
Robert Wilson	House of Commons
Mary Wood	RIIA
Patrick Worsnip	Reuters
Valerie Yorke	Economist Intelligence Unit
HE Mr Ghazi al-Rayez	Embassy of Kuwait

0070

Professor Akbar Ahmed
University of Cambridge

Professor Ahmed is the Iqbal Fellow at the Department of Oriental Studies at Cambridge University and a Fellow of Selwyn College, Cambridge. His last post in Pakistan was as Commissioner for Quetta, Baluchistan. His latest publication is 'Making Sense of Muslim History and Society' (Routledge, 1988) and he has just completed a new book 'Postmodernism and Islam', written in conjunction with Professor E Gellner, to be published shortly by Routledge. Professor Ahmed is the chief consultant for a major BBC TV series called 'Living Islam' based on his book.

Dr Henry Azzam
The National Commercial Bank

Henry Azzam joined The National Commercial Bank in Jeddah in February 1991 as the Bank's Chief Economist. He was born in Lebanon in 1949 and educated at the American University of Beirut where he got his BA and MA degrees in Economics and Finance and at the University of Southern California, Los Angeles where he earned a PhD in economics in 1976. Before joining NCB, he worked for 7 years with the Gulf International Bank in Bahrain, as the Chief Economist, writing GIB's Monthly Newsletter,'Gulf Economic & Financial Report'. Other previous postings include the Arab Fund in Kuwait and the United Nations Economic Commission in Geneva. He also taught international economics and finance at the American University of Beirut and at the University of Southern California, Los Angeles.

Dr Azzam is a leading economist in the region. He writes a monthly Newsletter 'The NCB Economist' analyzing economic and financial developments in Saudi Arabia and the Gulf and a weekly outlook on trends in the foreign exchange and credit markets. Dr Azzam has published several articles both in Arabic and English and he is the author of a book 'The Gulf Economies in Transition' (Macmillan, UK, 1988) and is the editor and co-author of a book 'Gulf Financial Markets' (GIB, 1988). His forthcoming book 'The Gulf in the 1990s: Challenges and Constraints' will soon be published.

Paul Barker
Paul Barker Associates

Paul Barker is the principal of Paul Barker Associates, a London-based economic and banking consultancy specialising in Arab world affairs. The consultancy was established in 1985 when the principal returned from a four-year stint as Chief Economist with ALUBAF Arab International Bank in Bahrain. Paul Barker was educated at Oxford University where he completed a master's degree and three years of advanced research; he has written and consulted extensively on Gulf affairs since the early 1980s in various capacities, and has a particular interest in banking, finance, energy and industrialisation in the Arab and developing world.

0071

Jonathan Crusoe
'Middle East Economic Digest'

Jonathan Crusoe has been writing about Iraq for MEED since 1979. He was born in Kuwait in 1953, and since joining MEED in 1978 has made regular visits to the Gulf region and Iraq. Apart from Iraq, he has also written about and and North and South Yemen for MEED.

Dr Mohamad Ghanim Al-Rumaihi
'Sawt Al-Kuwait' and 'New Arabia'

Dr Mohamad Ghanim Al-Rumaihi obtained his PhD in Social Sciences from the University of Durham in 1973. From 1973 to 1982 he worked at Kuwait University and held the following positions; Assistant Dean at the College of Arts and Education; Head of Sociology and Social Work Department; Associate Professor at the Sociology and Social Work Department; Professor of Sociology.

From 1982 to the present day he has acted as Editor-in-Chief of the Arabic Monthly Al-Araby Magazine, Al-Araby Children's Magazine and Al-Araby Book Quarterly. In August 1990 he became Chairman of Kuwait Research and Advertising Co Ltd and Editor-in-Chief of 'Sawt Al-Kuwait' and 'New Arabia'.

In 1980 Dr Al-Rumaihi was award the Kuwait Sociology and Economics Award by The Kuwait Foundation for the Advancement of Science and in 1990 the IBN SINA Award in Moscow.

Liesl Graz
'The Economist'

Liesl Graz was born in Germany, educated in America and in France, lives in Switzerland, and is a correspondent of 'The Economist'. She has been a passionate, if largely self-trained, observer of Middle Eastern affairs for over fifteen years with a special predilection for the Gulf and the Arabaian Peninsula. Besides innumerable articles in 'The Economist' and elsewhere, she has written 'L'Irak au présent' (published in French by Les Trois Continents, 1979), 'The Omanis: Sentinals of the Gulf', (Longman, 1982) and 'The Turbulent Gulf' (I.B. Tauris, 1990). Always ready to talk to anyone who listen on her favourit subjects, she has participated in university seminars and conferences in Louvain, Paris, Exeter, Tehran, Geneva etc. and is in frequent demand as a commentator on radio and television in Switzerland and abroad.

0072

John Grundon
British Petroleum Plc

John Grundon has worked for the British Petroleum Company in New York, Trinidad, Abu Dhabi and Libya, with a year in the Lebanon to learn Arabic. In various posts in London he was involved in BP's activities in West Africa, North and South America and the Middle East, particularly during the period of nationalisation following the first oil price crisis.

In 1975 he took charge of the commercial side of BP Exploration, with responsibility for BP's entry into new exploration areas.

In 1982 he became President of BP Alaska Exploration, controlling BP's wholly-owned interests in Alaska. He returned to London in mid-1985 to take up his present post, which initially covered regional responsibility for North Africa, the Middle East and the Indian Sub-continent but which, following BP's reorganisation last year, now also covers Central and South America, Canada and South Africa.

He is currently Chairman of the Advisory Board at the Middle East Centre of the School of Oriental and African Studies; in 1989/1990 he was Chairman of the Middle East Association.

Professor Fred Halliday
London School of Economics

Professor Fred Halliday studied Politics, Philosophy and Economics at Oxford and later took an MSc at the School of Oriental and African Studies, London and a PhD at the London School of Economics. He was from 1974 to 1982 a Fellow of Transnational Institute, Amsterdam and Washington, and since 1983 been teaching at the International Relations Department of the London School of Economics. Since October 1985 he has held a Chair in International Relations at the LSE. His books include 'Arabia Without Sultans' (1974), 'Iran: Dictatorship and Development' (1978), 'Threat from the East?' (1982), with Maxine Molyneux, 'The Ethiopian Revolution' (1982), 'The Making of the Second Cold War' (1983) and 'Cold War,Third World' (1989). His most recent work is 'Revolution and Foreign Policy: the Case of South Yemen 1967-1987' (1990). He has travelled widely in the Middle East and other areas of the Third World and has also undertaken research in the United States and the Soviet Union.

Noriko Hama
Mitsubishi Research Institute

Noriko Hama completed her University education at Hitotsubashi University, Tokyo where she studied international economics and finance. Ms Hama graduated in 1975 and joined Mitsubishi Research Institute becoming one of the Institute's first fully qualified female researchers. Her major area of expertise has been the economy of the United States, international trade and finance, and monetary issues in general.

0073

In April 1990 she was appointed to her current position as the Institute's first representative and resident economist in Europe. In this capacity Ms Hama covers macroeconomic issues relating to European integration with emphasis on the monetary union aspect and financial issues relating to the integration process.

Ms Hama has written and co-authored books on the United States, Japan and various currency issues. She regularly contributes to economic journals and periodicals.

Roger Hardy
BBC World Service

Roger Hardy has been interested in the Middle East for some 17 years. Formerly editor of the monthly magazine 'The Middle East', he has for the past five years worked as a Middle East specialist with the BBC World Service. His five-part series 'The Making of the Middle East' was first broadcast last year, and will be repeated in July and August. Roger Hardy is a Middle East Specialist for the BBC World Service.

George Joffe
Economist Intelligence Unit

George Joffe works for the Economist Intelligence Unit as their Middle East Editor and previously as Consultant Editor for North Africa and Middle East affairs.

He is Director of Research at the Geopolitics and International Boundaries Centre at the School of Oriental and African Studies, University of London, and specialises in border disputes and economic arbitration in the Middle East. He has written numerous articles on the Middle East and has co-authored books on the Iran-Iraq conflict with Dr Keith McLachlan.

Ambassador Kharrazi
United Nations

Dr Kamal Kharrazi is the Permanent Representative of the Islamic Republic of Iran to the United Nations in New York. He has held a number of governmental, diplomatic and academic posts. Since July 1980 he has been Managing Director of the Islamic Republic News Agency. From September 1980 to September 1988 he was a member of the Supreme Defence Council of Iran and the Head of the War Information Headquarters. He was also a Professor of Management and Psychology at Teheran University from 1983 to 1989.

Prior to his service in those posts he served as Deputy Foreign Minister for Political Affairs from May 1979 to March 1980. From August 1979 to July 1981, Dr Kharrazi was Managing Director of the Center for Intellectual Development of Children and Young Adults. He was Manager of Planning and Programming of National Iranian Television from March to August 1979 and was a teaching fellow at the University of Houston in the United States from 1975 to 1976.

0074

Dr Kharrazi was founding member of the Islamic Research Institute in London and a member of the American Association of University Professors. He has written a number of textbooks and journal articles and earned a doctorate in education and Management Psychology from the University of Houston in 1976. He also holds a master's degree in education from Teheran University, where he received his undergraduate education.

Dr Keith McLachlan
University of London

Keith McLachlan is a senior lecturer at the School of Oriental and African Studies, University of London. He is President of the British Institute of Persian Studies and Chairman of the Society for Contemporary Iranian Studies. His professional interests include the study of international borader issues and he is a director of the Geopolitics and International Boundaries Research Centre at SOAS.

Dr McLachlan has been a student of Iranian affairs since 1963 and continues to visit the country on a regular basis. He was a research advisor and participant in recent procedings of the Iran-America claims Tribunal at The Hague. Recent writings include 'A Bibliography of the Iran-Iraq Borderlands', (1988), 'The Neglected Garden: the Politics and Econology of Iranian Agriculture', (1988), 'Oil and Economic Development in the Gulf', (1989), and 'The Iranian Oil Industry 1954-73', (1991).

Professor Laurence Martin
The Royal Institute of International Affairs

Professor Laurence Martin was educated at Christ's College, Cambridge and Yale University where he obtained his PhD.

He was a Flying Officer in the RAF from 1948-50. He taught at Yale University, Massachusetts Institute of Technology and SAIS, Johns Hopkins University in the USA from 1955-64. From 1964-68 he was Woodrow Wilson Professor of International Politics at the University of Wales, followed by 9 years (to 1977) as Professor of War Studies at King's College, London. During the King's years (1969-75) he also held the posts of Chairman, Political Science Committee and Chairman, Research Grants Board of the Social Science Research Council. From 1978-90 Professor Martin was Vice-Chancellor of the University of Newcastle upon Tyne. As well as his current post of Director of The Royal Institute of International Affairs, Professor Martin holds the following appointments; Honorary Academic Advisor, Joint Services Defence College, UK; Honorary Professor of International Politics, University College of Wales; Member of Research Council, Center of Strategic and International Studies; Foreign Office Advisory Panel on Disarmament; Member of the Organising Group, European Strategy Group; Director, Tyne-Tees Television Ltd. Professor Martin is the author of many books and articles on security strategy including 'The Changing Face of Nuclear Warfare', (1987); 'Before the Day After', (1985) and'The Two-edged Sword', (1982).

0075

Edward Mortimer
'Financial Times'

Edward Mortimer was educated at Eton and Balliol College. He graduated with a first class honours degree in Modern History. In 1962 he completed a period of Voluntary Service Overseas in Senegal. He was a Fellow of All Souls College, Oxford from 1965-72 and 1984-86. He was also Assistant Paris Correspondent for 'The Times' from 1967-70, Foreign specialist and leader-writer 1973-85, and Senior Associate, Carnegie Endowment (New York), 1980-81. He has been a Assistant Foreign Editor, 'Financial Times' since January 1987.

Mr Mortimer is the author of 'France and the Africans 1944-60' (1969), 'Eurocommunism, Myth or Reality?' (1979 with Paolo Filo della Torre & Jonathan Story), 'Faith and Power - the Politics of Islam' (1982), 'The Rise of the French Communist Party 1920-47' (1984), 'Roosevelt's Children - Tomorrow's World Leaders and Their World' (1987). He has been a member of the RIIA Meetings Committee since 1984 and the RIIA Council since 1987. He is currently a Research Associate at the International Institute for Strategic Studies.

Dr Timothy Niblock
Exeter University

Dr Niblock is a Senior Lecturer in Politics and Joint-Director of the Research Unit for the International Study of Economic Liberalisation and its Social and Political Effects, University of Exter. He obtained his BA in Philosophy, Politics and Economics from New College (Oxford) in 1965. His first postgraduate work was undertaken at the College d'Europe (Bruges), and he obtained his D. Phil in International Relations from the University of Sussex. Dr Niblock has taught previously at the University of Dar-es-Salaam (in a temporary capacity while persuing research), at the University of Khartoum 1969-77 (ultimately becoming Associate Professor) and the University of Reading 1977-78. He served for 3 years as Deputy Director of the Centre for Arab Gulf Studies (University of Exeter) which he helped to establish. He is currently working on a general book on Arab politics. For the 1990-91 academic year, he holds a Canon Foundation Research Fellowship for work on the social and political effects of economic liberalisation in the Arab World. His publications include 'Social and Economic Development in the Abrab Gulf', ed., 'State, Society and Economy in Saudi Arabia', ed., 'Iraq: the Contemporary State', ed., and 'Class and Power in Sudan'. He served as Secretary of the British Society for Middle Eastern Studies between 1986 and 1990.

Dr Philip Robins
The Royal Institute of International Affairs

Dr Philip Robins has worked as a full time member of the staff of the Institute for the last three years. His formal position is that of Head of the Middle East Programme. His last book, which was published in May 1989, was entitled 'The Future of the Gulf: Politics and Oil in the 1990s'. He has written a number of articles and written extensively on Iraq, Jordan, Saudi Arabia, the Arab Cooperation Council and the Gulf in general over the past three years. He has a PhD in Middle East politics from Exeter University. He lived in the Middle East in

0076

the early and mid 1980's, and has travelled extensively throughout the Gulf and the Mashreq in the recent past.

Silvan Robinson
The Royal Institute of International Affairs

Silvan Robinson CBE was educated at Marlborough College and Oriel College Oxford where he was awarded a First Class Honours Degree in Classical Studies.

He worked for two years as a journalist on the editorial staff of 'The Economist' before joining Shell in 1954.

He has held a number of positions in Shell dealing with production, economic and supply matters in Brazil, USA and Nigeria. He then moved to Joint Ventures Division in London and in 1970 joined the Middle East Co-ordination, becoming involved in concession negotiations and the development of Shell's Saudi Arabian Refinery venture.

He was responsible in 1979-81 for Shell's international crude oil procurement in Shell International Trading Company and President of Shell International Trading Company from 1982 to 1987.

He is Chairman of the Energy and Environmental Programme at the Royal Institute of International Affairs since 1988 and Chairman of NEDO Electronics Sector.

Eberhard Rhein
Commission of the European Communities

Eberhard Rhein is Director in the EC Commission (Mediterranean, Near and Middle East). His previous positions include the following: Chef de Cabinet of Vice-President Wilhelm Haferkamp, Commissioner in Charge of External Affairs, Commission of the European Communities (1981-1984); Advisor and Deputy Chef de Cabinet of Vice-President Haferkamp (1977-80); Economic Advisor in the EC Commission (1976); Assistant to the Director-General for Development in the EC Commission (1970-75); Various posts in different services and institutions of the EC (1964-69); Economic Advisor to the Government of Afghanisatan (1962-63); Export Manager of HAKO Machinery Co., Bad Oldesloe, Germany (1960-61); Fellow at the Research Institute for Consumer and Distribution Economics, Hamburg, Germany (1960-61). Mr Rhein studied Economics and Political Science at Hamburg, Princeton and Paris Universities and obtained his PhD in Economics from Hamburg University in 1957.

0077

Stefano Ronca
Embassy of Italy

Stefano Ronca obtained his law degree in 1972, and spent two years as a Naval Officer before joining the Italian Diplomatic Service in 1974. He was appointed to the NATO Service at the Ministry of Foreign Affairs and dealt with various aspects of NATO defence until 1977.

He was posted to Brussels in 1977 to the Italian Delegation to NATO dealing with armament cooperation, press and information, political and economic committee. From 1981 to 1985 he was Economic Counsellor to the Italian Embassy in Libya and from 1985 to 1989 he was Head of the Crisis Centre of the Italian Foreign Ministry. He is presently First Counsellor at the Italian Embassy in London.

Dr Yezid Sayigh
St Antony's College, Oxford

Dr Yezid Sayigh is MacArthur Scholar and Research Fellow at St. Antony's College, Oxford University, working on international relations and Third World security. He has worked extensively on the politics and the military and strategic affairs of the Middle East, with special focus on the Palestinians and the Arab-Israeli conflict. His most recent publications include 'Arab Military Industry' (London: Brassey's, forthcoming 1991) and 'Confronting the 1990s: Security in the Developing Countries' (London: IISS, 1990).

Dr Paul Stevens
Surrey University

Dr Paul Stevens was educated as an economist and as a specialist on the Middle East at Cambridge and the School of Oriental and African Studies, University of London, where he received his PhD in 1974. For six years during the 1970s he lived in Beirut. For four of those years he taught economics at the American University of Beirut and for two years worked as an oil consultant. Since 1979 he has been at the University of Surrey where he is currently a Senior Lecturer in economics. He was a founder member of the Surrey Energy Economics Centre and joint creator of the Third World Energy Policy Studies Group. Dr Stevens has published widely in the areas of energy economics and development economics with the Arab world frequently acting as a bridge between the two interests. Since 1980 he has delivered more than 50 papers in 13 different countries. In the academic year 1989-90, on sabbatical from Surrey, he worked as Senior Economist with British Petroleum at BP's corporate headquarters. In addition to his academic work, Dr Stevens undertakes extensive work as a consultant for many companies and governments.

0078

$\mathcal{2}_0$

Fred Halliday

Resume of Presentation on 'Current and Future Issues in the Region'. RIIA Conference on The Gulf in the 1990s, 9 and 10 May 1991

1. Introduction

The recent Gulf war - the third inter-state war there in the last two decades - was a conflict that developed on several levels: it was an Arab civil war, a wider Middle Eastern confrontation, a challenge to the UN, a new chapter in Soviet-US relations, an upheaval in the world economy, a turning point in US politics. In one sense, the war achieved one thing only - it restored the status quo ante 2 August. Yet the impact on each of these levels was significant and may, over the space of months and years, be more substantial: we do not yet know.

2. The Arab World

Iraq has been defeated and put outside Arab politics for several years, yet its Ba'thist regime, based on party and security apparatuses, survives and may continue to do so, with or without Saddam. Prospects of political change in other states are dim. A new bloc of Arab victors - the GCC and Egypt and Syria - has been created, with military and economic implications. It will exclude others, but may not function so cohesively itself.

3. Regional Issues

For all the hopes of change, there is no certainty that there will be movement on the Arab-Israeli question. Turkey remains concerned about the Arab world, but does not want to be too closely involved - its main interest is improved relations with the USA. Iran, while now placed in a better position, remains excluded from the mainstream politics of the region.

4. East-West Relations

The most significant concomitant process of the Gulf crisis was the continued erosion of Soviet power. The 'new world order' now means not what it did in 1988-9, a new Soviet-US understanding, but a world in which US power is supreme, while not pervasive. Domestic pressures within the USSR oppose all-out cooperation with the USA, but cannot reverse the global trend.

5. International Economy

Two issues are central here. First, the impact of the Gulf war on the international economy - oil prices were less of a factor than a general depression of demand in late 1990 and early 1991

1

0079

as a result of uncertainty.   Second, the future of OPEC policy
oil prices.   GCC lowering of oil prices was one of the causes of
Iraq's invasion of Kuwait, and the long-run lesson should be not
to play politics with the oil price: but current Saudi policy
seems to be to keep prices below $20, to placate the West, keep
Iran and Iraq weak, and discourage development of non-Gulf
sources.

6. US Politics

Perhaps the greatest question is what use the USA will put, and
be able to put, its Gulf victory, at a time of increased decline
in Soviet power.   The prestige of the armed forces is higher, but
beyond that it is an open question what Bush and his successors
will be able to do, in terms of revitalising the US economy,
dealing with Third World issues, re-negotiating relations with
developed competitors in Japan and Europe.   Major opportunities
are there, but it is not evident these will be taken.   On one
issue a US response is clear: the Europeans, who played in
collective, i.e. EEC, terms a marginal role in the crisis, are
being discouraged from any development of an autonomous military
capability or set of institutions.   Many expected greater
economic leverage in the world economy: for all the talk of
enhanced US influence as a result of the Gulf war, there is
little sign of it in the current situation.

0080

INTO THE 1990S: AN ISLAMIC PERSPECTIVE

When Saddam Hussein invaded Kuwait in the summer of 1990 he destroyed more than Kuwaiti independence. He shattered the complacency of those who were dreaming of a stable and harmonious post-cold war New World Order which would set the stanchions in place for the projected political architecture of the 21st century. The war that followed had about it the inevitability of Greek tragedy.

In the future, major international crises would follow a pattern characterized by several facts: the involvement of the media which were seen and heard everywhere was one. Every gesture and every word of the main players, like Saddam, were news, to be discussed and analyzed. Another was the inter-connection of the world, both of people and economies: not only oil supplies to the West but the remittances of the South Asian workers were affected. Then, a feeling, a mood, grew that henceforth a crisis of this nature could escalate uncontrollably to a world disaster. A global perception therefore formed, not unanimous on cause and effect, but one that reflected concern for the interdependence of life on earth.

Most of this was new and frightening, but there was an eerie element of déja vu in the drama, as if half-awake we had seen some of it before. Over the last two years another crisis had been simmering. In it we had heard the principles

0081

of freedom of expression being defended - Voltaire was often cited - against those Muslims who felt their religious beliefs were outraged by The Satanic Verses. Muslims believed the Prophet and his family were insulted and the authenticity of the Quran challenged. Ayatollah Khomeini elevated the Muslim response into an international affair by issuing the fatwa which condemned the author to death. Then, by dying, he left the issue suspended in mid-air to eternity; no Iranian could revoke or cancel it.

We note that Islam is the common factor intertwining most of the people mentioned above and ask: is Islam to be isolated in the coming time as a force for anarchy and disorder? But then we consider other cases; that of the popular singer, Madonna, for example. Her songs, videos and stage performances, her use of the crucifix and the church, had incurred the wrath of the orthodox. In Like a prayer she appeared to deliberately provoke racial, sexual and religious controversy. The Pope himself was said to be outraged.

So besides Islam other traditional systems, too, were being disturbed. Something had changed fundamentally in the way people were responding to the world.

These crises were different yet in some ways similar. They brought together a bewildering collage of historical and contemporary images that bonded through communications technology the entire globe. The audio-visual

0082

media allowed, as never before in history, an instant access to news, an unsettling, dazzling, juxtaposition of diverse pictures, a variety of discourses. High philosophy and comic book ideas, historical facts and pop sociology jostled and mingled. The kinetic energy which was created in turn sparked ideas and prejudices, controversy and argument. The crossing of cultural boundaries created the misinterpretation of foreign idiom causing great offence and agitation, great misunderstanding, on all sides.

It was the media that juxtaposed for us images of people like Hitler and Saddam, Bush and young Stuart Lockwood, Rambo and Saladin, Khomeini and Rushdie, the Prophet and Voltaire, the Pope and Madonna, and places like Masada and Makkah, Babylon and Jerusalem. The Rushdie affair, the Madonna crisis, the manner of the Gulf confrontation were harbingers of things to come; it is the times and age we live in.

It is a period of dramatic change; structures that have held for decades are being pulled down. Changing, too, are notions of the self and of the other, of class, of ethnicity and of nation, although the nature and depth of these are still debatable. A perception is forming that we may be entering a distinct phase of human history, one following modernism and therefore tentatively called post-modernist.

However, although post-modernism is an explanation for some, it is also a cliché for others. Clearly the rupture with the previous period is not complete. For if recent events

0083

in the Soviet Union, East Europe and South Africa signify post-modernist impulses those in Tiananmen Square, the Baltic States and around Rushdie suggest the strength of tradition and authority.

How, then, are Muslim peoples reacting in the wake of the recent events in the Gulf? For this critical answer let us go not to the corridors of power in Muslim lands or their media (both to an extent influenced by the West) but to the core of their religious structure, the mosque.

This is a route that is seldom taken and therefore ensures that often even experts get it wrong (Iran in the 1970s being a famous example, when many experts were predicting a long reign for the Shah on the eve of Ayatollah Khomeini's revolution in spite of the overflowing mosques). The error is compounded by imposing simplistic labels derived from Europe, like 'fundamentalism', on Muslims.

Muslim political life in the main may be seen as a triangle. Socialism, based on the old-fashioned model of Moscow or its one party state Ba'athist variants in Syria and Iraq, the parasitic capitalist consumerism espoused by rich tribal dynasties (Saudi Arabia, Kuwait or not so rich ones like Jordan), and an Islamic order(Iran) are the three major points. They sometimes coalesce but are often in competition and provide the dynamics of society. Democracy, as in Pakistan and Egypt, has still to take firm root, although there is

0084

evidence of a rich and vigorous intellectual life in both countries.

The Gulf war has been a dramatic turning point for the Muslim world. For one it has exposed the bankruptcy of Arab socialism as represented by the Ba'ath party and Saddam Hussein. There is already unbounded cynicism about the workings of capitalism. This is because capitalism, for the ordinary citizen, is too directly linked with Washington; and Washington is seen as propping up Israel and, indeed, the Muslim dynastic rulers, generally seen as decadent and corrupt. The third point in Muslim politics, that centred around Islam, which has been gaining ground in the last decade, will further gain. Even Saddam, the erstwhile socialist, recognized this in the last days leading to the war by ordering the stitching of <u>Allah-u-Akbar</u>, God is great, onto the Iraqi flag. He was also shown regularly at prayer.

For us, then, Islam is not only theology, that is people's ideas about religion, but also sociology, that is, how Muslims act and behave and see their culture. Is there a coherent, unified and recognizable 'Islamic' perspective? And how do we identify its physical form in society? We do so through the little studied mosques and their networks. And it will be misleading to equate the mosque in Muslim society to the church in the West. The church simply does not carry the political and social clout among Christians that the mosque does among Muslims.

0085

A remarkably coherent perspective on major events, considering the variety of Muslim discourses, cultures and nations, is thereby created and sustained. The ideas that are generated on this network cut across national borders; they permeate the bazaar and the souk, the favela and the lower echelons of government. The mosque perpetuates customary values and lays out a strategy for action while expounding on the political and social issues of the day. During the month of fasting it feeds the poor, during crises it gathers resources and funds for the distressed and in normal times runs schools and organizes talks.

In mosques from Karachi to Cairo, in the Muslim world, and Seattle to Cambridge, in the non-Muslim world, I have been struck by the universality and similarity of themes expressed in the khutba, the sermon delivered on Friday to the congregation. About half an hour in length, the khutba is delivered before the main prayer. The audience in the mosque is highly receptive and a mood of quiet harmony usually prevails among it. It consists of anywhere from 50 to 50,000 people depending on the size of the mosque.

The main themes emerging in the sermons reflect the apocalyptic mood among ordinary Muslims. In Muslim countries the national language, in non-Arabic speaking lands often interspersed with Arabic, is used; English may be used in part in a mosque in London. The great days of Islam, the nobility

0086

of the past, are evoked; Quranic references support the arguments. The analysis is simplistic, the colours black and white and the expression hyperbolic. The audience largely rural and often illiterate, responds with heart-felt passion. Broad, atavistic themes comfort it in these times of rapid change.

Several clear themes are apparent: there is the eternal and universal struggle between good and evil. The world is seen as increasingly dominated by the power of the West, especially the USA, which represents moral and spiritual decadence. Sex, drugs and violence are what the West offers and Muslims must resist them with their piety and moral strength. Stereotypes and hearsay often pass as truth in the arguments; the VCR and some of its more vulgar exhibits are taken as exemplifying the West. The museums, parks and libraries, are seldom, if ever, mentioned. This is the reverse of the phenomenon known as Orientalism which Edward Said brought to our notice; the Orient as stereotype, as caricature, as decay, deceit and corruption. Here, in the Muslim world, we see the growth of Occidentalism.

Specific contemporary Muslim problems form another theme. The loss of Jerusalem and the fate of the Palestinians are on top of the list. Here political, racial and religious responses fuse. National issues are also raised. Corrupt rulers, the inequality between the rich and the poor, the malpractice of government are highlighted. They are also

0087

linked to the West, which is seen as supporting undesirable rulers to obtain concessions (for oil, a military base or strategic reasons).

Once we appreciate the vast networks of the mosques, their well established and organized nature, and the content of the sermons, we begin to throw light on some apparently confusing phenomena.

Take the Gulf war. Many people were confused by the way in which certain governments, like Egypt and Pakistan, supported the allies while large crowds in these countries demonstrated loudly in favour of Saddam. While many Muslim nations went along with the UN resolutions most Muslims remained cynical of the use of the UN, pointing out that UN resolutions continue to be ignored by Israel. Similarly, Western commentators are confused regarding the latest developments around Salman Rushdie. They ask if he has become a Muslim why is he still in hiding? The answers lie to a large extent in the mosque which has become a barometer for politics among Muslims.

Ayatollah Khomeini's revolution in Iran was perhaps the most dramatic example of the mosque overwhelming the secular palace of the ruler. But in other countries too rulers who may tune into the BBC for the main news are careful to listen to what is being said at the sermon.

0088

Although Imams in charge of mosques are amenable to pressures from government and often accused of being on their pay-roll, by and large, they act as the opposition voice. For this in many cases they have suffered terribly. But no one seen as deviating is spared. Even General Zia-ul-Haq, widely identified with the Islamic position, was often the target for scathing criticism from the mosque; earlier, Zulfiqar Ali Bhutto, Benazir's father, was toppled because of the intensity of the campaign spearheaded by the religious parties. Little wonder that Benazir's first trip abroad as Prime Minister was to Makkah; in public she covered her head and turned beads in deference to religious sentiment. Today, after the Gulf war, leaders not particularly associated with Islam, like President Mubarak in Cairo or King Hussein in Amman, pay special heed to the sermon.

It is in this context that we are able to understand Muslim support for Saddam Hussein or the continued condemnation of Salman Rushdie. Saddam, although many religious figures suffered at his hands, was seen as someone standing up to the West. Even those who opposed each other united behind him as a symbol, a rallying point. In an emotional meeting in Bradford the Supreme Council of British Muslims unanimously expressed their support for him. In Pakistan,where he was never popular because of his support for India over Kashmir, processions burnt effigies of Bush and Major. Maulana Noorani, head of a religious party, announced that 100,000 volunteers were ready to fight for Saddam.

0089

Similarly, Salman Rushdie remains a symbol of the cultural humiliation by the West of Muslims. In the mosques they remain suspicious of his declaration of faith in Islam. It is no surprise that the main mosque of British Muslims, at Regent's Park, London, remains in the forefront of the campaign to reject him. Indeed, its Imam, because he met Rushdie and accepted his conversion to Islam in December, was ostracised and prevented from delivering the <u>khutba</u>.

The policy statement published by the Islamic Research Centre, London, on 10 September, 1990, and titled "Crisis in the Gulf", thus reflects, as it sums up, the themes we are identifying. It points out what it sees as the "secret master plan" of "the only super-power, US". Some of this appeared far-fetched in September but to many is already appearing plausible today. It is worth repeating in full, for it holds wide currency among Muslims.

"The secret master plan thereafter [after the war] is:

1. Force Iraq to pay war compensation of $100 billion.

2. Disband the Iraqi Army, similar to the German and Japanese Army after World War II.

3. Allow the US forces to stay on Iraq soil for the next fifty years, again similar to post-war Germany and Japan.

4. Allow Iraq to keep only a police force.

0090

5. Dismantle Nuclear Reactors, Arms and industries, so that Iraq will have to purchase from the West.

6. Depose Saddam and his family after a Nuremburg type trial.

7. Keep several bases in the Saudi Peninsula and US troops to guard the oil fields.

8. Full control of OPEC from Arabs to control both production and world price".

But Islamic suspicion and rejection of the West come at a time when an argument is developing in the West itself for strong borders around national frontiers which would prevent interaction with the Muslim (indeed Third) world: thus Fortress USA and Fortress Europe. In the West this has powerful appeal, with resonances from the past. However this position ignores some important factors. There is the presence of about 10 million Muslims in the West. Most of these are now permanent citizens of the countries in which they live, with little real desire to go home. The argument also ignores the age in which we live - one we defined as post-modernist. With the developments in communications technology and transport it is practically impossible to isolate any part of the globe - or any group - successfully. Finally, there remains a moral argument, rooted in Christianity, but equally reflected in both 'left' and 'right' arguments: the need to interact with others, irrespective of race and nationality.

The contradictions and paradoxes will not soon be

0091

resolved. On the contrary, they will increase thereby increasing friction. Interconnected peoples and interacting events demand from us the need for an understanding of, and sympathy for, each other. Without these, as I have concluded in Post-Modernism and Islam (with Professor Ernest Gellner for Routledge), the global village will be increasingly susceptible to disruption and violence; and not only from the obvious dangers of a man with a bomb in his brief case but also, as we saw in the examples above, because of the actions of a military dictator, a pop singer or Booker prize winner.

0092

Conclusion:

In the light of the arguments above we sum up. In the age in which we are entering -- whether we call it post-modern or by some other name -- unless there is greater and more sympathetic understanding of Islam points of conflict with the Western world will be frequent; they will be cultural as well as political in nature. But even with all the goodwill of the West -- which in the present climate appears unlikely -- the major problems that exist within the Muslim world will continue to create unrest until they are seriously tackled. We have identified these as being on both an international and national level; of the former the problem of the Palestinians is paramount, of the latter the lack of democracy, the unequal distribution of wealth, and the poor education standards are just some. A sense of justice and balance are central to Islam; without these the sermons in the mosque will not be appeased.

There is the other emerging problem of the Muslims in the West; about 10 million live in the USA and Europe. These are for all practical purposes permanent citizens with little real desire to return to their Afro-Asian homes. But an increasingly apparent under-current of racism, cultural discrimination and intellectual isolation -- and their own preconceived notions, those we called Occidentalism -- prevent them from meaningful integration into or social harmony with

0093

the majority population.

Of course, this is not always true as there are numerous examples of Muslims living harmoniously with their own sense of identity preserved. The preservation of identity is critical for any immigrant community if it is to retain its sense of self and respect. Indeed, a Muslim is as near to God living in the East as he is in the West; the Quran underlines the universal nature of God who is everywhere. Muslims need to avoid the trap imposed on them by the notion of a West opposed to an East, and an Islam situated only in the East.

Muslims must also ask themselves with greater vigour what they can give or bring to their host populations? The answer is a great deal. Besides a stable family life, they express genuine concern for the aged, piety, good-will, balance and compassion; that is the Islamic ideal. No civilized -- however secular -- society would refuse to welcome these qualities. This is not, however, how Muslims are generally seen in the West. The resolution of the Western image with the Islamic ideal -- as much as the resolution of the substance of Islam with the rhetoric of the sermon --will surely be one of the great challenges to Muslims in the 1990s.

Akbar S. Ahmed

0094

4.

Marvin C. Feuerwerger

Dr. Feuerwerger is Senior Strategic Fellow at the Washington Institute for Near East Policy. At the Institute, Dr. Feuerwerger is responsible for strategic programs, and is the convenor of the Institute's Strategic Study Group on U.S. Interests in a Post-Cold War Middle East. He also is Professorial Lecturer in International Relations at the Johns Hopkins University's School of Advanced International Studies and serves as a consultant to the Office of the Under Secretary of Defense for Policy.

Dr. Feuerwerger previously served as the Acting Director of the Pentagon's Policy Planning Staff and as Director for Regional Policy in the Office of the Principal Deputy Under Secretary of Defense for Strategy and Resources. From 1986-1989, he was First Secretary at the American Embassy in Tel Aviv. From 1980-1986, Dr. Feuerwerger held a variety of posts in the office of the Assistant Secretary of Defense for International Security Affairs, rising to the level of Deputy Assistant Secretary for Policy Analysis.

Before joining the Pentagon, Dr. Feuerwerger served in the Carter Administration as Deputy Senior Advisor to the President and Secretary of State. Previously, he was a legislative assistant for foreign affairs and defense to Representative Christopher J. Dodd and to Representative Stephen J. Solarz.

Dr. Feuerwerger is a graduate of Columbia University (B.A. 1971), and received his doctorate from Harvard University (1977). He is the author of <u>Congress and Israel: Foreign Aid Decision-Making in the House of Representatives, 1969-1976</u> (Greenwood Press, 1979), and wrote <u>Restoring the Balance: American Interests and the Gulf Crisis</u> (The Washington Institute, 1991). His articles and essays have appeared in numerous publications, including <u>The Christian Science Monitor, Commentary, The New Republic, and Middle East Review</u>. He has served as a consultant to National Public Radio's "All Things Considered", and has appeared on such programs as The MacNeil/Lehrer News Hour, CBS Nightwatch, ABC Evening News, and CNN's Morning News. He and his wife, Debra Feuer, have three children.

Dr. Feuerwerger may be contacted at: The Washington Institute for Near East Policy/ 1828 L Street NW/ Suite 1050/ Washington, D.C. 20036; Telephone (202) 452-0650; Fax (202) 223-5364.

0095

THE CONFERENCE ON SECURITY AND COOPERATION
IN THE MEDITERRANEAN AND THE MIDDLE EAST (CSCM)

Stefano Ronca

1. The rationale underlying the proposal for a Conference on Security and Cooperation in the Mediterranean and the Middle East takes its inspiration from the need to create a stable system of regional cooperation, based on a set of rules and principles accepted by all the States concerned, along the lines of what Europe has been doing over the past two decades.

a) Globality

The area's problems require a global approach because security aspects are inseparable from development and mutual tolerance, and political stability cannot be achieved unless the economic shortcomings are tackled, or if it is only limited to some countries while ignoring others.

b) Graduality

The CSCM exercise must be viewed as a process which will become clearer as the members move ahead in a succession of increasingly complex stages, allowing for the initial diversity of stances and the weighty legacy of diffidence and hostility. CSCM must therefore be viewed as a long process, which obviously makes it advisable for the preparatory phase to begin as soon as possible.

In the course of the process of establishing a new order in the Middle East a variety of specific political and diplomatic initiatives are possible to deal with individual crises, from the Arab-Israeli conflict to Lebanon, as well as particular issues, such as security and economic cooperation. Initiatives of this kind would be complementary rather than alternatives to the CSCM, and could be included into the CSCM framework or in a collateral context.

0096

c) Universality

From Morocco to Iran, all the countries in the Mediterranean Basin and the Middle East should take part in the CSCM, both coastal States in the strict sense of the term and those with any kind of interest in the region (see Annex). This is because any destabilizing event anywhere in this area, as the Gulf crisis has demonstrated, is inevitably bound to send shock-waves throughout the region. In addition to this group of countries, we believe that it is necessary for the United States on the one hand, and the Soviet Union on the other, to be involved, at all events. Lastly, it may be expected that not only the European Community as such, but also individual Community countries will take part in the exercise, in addition to those who belong geographically to the area.

However, the fact that one or more countries do not participate must not be allowed to prevent the exercise from beginning.

d) Relations with the United Nations

The legal and diplomatic base for convening the Conference can be taken from the relevant decisions of the United Nations which has never issued so many pronouncements on any other region in the world. The United Nations will therefore be given a fundamental role in the CSCM, unlike the case of the CSCE.

This also applies to the participants, which should be both sovereign States in the region and the "national entities" recognized by the United Nations.

Given the political will, there is no reason why the UN should not be directly and explicitly involved in convening and organizing the CSCM, even as a preparatory stage for the peace Conference. It would be sufficient to add China to the list of countries given in the Annex.

e) Rules and principles

Rules and principles must be underpinned by the consent of the countries in the area. They will have the primary responsability for taking part in drafting them, since no new regional order could endure at length if it were imposed from the outside.

2. The CSCM and other international political and diplomatic initiatives/conferences on the Middle East are not mutually exclusive. These would flank, underpin and complement the CSCM. Outstanding unresolved issues (such as the Arab-Israeli, Iran-Iraq, Iraq-Kuwait disputes, Lebanon and Cyprus) as well as specific objectives such as economic cooperation and disarmament can be resolved with specific exercises, while the CSCM will be required to lay down rules that will remain valid through time. The principles agreed upon at the general negotiations could also encourage the search for points of equilibrium on specific issues: suffice it to mention the recognition of borders and the solution of the Arab-Israeli conflict. In turn, once the crises in the area have been solved, it will be easier to adopt and apply the general principles agreed upon at the CSCM.

3. The CSCM should lay down principles, bearing in mind a three-fold division along the lines of Helsinki, into the security, economic cooperation and human rights baskets, which could pave the way towards:

a) peace negotiations proper, particularly for the settlement of crises still awaiting a solution;

b) international peace conferences, such as the Arab-Israeli conference. In the conflict Israel has also demonstrated that it is capable of eschewing its traditional reflex reaction in the

0098

matter of its security. For the very first time, Israel has found itself on the same side as its adversaries in four wars, the Arab States which – apart from Egypt – do not even acknowledge its existence;

c) the creation of security structures in the region. A system based on the permanent presence of Western troops, or a special alliance with the United States and a few of the States in the region, such as Saudi Arabia, would not prove very stable;

d) the mobilization of European and Western resources, but also those of the most affluent Arab countries, in a new spirit of solidarity designed to ease the socio-economic tensions whose effects (such as the demographic effects) are already affecting Europe. This would appear to be an essential incentive to enlist the solidarity of the less fortunate countries, to prevent others from subsequently concealing their hegemonic ambitions behind a new confrontation between the "haves" and the "haves-not", as Saddam Hussein did;

e) the establishment of rules governing tolerance and respect for human rights. This is all the more essential today, after such a vast mobilization to restore the rule of international law.

4. It could take several years before the CSCM process manages to draft a set of principles comparable with those drawn up by the CSCE (a "Mediterranean Act" or something similar). We therefore consider that, in view of the urgent need to influence the post-war order in the Gulf and throughout the whole of the Middle East, it would be advisable to convene the CSCM Preparatory Committee as soon as possible. We believe that all the interested countries could immediately subscribe to a minimum package of principles as evidence of their individual commitment. This

package would, in practice, be a sort of "entry ticket" to the Conference which, even before it is formally called to order for the first time, could already exert a practical political effect on the post-war negotiations to settle the outstanding issues of specific relevance to the area.

This minimum package could comprise:

1. respect for the territorial integrity of States and the inviolability of borders;

2. economic solidarity with the less affluent countries in the area;

3. rejection of the use of force to settle disputes;

4. halting the arms race, particularly of weapons of mass destruction;

5. tolerance and dialogue in the political, cultural and religious spheres.

0100

COUNTRIES PARTICIPATING IN THE CSCM

(Tentative list)

EEC countries: (12)	Belgium, Denmark, France, Germany, Greece, Ireland, Italy, Luxembourg, Netherlands, Portugal, Spain, United Kingdom.
Mediterranean countries: (18)	Albania, Algeria, Bulgaria, Cyprus, Egypt, Israel, Jordan, Lebanon, Libya, Malta, Mauritania, Morocco, Romania, Soviet Union, Syria, Tunisia, Turkey, Yugoslavia.
The Gulf States: (9)	Bahrain, Iran, Iraq, Kuwait, Oman, Qatar, Saudi Arabia, United Arab Emirates, Yemen.
Other CSCE countries: (2)	Canada, United States.
UN-recognized entities: (1)	Palestine.

0101

Article appearing in the RUSI Journal, Summer 1991

NOT FOR CITATION UNTIL PUBLISHED

Dr Yezid Sayigh

Arab regional security: between mechanics and politics

"We are being manipulated by the Arab governments for their own advantage, and misunderstood by their peoples...
As the cold war began and intensified, more and more reliance was put on military bases which the United States and its allies could develop around the world.
Because geography and oil give the Middle East strategic importance, an extravagant courtship of the Arab governments was launched to preserve oil concessions and, more recently, to effect a military alliance with them.
In the process, we gave sanction to the neglect of the Arab populations".

Proposals submitted to the US President by an independent commission of American churchmen and laymen, April 1954.[1]

"It is important...that we build a regional security structure that is able to contain the aggressive tendencies of a leader like [Saddam Husein]...Certainly we [the USA] ought to play some role, and therefore there would be...some continuing [military] presence there".

US Secretary of State James Baker, 4 September 1990.[2]

Nearly 37 years separate these two quotes, yet little has changed in what they reveal about the basic thrust of US policy in the Middle East. The intervening period has witnessed an unceasing emphasis on the military dimension of security to the virtual exclusion of its other elements, token references to democracy, human rights and development and to other pressing political and economic issues notwithstanding. This approach is likely to be reinforced, if anything, as a result of the shock of the Iraqi

---

1. Security and the Middle East: The Problem and Its Solution, New York: n.p., 1954.

2. Hearing of the House Foreign Affairs Committee, 4 September 1990, London: The Refernce Center, USIS, American Embassy.

0102

invasion of Kuwait in August 1990, the focus on constructing and managing a war-waging coalition, and the subsequent success of the resort to force to liberate the emirate.

Yet how successful has the military orientation of security thinking been in the past, or is it likely to be in the future, given the immense depth and power of the underlying causes of conflict in the region, so vividly demonstrated by the Iraqi invasion and the diverse reactions to it of Arab governments and peoples? Conversely, what are the determinants of regional security, that must be addressed if appropriate mechanisms are to be found and lasting stability is indeed to be achieved?

The central argument here is that the basis of Arab regional security must be primarily political, rather than predominantly military. True, the need to stabilise the present situation and prevent further armed conflict is both undeniable and immediate. Yet equally, it will be difficult to achieve even temporary stability -- as the ongoing civil war in Iraq demonstrates -- unless the interim security measures adopted are based on an understanding of the root causes of conflict and are conducive to their resolution. More precisely, the opportunity provided by any suspension of overt conflict must be siezed rapidly to develop *political* solutions to the fundamental tensions and grievances of the region (which embraces diplomatic, social, or economic means of action as well), as part and parcel of attaining lasting security and stability. Otherwise, the partial steps taken as a matter of urgency or expediency in the initial post-Gulf war period will "gel" into permanent policy (or rather, non-policy), eventually re-establishing the regional *status quo ante* and perpetuating the causes of instability and conflict once more.

The distinct risk -- almost an inevitability, given past experience -- is that Western and Arab governments may succumb in practise (whatever the rhetoric) to the temptation of focusing solely on security "arrangements" and "structures", because these

2

0103

appear easier to establish and simpler to manage than attempting to address complicated or divisive political issues. Thus security "architecture" -- designing military pacts, deployments, arms controls, conflict-prevention mechanisms -- may supplant (rather than complement) security "thinking" -- analysis of the dynamics of conflict and change at both national and regional levels, and promotion of an integrated or multi-tiered approach to political, social, and economic problems.[3] Similarly, the managerial aspect of "geomechanics" -- the ordering of inter-state alliances according to self-interest -- might impede tackling core issues by obscuring "geopolitics" -- the understanding of the patterns of inter-state relations and their determinants.

In asserting the primacy of politics, the thesis of this article is that security in the Middle East is determined by four core linkages -- admittedly a word that fell in disrepute during the Gulf crisis, but which is worthy of rehabilitation in more contexts than one — + must be understood in their terms.

The first linkage has already been alluded to: geopolitics, or the inter-connections between the behaviour of different states in the Middle East regional system, stemming in part from the dictates of geography, material assets (natural and human resources), and strategy. The impact of the international system and main global powers on regional politics provides a second linkage (which will be treated last). Another component of regional security is the political-military linkage, that is, the causal relationship between various military phenomena -- conflict, conventional arms buildup, NBC and ballistic missile proliferation -- and their political driving forces -- Arab-Israeli dispute or

---

3. This broader approach to security is developed in Yezid Sayigh, Confronting the 1990s: Security in the Developing Countries, London: the International Institute for Strategic Studies, 1990.

Iraq-Iran competition, Arab inter-state rivalry, regional status and political prestige, consolidation of regime survival. The latter item points to the fourth linkage, between patterns of regional politics on the one hand, and the domestic structure of power in individual countries on the other: authoritarian or minority-based governments have a disproportionate impact on regional securities due to their monopoly over formulation of both domestic and foreign policies.

Geopolitics: post-crisis application

Suggestions have been made at various times since August 1990 for a Middle East regional security alignment that would include certain Arab states and either Israel or Iran (or both). The over-ambitious proponents of such proposals have invariably been non-Arabs, however. A few other commentators, realising the continuing difficulty of combining the Arabs and their erstwhile foes in formal alliance, have occasionally mooted the notion of a Western arrangement with Israel and/or Iran, bypassing all or most Arab states entirely.

At present, though, the initiative by the GCC countries, Egypt, and Syria (the Six-plus-Two) to form the nucleus of an Arab security framework -- by deploying peacekeeping forces from the latter two countries in the Gulf -- has pre-empted other proposals.[4] At the very least, the existence of this alliance will postpone Western -- primarily American -- efforts to construct broader military alliances. Ultimately, the likelihood is that the Six-plus-Two pact will form the basic building block on which

---

4. Official statement in al-Hayat, 7 March 1991. (In Arabic.)

4

0105

outside powers might seek to expand by introducing modifications or new partners. That, however, assumes the sustainability and viability of the Six-plus-Two coalition, which is not a foregone conclusion.

There are two immediate problems with the Six-plus-Two set-up. One is that it studiously ignores the vital function that Jordan played during the Gulf war as a buffer between Israel and Iraq (and the Gulf), a short-sighted and vindictive attitude shared by the USA. More fundamental is that the Six-plus-Two composition perpetuates longstanding Saudi policy of excluding both Iran and Iraq from formal structures concerned with Gulf security.[5] This may be understandable in the short-term, given the freshness of both Gulf wars, but it has grave implications. Exclusion of either Iraq or Iran, or of both countries, overlooks geographical and strategic realities and condemns the GCC states to permanent dependence on support from countries even further afield. It also implies an inability, or unwillingness, to alter the previous pattern of balance of power politics and to establish a new basis for cooperation and security in the Gulf sub-region. Furthermore, any long-term arrangement that fails to draw in Iraq is dangerous because it ignores that country's pivotal position (in both geographical and strategic terms) between the Gulf and Arab-Israeli theatres, suggesting that Iraqi involvement is necessary for the success of wider regional stability.

These are by no means the only potential flaws, though. Wartime solidarity and post-war rhetoric notwithstanding, the patterns of relations between the eight members of the Six-plus-Two coalition in previous decades suggest that their current alliance may

---

5. This aspect of Saudi policy, towards Iran especially, is discussed in Ghassan Salame, Saudi Foreign Policy since 1945, Beirut: Arab Development Institute, 1980, pp. 523-4. (In Arabic.)

prove ephemeral or at least subject to a strict ceiling. This is most obvious in the case of Syria, which was the least significant contributor to Gulf defence in real military terms. Lack of a common border and internal considerations in Damascus seriously delayed Syrian support and severely limited its extent. The Saudi leadership had long "bribed" its Syrian counterpart with large subventions to purchase its goodwill and moderate its foreign policy, in the words of one analyst, but at the end of the day it was opportunistic considerations (realisation that Iraq would lose, and the desire for better ties with the West) that swayed Damascus.[6] Above all, the Gulf crisis underscored the limited importance of Syria as either ally or foe of Saudi Arabia and the other GCC members.

Geopolitical realities affect Syrian-Gulf ties in another respect. This is the prospect of long-term disengagement between the GCC states and most Arab countries to their north in the post-war period.[7] For many years, the former group, oil-rich and population-poor, relied on Jordan, the Palestinians, Lebanon, Syria, and Iraq (among other Arab and non-Arab countries) for expatriate labour and professionals. The GCC states additionally depended on Jordan, Syria, and Iraq for varying forms and degrees of military assistance or strategic protection. The Iraqi invasion of Kuwait undermined this relationship, partly because official and grassroots reactions in many parts of the Arab region damaged ties, and partly because the "northern tier" Arab states were demonstrably unable to offer real protection or themselves posed the threat. This experience has prompted GCC government thinking (principally Saudi, followed by

---

6. Giacomo Luciani and Hazem Beblawi, The Rentier State, London: Croom Helm, 1987, pp. 79-80.

7. This and other aspects of Arab geopolitics are discussed in Yezid Sayigh, "The Arab regional system and its politics", International Affairs, July 1991.

6

0107

Kuwaiti) towards curtailing financial assistance to other Arab states still further and reducing dependence on their labour -- already over 800,000 Yemenis and some 200,000 Palestinians have been compelled to leave. For Syria, the implication is that it too will suffer, despite lipservice by GCC states to fraternal ties and token aid, as the peninsular Arabs disengage strategically and economically from their "northern tier" brethren.

Paradoxical as it may seem, similar considerations affect the relationship between the GCC and Egypt, which proved to be a more dependable, and militarily useful, ally than Syria during the Gulf crisis. Nonetheless, the absence of a common land border and the logistic difficulties of moving significant Egyptian forces to Saudi Arabia did not go unnoticed. This might suggest maintaining a substantial Egyptian contingent with pre-positioned armament and supplies in the kingdom (and Kuwait), as the Six-plus-Two have indeed largely confirmed, but two factors will probably limit the importance of this option in Saudi thinking. On one hand, there is an inescapable and marked contrast between the administrative, logistic, and technological superiority displayed by US/Western forces in the Gulf and more modest Egyptian capabilities. On the other hand is the traditional Saudi preference for military support by out-of-area powers over the physical presence of forces from regional neighbours.[8] The deep-seated attitude that "foreign" goods and experts are better than Arab or Egyptian ones has previously led GCC leaders to avoid the products of the Egyptian arms industry, for example.[9] Whatever the hopes of the Egyptian leadership, the distribution of Gulf reconstruction contracts since the latest war shows just how little Egypt counts for in GCC vision. The

---

8. Salame, op cit, p. 516.

9. Yezid Sayigh, Arab Military Industry: Technical Capabilities, Industrial Performance and Economic Impact, London: Brassey's, 1991 (forthcoming), Chapter on Egypt.

0108

GCC states understand full well that economic and commercial ties underpin security relations -- after all, that is how the Saudis have courted the USA -- but they do not seek so firm a relationship with other Arab countries.

These underlying realities point to further implications. Because its own sub-region -- embracing Libya and the Sudan (and to some extent the rest of the Nile Valley and Red Sea littoral, to include Ethiopia and Somalia) -- is strategically insignificant, Egypt has always sought to enhance its stature and thus attract financial and economic assistance by involving itself in the Arab-Israeli conflict and Gulf security. Already the Egyptian government has reflected this pattern by reviving its role in the Palestinian-Israeli peace process, mending relations with the PLO among others, and by insisting on rehabilitating the League of Arab States, which is the only regional body that offers scope for its leadership ambitions.[10] As "odd man out" in their respective sub-regions, moreover, Egypt and Syria have forged an axis since Spring 1990, which was the basis of their alliance during the Gulf crisis and now of their membership in the Six-plus-Two coalition. Yet the Egyptian-Syrian axis is the product of passing strategic circumstances and, given the experience of similar attempts in 1958-61 and 1971-73, is unlikely to last unless a common Arab policy is developed towards Israel, since that remains the principal common denominator between Syria and Egypt.

A final aspect of geopolitics that will affect the viability of regional security structures is the pattern of relations with the Arabian peninsula itself. The trend that evolved under Saudi impetus in the late 1970s and that became formally embodied in the creation of the GCC in 1981 has been inward-turning, and indicates the prospect of

---

10. Foreign Minister Butrus Ghali explicitly stated the aims and premises of Egyptian policy in interview, al-Hayat, 6 January 1991.

8

0109

continuing tension between the policy preferences of the "Six" versus those of the "Two" (Egypt and Syria). However, seclusion is not itself a viable prospect for the GCC. The anomalous position of Yemen, in the peninsula but not of it, is one case in point, while another is the persistence of bilateral disputes such as that between Qatar and Bahrain. More important is that GCC cohesion and effectiveness as a sub-regional security and policy-making agency -- hardly impressive during the Iraq-Iran war -- is dependent on Saudi peninsular hegemony. Yet the latter element depends on the internal stability of a fragmented tribal society, which will probably come under increasing strains in the post-Gulf war period and thus alter the nature of relations both within the GCC and between the GCC and its neighbours.

The political-military linkage: the issues

The need to prevent armed conflict, whether by controlling the means of waging it or by deterring its outbreak, is obviously a pressing imperative in the Middle East. It is made all the more urgent by the appalling civil war in Iraq and the prospects of further regional instability that that strife raises, as well as by the persistence of other more longstanding threats. Once again, however, the issue and its solutions are not clearcut: a mechanical approach that treats the military dimension as a practical or technical problem, in isolation of root causes and political tensions at both domestic and regional levels, risks placing the cart before the horse.

That said, there are three main categories of military issues that affect the search for regional security: prevention -- deployment of peacekeeping forces for early warning and "trip-wire" purposes, establishment of "hot-lines" and advance notification procedures of maneuvers and troop movements to avoid accidental conflict; deterrence -- deployment of outside forces or conclusion of defence and military assistance pacts,

0110

9

possession of non-conventional weapons or acquisition of advanced conventional systems; and arms control and/or disarmament, affecting NBC and conventional weapons and other areas of military technology or related industrial transfer.

Of the foregoing, preventive measures can only be based on agreement between the contracting parties if they are to be effective, and so appear as technical details that refine an established security arrangement. Deterrence is more contentious, since it presupposes continued tension or latent conflict with one or more regional actors, who are excluded from the arrangements proposed by the other side. Thus it only underscores the potency of political and strategic issues, that act as problems and threats rather than as the basis for promoting cooperation.

The third category, arms control and disarmament, best highlights the connection between prevention and deterrence or, more precisely, the inter-linkage between the military and political dimensions of security. Indeed, in many respects the debate about ways and means of suspending, or even reversing, the regional conventional arms buildup and the race to acquire NBC weapons and ballistic missiles is set to become paramount, both as a military issue and as a predominantly political one.

The most obvious instance of the complicating political-military linkage is the Arab-Israeli arena, the current focus on the Gulf and Iraq notwithstanding. For Israel, insecurity has been a prime driving force not only of conventional arms development but also of its clandestine nuclear (and possibly biological and chemical) weapons, ballistic missile and space programmes. In turn, this has fuelled Arab concern about the strategic balance and prompted counter-efforts to develop non-conventional weapons and their means of delivery, the most recent and public example being Iraq. At one level,

0111

10

therefore, the Western focus on dismantling the Iraqi NBC and missile infrastructure
misses an important part of the point when it ignores the far superior Israeli capability
and₍dismisses₎ Arab calls for making disarmament both reciprocal and across the NBC board.[11] At
another level, Israel and other Arab states (including Syria and Egypt) will neither curb
their military development nor disarm unilaterally. Indeed, they will not even
countenance a multi-lateral approach, such as a NWFZ, without a wide-ranging and
comprehensive settlement of their outstanding complaints and concerns, which above all
means obtaining a negotiated peace involving territorial concessions by, and security
guarantees for, Israel.

Important as it may be -- even central in the post-Gulf war period -- the
Arab-Israeli dimension is not the only factor. Were it so, then it might be easier to argue
that enforcing Iraqi disarmament (and similar controls on other Arab states, for that
matter) without rigorously pursuing controls on Israeli NBC efforts need not necessarily
prove destabilising, because Israeli behaviour could supposedly be moderated by the
USA. In reality, however, there are other contributors to the dynamic of regional military
competition. An evident example is the balance between Iraq and Iran. Late in the first
Gulf war the latter country revived its nuclear research programme – launched under the
Shah but suspended by the advent of the Islamic Revolution in 1979 -- and redoubled its

---

11. Details on Middle East capabilities in Frank Barnaby, The Invisible Bomb: The
Nuclear Arms Race in the Middle East, London: I.B. Tauris, 1989, Part One. Saudi
Defence Minister Sultan bin Abdul-Aziz and the Egyptian head of the UN
Secretary-General's Expert Committee on CW use, Ismat Izz, are among Arab officials
issuing such calls. Al-Hayat, 22 March and 14 April 1991.

ballistic missile development effort. This is a potential threat that Iraq, nor even Saudi Arabia and the other GCC members, can ignore. Arming to reduce their vulnerability would only threaten Israel, though, restarting the escalatory spiral.

Limiting the focus to conventional weapons is no less complicated. Major arms suppliers, especially in the West, will find it extremely difficult to restrict military transfers to their allies in the region, assuming they ever seriously consider doing so. Israel, Egypt, and Saudi Arabia will remain principal recipients of arms sales to the Middle East, given their security circumstances and proven loyalty; indeed, all three countries have benefitted from new deals since August 1990. This may be justified officially on the grounds that none of the recipients is likely to attack its neighbours, but even then such an argument is inherently political: it accepts the *status quo* and sidelines the demands of other actors, and so it enables the chosen recipients to maintain selfish policies, Israeli occupation of Arab land and denial of Palestinian rights being the foremost case in point. It also ignores the fact that local leaders might entertain regional ambitions, which would be enhanced by acquisition of advanced weaponry even if it was not actively employed. In all cases, a continued flow of arms will reinforce the marked military imbalances of the region, with attendant risks of restarting the arms race.

The risks are very real. Although the USA, Britain, and France have long been the leading arms suppliers to the Middle East, along with the USSR, there is substantial scope for smaller producers to export weaponry to countries that are supposedly under control. China is an important example, but a host of other countries are also involved in the arms trade, ranging from North Korea and South Africa, through Brazil, Switzerland and Austria, to the Netherlands and Germany. More significantly, although the USSR is likely to participate in collective control regimes, particularly in the NBC and ballistic missile spheres, it will probably prove more reticent concerning conventional weapons limitations if it feels that Western restrictions are one-sided. In such a situation, the

USSR would seek the political and commercial rewards of proving itself sensitive to the basic defence needs of such Arab states as Syria and Iraq. Nor should the need of Eastern European economics to export arms be overlooked in this context.

The foregoing treats the issue of arms controls as if it were a straightforward matter of government policy, but this is an unjustified assumption. In reality, the agendas of specific interest groups influence decision-making considerably, as the cases of the pro-Israeli lobby and the military, industrial and business communities (who back Saudi sales) in the USA demonstrate. As importantly, the scale of financial gains from arms sales will continue to influence Western (and other) governments and to attract private companies keen on earning large profits. An equally powerful incentive operates on the receiving side too. Arms deal are one of the most lucrative sources of commissions in the Middle East, along with oil and construction contracts, and so the temptation to employ government position to obtain private gain remains large. Such abuse of political power is most obvious in the Saudi case, where reportedly the convention is for middlemen to earn up to one-fifth of the value of contracts, though similar practises occur in Egypt and other Arab countries.[12] Transparency -- both supplier and recipient -- could be one way of curbing arms sales driven by the profit motive.

The purpose of these comments is to inject a note of realism into armchair proposals for arms controls and to temper self-righteousness among their proponents. And even given the political will, thorny practical questions arise: should limitations be discriminate or not, by country or weapon category? A blanket embargo on all arms sales to a specific country may be undermined because it may not adequately control third

---

12. Nor is Israel exempt. A recent scandal involving the Air Force head of acquisitions revealed major embezzlement. Jane's Defence Weekly, 23 March 1991.

0114

13

country transfers or transactions by private companies, especially those involved in transferring technology and components for use by recipient industries. Conversely, a discriminatory regime might be more effective in such categories as NBC weapons and ballistic missiles, because associated transfers can be more closely monitored and regulated at source, though it might prove inherently destabilising by perpetuating Israeli nuclear hegemony and Arab insecurity.

Once again, the inter-locking nature of the problems and the dynamic interaction between sub-regions and parallel security concerns across the Middle East suggest that a comprehensive, politically-founded outlook is necessary for an effective halt to the regional arms race. This is not to suggest that arms controls (or other security-enhancing military measures) must wait on solutions to intractable political conflicts. Rather, having noted the debilitating effect of short-sighted self-interest and partisanship on the commitment of outside suppliers to real controls, the argument here is that the active interaction of the political and military dimensions of security must be acknowledged in the policy proposals put forward for the region. Whether dealt with simultaneously or in tandem, and in whatever order, arms controls in both the conventional and non-conventional spheres have to be linked to resolution of the fundamental political issues. Security can only be an integral whole.

The domestic-regional linkage: implications

The nature of ruling elites in each country and of the political system (that defines the relationship between rulers and ruled) is a major determinant of inter-state relations in the Arab region. And because real power in most Arab countries rests with narrowly-based elites -- drawn from family, tribal, ethnic, or sectarian minorities, and

0115

14

almost invariably unelected and too often supported by Western nations -- incumbent regimes wield a disproportionate impact on the functioning and stability of the regional state system as a whole.[13] The ability of President Saddam Husein to launch his country virtually single-handedly into two vastly debilitating wars within a single decade reveals this linkage most starkly.

While Iraq provides an example of the more violent consequences of the domestic-regional linkage, its implications for post-crisis security are better demonstrated by the case of Saudi Arabia. The kingdom has long based its defence on a costly, high-tech front-line air force;[14] partly because of its limited population base, but more significantly because of its fear for its own survival. The ruling family has deliberately kept its standing army small, and balanced it with a parallel force, the National Guard.[15] Such a posture is untenable as a long-term option in the post-Gulf war period, though, even if outside forces provide a major share of defence transitionally.

---

13. Former Secretary-General of the League of Arab States Mahmoud Riad expressed this succinctly: "Arab fate is not decided by the Arab people. Rather, the fate of the nation is in the hands of individuals who insist on imposing their own views". In "The difficulties facing Arab joint action", al-Hayat (London), 11 December 1990. Much has been written on the nature of political systems in various Arab states, but a recent effort to cover a wide range of them is Berch Berberoglu (ed.), Power and Stability in the Middle East, London: Zed Press, 1989. Some of these connections are also drawn together in Valerie Yorke, Domestic Politics and Regional Stability: Jordan, Syria and Israel, London: Gower for the IISS, 1988, Conclusions.

14. Anthony Cordesman, The Gulf and the West: Strategic Relations and Military Realities, Boulder CO and London: Westview and Mansell, 1988, p. 200.

In order to be secure, Saudi Arabia must provide a greater degree of its own self-defence. Simply to rely on yet more high-tech weaponry, supported by a veritable army of foreign technical personnel, is inadequate. Expanding the standing army, possibly by conscription, is an alternative. But as the experience of the Hashemite throne in Jordan shows, this option subtly shifts the nature of allegiance, fostering a concept of citizenship and allegiance to the state rather than the ruling family *per se*.[16] The eventual result in Jordan was the riots of April 1989 among the tribal bedrock of the throne, who demanded electoral participation in the political system. The Saudi leadership cannot involve its citizenry in national defence more extensively without suffering strains in the social and political system. Already, the need to mobilise the home front during the Gulf crisis by stressing Saudi patriotism has altered the ideological basis of government legitimacy. From a broad and relatively focus-less Islamic stress, the ruling family had to promote the "national myth": seeing themselves as members of a defined national entity, ordinary citizens are more likely to expect a share in decision-making.[17]

---

15. Implied in ibid, p. 201. One writer suggests that the main fear was of the tendency of bedouin tribes to wage conflict. Abdulaziz Fahad, "Why Saudis Feared Defence and Are Reconsidering", International Herald Tribune, 13 February 1991.

16. Paul Jureidini and R.D. McLaurin, Jordan: The Impact of Social Change on the Role of the Tribes, Washington DC: Praeger for CSIS, Washington Papers No. 108, pp. 6-7 and 63, for example.

1984

17. Beblawi, op cit, pp. 74-5.

Neither can the Saudi security dilemma be resolved by maintaining a high level of dependence on outside military assistance. The Western nations might be able and willing, as long as costs are covered by GCC states, to deploy naval and air units in the Gulf on a permanent basis, along with prepositioned *materiel* for ground troops. However, funds are no longer as available as they used to be; the Saudi government has resorted to deficit spending uninterruptedly since the late 1970s, and now may have liquifiable assets worth no more than $30 billion.[18] The Kuwaiti government will be drawing down its overseas investment to cover its budget for at least two years to come. In light of the costs of the Gulf war, reconstruction, and Kuwaiti oil fires -- at a time of declining oil revenues in real terms -- the prospect is one of decreasing financial solvency throughout the Gulf (and by extension, the Arab World). Naturally, this also limits reliance on high-tech defence.

In this respect, Arab military assistance such as that offered by Egypt and Syria might appear more cost-effective. Conceivably, Arab troops would bolster Saudi and GCC defences in the initial phase of a crisis, until additional Western forces could arrive. But besides possible doubts concerning the effectiveness of Egyptian or Syrian troops and equipment, the GCC states cannot assure themselves that this will be a really lasting and dependable arrangement, unless they are in turn willing to guarantee their Arab partners certain rewards in exchange. The traditional problem of all Arab countries that are labour- or troop-donors to the oil-rich Gulf states is that they have had no assurance of dependable financial aid or forceful diplomatic support.

---

18. According to the director of the Oxford Institute for Energy Studies, Robert Mabro. Private discussion, 6 April 1991.

Put differently, the dilemma for the Gulf states is how to resolve the dichotomy between the innate and acquired dimensions of security.[19] At the domestic level, innate strength stems from such factors as political cohesion and social harmony, while military power is in this sense acquired. In regional terms, the parallel contrast is between armed defence that a given country provides itself and strength deployed by outside powers, for example. The fundamental problem in the Gulf is that ruling elites do not wish to dilute their power, nor distribute their wealth more widely, by developing the innate dimension of security at the domestic and regional levels. This is inherently self-defeating, since financial constraints are set to make reliance on acquired elements of security and on high-tech defence increasingly problematic.

A prime indication of this cupidity is the consistent refusal of Gulf states to integrate Arab expatriate workers and professionals into local societies. Such a process would have strengthened national security and provided the basis for stronger military defence: in part by removing the constant suspicion that guest communities harboured a potential "fifth column", and in part by enlarging the general population base and the skilled manpower pool.[20] By transforming a significant slice of the non-native support base -- already massively involved as foreign personnel in security, defence and administration -- into nationals, the host governments could have given them a real stake

---

Terms used in

19. Sunday Ochoche, "Towards the 'Habilitation' of the Concept of Security: Some Preliminary Sketches", unpublished paper, p. 15.

20. These issues are discussed in Saadeddin Ibrahim, The New Arab Social Order: A Study of the Social Effects of Oil Wealth, Beirut: Centre for Arab Unity Studies, 1982, pp. 190-1. (In Arabic.)

in the future of their adoptive countries. This would not only enhance security, indeed, but would also greatly benefit local economies by encouraging expatriates to commit themselves permanently to the host states.

However, an integrative policy would undermine vested interests. First and foremost is the "sponsor" system, under which no expatriate can work, keep a family, or start a business without paying commissions or majority interest to Gulf nationals and business partners.[21] This system is open to immense abuse. Integration would also implicitly undermine the existing basis of domestic power, by compelling ruling families to clarify the concept of citizenship, which would inevitably alter the traditional relationship with the original nationals. A recent example of the latter problem is the plight of the 100,000 "bidoons", bedouins who have long been refused Kuwaiti nationality -- although they form *much* of Kuwaiti Army manpower -- and who are now being persecuted, expelled, or refused re-entry to the emirate. It is hardly surprising, therefore, that official Saudi and Kuwaiti statements since August 1990 should have explicitly rejected the option of integration.

Role of the West

The potential role of the West in post-Gulf war regional security highlights the linkage between the international system and the main global powers on one hand and Arab regional politics on the other. More to the point, such a role has to be carefully judged, since it will have a critical effect on the three other determinant linkages described earlier (geopolitical, political-military, and domestic-regional).

---

21. Beblawi, op cit, pp. 55-6; and Ibrahim, op cit, pp. 33 and 175-6, for example.

At present, there appears to be little agreement among the leading Western nations on security proposals. The UK has no blueprint, and its attitude is summarised in three basic points: that the local states should get on with formulating and implementing their own ideas; that the USA and Britain are unable or unwilling to commit themselves to a long-term military presence, for reasons of finance and public opinion; and that in all cases Middle East security requires dealing with four issues, namely the Gulf, Palestine, arms controls, and economic development.[22]

The USA, conversely, has already committed itself to basing air and naval units in the Gulf, along with a permanent operational/logistic headquarters in Bahrain to coordinate the arrival of additional reinforcements and ground troops, when needed.[23] Yet there is little indication that American thinking has gone any further than the technical practicalities of such arrangements. Rather, the emerging pattern is one of forming policy as events dictate; this is the impression gained from the way in which the Gulf war ended, the nature of US reactions to the outbreak of the Shi'ite rebellion in south Iraq and the Kurdish revolt in the north, and the stop-start process of aiding Kurdish refugees and setting up a safe-haven for them. US policy-making in this *ad hoc* fashion is true to form -- witness the debacle in Lebanon in 1982-4. True, there are other consistencies: the stress on the US-Saudi military relationship and on managing ties with Israel and Egypt. However, a potential tension lies between the narrow focus on these partial constants and the need to grasp that US policy in specific areas can have much wider, unanticipated consequences.

---

22. Based on private discussions with a number of FCO officials, in March and April 1991.

23. Details in International Herald Tribune, 25 March 1991.

The latter comment holds the key to defining a balanced role in the Middle East for the Western nations or any other outside power or organisation. The critical requirement is an ability, on the one hand, to compartmentalise or distinguish certain aspects of security policy, while appreciating the inter-linkages and building on them to achieve much wider and deeper security, on the other.

Several examples illustrate the required balance. Most current security proposals focus on the Gulf sub-region specifically, whether relating to troop deployments, military assistance agreements, or formal defence pacts. But Gulf security will be compromised if no progress is made on the Arab-Israeli front, if only because three Arab actors involved in the former sub-region -- Iraq, Syria, and Egypt -- are also involved in the latter. The evolving US-Arab strategic relationship presses in that direction too, as does the desire of Gulf rulers to see a source of instability removed by resolving the Palestine problem.

Furthermore, both Israel and Syria, and to a lesser degree Egypt, are involved in various NBC weapons and ballistic missile development programmes, but are unlikely to accede to an arms control regime simply because the West wants to impose one on Iraq. And arms controls will not be accepted by regional actors unless they are linked to resolution of other political and territorial disputes. The point is not so much that the Arab-Israeli conflict and arms proliferation must be addressed along with the issue of Gulf security (which they must) in the interest of lasting peace and stability in the Middle East, but that advantage should be actively and deliberately taken of the various regional inter-linkages precisely in order to promote solutions to a larger basket of problems and threats than previously considered feasible.

0122

21

Naturally, broadening the range of issues that must be addressed by both local actors and outside powers raises questions about ways and means, and about responsibility. Is it up to Western nations to promote specific blueprints for the region? Is it theirs to impose solutions, and how? Where to draw the line?

The Western track record is not good: direct colonial rule, overt or covert intervention in the internal affairs of the region's states post-independence, active or tacit complicity in the excesses of authoritarian regimes, and general apathy to humans rights violations in Arab countries and the Israeli-occupied Palestinian territories. Western policy remains subject to the influence of special interests and commercial profit. Nor are Western nations, any more than local actors, suddenly more committed to standards of morality and international law in practise than they were before 2 August 1990, when business was going on as usual with Iraq.

That said, the West is deeply involved in the Middle East, economically, commercially, politically, and militarily. Its moral and strategic responsibility is therefore commensurate with the extent of its actual presence and influence. In practical terms, this responsibility should be enacted at three levels. First, any military commitment to regional (or sub-regional) security should distinguish clearly between defensive or deterrent strength and compellent power. It is one thing to deter aggression and help repel it, but another to exert leverage on certain states through the implied threat of force. This is particularly important because Western military presence in the region may ultimately encourage local allies to pursue their own regional ambitions, relying directly or indirectly on the added clout imparted by out-of-area forces.

A related responsibility, secondly, is for self-restraint in using the Middle East as a means of maintaining life in Western political and military bodies. Already, the search for a role for NATO has led some commentators to suggest a relocation of its focus to

22   0123

Turkey. The Canadian Defence Minister reflected such thinking when he suggested that NATO should develop an out-of-area capability because the world had become less stable.[24] WEU Secretary-General van Eekelen was even more forthright, arguing that the EEC should have a foreign and security policy or risk being sidelined in history.[25] Besides the evident failing that such statements reveal a continued inability (or instinctive unwillingness) to grapple with fundamental political and economic problems, they overlook the possible consequences of further militarising that part of the world and of confronting the USSR, Iran, and the Arab states with what will become a heavily-armed and potentially revanchist Turkey.

Indeed the example of Turkey raises the third aspect of Western responsibility, namely to avoid shoring up the inequitable regional *status quo* or propping up authoritarian regimes. The Turkish Army was able to raze dozens of Kurdish villages, unnoticed by Western media, while the Allies dealt with the Gulf crisis: how would greater NATO commitment to Turkey affect its internal situation and human rights record? Pious assurances aside, how can Western contributors to regional security structures ensure that their presence will not enable Arab regimes to ignore internal pressures for reform even longer, or Israel to resist Palestinian independence? Indeed, given the degree of government dependence on the West, it has considerable room for leverage in support of political liberalisation in the Arab states and Israel.

---

24. Jane's Defence Weekly, 20 October 1990.

25. Ibid, 27 October 1990.

23

0124

Is a CSCME utopian? (Can we afford fatalism?)

A variety of proposals for Middle East regional security have been proposed in different quarters: US policy has veered since the Gulf war towards the notion of a series of bilateral agreements with local states, while independent experts have suggested reimposing a UN mandate or creating functionally-related or regionally-differentiated institutions which are "kept as discrete and limited in their agenda and membership as their subject-matter permits".[26]

This article has argued that a rigidly de-linked approach to regional security is inadequate because it leaves core problems unresolved, and so may prove to be destabilising in the long-term. As seriously, a stress on mechanics (management) and on the military dimension of regional security overlooks its other determinants, especially the structure of domestic power in local states, which has an immense impact on internal stability and on inter-state politics. The tendency of Arab ruling elites to treat national security and regime security interchangeably complicates the establishment of viable regional organisations. At the same time, the economic crisis and political *malaise* of most countries in the region suggests that the need for development and democratisation will impinge increasingly on security and reinforce the linkages at all levels. Ultimately, regional security is an aggregate that is no better than its individual parts, but most local states have yet to accept that their national security may be best served by enhancing, and making concessions to, collective security.

---

26. The UN mandate idea is from Abdul-Monim Said Aly, in private discussion, March 1991. *The quote is from* Shahram Chubin, "Post-war Gulf security", <u>Survival</u>, March/April 1991, pp. 154-5.

24

0125

What is needed, therefore, is an approach that allows separation of issues (when needed) and accommodation of linkages at one and the same time, and that propels both the regional and the domestic levels of security in parallel. A relevant model is the Conference on Security and Cooperation in Europe (CSCE), suitably modified to Middle East realities.[27] Just how instrumental the CSCE forum was in propelling change in Europe is open to debate, of course, and it may only have crowned what had already been decided on the ground. But all the more reason, then, to build on the momentous changes in regional balances and dynamics heralded by the Gulf crisis and war, and to assert a CSCME as the broad framework within which narrower bi- or multi-lateral structures can operate. It could also come about at the initiative of the UN or overlap with it on certain issues, but would not be subject to the same membership and voting rules.

A distinct advantage of a CSCME is that it incorporates three principles: it combines all parties and recognises their concerns, fears and needs, but without compelling any to concede anything *a priori*; it accepts the asymmetry of capabilities and problems, yet seeks balance; and it encourages reciprocity. Furthermore, a CSCME framework would be multi-tiered and multi-layered, allowing various issues to be dealt with separately, collectively, or in varying combinations. Gulf security is an example: the Six-plus-Two alliance could provide basic military defence for the GCC states, while a broader committee including Iraq and Iran (and maybe Yemen) would tackle wider issues of security and cooperation in the sub-region. Another example is the Arab-Israeli conflict and arms controls: conventional and non-conventional weapons could be dealt

---

27. In the West, Italy and Spain have proposed adaptation of the CSCE model to the Middle East. See remarks by Italian Foreign Minister De Michelis, International Herald Tribune, 18 February 1991.

0126

with separately from each other, yet also in connection with movement on overall peace, Palestinian rights and Israeli security. Similarly, CSCME would provide a forum in which human rights and political and civil freedoms would be accorded status and actively promoted; it might also be the umbrella for a dedicated human rights agency or a regional reconstruction and development bank, allowing for some conditionality between trade or assistance and democratisation.

To deal with Gulf security, the Arab-Israel conflict, arms controls and disarmament, economic development, and democratisation might seem too much to ask for, or rather too much to expect. Yet the accumulated strains and tensions within the domestic and regional systems in the Middle East are as great now as they were in Eastern Europe at the end of the 1980s, if not worse, and demand as sweeping an approach. Of course, in the European case there was a long record of negotiations, and the CSCE arguably only succeeded once the East-West balance had shifted and the principal parties to it had changed their priorities. But all the more reason, then, that Western involvement in Middle East regional security structures should not help re-impose the *status quo ante*, in the way that Soviet power maintained an artifical balance in Central Europe for over four decades.

In any event, whatever the Western role or the fate of particular proposals, it is incumbent on the Arabs themselves to alter the basis of the conduct of their domestic and regional politics. Their civil society has been marginalised or brutalised for far too long, but it is only by its reactivation and empowerment -- through appropriate institutions and reforms -- that their region can eventually achieve peace and security.

0127

26

7₀

ISLAMIC REPUBLIC OF IRAN
Permanent Mission to the United Nations

622 Third Avenue, New York, NY 10017 • 212/687-2020

P R E S S   S E C T I O N

Statement on "Perspectives on the future of the region"

By His Excellency Dr. Kamal Kharrazi

Permanent Representative of the Islamic Republic of Iran

to the United Nations

At

The Royal Institute of International Affairs

Chatham House, London

(May 9 & 10, 1991)

Third Middle East Conference

Beyond the Crisis: the Persian Gulf in the 1990's

Please check against delivery

- May 9, 1991

0128

In the name of God, the Compassionate the Merciful

Perspectives on the future of the region

9 May 1991

Sir John Moberly, Ladies and Gentlemen,

I am privileged and delighted to be here this afternoon. Thank you for inviting me, and thank you all for your interest.

By now, I am sure, it is clear to everyone that the Persian Gulf is a hot-spot on the globe, if there was ever any doubt. Persian Gulf is a strategic area where the fashionable concept of "new international order" will be tested. It will be a gloomy world order if the U.S. - led war against Iraq were to become a precedent. It will be gloomy because U.S. policy during and after the war has created the following unholy conditions upon which the U.S. administration intends to build the structure of the new world order:

-Destruction of Iraqi infrastructure beyond the limits authorized by the Security Council resolution which resulted in close to 200 thousands Iraqi deaths,

-Undermining the United Nations by misusing the Security Council machinery during the war and, as the victor, circumventing the United Nations after the war,

-American intolerance vis-a-vis the inherent uncertainties of popular uprisings in southern Iraq and in the north which allowed Saddam Hussein to massacre thousands of Iraqi people and to uproot more than 2 millions,

-Continuation of the old contradictory policy by the United States with respect to the Middle East; further provision of advanced weapons and financial assistance to Israel, the sole winner in the war despite its decades of aggression against Palestinians,

-Escalation of arms-race in the Middle East and the Persian Gulf,

-Extension and expansion of foreign military presence, leading to further escalation of tensions among the regional states and overall destabilization of the Persian Gulf.

To draw a clearer picture of the future of the Persian Gulf, I begin with a brief exposition of the U.S. role and objectives in the recent crisis, and then I will proceed to discuss the issues

1

0129

related to the future security of the Persian Gulf.

I would suggest that the United States became involved in this crisis in order to secure its own long term interests. The objective was for the United States to become the final arbiter in the political and economic life of the region. The U.S.-led war to force Iraq out of Kuwait resulted in expansion of U.S. power and influence in many of the regional states. This power, Washington thought, will enable the administration to shape the future of not only the Persian Gulf area but also the entire Middle East. Furthermore, it would give the U.S. Government a strong leverage for extending its influence over Europe and Japan through a tacit control of the supply of energy from the Persian Gulf area. This was the frame of mind in Washington on 2 August 1990, if not before it.

With the Soviet Union practically out of the picture, the U.S. administration realized that it could give an international flavor to its national policies by using the mechanism of the United Nations Security Council. There are many examples that one may cite concerning the United States misuse of the United Nations machinery to secure its objective.

The United States rush to use military force was one of the aspects of the influence and power wielded in the United Nations to pass resolution 678. Comprehensive economic sanctions against Iraq were more effective than any other sanctions in the history of international relations. American influence and power in the Security Council thus deprived the United Nations to explore all facilities at its disposal, including the economic sanctions, before it was pushed to authorize the use of force to repel Iraqi aggression.

The discrepancy between the objective of U.N. resolutions and the allied military actions is another example of the abuse to which the United Nations was subjected. The ultimate objective of the 14 resolutions adopted by the United Nations Security Council was limited to evicting Iraq from Kuwait. However, this objective was expanded to include the destruction of Iraq's military capability and civilian infrastructure by the allied forces.

In fact, the unbridled use of force by the allied forces has opened debates within the United Nations and academic circles as to the prudence of authorizing the use of force without designing a mechanism to have control over the actual operation of the implementation of the U.N. resolutions.

An alternative that has informally begun to be discussed and has been the subject of recent scholarly essays, is the revitalization of the United Nations Military Staff Committee. This option could have been explored in dealing with Iraq's invasion of Kuwait -- because the rivalry between the Soviet Union

2

0130

and the United States was absent in this case.

These are but a few examples of the United States tactics in the recent crisis that have alerted not only the people in the Middle East but all peoples of the developing countries. These points do not testify, as far as we are concerned, to a bright future for the Persian Gulf region where the U.S. administration claims a new world order came into existence. In view of the people of the region, Arabs and non-Arabs alike, the elements involved in the U.S. - led war against Iraq were the same old elements of hegemony, and pursuit of a super-power interest in the Persian Gulf. What makes this experience distinct from those during the cold war is that the entire experience of the Persian Gulf war was under a superficial banner of international endorsement.

The actual conduct of war against Iraq to evict it from Kuwait is over, albeit with problems I listed above. However, the management of politics of the region and the unresolved differences are yet to be started. These, I am sure, will prove to be a more difficult task to accomplish. They are also better indicative of U.S. policy in the Persian Gulf. It will soon be further clear whether the United States will promote cooperation or confrontation among the states in the region, whether it will promote arms limitation plan in the area or will sale weapons to its preferred clients.

In this context the question of future security arrangements for the Persian Gulf will become a fundamentally important issue, on which I will now focus.

In this era of growing interdependence, it is imperative to have a broader definition of security. Various elements of security at individual, national, regional, and international levels are organically intertwined. National security influences and is influenced by security at other levels.

The notion of National Security, in its limited military dimension, raises a problem which is, the theoretic concept of security dilemma. The more a state enhances its military strength to achieve its national security goal, the more it might encroach on the security of other states, particularly its neighbors. Hence, a state in pursuit of its national security has to consider the security of other states.

In this age of interdependence, security ought to be defined in terms of a comprehensive scheme encompassing political, social, economic, cultural, environmental, and military dimensions. Such a comprehensive arrangement is the ultimate objective for which the Islamic Republic of Iran is working hard to achieve. We have to work hard to convince the entire region about this inclusive notion of security. Understanding the restraints of reality in the Persian Gulf and the difficulties to change the habits of the old

3

0131

way of thinking about national security, we are prepared to work very hard.

After this introduction and before proceeding to talk about security arrangements for the Persian Gulf I would like to make two general observations. Any security plan for the Persian Gulf, if it is expected to be viable and conducive to the stability of the Middle East and the rest of the world, should have the following two qualities:

First: The Persian Gulf should be treated as a total unit with its own particular problems and peculiar characteristics. It should not therefore, be expanded to include the entire Middle East. For, the problems in the Middle East have their own independent history and dynamics. However, unresolved conflicts in the Middle East could influence the security and stability of the Persian Gulf.

Second: The security plan for the Persian Gulf should not be imposed or glued together by the outside states and on the basis of military presence of foreign powers. It should be regional and grass-root. For foreign presence will only increase the already existing tensions among the populations and thus escalate the instability of the region.

Unfortunately, the predominant thinking in the Persian Gulf in the context of security has long been centered around military strength. This exclusive concept of security at the expense of social and economic development, has cost the Persian Gulf region the destruction of three countries, Iran, Kuwait and Iraq. By this proposition I do not intend to white-wash the role of international politics in Iraq's decision to invade Iran or Kuwait. I am simply portraying the mind frame in the Persian Gulf which allowed itself to become the victim of expedient world politics.

However, in the aftermath of the allied war against Iraq, it seems that some regional leaders and publicists have come to question the prevailing notion that equates military strength with security. The question, now, is: how much military power is sufficient to preserve one's security? Iraq's military is destroyed now. Iran has been under sanction during the eight years of war, and since the cease-fire in 1988, it has been preoccupied with reconstruction and economic development and not with building up its miliary forces. Under such circumstances, one wonders about the intentions behind U.S. major arms sales to the Persian Gulf and other states in the Middle East. What will happen to allied weapons already in place in Kuwait and Saudi Arabia? What are the perceived threats against which arms procurements are supposed to provide security? Of course, I am cognizant of the pressure that military industry wields against their governments to export weapons, but it would be naive to believe that as the whole story. Answers to these and other questions will have to be among the

4

0132

guidelines for some kind of arms limitation plan for the states in the Middle East and the Persian Gulf. Further arms sales by Western countries and third world arms - producing countries will be detrimental to the security of the Persian Gulf. We should take advantage of the current situation and devote more attention to arms control for the Middle East and the Persian Gulf.

Of course, the differential treatment of Non-Proliferation Treaty in respect of Israel is a pointed problem which need to be addressed separately. This situation would naturally compel other states in the region to seek nuclear weapons and other weapons of mass destruction. It may be high time, after the war in the Persian Gulf where Iraq's weapons of mass destruction is destroyed to pursue the idea of Nuclear Free Zone in the Middle East very seriously. The International Community should put pressure to bear upon Israel to sign and conform with the Non-Proliferation Treaty.

In view of the Islamic Republic of Iran time has come for the countries in the region to give serious thoughts to allocation of their resources in a fashion that provides a greater degree of economic, social, and cultural developments. Otherwise, the Persian Gulf will become a warehouse of military hardware to the detriment of growth and higher standard of living. A situation that breaths suspicions and creates instability. This new thinking will not bear fruits unless there is effective communications between the littoral states to reach mutual understanding on the security of the region.

Another major consideration in prospect of security in the Persian Gulf is economic and cultural cooperation. The states of the region have a vast potential for economic cooperation. It needs political will and confidence to explore the possibilities. At the broadest level, I would like to suggest that the regional states as the oil producers have common interests with the consumer states. Oil producers and consumers will both benefit by maintaining the freedom of shipping lanes in the Persian Gulf and by a stable market. A market that is stabilized by the principle of supply and demand, free from non-market variables. At any rate, any future Persian Gulf security arrangement should be attentive to the common interests of the oil producing states and their consumer states.

In the context of economic cooperation, the question of Haves and Have-nots in the broader region should not be over looked. If we are to root out the underlying sources of tension, this issue should be seriously addressed. Future economic planning in the region should lead to redistribution of the economic resources within the region and the closing of the gap between the haves and have-nots.

It is expected that economic cooperation, social, and cultural exchanges will promote a better atmosphere of political

5

0133

cooperation, but realistically speaking, competition is likely to continue, however at a slower pace and hopefully in a constructive manner. Cooperation will likely remain conditional in the future. Regional countries must still be convinced, that in certain areas, they could maximize their own interests through cooperation rather than by individual efforts or confrontations. One such example of cooperation is the common efforts by regional states to ensure the security of their environment. No one state in the Persian Gulf can effectively deal with the huge problem of pollution that has befallen the region. Expansion of the volume of trade in different fields is another potential for economic cooperation. The underlying incentive and criteria for the future relations between the states in the region ought to be cooperation and perhaps constructive competition but never confrontation. Regional countries must be convinced that no one party can maximize its own self interests at the expense of the others. These are assurances that parties concerned need to provide, in good faith, both in words and deeds to one another.

There are some political considerations that have direct bearings on the question of future security of the region. The extent and strength of a regional security is an outcome of the perceived external threats by a member and the degree of internal instability and/or discontentment. One major problem in formulating a viable regional security arrangement is the problem of internal discontentment that may threaten some of the states in that region.

History is the best reminder of the old aged technique of diverting attention from internal problems by making far - fetched external threat or exaggerating about external threat to unite people against a foreign enemy.

A lesson to be learned from the crisis in the Persian Gulf is that dictatorship is very costly. A high price is to be paid by all, when massive external supports are provided to a regime which is not restrained by domestic forces and lacks public legitimacy. Therefore, public participation of people in their collective affairs will guarantee internal security which in turn leads to a stronger regional security. In this connection, democratic institutions as well as checks and balances on government behavior and procedures such as public elections and parliaments have to be promoted and strengthened, if the regional security is to be effective and long lasting in the Persian Gulf.

Following the establishment of the cease-fire between Iran and Iraq, despite all odds, my Government has strived to promote the idea of regional security along the preceding principles that I have mentioned. Ideas that are marked by cooperation rather than confrontation. Iraq's invasion of Kuwait and the war that followed are indicative of the validity and the urgency of the need to further promote and implement a new thinking about the problems and the security arrangements so that similar crisis could be

6

0134

prevented. Many positive steps have been taken and yet many more
are still needed.

7

Eberhard RHEIN, Brussels

Europe and the Gulf region: a long-term perspective[1]

1. Europe iis vitally dependent on stable, secure oil supplies from
    the Gulf region. It has an overriding interest in an unimpeded
    flow of oil from that region.

    It shares that interest with the USA, Japan and a growing number
    of developing countries.

2. This interest seems best secured in the absence of military
    conflict, severe political tension or other turmoil likely to
    lead to an interruption of oil flows or, even worse, to a
    destruction of oil reserves.

3. Political stability in the Gulf region has therefore always been
    the primary objective of western policy over the last 40 years.
    In the past, such stability has been sought by

    —   maintaining a strong western, essentially US, political
        influence in the region and building strong ties with one or
        the other major power in the region, up to 1979 Iran, since
        then Saudi Arabia plus the GCC,

    —   preventing non-friendly external powers (i.e. the Soviet
        Union) from establishing a dominant influence in the region,

    —   preventing any single country from gaining a controlling
        influence over the Middle East oil reserves and thus reaching
        a monopoly position in the world oil market.

---

(1) Chatham House Conference, 9 May 1991.

0136

4. In the future, political stability in the Gulf will have to remain a key objective of European foreign policy.

How is such political stability to be best secured in the next decades, what rôle for Europe in that respect?

4.1 Political stability will be best achieved, if and when the "three pillars" of the Gulf - Iran, Iraq and the GCC - establish a more cooperative relationship instead of the traditional rivalry for regional supremacy.

As long as the traditional power struggles do not cease, there will be no end to the arms race which, if left unheeded, is bound - sooner or later - to erupt anew into military conflict, as the two Iraqi aggressions have sorely demonstrated.

4.2 Political stability between the countries seems less and less secured without internal political stability.

There will not be internal political stability in the long run without democracy and respect of fundamental human rights.

Power and wealth will need to be shared more equally; minorities, whether ethnic or religious, will have to be given their say in government. Profound social changes are bound to take place in the Middle East; it is essential that these take place smoothly, by reform instead of by revolution!

4.3 Europe's rôle in working for greater stability in the region is bound to be limited. We cannot substitute lacking political will or maturity by advice or example. We cannot force anyone to what we believe to be the path of virtue!

With such - important - qualification Europe has a triple rôle to play.

0137

4.3.1 We should try to persuade the three Gulf powers to institute contractual forms of regional cooperation, or better integration among themselves.

The GCC is a good example; but as long as its thrust is directed more against the two neighbours in the north, and not conceived as the hard core of a wider cooperation with Iraq and Iran, the germs of distrust and power struggle remain in place; and the GCC will only remain an instrument for changing the balance of power in favour of its six members. What sort of cooperation to install?

There seem to be at least three fields, environment, trade and energy:

- the environmental protection of the Gulf is a common goal of all the surrounding countries;

- there is plenty of room for expanding trade among the Gulf countries. The example of the GCC demonstrates it. Why not strive for an FTA between the GCC, Iraq and Iran?

- there is room for more cooperation in the field of energy. Is it inconceivable to admit Iran as an associate member to the OAPEC?

4.3.2 Europe must, with even more vigour, lend its moral support to all those who fight for more democracy and human rights. This corresponds to our moral and political convictions, but it is also in line with our self-interest.

4.3.3 Finally, Europe must pay more than only lip service to the reduction of the level of arms supplies to the region. A "Gulf Community" will not take shape in the near future, if ever. Should we not try, in the meantime, to achieve instability at the lowest possible level of military weaponry? Must Europe therefore

0138

not take the initiative or support at least other initiatives to control the export of arms to the region, within a multilateral framework, however difficult this may be?

5. How to implement such broad and long-term objectives?

5.1 In the most general way, Europe must step up - substantially - the level of interaction with the countries and people of the Gulf.

Compared to its vital strategic importance, the region has been neglected or, at best, been considered as an attractive market for European equipment, luxury car or arms producers. We have not been able to institute a meaningful political dialogue (not necessarily because of our fault only). This is bound to change, for the EC even more than for member states.

It is a sad anachronism that, among the 100 odd Delegations that the Community maintains throughout the world, there is none in Teheran, Riyadh or Baghdad. This is going to change as of 1992.

5.2 It is equally strange that it took the Community until 1990 to establish contractual relations (in the form of cooperation agreements) with at least one of the regional powers, the GCC[1]. The relations between the Community and Iran have sufficiently warmed up recently to warrant the negotiation of a similar agreement with Iran in the not too distant future, to be followed by an Iraq-EC agreement, as soon as the internal political conditions will be ripe for such a major political gesture.

5.3 Much more important for the future EC-Gulf relations will be the outcome of the ongoing negotiations between the Community and the GCC on a FTA.

(1) Leaving aside an insignificant trade agreement with Iran concluded in the early sixties.

0139

If concluded, such an agreement will no doubt usher in a very intimate economic relationship between Europe and the GCC. Geopolitically, it will be also Europe's reaching out for a more important political rôle in the Gulf region.

6. Supposing close economic cooperation being established between the three Gulf powers and thereby a high degree of political stability, is there not a danger for Europe becoming the victim of monopolistic oil price policies by the three powers who will control an important and increasing share of the world's oil supply? Is therefore the aim of political stability and security of oil supply only to be achieved at the price of a higher oil price?

Such a reasoning overlooks certain fundamental long-term factors:

- first, the price of oil is bound to increase substantially in real terms over the next decades, as we move closer to depletion of resources (in much less than a hundred years!).

- secondly, the sooner Europe (and the world at large) grasps this fundamental, however unpleasant truth the better can it prepare for the post-oil era of more expensive energy.

- thirdly, the power of a Gulf "oil monopoly" will be restrained by the countervailing power of the future "gas monopolist" of the Soviet Union.

- fourthly, the better the Gulf powers are able to smooth the inevitable long-term rise of the oil price, the better should Europe be able to develop the substitution energies necessary for its survival as a region of prosperity.

6. Political stability in the Gulf will not be reached, as long as there is conflict or threat of conflict in the immediate neighbourhood.

0140

Two main areas of conflict will have to be addressed, the Israeli-Arab conflict and the potential Turkish-Syrian /Iraqi discord over water supplies.

What solutions for either?
What, if any rôle for Europe?

6.1 The solution for the Israeli-Arab conflict is well-known: peace against land. The devil lies in the detail. Successive US Secretaries of State have become sorely aware of the very intricate nature of the peace process.

Europe has so far not played an active rôle in bringing peace to the Near East. It will continue to be only an interested, well-intentioned observer. It has never tried to wield its own (usually underestimated) leverage.

Europe's rôle can be one of economic and financial support to the parties, once an agreement is reached. It can - and must - shoulder a major share of the financial burden necessary to secure peace and economic cooperation between the partners.

6.2 Turkey's GAP project will substantially reduce the quantity and the quality of the Euphrates and Tigris water flowing presently into Syria and Iraq.[1] This is bound to impair good neighbourly relations. It may produce a collision ending in military confrontation.

There is only one safe way of at least softening a major water conflict between Turkey and its two downstream neighbours: a Euphrates/Tigris regional water authority, under which the three countries will jointly operate the overall water resources and share them.[2]

---

[1] by at least one third of the total water volume of ± 48 billion m^3/year.
[2] The Nile river agreement is an example of what may be done.

0141

Europe's rôle is again very limited. It should help to bring the three parties to the negotiation table, so as to allow the necessary adjustments, including joint dams where feasible.

7. The Gulf region constitutes Europe's life blood; it will continue to do so for at least another 50-80 years.

Europe can therefore not afford to neglect that region which — in geopolitical terms — will remain the most sensitive one in the world. It has to understand what goes on there. It has to try to influence developments there whenever these threaten to be contrary to European interests.

It has, above all, to establish a close relationship of economic, political, technological and cultural cooperation with the three Gulf powers.

Geographic proximity and existing cultural ties should facilitate the setting up of a close network of interdependence. We are at the very beginning of that process. The challenge before us is important, far too important to be left only to diplomats, government officials or Middle East traders. The Gulf region must become one of the priority regions of European foreign policy, by the same token as the USA, the Soviet Union or Japan.

We cannot afford any longer to be taken by surprise. Let us learn at least one lesson from August 2, 1990: the Gulf is of vital interest to us. We need friends there!

0142

9. Oil Supply and Price - The Potential for Partnership with the West

Summary

There have been three main reactions to the consequences of the recent Gulf War:
(a) Some people see it as proof that markets work if left to themselves - and things should be left that way.
(b) Others are calling for a Consumer/Producer conference or dialogue: things are too dangerous to be left to the market.
(c) A further view is that the crisis was indeed dangerous, but that corrective action for the future is a matter for quiet diplomacy and bilateral discussion.

In my view, a major oil crisis was avoided at least as much by luck as by judgement. However, the issues of real concern to consumers are not identical with the interests of the producers.

Consumers need, or ought to feel the need for:
(a) Better emergency security arrangements including much larger and more widely spread, strategic stocks. There should be a willingness to use some of these stocks to contain damaging price rises in a crisis. The LDCs need to be involved, not just the OECD.
(b) Policies that limit increases in demand for crude (and products) from the Middle East.
(c) Assurance that adequate spare production capacity will be available to cope with future disruptions with the involvement of risk capital investments by western firms.
(d) Acceptance that environmental greenhouse gas containment will result in reduced calls for crude oil.

The producers shopping list is rather different. It includes:
(a) Management of prices and assurance of growing markets so as to meet the budget needs of reconstruction and growing populations.
(b) Access to overseas funds to develop extra production capacity.
(c) Continued downstream intergration.

The idea that some sort of consumer-producer buffer stock could smooth out prices is a non-starter. Only the producers can manage prices by careful matching of supply and demand.

The short term prognosis is uncertain. Extra capacity was brought on stream in the emergency. Demand is not going up fast and Iraqi and Kuwaiti oil will be entering the market. However, in the longer term, unless consumers take positive action, the World will become increasingly reliant again on the Middle East with all the risks that entails, including reliance on Iraqi crude.

Positive policies are therefore urgently needed. A cumbersome international conference is unlikely to produce valuable results. But individual actions and a degree of mutual understanding are highly desirable.

Silvan Robinson

0143

THE MIDDLE EAST CONFERENCE - Thursday 9 May 1991
(Royal Institute of International Affairs)

HOW MUCH INFLUENCE WILL THE US AND ITS ALLIES HAVE ON OIL POLICY
by Peter Bild - Chief News Editor AFX News

* A little over two months ago at the end of February this year, Algeria's mines minister Sadek Boussena, the man responsible for his country's oil industry, was asked some questions by Italian journalists about the future of Opec in the wake of the Gulf war. What sort of organisation would Opec be following the invasion and occupation of one member by another? Could Opec, he was asked, ever again be an effective and collectively wielded instrument of the oil policies of its member states?

* The question was posed about 10 days before Opec members were due to meet in Geneva for their first ministerial get-together as the dust and sand were still settling in the wake of Operation Desert Storm.

* As a sensible and intelligent individual would, he did not pretend that Opec - though founded and run as a purely economic organisation - could escape the political fall-out of the Gulf crisis and war. He replied, not unreasonably, that this would depend on a number of factors. One of them, he said, related to Saudi Arabia's perception of its interests after the upheavals of the Gulf war. A question that would have to be answered, he said, was this: to what extent could Saudi Arabia (which had been the base for nearly half a million largely western forces) be expected to pursue an oil policy independent of the interests of the United States?

* This generally unremarkable interview was carried in a daily Italian newspaper where it was spotted by the correspondents of a number of international news agencies. How did the newshounds respond? Alert as they are to the sensitivities of the oil markets, anxious as any journalist would be to the potential for frontpage-grabbing headlines of international conflict - how did Reuters, AP-Dow Jones and the others react that day? They ignored the story. It was, after all, a statement of the obvious.

* The Saudis, however, did not ignore M Boussena's remarks. Their response was startling in its vehemence. A few days later in the run-up to Opec's Geneva session, it became clear just what an explosive issue this was for the world's largest oil exporter. Let me quote from the Oil Daily Energy Compass of 9 March 1991 which received an unsolicited phone call from a Saudi oil policy official. Middle East Economic Survey (MEES), Petroleum Intelligence Weekly and others received similar calls. The Saudi oil official said about M Boussena:
" He tells us to keep politics out of Opec and then accuses of hatching an oil price conspiracy with the United States. Sadek Boussena implies we are simply carrying out US oil price policy. But if he knows what official US policy is on prices, I wish he would share the secret with me because I haven't a clue what it is."

0144

* So now we know the answer to the question posed as the title for these remarks: "How much Influence will the US and its allies have over Oil Policy". The answer obviously is "None" - and that's official.

* It may be official, but is it really the answer? Ever anxious to avoid making up answers when there are policy-makers and former policy-makers around who should know, I decided to ask one of them. What would Sheik Zaki Yamani have to say? I asked him. "No comment" he replied "But, please, Peter. That is off the record". Bearing in mind Chatham House rules, I must ask any fellow reporters to keep that illuminating response "off-the-record".

* I tried elsewhere and asked other less exalted individuals, who are still oil policy makers, the same question. Their answer: "Its obvious. Washington runs Saudi oil policy. While King Fahd is in power, George Bush, Dan Quayle, or General Norman Schwarzkopf have only to pick up the telephone to determine Saudi oil production and the world price of oil."

* So there you have it again. The answer is "The US and its allies have total influence on Opec and Middle East oil policy." This time, it is unofficial, even though an official said it.

* But is that really true? Even if it were, would it or could it happen like that? And even if the answer were to be a qualified "Yes", how much impact would such a phone call have on the world's oil price? How big a role does "policy" play in world oil and energy developments compared with other forces?

* Starting with the extreme views expressed by two policy makers, are views really so divided? Was, for example, Sadek Boussena suggesting that oil producers should or could determine their oil production and price policies in a political vacuum or without some regard to the interest of consumers in the US and its allies?

* It is worth quoting another argument presented at an Opec gathering in December when members confirmed their earlier decision to unilaterally raise production:
"The Opec ministerial monitoring committee was therefore imbued with this spirit of collective market responsibility when it declared that the burden of tackling the crisis (arising out of the loss of Iraqi and Kuwaiti oil supplies) lay not with Opec, nor even with the producers alone, but also with consumers from the industrialized world...".
Who was this toady of the west who suggested that policy must take account of consumer interests and should be responsive the consumers' policy initiatives? None other than Opec President Sadek Boussena.

0145

* Lets return to my vehement Saudi: "If somebody can tell me what official Saudi policy is on prices, I wish he would share the secret with me". The vehemence tells us merely that however great US and allied influence really is, we are unlikely to find that influence publicly expressed or acknowledged. Because of political, cultural and religious sensitivities - and this tells us a great deal about the robustness or fragility of political regimes in the Middle East - influence publicly expressed is likely to be counter-productive.

* Before returning to the question of influence over policy, I should like to raise the question, at least, as to how big a role national "policy" or "policies" actually plays in oil market and oil industry developments. It is clear that oil policy, both its expression and implementation, affect the political stability and future of many Middle East countries. In its simplest form, it is obvious that the oil price is crucial to the economic and thus the political welfare of a number of Middle East countries. It is less clear that the reverse is true, that "policy" per se is a major influence on price.

* Lets focus for a moment on the price of oil. A few days ago, Robert Mabro led a discussion in Chatham House on the subject of what actually determines the oil price. Let me pick up some of the highlights of that discussion. There are all the obvious difficulties of determining which oil price is important, crude or products, and then which crude or which products.

* While it might be clear to some free-market purists
that the price of crude is determined by the price of products, the price of most Opec crude is actually set day-to-day by reference to the price of non-Opec crude such as North Sea Brent or in the states Alaskan North Slope or WTI. Even if we home in on the relationships between those crudes and products, it is obvious that these vary over time and in response to market pressures. It is not inevitable that this should be so, and for many years while Opec tried to determine both absolute and relative selling prices of their crudes, it was not the case. But if we accept market pressures as the simple answer, it is obvious that the relative attractiveness of one crude over another in response to product demand is in some way linked to the policies of consumer governments. Growing environmental awareness and the implementation of environmentally aware energy policies in the US and its allies clearly has an influence on Middle East and other oil producers, whether deliberate or not.

0146

* Even if we look at the obvious interaction of supply and demand, the free marketeers who deny the influence of Opec policies have a lot of explaining to do. It is obvious that Opec actions or intentions, even if their impact is via the price expectations of buyers, sellers and traders, DO have an influence on the oil price. Rather than getting lost in a sterile and ultimately semantic debate about what constitutes a market, let us just accept that the "market" incorporates in some way the activities of those groupings like Opec and consumer governments that wittingly or unwittingly have an impact on both supply and demand for oil.

* Before returning to western influence on Middle East oil policy, we have to ask what sort of policy choices Middle East and other Opec producers are likely to have in the short to medium term. Right now, Opec members are producing at or near their limits. This means that the only real choice they face right now is to reduce their production significantly in order to raise oil prices significantly. If they did that, consumer governments would doubtless start to worry. Individually or collectively through the IEA they would make noises about the impact on inflation or world recession and the third world. In this hypothetical scenario, its a safe bet that pretty soon, King Fahd's phone would start ringing and instructions would go out to Aramco to increase production. That would indicate strong US and allied influence on oil policy. Could this happen?

* Its worth looking for clues in the events of 1986. Opec had launched a price war, in effect if not in name, by setting "market share" as its policy priority at the end of 1985. A succession of long drawn-out ministerial meetings in Geneva and Vienna had failed, or not even tried, to halt the slide which took prices from around $30 a barrel in late 1985 to under $10 in late spring 1986. If we are talking about policy, it was clear that the so-called "Opec monopoly", sometimes referred to as the world's most powerful cartel, had totally failed to have any significant impact on the oil policies of the US and its allies. Pleas for joint measures to stabilise oil prices, for help in reducing the supply surplus, had fallen on deaf ears.

* During Ramadan, in the Saudi summer capital of Taif, Sheik Yamani assembled an informal but influential group of ministers and officials from other Opec countries. The magic number "18" began to emerge. 18 million b/d was the sort of market share that Opec could live with. $18 a barrel, give or take one or two dollars, was a reasonable price range to aim for. At the official Opec level, however, nothing happened for several months to turn this concept into reality. Opec members argued over the criteria to be adopted for distributing market share and an official price of $28 remained the official, but officially suspended, Opec price. Not until the beginning of August did Opec take any effective action to end the price war when its members agreed, apparently out of the blue, to reinstate temporarily the quotas that had previously supported a $28 price.

0147

* Was it really out of the blue? Or was it, as some observers believe, out of the blue eyes of Vice-President George Bush who had visited Saudi Arabia and King Fahd some months earlier? Was the Taif session at which the $18 and 18 million b/d consensus emerged a result of US influence on Saudi and thus on Opec oil policy? Or was that merely the result of intolerable financial pressures on all Opec members?

* I believe George Bush and his visit to Saudi Arabia did play a role. Whether it affected the course of developments or merely affected the timing is a question to which the answer is more difficult to find. In the end, one can argue, the distinction is immaterial. Timing is crucial in history, just as it is for market players. Bush's influence, if it was exercised, was only able to play a role because prices had fallen so far and so fast. Times were exceptional. Without the financial pressures on Opec, the influence would have been rejected.

* This is I believe is the crux of the matter if we look at the situation today. Is the current price of oil and its prospective availability sufficiently uncomfortable for either consumers or producers to provoke the exercise or even the attempted exercise of direct influence on oil policy? I believe not.

* How long will this be true? Are we likely to see a situation arising in which the US and its allies are likely to want to exercise influence over policy?

* Obviously, no one can predict political developments in the Middle East which are likely to overthrow all calculations of what is likely to emerge. But again I believe that the perceived need for direct allied influence on Opec oil policy is unlikely to emerge even in the medium term. There are two reasons:
1> The exercise of external influence is unpopular and would be uncomfortable both for the the U.S. and for the recipient of such advice. It raises divisive debate within the U.S. which is itself a coalition of producer and consumer interests and does little to enhance any President electoral or re-electoral chances. For Saudi Arabia or any Opec government, suggestions that its oil policy strings are being pulled from outside are destabilizing and -- as we have seen in the case of Kuwait -- can give rise to powerful movements that throw into doubt the legitimacy of family regimes.
2> Second, I believe Opec countries and governments have learned some lessons from the past. "Policies" can be extremely damaging in the long term, however attractive they look in the short run. An excess of "policy" can be damaging to one's economic and political health. It may have been the market that took oil prices up to nearly $40 a barrel in the early 1980s. But it was a deliberate act of policy by Opec members to keep them there. Even the most traditionally hawkish of Opec governments is now willing to admit to the error of such policies. Again let me quote Algerian minister Sadek Boussena who as President told Opec ministers as they took action to increase rather than curtail supply:

0148

"Uppermost in our concerns were the experiences of the previous ten years when increases in oil prices were followed by a sharp drop (both in demand and price - my insertion) which then dominated market affairs in the 1980s.

* Putting aside occasional outbursts of rhetoric, I believe the days of Opec policy "activism" are over. The policy is to desire stability, but to do only just enough to bring it about.

* That realisation will be the factor which most limits US and allied influence on oil policy. The policy will be too hard to find, let alone to influence.

* The oil policy will be to avoid oil policy. The policy will be: Policy is dead...long live that policy." Even the U.S. will have a hard time influencing that.

0149

POST-WAR ECONOMIC OUTLOOK
IN SAUDI ARABIA AND THE GULF

HENRY T. AZZAM
CHIEF ECONOMIST

THE NATIONAL COMMERCIAL BANK
JEDDAH, SAUDI ARABIA

MAY 3, 1991

0150

POST-WAR ECONOMIC OUTLOOK
IN SAUDI ARABIA AND THE GULF

1. INTRODUCTION:

The economies of Saudi Arabia and the other Gulf states have proven their resilience during the Gulf crisis. Whatever damage afflicted has been contained and the economies of the region are now regaining the momentum that was building up before the Iraqi invasion of Kuwait. Peace in the region removes a major element of uncertainty and encourages Gulf businessmen to reconsider investment decisions put on hold because of the crises. It will also help boost consumer confidence and encourage more relaxed spending patterns. It will take sometime before Kuwait and Iraq are able to resume their pre-war oil production levels. This should lend some fundamental strength to the world oil market. Oil price are unlikely to tumble and Saudi Arabia, UAE, Oman, Qatar and Bahrain could maintain oil production close to recent high levels. Stable oil revenues will make it possible for the governments of the region not to cut fiscal expenditures thus maintaining steady domestic economic growth.

With the end of the crisis, a major risk element that had daunted the Gulf countries in the later part of 1990 has now been removed and focus is shifting back to the region's more positive economic fundamentals. International business outlook to the Gulf countries is changing. The region now out of the news limelight, is no more viewed as being in a war zone. The crisis has demonstrated that the world is committed to the security and territorial integrity of the Gulf countries and to the free flow of oil from the region. Saudi Arabia and the other Gulf states have emerged from the crisis as a major regional power, capable of reasserting themselves in OPEC and other regional and international bodies. The bold decisions taken by the Gulf governments during the crisis, the improvement in the regional geo-political atmosphere, the growing sense of national identity, unity and self-confidence in the region, and the gradual rise in consumer spending should translate into better business opportunities for the region's private sectors.

Solution of the Gulf crisis has had global dimension as well. It boosted consumer and business confidence worldwide and encouraged people to invest and spend. It had also lessened the chances of higher oil prices, thereby dampening inflationary pressures in the major industrial states and brought forth lower oil import bills. International and regional businesses will benefit from the rebuilding of Kuwait's war ravaged economy and from the resurgence of exports to the Gulf region. Equally important, developing countries especially those in the Middle East who had suffered because of the crisis will be able to resume normal growth path.

0151

- 2 -

Most industries in Saudi Arabia and the other Gulf states will benefit from the additional demand generated by the reconstruction process in Kuwait and later on in Iraq. Those industries that are especially sensitive to transportation costs and quick deliveries (e.g. cement, steel, aluminum and other construction related materials) should prove competitive. Gulf engineering and construction companies will be drawn upon especially for small and medium size construction projects and sub-contracting for international companies. Banking, aviation, insurance and shipping will also benefit as the process of reconstruction and development proceeds and re-export trade will witness a major boost.

While economic growth prospects for Saudi Arabia and the Gulf in the coming twelve months are encouraging, the cost incurred because of the Gulf war will continue to weigh on the governments' financial position this year. The region has incurred additional costs because of the crisis, far more than the extra revenues generated from last year's higher oil prices and production levels. The financial commitment to the multinational Gulf war effort, the aid and long term loans extended to friendly developing countries, the new requirements of the defence sector in light of the Gulf crisis and the planned investment to boost the region's oil production capacity are significant additional expenditures that will be accounted for in this year's finances. Government expenditures are unlikely to be cut much inorder to preserve steady growth in domestic economic activities. The current oil production levels are, therefore, expected to be maintained which together with burgeoning petrochemical, aluminum and other non-oil exports will help boost the overall trade surplus of various Gulf states. However, the heavy financial commitments will continue to weigh on Gulf states' budgets and current account balances. Projected deficits will be financed mainly by drawing down on reserves supplemented by internal borrowing, privatization, gradual liquidation of foreign assets and some international borrowing.

2. IMPACT OF THE CRISIS ON THE ECONOMIES OF THE REGION.

Economic indicators in Saudi Arabia and the other Gulf states pointed towards solid growth in the first seven months of 1990, continuing the uptrend that started in the year before. Nominal GDP moved higher, inflation remained subdued and by July last year, share prices reached an all time high. Exports of petrochemicals and other non-oil products were on the rise, refineries and industrial plants were operating close to full capacity and commercial banks reported better mid-year results with a noticeable resurgence in deposits and demand for bank credit. Commerce and retail sales activities were generally up and the countries of the region were making steady progress towards attaining

0152

- 3 -

economic diversification and reducing the dependence on oil as the primary engine of growth. However, the thrust of activities slowed down following Iraq's invasion of Kuwait last August. Less sanguine post-August economic indicators were more visible in certain non-oil sectors, while growth in oil revenues remained buoyant reflecting firmer oil prices and higher production levels.

Economic growth during the period August-December 1990 was lopsided. the oil sectors and those domestic activities benefiting from the multinational military buildup and the arrival of thousands of Kuwaiti nationals to the other GCC states recorded sizeable growth rates, while other non-oil sectors remained generally subdued. The uncertainty created by the crisis reduced domestic consumption of durable and luxury good items, delayed long term investment plans and brought forth retrenchment in such services as shipping, aviation, banking and consulting. Several projects were either delayed or put on hold pending a solution to the crisis. Traders ran down stocks rather than pay for high war risk premiums on imported cargoes and the increased cost of credit. Capital outflows were recorded during the first few weeks following the invasion, but have subsided later on. Although the data are sketchy, indications are that there have been substantial reflows of capital since August and by the end of the first quarter this year bank deposits were heading towards pre-crisis levels.

The region's stock markets which performed quite well during the first half of the year tumbled following the crisis. Before the Iraqi invasion of Kuwait, activities on the newly established Bahrain and Oman stock exchanges were performing better than expected with prices generally firming. Share prices in Saudi Arabia also soared in the first half of the year and by May 1990, the official share price index reached an all time high of 118.3, up 8% from its level at the beginning of the year. By July 30, 1990, Kuwaiti shares as well as shares traded in the UAE were also up on their corresponding 1989 levels. The first public issue of Arab Banking Corporation was a success and several new public companies were established namely Alujain, the Saudi Industrial Development Company, and the Arabian Industrial Development Corporation.

Gulf share prices assumed a declining trend from August to November 1990, but recovered somewhat by the end of the year. In Saudi Arabia for example, the official price index dropped 22% during the last five months of the year, and the value of shares traded was also down by almost 50% on levels recorded in the first half. For the whole of 1990, the market's share price index declined by around 10 percent. The drop in Saudi and other Gulf share prices compares favourably with declines of share prices in the world's major financial centers. In Tokyo, for example, the market index declined by 38% in 1990, in Germany it fell by 20.9%, in France it was down 25.2%, in the UK it lost 12% and the Dow Jones Industrial Average in the US dropped 6.4% on the year.

0153

- 4 -

OPEC's crude oil production was higher than the organization's quota of 22.5 mb/d during the first seven months of the year. By July 1990, OPEC's production reached 23.5 mb/d, up from 22.8 mb/d at the beginning of the year, setting the scene for a sharp downward adjustment in the price of oil. The spot price per barrel of OPEC's basket of seven crudes dropped from $20.5 in the first week of January to a low of $13.67 in the third week of June. In the first seven months of the year, OPEC's basket price averaged $16.78 a barrel compared to $17.31 for the whole of 1989 and $14.24 in 1988. During August-December 1990, the price rose to an average of $29.74 a barrel, giving an average price per barrel for the year as a whole of $22.25 . While Kuwait's oil production following the invasion dropped to 100,000 b/d (mainly for local consumption) and Iraq's output did not exceed 450,000 b/d, Saudi Arabia boosted production to 8.5 mb/d with an average for the year of 6.45 mb/d, 28% higher than in 1989. UAE production was up 11% on the year before with an average for 1990 of 2.065 mb/d. Qatar's output was up to a yearly average of 382,000 b/d, Oman boosted production to 683,000 b/d while Bahrain maintained the 43,000 b/d production level attained in 1989.

Even though the higher price and production levels in the last five months of 1990 boosted Gulf states revenues from oil exports, however, the additional expenditures incurred because of the Gulf crisis exceeded the extra income generated. Saudi Arabia, for example, provided ample support to multinational forces including full coverage of fuel, water, food, local transportation, host country facilities and several other expenses incurred. Military spending surged as well to foster the region's own defence capabilities and more than $5 billion was spent to raise oil production capacity of Saudi Arabia and the UAE in order to compensate for the loss of Kuwait's and Iraqi output. Furthermore, a significant portion of Saudi Arabia's incremental oil production was supplied either free of charge to the multinational forces or sold at concessional terms to developing countries in the region who had suffered as a result of implementing the embargo on Iraq.

Since the beginning of the crisis, Gulf governments brought themselves up to date in their payments on contracts, boosting private sector confidence and further easing overall liquidity conditions. There has been a stimulus as well from the multinational military build up in the Gulf. This has generated a sizeable increase in demand for local food and beverage industries, procurement and catering activities, transportation and retail sales in general. The arrival of multinational forces, together with thousands of Kuwaiti national and hundreds of journalists led to heavy demands in the property market especially that of Saudi Arabia's Eastern province, raising rents there. Hotels,

0154

restaurants, trucks and construction equipment owners, car hire and catering companies, food manufacturers and bottled water plants as well as clothing and electronics among others recorded booming business conditions in the second half of the year. The need to provide coalition forces with accommodation led to the award of large number of contracts to local firms giving a boost to construction activities especially in the Kingdom's Eastern provinces.

Even though certain non-oil economic activities in the industrial, trade and construction sectors remained subdued during the August-December period, the overall positive growth recorded in the first seven months of the year and the sizeable rise in oil exports following the crisis, coupled with the stimulus generated from the spending of foreign military forces and the expenditure of Gulf governments to accommodate these forces suggest positive GDP growth rates for the various gulf countries in 1990. With the exception of Kuwait, 1990 growth rates are estimated to have exceeded those of the previous year, with the higher output in the hydrocarbon sectors more than compensating for the slowdown in non-oil GDP. (Table 1)

Inflation in the region edged up in 1990, given the strong economic conditions in the first seven months of the year and generally rising prices of imported goods reflecting higher inflation world wide. The 20% drop in the value of the dollar (to which the Gulf currencies are unofficially pegged) vis-a-vis the currencies of the region's major trading partners of Western Europe and Japan contributed as well to the higher import prices. War risk insurance surcharges and higher fuel prices during August-December period raised marine and air transportation costs and further accentuated the higher prices of imported goods in the region's markets. However, government subsidies on basic goods and services including gasoline, electricity, water, basic food items, education, health and other public services were maintained throughout the year and little or no increase in prices of these items was reported. This had dampened overall inflation figures for the year (Table 2).

3.   THE OIL MARKET OUTLOOK:

The average spot price of OPEC basket of seven crudes dropped to $16.77 per barrel in March down from $17.55 a barrel in February and $22.38 a barrel in January. The March price level is the lowest since the Gulf crisis began last August. The basket price reached a peak of $34.58 per barrel in October last year and has been trending downward since then. Prices are now back to pre-crisis levels and the average for the first quarter this year is $18.9 a barrel for OPEC basket. Led by Saudi Arabia, those OPEC countries unaffected by the

- 6 -

UN embargo, have been successful in making up for the lost Iraqi and Kuwaiti oil. OPEC crude oil production averaged around 23 mb/d in the first quarter this year, up from around 21 mb/d last August. The firm production combined with demand declines in major oil consuming countries, especially the US because of mild weather and economic recession, widened the gap between the call on OPEC oil and the Organization production levels and exerted downward pressure on prices in the first quarter of this year.

With the beginning of the second quarter in April, the seasonal weakening of petroleum demand is expected to reduce demand for OPEC oil by 2 to 3 mb/d compared to the first quarter (Table 3). With non-OPEC supply relatively stable at 28.6 mb/d, the call on OPEC oil is forecast to decline to 23.3 mb/d in the second quarter. However, no dramatic price collapse is expected in the coming few months. Iraq and Kuwait are unlikely to resume production any time soon and OPEC has already started to implement a new production quota for the second quarter with a 5% cut in the organization's output to 22.3 mb/d. The very fact that OPEC did reach a deal on reducing second quarter supply could be sufficient to keep prices relatively steady for the time being. OPEC's third quarter production is expected to reach 22.6 mb/d up from 21.9 mb/d in the second quarter. Supply and demand condition will allow the organization to boost production to 23.4 mb/d in the fourth quarter giving an average for the year of 22.7 mb/d.

It will be sometime before the present embargo is lifted against Iraq's oil exports, previously running at about 2.7 mb/d. Even if all goes straightforwardly in the implementation of the UN ceasefire to end the Gulf war, it will be the third quarter at the earliest before Iraq will be allowed to start exporting oil to the international market, and even then at a much lower level than before. Iraq's crude oil export capacity has been curtailed by more than two thirds as a result of the Gulf war. Extensive damage was inflicted on the country's southern export installations. The pumping station south of Zubair, used to dispatch 1.6 mb/d of crude across Saudi Arabia via IPSA pipeline was destroyed. Parts of Iraq's oil pipelines to Saudi Arabia and Syria were damaged together with surface facilities and pipelines in the southern part of the country. However, Iraq's export installations in the northern part of the country, and in particular, the K-2 pumping station remained mostly intact. After the embargo is lifted, Iraq would be able to export around 800,000 b/d of Kirkuk crude oil via the Iraqi-Turkish pipeline from the Mediterranean. The pipeline will not be used at its full capacity of 1.6 mb/d because of the damage inflicted on the K-3 pumping station of Haditha which used to pump Basra light crude through the Northern outlet.

0156

- 7 -

As regards Kuwait, the prospects of a resumption of oil exports is even more remote. The latest assessment is that it will take a minimum of one year to extinguish the 500 or so burning oil wells. Some 700 oil wells out of a total of 1,080 sustained considerable damage during the Iraqi occupation. Up to 6 mb/d of oil (about 10% of world consumption) are burning out daily and it will take at least two years before Kuwait returns to major oil production. The longer term effects on Kuwait's production potentials are quite serious. It is estimated that around 5% of the country's 100 billion barrels of recoverable reserves may be lost from the fire. In addition, diminishing oil field pressure, loss of water and gas drive and other technical factors may reduce recovery ratio and could raise oil production cost. If every thing goes according to plan, Kuwait may be able to produce by next year some 500,000 b/d, the bulk of which will be for export.

The implications for OPEC and the world oil market is that there is less need to worry about an accentuated oil surplus, at least throughout 1991. This has become more evident following the declaration of the Soviet Union that it will be able to set aside for exports only 1.5 mb/d in 1991 compared to Soviet oil exports (both crude and oil products) of around 3 mb/d in 1990 and 3.76 mb/d in 1989. USSR's crude oil production in 1990 averaged 11.4 mb/d compared to 12.14 mb/d in 1989, a decline of 6.1%, with projections for a further fall in 1991 to 10.56 mb/d. Supply and demand conditions in the world oil market suggest a tendency for market prices to remain stable this year. We are forecasting an average price for OPEC basket of crude of around $17 a barrel for 1991. Prices could ease a bit in the second quarter from the $19.14 a barrel average in the first quarter before rebounding later in the year.

According to the International Energy Agency (IEA), OECD oil consumption in 1991 is projected to remain unchanged from 1990 at 37.6 mb/d. Non-OECD consumption is expected to rise by 0.5 mb/d to 15.8 mb/d, giving a total world demand this year of 53.4 mb/d around 1% higher than last year's level. The projected total demand of 53.4 mb/d will be met by 28.6 mb/d from non-OPEC production (close to the previous year's level), a small drawdown of oil stocks of (0.2) mb/d and a residual OPEC production of 24.6 mb/d of which 22.7 mb/d comprises crude oil and 1.9 mb/d natural gas liquids. The relative stability of non-OPEC supply is due to counter-balancing factors. While USA production and net CPE exports, mainly from the USSR will decline further this year, UK's output will adjust slightly upwards and production from other less developed countries (Brazil, Syria, India, Malaysia, etc.) will record a marginal increase of 0.1 mb/d. (Table 4).

0157

- 8 -

4. OIL REVENUES AND ECONOMIC GROWTH PROSPECTS IN THE REGION.

The 28% average rise in oil prices last year and the increase in GCC oil production especially for Saudi Arabia and UAE boosted the region's oil revenues. Total revenues of the six GCC states are estimated to have increased by 30% in 1990 to $63.041 billion from $48.463 billion in the year before (Table 5). Excluding Kuwait, the combined oil earnings of the Gulf states is estimated at $58.83 billion, 49% above the corresponding $39.54 billion in 1989. Saudi Arabia's earnings from oil exports are put at $35.68 billion, an increase of more than 56%. UAE's earnings are estimated to have reached $14.5 billion, up 40% on the year before. Qatar's earnings rose 48% to $3.32 billion, Oman's earnings up 32% to $4.5 billion and Bahrain's earnings are put at $845 million, or 28% higher than in 1989.

Projections of 1991 crude oil production and earnings are given in Table 5. The average price per barrel of OPEC's basket of seven crudes is forecasted at $17, while the postulated average daily production levels are those agreed upon in the latest OPEC meeting of March 1991. It is assumed that the ban on Iraq's exports of oil will be lifted in the third quarter but the country will not be able to export more than 800,000 b/d. This could easily be accommodated by a pro-rata cut in the daily production of the other OPEC countries. The second quarter quota is taken as an average for the year as a whole assuming that the lower production levels of the second half necessitated by resumption of Iraq's oil exports will be more than offset by the higher production levels of various OPEC countries already recorded in the first quarter. Under the assumed price and production scenario for 1991, oil revenues of Saudi Arabia will be marginally higher this year than in 1990, because the postulated percentage increase of the Kingdom's average daily production (24.5%) exceeds the expected decline in average oil prices (23.6%). Oil revenues of UAE, Oman, Qatar and Bahrain will be lower in 1991 compared to corresponding levels in the year before but higher than in 1989.

Estimates of 1991 GDP and non-oil GDP growth rates for Saudi Arabia and the other Gulf states are given in Table 1. Less buoyant economic growth conditions may be recorded this year than in the year before. However, growth will remain positive with several non-oil economic activities in the industrial, trade and construction sectors picking up following the end of the crisis. Already a sharp increase in consumer and durable goods orders has been witnessed in the market of Saudi Arabia and the UAE during the first quarter this year. The Kingdom's agricultural sector is set to record another bumper year in 1991.

0158

- 9 -

Share prices in Saudi Arabia and the other Gulf states have been moving higher with the official Saudi stock market index up 10.4% in March this year following gains of 4.2% in February and 1.4% in January. Most of the improvement was recorded in the banking, industry and other services sectors reflecting a surge in business and consumer confidence in the region's growth prospects.

Non-oil GDP which accounts for around 75% of total economic activities in Saudi Arabia is forecast to record positive growth rate of 3% this year. Given the projected 1.2% growth in the Kingdom's oil GDP, this gives an annualized growth rate of 2.5% in total GDP for 1991. Oil and non-oil GDP growth rates vary from one Gulf country to another, but in general, we are forecasting negative growth in the oil sector and a continuation of a positive growth in the non-oil activities. Inflation in the various Gulf countries is expected to ease a bit this year. The firmer tone of the US dollar and therefore the Gulf currencies vis-a-vis currencies of the region's major trading partners should translate into lower domestic import prices. The less buoyant domestic growth conditions compared to the year before will also help dampen overall inflationary pressures.

5. NEW BUSINESS OPPORTUNITIES IN THE POST-WAR PERIOD.

Ample business opportunities will be generated in the post-war era from additional defence spending, reconstruction in Kuwait, expansion of oil production capacity and other related public sector projects. Private sector activities will gradually regain their pre-crisis vigor and several projects and investment decisions that were put on hold following the Iraqi invasion of Kuwait may now be reconsidered. For example, the Arabian Industrial Development Company (AIDCO) is going ahead with plans to establish a $200 million petrochemical projects, one of the largest in the Kingdom. The $750 million scheme to build the third phase expansion of Al-Khobar power and water complex has now been approved. The go ahead sign has also been given for the expansion of Madina-Yanbu power and water facilities. Work on Qatar's North Field gas scheme and Bahrain's aluminum expansion project are now proceeding at full steam. A number of major contracts signed before the war have started to be implemented. These include Japan's Chiyoda's $306 million contract with Saudi Arabia Fertilizer Company (SAFCO) to construct an ammonia-urea plant in Al Jubail; an SR908 million contract to build a soda ash plant for the International Chemical Industries and Trading Co. of Jeddah and other industrial projects associated with the offset schemes of the US Peace Shield and the UK Al-Yamamah defence contracts.

0159

- 10 -

In the post-war era defence and security will be given greater importance. Expanding GCC forces will open additional employment opportunities for Gulf nationals and generate more business for contractors working on defence related projects. Raising the oil production capacity of Saudi Arabia, UAE and other Gulf states has already started and there are plans to increase the region's capacity by more than 30% during this decade. This requires massive capital expenditure that could reach $15 billion in Saudi Arabia and $4 billion in the UAE. Ample business and employment opportunities will therefore be created due to the forward and backward linkages that such expenditures will have on the rest of the economy.

Gulf companies and financial institutions will undoubtedly benefit from the huge reconstruction requirements developing in Kuwait. Although initial estimates of the total reconstruction costs were put at more than $100 billion, these have been scaled down to $30 billion for major rebuilding projects. If Gulf firms arrange to get 10% out of that (or $3 billion) they will be in a good shape. It is heartening to know that Kuwait's refineries did not endure much damage. Of the four major power stations, only one has been totally destroyed. A lot of the infrastructure has been abused but not structurally damaged so that it can be cleaned up instead of demolished and rebuilt. The sectors that are most likely to benefit from reconstruction expenditures in Kuwait are oil and gas, telecommunications, water, power generation, desalination, ports, the airport, few hotels and public buildings. Sooner than later, the private sector will become active again especially when essential services are restored and will begin awarding contracts for the repair of building.

The progress achieved by the large Saudi and other Gulf based engineering and construction companies during the past years and the experience they have in executing projects in an atmosphere similar to that of Kuwait will enable them to compete for reconstruction projects there. They stand to benefit from their proximity to the country and their ability to mobilise the required technical and financial resources for the projects. Although it was generally stated that US and other western companies would be given priority in major reconstruction contracts, immediate preferences will go to GCC contractors, especially the small jobs that could easily be executed by them. The combined annual capacity of the Saudi contractors for example, exceeds SR70 billion in addition to the wide experience gained over the past two decades through working closely with foreign companies. Furthermore, Gulf contractors benefited from government's policies of limiting civil projects under $50 million to local contractors. Several joint venture arrangements between Gulf and foreign contractors may soon be established to undertake major reconstruction works.

0160

- 11 -

Saudi and other Gulf manufacturing industries will also benefit from the opportunity arising in Kuwait. The construction material industry, both metal and non-metal, which is suffering from excess capacity in some areas, should be able to offer some very competitive prices. Cement produced in the Gulf for instance, currently selling below average world prices coupled with lower transportation costs and quick deliveries should prove very competitive. the metal fabrication industry, including steel, pipelines, pipe equipment, aluminum products, valves and fixtures, and road signs among others are equally sensitive to transportation costs and this should provide the edge to many producers in the region. Another advantage to Gulf producers is the unified economic agreement that allows free flows of goods and services among GCC member countries and guarantees locally manufactured goods a long term future in the Kuwaiti market.

The services most likely to be called for are obviously those of the trading firms, which have long established commercial links with Kuwait. The proximity of the Gulf countries and their strong trading base will mean many firms engaged in reconstruction will prefer to rely upon supplies from here rather than their domestic countries. Gulf suppliers who are able to provide Kuwait with US and European products are likely to be big winners. Many consumer durable items (cars, household appliances, furnishings, light fixtures, etc.) that have been looted or destroyed will need to be resupplied. Contracts will also be awarded for restocking of everything from banks and schools to hospitals and public sector enmities. Gulf shipping, consulting, aviation, training, insurance, trade and banking will also benefit from post war reconstruction in Kuwait. Leasing of equipment to foreign companies starting operation in Kuwait will also be in demand. Environmental clean up, waste management, servicing and spare parks for earth moving equipment will also do well. Ports in the Gulf states and the Eastern province of Saudi Arabia will once again re-emerge as trans-shipment points for the cargo headed especially in the first year or so. The relaxed economic and social climate in Dubai and Bahrain, should help lure international companies seeking a staging post from which to service Kuwait.

On the commercial banking scene, bonding and trade finance are the two main activities that could witness some resurgence. Saudi banks for example will be providing such services to their clients involved in projects or doing business with Kuwait. Syndicated or project loans to Kuwait, Bahrain and Saudi Arabia should not be ruled out, especially as some countries of the region may opt for international borrowing instead of asset liquidation to generate revenues. The Gulf region has become a net importer of capital in 1990 and may continue to be so in the foreseeable future. Markets here are switching from cash to credit to finance imports and with the surge in demand for project finance ample opportunities will be created for the enterprising financial institutions.

0161

- 12 -

6. CONCLUSION:

Prediction of a fairly smooth recovery in the economies of the region after the war should be qualified by the prospects of weaker government finances. The euphoria of peace may boost private expenditure and consumer confidence but the war-related obligations will continue to weigh on governments' financial position this year. Even though Gulf countries enjoyed higher oil revenues in 1990, however, the extra expenses incurred because of the crisis exceeded the additional income generated. The anticipated deficits in the 1990 budgets of various Gulf states are expected to have either expanded (Saudi Arabia, Bahrain and Qatar) or shrank a bit (UAE and Oman) but have not necessarily turned into surpluses. The financing gap is believed to have been made for by internal borrowing and drawing down on foreign reserves.

The extent of the Gulf war obligations, the additional outlays to boost the region's defence capabilities, the loans and grants given or pledged to friendly countries, the planned expenditures to raise oil production capacities and the need to maintain domestic economic growth are expected to greatly increase governments' expenditures this year. The additional financial requirements at a time when oil revenue are unlikely to match those of the year before raise the prospects of even higher government budget deficits in 1991. While the additional revenues from increased oil prices and production in 1990 did not exceed $12.7 billion for Saudi Arabia and $14.6 billion for the region as a whole, the extra expenditures incurred because of the war effort are estimated at around $20 billion. The generally tight budgetary conditions could mean contracts for operation and maintenance or priority projects will go ahead but work on several mega-project schemes may be delayed.

The Gulf crisis has unveiled several structural factors and risk elements that will undoubtedly affect business climate in the region for some time to come. While it may take longer for private sector to regain its pre-crisis vigor, ample opportunities will continue to be generated from additional defense spending, reconstruction and exports of goods and services to Kuwait as well as gradual resurgence of domestic economic growth conditions. Businessmen in the region and abroad are expected to reassess the new risk/return profile and position themselves to benefit from the potential opportunities arising. Those who are hesitant will be at a disadvantage and could lose out to the competition. According to the Ministry of Commerce in Saudi Arabia, 12,000 new commercial records were opened in the Kingdom in the second half of 1991 compared to 10,000 during the same period 1989. Licenses for more than 100 factories with combined investment of SR5.7 billion were issued in the second half last year,

0162

- 13 -

compared to 94 licenses with total investment of SR1.5 billion during the same period 1989. Furthermore 27% of last year's industrial investments have been earmarked by foreigners. Uncertainty is likely to remain a salient feature of this market, as it is the case elsewhere in the developing countries, but at least external risk has been greatly reduced and the internal stability and unity demonstrated during the crisis has proven many doubter wrong. The challenge is to learn to operate in such an environment and reap the benefit of rates of return more than commensurate with the risk involved.

******

0163

TABLE 1

NOMINAL GDP GROWTH RATES IN THE GCC STATES
(% CHANGE)

	1985		1986		1987		1988		1989		1990		1991	
	Non-oil GDP	Total GDP	Non-oil GDP	Total GDP	Non-oil GDP	Total GDP	Non-oil GDP	Total GDP	Non-oil GDP	Total GDP	Non-oil GDP	Total GDP	Non-oil GDP	Total GDP
S. Arabia	-2.3	-12.4	-7.0	-16.0	1.1	1.6	1.9	4.3	4.6	7.8	1.5	4.0	3.0	2.5
Kuwait	-4.5	-8.6	17.6	-13.8	8.3	16.5	-1.5	-4.9	3.6	21.3	---	---	---	---
UAE	-0.2	-2.4	5.7	-17.5	2.4	8.3	3.8	-1.2	5.0	14.3	2.0	15.0	5.0	1.7
Oman	12.8	13.2	-15.2	-19.0	-8.4	7.6	8.3	-2.9	2.3	10.5	4.0	9.0	4.5	1.5
Bahrain	-11.9	-7.0	-4.6	-13.8	7.1	-6.4	2.0	2.0	3.5	2.5	1.5	2.8	1.5	-2.0
Qatar	-6.4	-10.4	0.5	-18.5	0.6	1.7	0.5	-2.0	2.5	8.0	2.0	10.0	2.0	-1.5

0164

- 15 -

TABLE 2

GCC INFLATION RATES
(CONSUMER PRICE INDICES % CHANGE)

	1985	1986	1987	1988	1989	1990*	1991**
S. ARABIA	-3.1	-3.1	-1.6	1.0	0.9	1.5	0.5
KUWAIT	1.5	1.0	0.6	1.5	2.5	----	----
U A E	2.0	-1.0	5.5	5.0	8.7	8.0	4.0
OMAN	-1.1	6.4	0.3	-0.6	2.3	3.6	2.5
BAHRAIN	-2.6	-2.3	-1.5	-0.2	1.5	2.0	1.0
QATAR	1.9	1.6	3.6	2.0	4.0	5.0	3.0

*   Our estimates
** Our forecast

0165

- 16 -

TABLE 3

THE WORLD OIL MARKET: 1991
QUARTERLY SUPPLY & DEMAND FIGURES (mb/d)

	Q1	Q2	Q3	Q4	1991 (Yearly Ave.)
World Oil Demand*	54.4	51.8	52.7	54.9	53.4
Non-OPEC Supply	28.9	28.5	28.5	28.6	28.6
Additional Requirements	25.7	23.3	24.2	26.3	24.8
Change In Stocks	- 0.7	+0.5	+0.3	- 1.0	- 0.2
Natural Gas Liquids	1.9	1.9	1.9	1.9	1.9
OPEC Crude Oil Production	23.1	21.9	22.6	23.4	22.7

* excluding USSR, China and East European countries.

Source: International Energy Agency,
Monthly Oil Market Reports, Jan-Apr, 1991

0166

- 17 -

TABLE 4
WORLD OIL SUPPLY AND DEMAND (mb/d)

	1988	1989	1990	1991*
Spot Price of OPEC Basked ($/b yearly ave)	14.24	17.31	22.25	17.0
World Demand (excl.USSR, China & East Europe)	51.2	52.2	52.9	53.4
N. America	19.2	19.3	18.9	18.6
Europe	12.5	12.5	12.7	12.9
Pacific	5.5	5.8	6.0	6.1
Non-OECD	14.0	14.7	15.3	15.8
Non-OPEC Supply	29.2	28.7	28.7	28.6
USA	9.8	9.2	8.9	9.0
Canada	2.0	2.0	2.0	1.9
U.K.	2.4	2.0	2.0	2.1
Norway	1.4	1.6	1.7	1.6
Other OECD	1.1	1.2	1.3	1.3
Mexico	2.4	2.5	2.5	2.5
Oman	0.6	0.6	0.7	0.7
Egypt	0.9	0.9	0.9	0.9
Other LDCs (1)	6.0	6.5	6.8	6.9
Net CPE Exports (2)	2.6	2.2	1.9	1.7
Change In Stocks	- 0.1	- 0.1	+ 0.9	- 0.2
Requirements from OPEC	21.6	23.2	25.1	24.6
Natural Gas Liquids	1.8	1.9	1.9	1.9
OPEC Crude Oil Prod.	19.8	21.3	23.2	22.7

*   Our projections
(1)   Oil production of other non-OPEC developing countries include that of Brazil (0.63 mb/d in 1990), Syria (0.39 mb/d in 1990), India (0.66 mb/d in 1990) and Malaysia (0.6 mb/d in 1990).
(2)   Net exports of USSR, China and Eastern European countries.

Source: International Energy Agency, Monthly of Market Reports, Jan-Apr 1991.

0167

- 18 -

TABLE 5
OIL PRODUCTION AND REVENUES IN THE GCC STATES

	1989		1990		1991 (1)	
	Prod. (mb/d)	Revenues ($ mm)	Prod. (mb/d)	Revenues ($ mm)	Prod. (mb/d)	Revenues ($ mm)
Saudi Arabia*	5.064	22,900	6.540	35,678	8.034	36,035
Kuwait*	1.463	8,922	1.178	4,210	--------	--------
U.A.E.	1.858	10,359	2.065	16,072	2.320	12,863
Oman	0.640	3,375	0.668	4,482	0.700	3,635
Qatar	0.320	2,249	0.382	3,324	0.399	2,692
Bahrain	0.043	658	0.043	845	0.042	627
Total	9.388	48,463	10.801	63,04	11.495	55,852
Total less Kuwait	7.925	39,541	9.623	58,831	11.495	55,852

* Including 50% of neutral zone output of 300,000 b/d in 1989. The same applies up till August 1990 followed by an average Neutral zone output of 260,000 b/d for Saudi Arabia with no neutral zone production for Kuwait.

(1) Projections based on an average price of $17 a barrel for OPEC basket of crude oil and countries producing their respective 1991 second quarter quota.

Source:
Annual Reports of GCC Central Banks and Monetary Agencies, OPEC Statistical Bulletin, 1990, MEES (various issues), International Energy Agency, Monthly Oil Market Reports, Jan-Apr 1991.

0168

THE SIZE AND DISTRIBUTION
OF
OIL WEALTH IN THE REGION

George Joffe

It is commonly assumed that the Gulf states enjoy a level of income and reserves, as a result of their role within the international oil market, which places them very high in the hierarchy of national wealth throughout the world. While this may well be true in per capita terms, it is certainly not the case at the level of national accounts. In GNP terms in 1987, the Japanese economy was 25 times greater than that of Saudi Arabia, for example, while the French economy was ten times greater and the German economy was twelve times larger. The same is true of the Gulf states' balance of payments positions: Germany's balance of payments surplus in 1988 was 3.5 times greater than that of Kuwait, while Japan's was 5.5 times greater.

GULF STATES EXTERNAL ACCOUNTS - 1989
($ bn)

Country	exports†	imports†	current a/c	reserves	debt	GDP
Bahrain	2.69	2.80	-0.17	1.05	†††	3.48
UAE	15.89††	10.16	3.87	4.46	10.97	27.27
Iran†††††	13.60	14.75††††	-3.20	na	5.90	454.67
Iraq†††††	14.60	7.68	2.85	na	23.79	212.83
Kuwait	11.49	6.30	9.32	3.10	7.25	23.06
Oman	3.93	2.25	0.45	1.35	†††	8.40
Qatar	2.78	1.33	0.18	0.53	0.91	7.45
Saudi Arabia	48.06	20.81	-3.98	16.75	†††	78.40

Source: EIU-BI, Country Report No.1-1991, for these countries.
† exports - fob: imports - cif.
†† including re-exports.
††† Bahrain - $1.27 bn in 1988
   Oman - $2.94 bn in 1988.
   Saudi Arabia - $15.15 bn in 1988.
†††† fob figure.
††††† GDP figures calculated at official exchange rates; at unofficial rates, Iran's GDP would be of the order of $45 bn and Iraq's would be around $27 bn.
Note: Debt figures are taken from the World Bank's Debt Tables.

However, once these figures are reviewed in per capita terms, the picture looks very different. The combined populations of the GCC states in 1986 were 15.71 mn persons, of which 6.9 mn were estimated to be temporary migrants. The populations of Iran and Iraq over-shadowed these figures, with Iraq having a population of 16.1 mn and Iran a population of 49.94 mn, which was growing at over 3 per cent annually. Measured in per capita terms, then, the conventional view of the Arab Gulf states' wealth appears to be more justified. Furthermore, it is the smaller states that appear to be the most wealthy in this respect.

1

0169

It is also the case that several Gulf states have major
investments abroad or have consistently spent large sums on
foreign aid. Saudi Arabia and Kuwait have dominated the foriegn
investment picture. Saudi Arabia, for example, is estimated to
have had around $48 bn in foreign investments in 1989, out of
total reserves of around $64.8 bn. Although the overall figure
reserves figure was less than half the 1982 figure of $145 bn, it
was still a substantial amount. The decline, however, indicates
the problems faced by some Gulf states during the 1980s, as oil
revenues declined.

Kuwait, before August 1990, was believed to have had foreign
investments of $100 bn (net book value figure) to $200 bn
(assumed market value figure). The actual figures are unknown
but in 1985 Kuwaiti state investments were stated by the
government to be $48 bn - $35.7 bn in the non-Arab world and the
balance in Arab countries. In 1989, Kuwait's total reserves (in
the Reserve Fund for Future Generations - RFFG - and in the State
General Reserve - SGR) were $91.17 bn, most of which was believed
to have been invested. Some 60 per cent of the SGR, which was
one third of the total at $32.09 bn, was invested in Kuwait
itself, but only 23 per cent of the RFFG, which formed the
balance, was invested locally. The foreign income from the two
funds was $4.16 bn in that year. There are also, of course
substantial private investments abroad.

Oil - the source of wealth

Despite the recent conflict in the Gulf, there is little doubt
that the revenue and investment levels of the past will
eventually be restored. Not only are all the Gulf states richly
endowed with oil reserves - the region contains 64.5 per cent of
the world's proven reserves and, during the 1980s, provided
between 20 and 25 per cent of world demand - but they will also
continue to be major producers for the foreseeable future.

GULF OIL RESERVES AND PRODUCTION - 1989

Country	reserves (bn bbls)	% total	production (mn b/d)				% total
			1986	1987	1988	1989	
UAE	98.1	9.6	1.65	1.70	1.78	1.78	3.1
Iran	92.9	9.2	1.91	2.31	2.27	2.27	4.6
Iraq	100.0	9.9	1.75	2.09	2.60	2.60	4.5
Kuwait	99.7	9.8	1.60	1.47	1.66	2.00	3.3
Oman	4.3	0.4	0.56	0.58	0.60	0.59	0.9
Qatar	4.5	0.4	0.36	0.34	0.36	0.40	0.6
Saudi Arabia	255.0	25.2	5.15	4.36	5.26	5.26	8.3
Gulf Total	654.5	64.5	12.98	12.85	14.53	14.90	25.3
World Total	1,011.8	100.0	60.38	60.15	62.35	63.56	100.0

Source: BP Statistical Review of World Energy; 1990

0170

2

Reserves-to-production ratios range from 20 years for Oman up to more than 100 years for Abu Dhabi, Kuwait and Saudi Arabia. Iraq and Iran are in the same league, with reserves-to-production ratios of 89 years (Iran) to 97 years (Iraq). Even the damage done to Kuwait's oil fields by the conflict and by Iraq's firing of the majority of its wells will not substantially affect the reserves-to-production picture.

Of course, actual levels of earning power in the wake of the conflict will depend on the call on Gulf oil supplies and on the market price. That, in turn, will depend on Opec discipline - an issue that the Gulf states will now, no doubt, be anxious to address, particularly once Kuwaiti and Iraqi crudes return to the market. However, if production levels do not substantially increase over the next five years, for example, and prices fluctuate between $20 and $25 per barrel - the range that has been suggested by several commentators - than Gulf crude revenues will fluctuate between $110 bn and $137 bn annually. In 1989, overall Gulf income - dominated by crude but including refined product sales and other visible exports - totalled $115 bn. In short, the 1989 figures provide us with a good guide as to how the costs of the conflict and of reconstruction will be met.

Iraq's costs of reconstruction

Not surprisingly, Iraq's reconstruction costs after hostilities are completely over are expected to be massive. International oil industry sources have suggested that damage to the oil sector should be costed at least $10 bn, while, if the damage to the petrochemical industry is included, the costs rise to $20 bn. It would take three years for reconstruction to be completed. Other reconstruction costs - to Iraq's infrastructure, articularly to communications, power generation, urban structure and water supply - have been estimated by similar sources to raise the total cost to around $110 bn.

The costs of the Gulf war compared

These figures can be contrasted with Iraq's losses during the Iran-Iraq war. According to Iraqi sources, at least $208 bn was involved (military expenditure $102 bn and lost oil revenues $106 bn).[1] Another authoritative source suggests a figure of $452.6 bn for GDP losses, $197.7 bn for lost oil revenues and $67 bn for direct war damage - a total of $717.3 bn.[2] The GDP losses include a figure of $55.3 bn for additional military purchases attendant of the war, on top of the $23 bn that would have been spent over the eight year period had there been no war at all. According to this source, therefore, Iraq's direct military costs during the Gulf war, therefore, are estimated to have been $78.3 bn - somewhat less than Iraq's own claims.

In the wake of the war, Iraq was prepared to devote massive sums to reconstruction and to further development. One source recently estimated the sums involved to total $63 bn over a ten year period, with 1,200 development projects being launched in

3

0171

1989 alone. Yet oil revenues averaged only $15 bn, while foreign currency expenditures averaged $20 bn - $11 bn for civilian imports, $5 bn for military imports, $3 bn debt repayments and $1 bn for workers' remittances abroad.[3]

Other sources point out that the reconstruction plan launched in 1989 was to cost $37 bn over five years - $3-$4 bn being spent on the reconstruction of Basra alone ($2.5 bn on its infrastructure), $2 bn on the reconstruction of the Basra refinery complex (now destroyed once again), $2 bn on a new petrochemical complex at al-Moussayib outside Baghdad, $13 bn on delayed heavy industrial projects, $11.5 bn on other delayed industrial schemes (both originally projected in the pre-Gulf war period), $4 bn on import substitution schemes and $1.5 bn on new port schemes to replace Basra. They also proposed a balance of payments projection for Iraq during the first half of the 1990s that gives some idea of the financial shortfall expected even then. That, no doubt, contributed significantly to the ultimately calamitous decision by the Iraqi leadership to invade Kuwait on August 2, 1990.

IRAQ - EXTERNAL ACCOUNT PROJECTIONS: 1988-1993
($ bn)

	1988	1989	1990	1991	1992	1993
Revenues	13.86	15.05	16.24	16.96	16.56	20.07
Oil	13.16	14.25	15.29	15.56	19.11	18.62
Non-oil	0.70	0.80	0.95	1.40	1.45	1.45
Imports	12.42	15.66	15.97	16.37	15.86	16.95
Civilian	7.42	8.16	8.97	9.87	10.86	11.95
Military	5.00	5.00	4.50	4.00	2.50	2.50
Reconstruction	-	2.50	2.50	2.50	2.50	2.50
Trade Balance	1.44	-0.61	0.27	0.59	3.70	3.12
Current Account	-2.56	-3.71	-3.13	-2.81	0.10	-0.78
Invisibles	-1.00	-1.00	-1.10	-1.20	-1.20	-1.50
Transfers	-1.20	-1.10	-1.10	-1.00	-1.00	-0.90
Debt interest	-1.80	-1.00	-1.20	-1.20	-1.40	-1.50

Source: Joffe E.G.H. & McLachlan K.S. (1988) **The Gulf War: building on the stalemate**, EIU (London); 30-37
Note: These estimates reflect the position before the invasion of Kuwait on August 2, 1990.

The financial implications of reparations

There are two major factors involved in in the pattern of any reparations which Iraq may be forced to pay. One of these reflects the costs of the damage done to Kuwait. The other reflects outstanding debt incurred by Iraq as a result of its war against Iran. In view of international condemnation of the Saddam Hussein regime for its actions in Kuwait and over the actual invasion itself, there is a strong possibility that some,

4

0172

at least, of these debts will be included in the eventual figure established for reparations.

(1) If Iraq is obliged to pay Kuwait's reconstruction costs the total cost to Iraq could reach between $130 bn and $200 bn. Kuwait's reconstruction costs were estimated by Abdelrahman al-Awadi, Kuwait's cabinet affairs minister up to the recent cabinet reshuffle, to have reached $64 bn in mid-January. Other Kuwaiti sources have put them at between $20 bn and $50 bn, of which $10 bn was said to have been caused to the oil sector before Kuwait's oil wells and installations were fired in late February.

According to Kuwaiti oil industry sources in mid-February, the firing of half of Kuwait's 1,000 oil wells would cost $5 bn to repair, while lost oil exports would probably total $40 bn, thus increasing the total to between $165 bn and $235 bn.[4] Of course, these figures are speculative, but there is a growing consensus that the are of the right order of magnitude.

(2) Iraq's foreign debt was conservatively estimated to have been $75 bn before the crisis began on August 2, 1990, of which $14 bn alone is due to Kuwait. Even if $20 bn-worth of debt to OECD countries - this is a 1989 figure and is now estimated to have risen to $35 bn[5] - were abandoned, that would still leave $55 bn to be repaid to Arab Gulf states, $25.7 bn of it to Saudi Arabia alone.[6] In fact, foreign debt repayments to the OECD world cost $3.34 bn in 1986 and $2.84 bn in 1987, when OECD debt stood at $15.817 bn. As a result of rescheduling, debt repayment fell to $1.8 bn in 1988 and was expected to continue at this level until 1993 when rescheduled debt would become due and repayments would rise to between $3 bn and $4 bn annually.[7]

(3) There may also be claims for the repayment of the military costs incurred by the Allies - estimated at as much as $50 bn overall.[8]

Kuwait's reconstruction costs

There have been several estimates of the cost involved in restoring the damage done in Kuwait. It is impossible to establish a definitive figure at present, although the estimates are continually becoming more precise. An indication of the most widely quoted estimates is given below.

(1) Middle East Economic Survey (MEES) suggested in early March that Kuwait had already disbursed around $20 bn on war-related costs and in aid to friendly countries by the end of March 1991. It also pointed out that the basic reconstruction programme would cost at least $800 mn and that overall reconstruction costs would run into "tens of billions of dollars".[1]

---

[1] MEES, 34:24, 11.03.1991   5

0173

걸프사태 : 자료 및 언론보도, 1990-91. 전3권 (V.2 자료, 1991.4-5월) 377

(2) At about the same time Middle East Economic Digest (MEED)
claimed that reconstruction costs for the oil refineries and
related facilities would cost $5 bn, while putting out the
oil field fires - 500 wells on fire and a further 300 mined
- would cost a further $600 mn to $1 bn. Kuwait was losing
5 mn b/d, worth $100 mn/day, through the fires, which would
take between one and two years to extinguish, an implied
loss of $4-$8 bn at least.[2]

This would be amplified by the fact that it would take
between six and eight years to restore Kuwaiti production
capacity, although it could never reach prewar levels
because of damage done to the pressure reservoirs. MEED
estimated that minimum reconstruction costs would be $20 bn,
with military costs to the USA adding on $13.5 bn and to the
UK an additional $1.32 bn.   Promised aid to the Gulf
Financial Crisis Coordination Group was set at $3.684 bn,
while aid to Kuwait exiles during the hostilities had cost
$1.5 bn. The total cost to Kuwait - which, no doubt, it
would try to recover as reparations - was, in MEED's view,
$39.32 bn.

(3) MEED also estimated that the oil fires would mean that
Kuwait would lose around 5 per cent of its overall reserves.
This figure was challenged by the authoritative French
daily, Le Monde, which claimed that up to 10 per cent of the
reserves would have been destroyed[3].   Other sources have
suggested that the correct figure would eventually be 15 per
cent of total reserves. It has to be said that the actual
figure will depend on the eventual international price of
oil, as well as the actual destruction caused.

(4) The most recent report of likely reconstruction costs, from
the United Nations, suggests that reconstruction will take
up to ten years. It claims that Kuwait lost $8.5 bn during
the Iraqi occupation as a result of embargoed oil exports
and is currently losing between $40 mn and $120 mn per day
as a result of the damage done to its oil fields. Damage to
refineries and petrochemical sites has been evaluated at
$7.8 bn. The electricity generating sector will cost $1 bn
to restore, $2 bn will have to be spent on port and airport
reconstruction, $1 bn on telecommunications and $5 bn in
replacing damaged and destroyed vehicles. A further $3.7 bn
will be required to restore buildings.[4]

In short, total reconstruction costs to date are $20.5 bn.
To this must be added the financial losses, which include
$500 mn-worth of gold stolen from banks, and the damage done
to the hospital and educational sector, as well as losses

---

[2] MEED; 22.3.1991

[3] Le Monde; 15.3. 1991.

[4] Reported in Le Monde; 4.5.1991

6

0174

from the private sector and lost oil revenues. In effect,
the early estimates of between $60 bn and $100 bn seem
likely to be close to the eventual costs.

Iraqi repayment patterns

Overall Iraq may have to pay as much as $260 bn to $330 bn, as a
result of this crisis, in reconstruction costs and war
reparations:-

IRAQ - POSSIBLE RECONSTRUCTION AND REPARATION COSTS
($ bn)

Reconstruction		
Iraq	110	
Reparations		
Kuwait	95	
infrastructure	(40)	
lost oil exports	(40)	
oil sector repairs	(15)	
Allied military costs		
(net of contributions)	50	
Outstanding foreign debt		
Gulf states	55	
OECD	20	
SUB-TOTAL	330	
Miscellaneous		
Soviet loans	9	
French military loans	6	
Iran reparations‡	150	
TOTAL	495	

‡ These stem from the 1980-88 Gulf War

It has been estimated that it would take up to 15 years for this
sum to be paid off on the most optimistic projection of oil
prices. However, at a more realistic scenario of an average oil
price of $20/barrel, Iraq's annual oil income would be of the
order of $15 bn, at a restored oil production level within a new
Opec discipline of no more than 2.5 mn b/d and exports at 2 mn
b/d. If production were permitted to rise to 3 mn b/d - Iraq's
original target for 1991 (its Opec quota in 1990 was 3.14 mn
b/d), then revenues will be $18 bn annually.[9]

Not all of these sums could be available for reparations,
for Iraq will have its own reconstruction programme to consider
and will have to maintain the flow of essentail imports. Imports
would run annually at at least $10 bn (the level in 1988 and
1989), with around $2.5 bn being devoted to food imports (27 per
cent of total imports in the past). Service and capital costs
would add at least $2 bn to that figure, leaving between $3 bn
and $6 bn available annually for reconstruction and reparation
payments. Thus, in the worst case scenario, Iraq could be

7

0175

burdened with foreign debt obligations for between the next 50 and 100 years, as a result of the current hostilities.[10]

Iraq does have some limited assets that could be used to cover part of the reparations bill. The assets blocked by the UN embargo in August 1990 are believed to have been around $3 bn ($3.042 bn in December 1989, according to the Bank for International Settlements). There is also considerable Iraqi oil in storage outside Iraq. Iraq has already requested the United Nations Sanctions Committee to allow it to use $942.5 mn-worth of this crude to purchase essential foodstuffs and medicines - a move which is oposed by the United States.[11]

Kuwait has also claimed that an additional $5 bn has been concealed in clandestine accounts in London and Switzerland. These have been created through the Iraqi holding company network of arms-related manufacturers in Europe built up between 1988 and 1990 and dedicated towards acquiring nuclear, missile and chemical weapons technology. They were apparently operated through a UK clearing bank, two Swiss banks and a Euro-Arab consortium bank and were coordinated by Barzan al-Tikriti, Saddam Hussain's half-brother and Iraq's ambassador in Geneva to the UN. Some of the sums involved came from the fraudulent activities of the Atlanta branch of the Banco Nazionale del Lavoro (BNL), involving around $4 bn, and from clearing activities directed by the Bank of Credit and Commerce International (BCCI) in the USA. Other sums apparently came directly from Baghdad.[12]

There have also been anxieties expressed in France that "first-call guarantees" guaranteed by French companies against successful completion of contracts in Iraq might be called in, once the UN embargo is lifted. The sums thus collected could then be used by Iraq to pay off debt and reparations. These are officially set at around $1 bn but are, in reality, between $1.2 bn and $1.6 bn. The reason for such anxieties is that, under Iraqi law, all delays to contract completion are the responsibility of the companies involved and the contracts concerned had not been completed before the UN embargo was imposed. The French government is currently examining the situation, which could affect companies of other countries as well, although Baghdad has recently indicated that such guarantees will not be invoked.[13]

All in all, therefore, there may be as much as $10 bn available for immediate repayment to Kuwait. Iraq has already agreed to return property seized from Kuwait, which includes gold worth $800 mn and currency worth KD 365 mn ($1.25 bn) - a total of around $2 bn.[14] However, these figures fall far short of what will be required and reparations are bound to be a very heavy burden for many years to come. Indeed, these figures may suggest that some thought may have to be given to the wisdom of exacting reparations payments once military defeat is complete, whatever the government in power in Baghdad. In fact, reparations are likely to be collected by impounding a proportion of Iraq's oil production, once sanctions are finally removed. No actual level

8

0176

has yet been set, although figures of between 10 and 25 per cent of total production have been suggested.

Oil, the source of funding

Even before the conflict over Kuwait began, Iraq's economy was heavily oil dependent, with around 65-70 per cent of GDP being derived from the oil sector. The figure was masked, in the conventional method of GDP calculation, both by the assimilation of oil processing and transformation into the industrial sector and by the misallocation of oil revenues to current "value added", rather than being correctly treated as capital depletion of a finite, non-renewable resource.[15] The result was that, as the table below shows, oil's contribution to GDP by industrial origin was conventionally set at 36 per cent for 1988 - the most recent year for which figures are available.

IRAQ - STRUCTURE OF GDP 1988
(Conventional measure)
($ bn)

Sector	Value	Share (%)	Annual growth rate (1986-1990)
Agriculture	1.54	7	1.8
Industry	2.39	10	10.0
Services	10.92	47	6.2
Petroleum	8.51	36	13.4
GDP TOTAL	23.36	100	8.7

Source: EIU

More recent estimates from within the Iraqi administration support the conclusion of Iraq's growing oil dependency:-

IRAQ - OFFICIAL GDP ESTIMATES
(%)

Sector	Contribution				Annual growth rate			
	1976	1980	1988	1989	1986	1987	1988	1989
Oil	59.6	63.0	60.5	61.3	24.5	60.8	-4.0	27.0
Agriculture	8.4	7.0	6.3	5.1	-6.5	-8.1	2.8	1.7
Industry	7.8	5.0	10.4	11.6	-7.0	11.2	-22.6	41.5
Services	24.2	25.0	22.9	22.0	11.1	-0.3	-20.1	20.9

Ministry of Planning, Annual Abstract of Statistics 1990, Baghdad

These estimates make it clear that oil will have to be the major foreign currency earner in future and the vehicle through which reconstruction and reparations are paid for. Iraq also has considerable gas reserves, consisting of associated gas and estimated at 2,690 bn m^3 in 1988. Gas sales increased tenfold between 1984 and 1988 to 5.7 bn m^3 annually, including 50 mn m^3/day to Kuwait. In 1984, on 12 per cent of the associated gas produced was marketed, but by 1988, this had risen to 54 per cent and the proportion of flared gas was cut by 22 per cent between

9

0177

1986 and 1988. Since 1986, a nationwide gas pipeline network has been under construction by Soviet contractors.

There is little doubt, however, that Iraq's production will be restrained to within quotas set for it by Opec. Its export outlets all depend surrounding states:-

(1) Apart from tanker transport across Jordan, the major mode of oil export is by pipeline. The doubled Kirkuk-Dortyul pipeline across Turkey can carry 1.6 mn b/d, while the IPSA-1/2 lines across Saudi Arabia provide a further 1.6 mn b/d. Iraq unilaterally cancelled its pipeline agreement with Saudi Arabia last year and will now have to negotiate new terms. These may include transit fees, which were not paid originally. The Kirkuk-Banias pipeline (900,000 b/d) across Syria has been closed since April 1982 and is now used for Syria's own fields at Deir ez-Zor.[16]

(2) Other export outlets can also easily be controlled. Movement from restored oil export terminals (2 mn b/d) would be through the Gulf and thus open to naval control. It is therefore unlikely that Iraq will be able to reduce the period required to liquidate reparations by increasing production and exports beyond levels permitted by Opec in the future.

Nonetheless, it should not be forgotten that, up to the invasion of Kuwait, Iraq was an aggressive exporter of crude. It only agreed to abide by its Opec quota of 2.64 mn b/d at the end of 1988 and of 3.14 mn b/d at the start of 1990 with reluctance - at a time when production was accelerating and Iraq's capacity to exceed the quota had become a realistic possibility within the short-term. Projected export capacity was said to be 3.5 mn b/d at the start of 1990 and was expected to rise to 5 mn b/d by the end of the year as the Gulf offshore terminals at Mina al-Bakr were reconstructed.

IRAQI OIL PRODUCTION AND EXPORTS 1978-1990
(mn b/d)

Year	Production	Export	Domestic Consumption
1979	3.475	3.275	-
1980	2.645	2.459	-
1981	0.895	0.746	-
1982	1.010	0.811	-
1983	1.105	0.725	-
1984	1.225	0.856	0.234
1985	1.440	1.095	0.256
1986	1.745	1.388	0.272
1987	2.090	1.779	0.283
1988	2.600	2.354	0.300
1989	2.825	2.541	0.300
1990	1.695	1.395	0.200

Sources: Opec, Annual statistical bulletin
BP, Statistical review of world energy 1990, (London)

10

0178

There is also little doubt that economic sanctions would provide a potent weapon against future Iraqi behaviour which was considered hostile. The sanctions imposed by the UN in August 1990 under UN Security Council Resolution 661 were 90 per cent effective on Iraq's imports by December 1990 and 95 per cent effective on Iraq's exports, according the CIA Director William Webster, while 60 per cent of Iraqi industry had been closed down as a result of the lack of adequate inputs. Despite improved cereal harvests, the CIA also calculated that food stocks would have been exhausted by early summer 1991. Even when sanctions are removed after the end of hostilities, they will remain a potent threat to guarantee future good behaviour.

The financial consequences of the conflict

Quite apart from the cost of repairing the damage done to Iraq and Kuwait by the conflict, there have been far wider financial ramifications for the Gulf states.

<u>Direct military costs</u>

The Gulf states also financed the conflict, together with Germany, Japan and South Korea. They provided 67.55 per cent of the total pledges and disbursing 53.12 per cent of total disbursements by the end of March 1991.[17] Saudi Arabia pledged $16.839 bn, Kuwait $16.006 bn and the UAE $4 bn of the total estimated cost of $54.545 bn of Operation Desert Storm, according to the US Senate Appropriations Committee. By the end of March, Saudi Arabia had paid out $6.102 bn - 36 per cent of its pledge- $1.566 bn in kind and $4.536 bn in cash; Kuwait had paid out $5.510 bn - 34.4 per cent of its pledge - $10 mn in kind and $5.5 bn in cash; and the UAE had paid out $2.010 bn - 50.2 per cent of its pledge - $140 mn in kind and $1.87 bn in cash.

Different US sources give figures for the contributions made which differ slightly from source to source. The US House of Representatives Appropriations Committee, for example, has claimed that the combat costs of the conflict were $31.5 bn, while non-combat costs were $38 bn. It also suggested that the amount of assistance raised from other states for the US initiative was $53.6 bn, of which $14.9 bn had been received by early March. At the same time, the US government has raised a further $15 bn from domestic sources towards the overall costs- which include special aid packages, such as the $4.1 bn package approved by the Committee which included $650 mn for Israel. Nevertheless, all these sources make it clear that the Gulf states provided by far the biggest contribution to the costs of "Operation Desert Storm".

According to the chairman of the House of Representatives Armed Services Committee, 75 per cent of US incremental costs in the operation will be met by such contributions. Britain has reported a similar situation. Overall British war costs were $4.75 bn, with direct military costs reaching $2.5 bn. Around

11

0179

$3.9 bn of this figure will be met through pledges. Saudi Arabia has pledged $1.09 bn ($200 mn paid by May), Kuwait has promised $1.25 bn ($180 mn paid by May) and the UAE has contributed $332 mn. The balance is to come from Japan (which has already paid $270 mn), Germany and South Korea (which has provided $30 mn).

CONTRIBUTIONS TO US MILITARY COSTS
($ mn)

	Total Pledge	Received	(Cash)	(In Kind)(1)
Saudi Arabia(2)	16,839	6,924	4,536	2,388
Kuwait	16,006	7,016	7,000	16
UAE(3)	4,090	3,049	2,870	179
Japan(4)	9,840	7,279	6,646	633
Germany	6,572	6,401	5,772	629
South Korea(5)	38	138	110	28
Other(6)	3	3	0	3
TOTAL	53,645	30,810	26,934	3,876

Source: MEES, 34, 28 (15.04.1991)
Notes: (1) As of March 19, 1991.
      (2) Host nation support is open-ended and totalled $3,339 mn for 1990.
      (3) The USA considers that the UAE's contribution should be increased to reduce the burden on Kuwait.
      (4) The USA has noted with annoyance that it will receive only 90 per cent of Japan's contribution. Furthermore, the contribution is in yen and is thus susceptible to adverse currency movements.
      (5) $15 mn of this figure will not go to the USA.
      (6) This includes Denmark ($1 mn), Bahrain ($1.2 mn), Oman ($600,000) and Qatar ($200,000).

Aid provision

The Gulf states have also generated most of the aid required for the US-inspired Gulf Financial Crisis Coordination Group, providing 62.25 per cent of the total funding. To date, $8.3 bn has been paid out by the group, mainly to Egypt, Turkey and Syria. There has also been an additional $900 mn sum paid by Kuwait to Turkey last December to compensate for losses incurred by Ankara after imposing the trade embargo on Iraq. Kuwait has also paid a sum of $300 mn to Syria, although it is not clear whether or not this forms part of its GFCCG committment.

Kuwait has also provided $800 mn to Egypt as compensation to 69,000 Egyptian workers of the total 89,000 Egytian workforce in the Amirate who lost bank deposits in there when they fled the invasion, on top of $50 mn-worth of compensation paid to them last October. Kuwait has also agreed to make additional payments to France ($1 bn) and the UK ($1.3 bn - see above) for their participation in Operation Desert Storm, in addition to the sums already promised to the USA. The UAE has also promised an additional payment of $500 mn to the UK for the same purpose.

12

0180

GFCCG FUNDING: MARCH 1991

($ bn)

Aid to from	Egypt, Turkey and Jordan	Others, inc. Syria	Total
Saudi Arabia	2.848	1.773	4.621
Kuwait	2.500	1.184	3.684
UAE	0.850	0.619	1.469
Total	11.741	3.959	15.700

Source: Middle East Economic Digest; 22.03.1991

In short, between funding the conflict and providing aid, the three Gulf states have pledged enormous sums. Saudi Arabia has committed itself to $21.460 bn, to which should be added a $4 bn loan to the Soviet Union now under negotiation and $500 mn to Egypt to help resettle Egyptian refugees from Iraq and Kuwait. Kuwait has pledged $23.190 bn and the UAE a further $5.465 bn.

Other costs

However, the Gulf states' committments have not ended there. There have also been other direct costs in addition to those caused by war damage or lost oil revenues. In addition to the military and aid provisions, as well as its reconstruction costs - $15 bn of which will have to be paid out during this year- Kuwait has had to provide $1.5 bn which was paid out to Kuwaitis exiled abroad during the conflict. There has also been a further sum of $3.9 bn paid to compensate the Kuwaiti industrial sector and the recent write-off of internal Kuwaiti debt will add a further $4.75 bn to the total cost of the Iraqi invasion.[18]

Saudi Arabia has suggested that up to $20.95 bn additional expenditure has been incurred as a result of the war and that, despite an increase in oil revenues from a projected $20.3 bn to $31 bn, the Kingdom would still face a $10.25 bn "crisis" deficit in 1990. These domestic costs are in addition to promised aid and contributions towards the military expenses of the Coalition. They include $4.7 bn used to increase oil production levels towards 9 mn b/d with a short-term surge capacity of up to 10 mn b/d (although most professional observers consider this a vast over-estimate); arms purchases of $12.6 bn, of which $7.6 bn were purchased from the USA; and direct Saudi military costs of $1.7 bn.

Debt forgiveness for Egypt

Saudi Arabia has recently made a further $1.5 bn available to Egypt for balance-of-payments support and for new development projects. This sum is in addition to the decision by the Gulf Cooperation Council (GCC) to forgive all its official debt with Egypt in return for the military aid provided by the Mubarak government during the conflict. In fact, Egypt was able to reduce its foreign debt burden significantly during the conflict, since the GCC initiative was followed by other creditors.

13

0181

EGYPT'S FOREIGN DEBT & DEBT FORGIVENESS
($ bn)

	WB Figures	OECD Figures	Forgiven
External Debt (1989)			
Total debt	48.799	52.203	
Offical debt	33.586	-	
Bilateral debt	28.421	-	
Debt service	2.992	-	
Debt/GNP	150%	-	
Forgiven Debt (1990)			
US military debt			7.100
GCC debt			7.700‡
G-7 debt			9.000‡‡
Other debt			0.739‡‡‡
TOTAL			24.539
Outstanding Debt (1991)			
Egyptian claim	28.000		
Observers	35.000		
EIU forecast	33.000		

Sources: World Bank, World Debt Tables 1990-91,
         OECD, Financing and External Debt of Developing
            Countries,
         EIU, Egypt - Country Report No.1-1991,
            Business International (London).

Notes: ‡ This is an official Egyptian figure, other sources
           quote between $6.1 bn and $7.1 bn. It includes $4.5
           bn-worth of Saudi debt.
         ‡‡ This figure is an estimate, set at one third of total
           Group-of-Seven debt which is believed to include the
           vast majority of official bilateral debt. France is
           owed $8 bn and the USA $7 bn alone.
         ‡‡‡ This includes Spain ($650 mn); Canada ($78 mn) and
           Finland ($11 mn).

Future GCC financial committments

On March 6, 1991, President Bush, in his annual State-of-the-
Union message to Congress, outlined plans for a new international
order, particularly in the Gulf region. Apart from committments
to regional disarmament, the US president also made it clear that
regional security would have to guaranteed by regional states and
that there should be a new drive for regional economic
development. On the same day, in Damascus, the GCC states,
together with Egypt and Syria - the so-called "Group of Eight"
(G-8) - announced that they intended to create a regional
security organisation.

    The new organisation was to use the military muscle of
Egypt and Syria, in addition to that of the Gulf states
themselves. Saudi Arabia has also decided to double the size of
its armed forces and other Gulf states anticipate considerable
spending on new armaments. Furthermore, the GCC decided that it
would under-write the costs of the proposed security operation,
estimated at between $15 bn and $18 bn for a five year period.

14

These figures seem to be a serious under-estimate for the overall costs that will be involved in regional security.

This conclusion is reinforced by the fact that the USA intends to provide $18 bn-worth of new arms to the Gulf during 1991, according to the latest Jarvits Report submitted to Congress in March 1991. Furthermore, Saudi Arabia alone anticipates spending $20 bn on new arms during the year. Yet, the Gulf region is already one of the largest purchasers of armaments in the world.

According to a report being prepared for Michel Camdessus, the director-general of the IMF, ten states in the Gulf region figure among the twelve states worldwide which have the greatest expenditure on arms. On average, 13 per cent of their GNPs is committed to military expenditure, compared with the world average of 5 per cent. If their expenditure were reduced to the average level, the Gulf states would immediately benefit from an additional $30 bn for development.[19]

The first steps towards providing for regional economic development were taken at a GCC meeting in Riyadh on April 22, 1991.[20] The new fund proposed at the meeting is to be capitalised by the GCC at $5bn over the next three years and at $10 bn within ten years. Eventually, it is expected to reach $15 bn. However, it is not clear whether this will be done by consolidating current GCC aid programmes in the new fund - so that the actual committment of new funds will be correspondingly reduced.

Furthermore, the new fund will not make a significant difference to Middle Eastern development, if it is not in addition to existing GCC aid committments. Currently, Arab aid is only 6 per cent of the total development aid entering the Middle East. Furthermore, it is feared that the major beneficiaries will be, Egypt and Syria which are also members of the "Group of Eight". It will thus do little to alter living standards and economic development levels throughout the Middle East and North Africa, despite the massive disparities that exist.

The consequences

Quite apart from the costs the GCC has already incurred, it seems inevitable that there will be significant financial problems for the Gulf in funding all the committments it has undertaken for security, rearmament and economic development. Saudi Arabia, for example, has had to face a decade of declining reserves, as oil prices stagnated and then declined and as it has had to play the role of "swing producer". The attempt to create stable prices in 1985 cost the Kingdom $6 bn in oil revenues and the constant need to balance the Kingdom's current account deficit has eaten deeply into its reserves.

15

Its liquid reserves have been halved since 1984 from $24.748 bn to $12,296 bn in 1990. Overall assets, including foreign investments, were estimated by SAMA to be $64.8 bn in 1989, compared with their maximum level of $145 bn in September 1982. As far as Kuwait is concerned, its foreign assets, conventionally set at $100 bn, are now thought to have been halved as a result of the conflict with Iraq. It is known that at least $10 bn-worth of assets have already been liquidated. Nonetheless, Kuwait's central bank only has $bn in liquid assets and, in order to avoid too hasty sales of foreign assets, the Amirate is anticipating raising discrete loans of around $5 bn each up to a maximum of $20 bn to finance reconstruction.[21]

GLOBAL GCC COSTS INCURRED BY THE GULF CONFLICT
($ bn)

Item	Kuwait	Saudi Arabia	UAE	GCC Total
Reconstruction	60-95	-	-	60-95
Military costs	16	17	4	37
Aid	9	9	6	24
Other	10	21	-	31
Egyptian debt	‡	‡	‡	9
G-8 security	‡	‡	‡	15
Economic aid	‡	‡	‡	15
TOTAL	‡	‡	‡	191-226

At the same time, the three major Arab Gulf oil producers-Saudi Arabia, Kuwait and the UAE - have taken on obligations of around $30 bn in addition to the costs associated with the conflict of over $90 bn. These sums cannot realistically be financed from capital reserves, and it seems unlikely that current earnings could bear such a burden either - unless oil prices rose significantly. It thus seems unlikely that the proposals for Gulf-financed security and for new economic development programmes also financed by the Gulf will actually be realised - unless there is a significant and permanent increase in oil prices and revenues. The likelihood of that, however, seems remote.

1. Middle East Economic Survey, 33:42; 23.7.1990; D6.

2. Mofid K. (1990), "Economic reconstruction of Iraq: financing the peace", Third World Quarterly, 12, 1; January 1990; 53.

3. Mauras V. (1991) "L'Irak, est-il pauvre?", Le Monde, 26.02.1991: 21,23.

4.

0184

5. According to Mehran Nakhjavani (War Report; 23.3.1991), by the end of 1991, Iraq's OECD debt will have reached $35 bn, debt to the USSR and Eastern European countries will be $15 bn and financial debt to the Gulf states (in other words, direct loans in cash, arther than aid in kind) will be around $30 bn. Iraqi arrears in interest payments to Western commercial banks at the end of March 1991 stood at $560 mn (MEES; 34:30, 29.4.1991).

6. **SAUDI AID TO IRAQ 1980-1990**

($ bn)

Direct aid	
grants	5.843
soft loans	9.247
Oil in aid	6.751
Equipment*	3.739
Other	0.048
Total	25.734

*military and transport equipment

Notes: Kuwait provided $9 bn in cash at the start of the war
and $6.751 in oil aid - a total of $15.751.
The UAE provided $3 bn in cash aid.

Source: **Middle East Economic Survey**, 21.01.1991; B3, quoting official Saudi sources.

7. EIU (1990), **Country report: Iraq**, Business International (London): Nos. 1-4 inclusive.

8. MEES (34:24); 11.3.1991; B2.

9. Financial Times, February 16-17, 1991.

10. There are suggestions that the UN Security Council resolution for a permanent ceasefire recognises that total reparations of this kind are unrealistic. It apparently suggests that 250,000 b/d of oil should be directly used to cover reparation costs. This would generate $1.8 bn annually at international crude prices of $20 per barrel. Saudi Arabia is also expected to push for a permanent oil price "in the low twenties" and, oil analysts believe, now has the clout to enforce such a price through OPEC (Christian Science Monitor; 7.3.1991).

11. MEES, 34:30, 29.04.1991; A2.

12. Financial Times; 21.3.1991

13. Le Monde; 20.3.1991.

14. MEES; 11.3.1991; B4.

15. Stauffer T.R. & Lennox F.H. (1984), Accounting for wasting assets: income measurment for oil and mineral exporting rentier states, Opec (Vienna).

17

0185

Stauffer T.R. (1987), "Income measurement in Arab states" in Beblawi H. & Luciani G. (eds), **The rentier state**, Croom Helm (London).

16. Economist Intelligence Unit, Iraq: Country Profile 1990-91; 24

17. MEES, 34:27; 8.4.1991.

18. The Independent, 4.5.1991.

19. Le Monde; 3.5.1991.

20. MEES, 34:30; 29.4.1991; B1-B2.

21. The Independent; 4.5.1991.

Paul Barker ASSOCIATES

ECONOMIC AND
BANKING CONSULTANTS

13. Financing Reconstruction in Kuwait and Iraq

by

Paul Barker, Paul Barker Associates

Friday, 10 May 1991

Royal Institute for International Affairs
London

Unit 35, Finsbury Business Centre
40, Bowling Green Lane, London EC1R 0NE, UK
Telephone: 071-278 0333 x 206
Telex: 267247 FINSEC Fax: 071-837 7612
VAT 440 5846 53

0187

Before discussing the financial ways and means to reconstruct either Kuwait or Iraq I think it is clear that we need some idea of the extent of the damage incurred and of the nature of the replacement articles (or economies) that are to be installed.

PHYSICAL DAMAGE
Starting with the physical aspects of the destruction wrought on both Kuwait and Iraq, I should like to project summaries from the mission report of UN Under Secretary General Marti Ahtisaari, who was sent to the two countries to assess humanitarian needs. His dramatic language may be out of character with what one had come to expect from international bureaucrats, but precisely because of that, it warrants attention.

I should like to use the findings of the UN document to give a brief breakdown of the breakdown of the two economies. Many of these findings have been substantially corroborated by secondary reporting, and in each case they are divided into four main categories: food and agriculture; water, sanitation and health; transport and communications; and energy and industry.

In the case of Kuwait I would single out the following factors:

- Kuwait's six month strategic food reserve was substantially looted during the war, but since liberation a state-run importing and distribution system has been established under the guidance of the Kuwait Supply Company and 40 consumer cooperatives. Staples are, it appears, still being handed out free and most other food is subsidised. Indigenous agriculture and fishing has been affected by marine pollution, the minefields and the spreading of oil lakes across the country.

- One desalination plant is reported to have been wrecked, but the remaining water infrastructure incurred only moderate damage and mains supplies have been restored in many areas. Kuwait's three major sanitation plants suffered only superficial damage. There was little structural damage to health facilities, although some advanced equipment was removed. The major problem with hospitals is to persuade the largely expatriate medical staff to return. There exists an unquantifiable health hazard because of the degrading of the environment and this will require constant monitoring to identify potential outbreaks of disease and the seriousness of already noted skin, eye and lung ailments.

- Oil may be spilling out of the ground and/or burning at a rate of 4 to 6 mn b/d. The task of ridding the country of mines was considered one beyond the task of the Allied forces and therefore requiring commercial engineering assistance. Many mines are of a non-ferrous type and very difficult to detect. The UN report believes the problem of unexploded ordnance is one of the gravest facing Kuwait.

- As far as transportation is concerned, there was only moderate surface damage to most of Kuwait's roads and only three bridges were damaged. At the airport the runaways and taxiways are only slightly damaged but the landing system, terminals and other buildings have undergone serious damage and the control tower has been destroyed. The two ports of Shuwaikh and Shuaiba have suffered serious dock facility damage and require wrecked hip and mine clearing exercises. Two thirds of Kuwait's vehicle fleet of around 800,000 has been reported stolen, looted or vandalised. All Kuwait city's fire engines and all the government's stock of ambulance were removed.

1

0188

About one third of the country's telecommunications facilities were moderately to severely damaged, but as of 15 March 57 per cent of capacity had been installed and free calling had been offered widely.

All of Kuwait's four power stations were damaged, and 40 substations incurred varying degrees of damage.

What is perhaps surprising about this tale of woe is the apparent low cost of restoring the damage mentioned. Although no figures are given for payments to oil fire fighting teams, contracts to restore order in the other areas mentioned were said to have been covered by contracts worth a relatively modest $550 million. This figure is quite clearly of a different order from the $23 billion minimum figure put forward another UN mission, as shown on the next slide. The number for oil earnings not received during the period of occupation is an opportunity loss, while in all cases the UN mission suggests that its estimates are of what would be needed to return Kuwait to its former capacities.

Turning to Iraq, the catalogue of physical destruction lengthens considerably, reflecting the size of the country, the allied forces' bombing strategy and both the accuracy and inaccuracy with which the latter was implemented.

- on the food and agriculture front, stocks of basic foodstuffs were reported critically low. Livestock farming has been seriously affected because of the absence of imported feed products. The country's sole veterinary vaccine plant was destroyed along with all stocks of vaccine; powdered milk was being rationed to babies only. Seed warehouse for vegetables and potatoes have been destroyed, jeopardising next season's planting. The June grain harvest has already been seriously compromised largely because of the absence of fuel to run irrigation systems and harvesting machines.

- The entire water purification system in Baghdad came to a halt because of lack of electrical supplies, which has even prevented adequate water testing to determine the extent of contamination. Garbage and sewage treatment has virtually halted, largely because of lack of fuel.

- 83 road bridges were destroyed during the war. All internal and external telephone systems were destroyed. Bombardment is reckoned to have paralysed oil and electricity sectors almost entirely. The UN mission reckoned that Iraq must be assured 25 per cent of pre-war civilian domestic fuel consumption through imports to fulfil even basic humanitarian activities. Without energy to run refrigeration units, irrigation systems, or water plants, much relief work is bound to be hampered. The problems of disease and starvation will start to mount rapidly as the summer approaches and as stocks are run down even further.

FINANCIAL DAMAGE
There are many ways of approaching the problem of putting a financial or economic price on the damage the Gulf war has done to regional economies, and particularly to Iraq and Kuwait. I shall make a distinction between current earning losses and capital damage and hint at the more problematic issues involved in trying to put figures on long-term opportunity losses, economic costs and unrealised investment yields. In fact My next slide compares the war-related current account gains and losses incurred by

2

0189

Saudi Arabia, Kuwait and Iraq. In the case of Saudi Arabia, we see an approximate balance between the oil earnings gains of 1990/91 over 1989 and the losses from payments to the Allied forces, for extra armaments, larger volumes of worker remittances etc. If this picture tends to suggest that Saudi Arabia may have emerged relatively unscathed from the war, let me just caution that 1) this is a purely economic picture and 2) by running 1990 and 1991 into an aggregate, I conveniently ignore the problem of quarterly cash flows and the liquidity crunch the Saudis faced in the first months of this year. The non-war economy may also have continued to run at a small deficit during the period.

The Kuwaiti loss from the war as shown, at some $35 bn, includes an element of short-term opportunity cost as it is derived from the difference between the anticipated 1990/91 current account surplus and the realised current account deficit. I shall dwell on the components of this figure when I come shortly to discuss the Kuwaiti balance of payments.

The situation in Iraq as regards figures has become so hopeless that any attempts to derive a 'current war balance' figure would be meaningless. Instead, I illustrate as a short-term gain the $6-7 billion current account deficit projected for Iraq for the seventeen months from August 1990 on a peace basis, and which airtight and continuing sanctions and a financial freeze would presumably prevent the country from incurring. On the loss side I show the $22 bn of foregone oil export revenues - assuming no requited exports prior to 1992.

One last point vividly illustrated by this graph is the seemingly obvious but sometimes overlooked fact that any windfall earnings raised by Saudi Arabia, especially in 1991, have been derived from the absence of Iraqi and Kuwait crude from the market not from prices. Saudi Arabia has experienced a volume windfall, and the implications of this for the reintegration of Iraqi and Kuwaiti oil into the world market and for these countries' future revenue prospects should not be underestimated.

Turning to the assessment of capital losses, the figures for Kuwait and Iraq tend to mount rapidly and in a curiously rounded fashion. Thus the most common figure for Kuwait (including current losses as well) is $100 bn. For Iraq - according to finance minister Mohammed Saleh - $200 bn, of which at least $20 bn is a current opportunity loss of oil revenue. Kuwait's capital costs could include not only wrecked industrial plant, aircraft etc. but also items such as the writing off of loans to Egypt, the burden on government reserves of financing capital flight after the promised June lifting of exchange controls, the backing needed for a new currency, and the cost of the estimated 6 mn b/d of oil that has been either burning or spilling over into apparently unretrievable oil lakes in Kuwait.

A recent World Bank study on the possibility of a world capital crunch by Chief Economist Lawrence Summers provided estimates of a more strictly-defined capital requirement for Kuwait and Iraq at US$25-50 billion for the former and US$100 billion for the latter. In the same report Saudi Arabia is judged to have a capital requirement of US$20-30 billion and Iran one of US$10-20 billion. Bang goes the concept of an Opec surplus, apparently. Summers does point out that not all these 'needs' will be necessarily met. Financing is clearly one of the arts of the possible.

Realistically, there is little way of testing these ballpark figures for accuracy, and as a

3

0190

totally untrained damage assessor I would only point to several clear problems of valuation. What value do you put on a hospital that was destroyed but which in the post-war situation of a lower Kuwaiti resident population is no longer needed and is not to be rebuilt? Do you assess damage on the basis of reconstruction costs alone or do you add in an element for loss of business? More theoretically, how do you assess any non-oil sector values in a rentier economy where businesses do not exist on stand alone basis but as a function of oil revenues? And in terms of attributing liability, how can we be sure that the retreating Iraqi army inflicted all the damage to Kuwait's industrial installations, for instance?

Taking the insurance worlds' terminology into the more concrete world of actual reconstruction contracts and financing, can we expect to be operating on a 'new for old' basis and if so what does it mean? And what sort of excess policy, or percentage of cost, should the financiers of reconstruction be looking to impose upon the claimants to impose some form of joint responsibility to make sure the wholly bloody mess does not reoccur?

'New for old' policies, as I understand them, mean that if you write off a 1950s Ford in a pile up, the insurance company would probably cough up to the tune of the latest model of Ford. On the much wider reconstruction front that we're looking at, does this mean that we can expect a totalled desalination plant to be replaced by an old model or by the most recent technology? Taking the 'new for old' concept one step further, I wonder whether in certain cases old prices might not in fact be higher than current ones. You will remember that much of Kuwait's and Iraq's major infrastructural development was contracted at a time when prices in the Gulf were ludicrously inflated to cover for inexperience, massive kick-backs, huge profit margins, and a very much overstretched transport infrastructure.

Although some of these conditions might prevail again, I would suggest that part of the urgency and overextension of personnel and facilities will be mitigated, both by financial and other constraints. It also has to be realised that original prices for industrial plant contained the costs of licensing, design and engineering. One would not expect to have the Iraqis and Kuwaitis pay for these again. All of which is to say that simply totting up these states' development budgets over the last ten years and putting that forward as a reconstruction bill is likely to be very misleading!

KUWAIT:
FINANCIAL RESOURCES
My next slide represents some basic estimates of how the Kuwaiti current account situation might be turning out under the pressures of the invasion and the cessation of almost all economic activity. I think the main point to be stressed here is that Kuwait's worst moments are likely to be concentrated in 1991. From then on, depending on the means of financing this year's large current account deficit and subject to a relatively slow reconstruction and rehabilitation effort, the current account financing needs are likely to moderate. For 1992, I am assuming Kuwaiti oil exports or other countries' compensatory oil exports at a quarter of 1989 levels and imports at 70 per cent of 1989 levels. Kuwait thus continues to run a small trade deficit against tradition, but one

4

0191

the US governments and other allied forces, payment to neighbouring states, in 1991 the freeing of remittances, and in both years the weekly cash handouts to exiled Kuwaitis. Transfers are projected to fall off significantly in 1992 but to still come in at over US$1 billion more than in the 1989 base year.

It is on the services balance that we see a steady deterioration, reflecting a drop in investment income on a declining volume of foreign assets and the assimilation into services payments of much of the reconstruction contracts and increased insurance and freight charges on imports. From a current account standpoint it is somewhat irrelevant whether the large 1991 deficit is financed by reserve drawdowns or loans: in 1992 the interest cost of servicing say US$15 billion of loans would be roughly equivalent to the lost income to be realised if there was an assets disposal of US$15 billion.

I think the implication of this scenario is clear: that from 1992 onwards, borrowings by Kuwait in excess of US$3 billion a year are likely to be financing capital account transactions such as capital flight, reserve replenishment, and loan and investment write-offs. One would hope that some of these write-offs might pass through the income account, but Gulf accounting standards would suggest they will not. I think that bankers might have learnt from their Latin American experience that there are certain inherent risks in this type of financing.

Turning to the question of how much money the Kuwaiti government has at its disposal - both in general and on a liquid basis - I present three evaluation methods on the next slide. The first - the cumulative current account approach - indicates that the Kuwaiti economy should have generated US$110 billion in overseas assets since balance of payments statistics began in the early 1970s. Kuwait has tended to reflect fairly accurately the appreciation of past years' investment through the balance of payments, but some capital growth has inevitably be missed. The main problem with the cumulative current account method is that it gives no indication of the current ownership of these overseas reserves, and even as official statistics show government money flowing out, they lump together assets of the government reserve funds, the Kuwait Petroleum Corporation and Kuwait Airways.

The next method takes a Kuwait government figure for 1988 for the Reserve Fund for Future Generations (RFFG) and extrapolates onwards. For those of you who do not already know, the Kuwaitis established the RFFG in 1976, with the stipulation that 10 per cent of the government's annual revenues from oil and non-oil sources within the economy should be invested in it, and that capital and accrued income in this fund should remain intact until 2001. Well, as my figures indicate, I believe that the fund has been raided to the tune of as much as $20 billion since 2 August, but could still stand at US$77 billion. This would all be government money, but there are principled and practical question marks about how much could be made available immediately as I shall explain. Kuwait has also run a state general reserve in which other budgetary surpluses were held. But following years of budget deficits, local share rescue operations and injudicious deployment, I assume there is not much left of immediate hard currency value in this account.

My third estimation method draws on my own close study of the Kuwait Investment Office's (KIO's) activities over the years, and extrapolates from the KIO's UK quoted equity portfolio. My analysis of this portfolio has consisted of tracking stakes held by the KIO's nominee companies to percentages as low as 0.16 per cent of any particular

5

plc, and therefore hopefully can claim a certain comprehensiveness. Taking this figure, I then multiply by three to include the KIO's sterling bond, property and private company holdings, and then multiply by 6.7 per cent on the assumption that the KIO holds no more than 15 per cent of its assets in sterling.

This method, as you will appreciate, has the advantage of being based on certifiable share stakes and established market values, but as my figures show, it also highlights the extreme volatility of Kuwait's foreign assets. Within three months of 1991 on this basis, Kuwait's foreign assets holding would have shown an appreciation of over 26 per cent in sterling terms but only 11 per cent in dollar terms. The overall figures are high and provide some comfort, but does such a movable feast provide secure collateral?

A final problem with assessing the liquidity of Kuwait's foreign assets can be shown by the next slide, representing the distribution of the KIO's UK equity portfolio. The Kuwaiti BP stake makes up 68 per cent of the KIO portfolio. This not only confirms to me the intermingling of foreign asset holdings between the KIO and the KPC but also suggests that certain assets are of a strategic nature and would only be liquidated under extreme duress.

FINANCIAL OPTIONS

The above picture of liquidity, currency and investment strategy uncertainties perhaps explains why the Kuwaitis have such a hard choice in deciding how to finance their present current and capital account needs, and why a certain amount of personal blood is being spilt in an effort to get control of this decision making process. Apart from the choices of how best to raise money, there is also the question of how much should be released for current spending?

Many of you are, I'm sure, well aware of the great financial schism in Kuwait state investment circles between the Kuwait Investment Authority and the Kuwait Investment Office - the KIA and the KIO. The KIA was set up in 1982 as a major offshoot of the Ministry of Finance, charged with the overall management of all funds vested in the State General Reserve and the Reserve Fund for Future Generations. As such it became nominally in charge of the KIO in London. The KIA was essentially a sop to nationalist elements in the increasingly vocal National Assembly. These were demanding more local say in the management of Kuwait's financial legacy, greater accountability, and a deal more money invested in the Arab world and the Kuwaiti economy; they were basically saying they did not trust the al-Sabahs with the nation's money. The KIO has struggled ever since 1982 to keep its independence, and it is easy to see why in the present atmosphere of heightened political debate on Kuwait's future, the KIO/KIA feuding has broken into the open again. The problem was not eased when after the invasion large numbers of KIA officials upped it to London and planted themselves in St Vedast House, the KIO's highly self-effacing headquarters close to St. Pauls.

One of the immediate areas of conflict between the KIA and KIO following the invasion seems to have been over the degree of support to give to the Kuwaiti international banking network. Many overseas Kuwaiti banks are indirectly owned by the KIA, but to meet immediate liquidity problems in these banks, the KIA appears to have pushed KIO money into deposits with these banks as it had none or precious little of its own to help out. The KIO in the past has been extremely wary of dealing with Arab banks.

6

0193

These demands on its funds will come on top of other requests to pour money into refloating the local economy and financial system, and there clearly has to be some questioning of how money should be paid out. The KIO may have temporarily broken its trust status to help out, but there are bound to be those who question how long it should go on being raided. The appointment of Abdullah Gabandi as head of the KIA is an intriguing one. As managing director of the KIA's 99 per cent owned Kuwait Foreign Trading Contracting and Investment Company (KFTCIC), he had been responsible for trying to keep several ailing banks afloat and for dealing with KFTCIC's large sovereign loan problems largely by making extra equity calls on the KIA. The first indications are that he may have begun to reassess priorities.

Turning to the problems likely to face the Kuwaitis if they decide that borrowing is their better or politically more acceptable option, I have already alluded to many of the concerns likely to face commercial lending officers. These are: uncertainty as to the purpose of lending and the overall size and time horizon of the financial plug needed; unfamiliarity with some of the new names likely to be negotiating loans; and the fluctuating value of any collateral base assumed or offered. To elaborate briefly on the personality point, which is of extreme importance in the world of finance, I am sure that many bankers will be mourning the passing (in functional terms) of Sheikh Ali Khalifa, the former oil and finance minister and Fouad Jaffar, ex-executive head of the KIO.

The former certainly commanded genuine respect of the highest order in banking circles, and his presence in the new government would have certainly helped banks wavering on whether or not to lend to Kuwait. There are other uncertainties over personnel that will have an important impact on Kuwaiti commercial banks' ability to restore credit lines. Certain highly respected Palestinians have moved to jobs outside of Kuwait, for instance.

Apart from the problems raised above, there are others that will confront Kuwait in any attempt to borrow funds commercially. On the official level there is the problem of whether the KIO would be prepared to pledge assets formally against loans. This would seem unlikely, but if banks do not hold the KIO's share certificates in their own safes, they will feel uneasy about waking up the morning after and finding that a major disposal has been made. Other problems in terms of state borrowing surround the tenor of loans - even if the Al-Sabah reestablish their authority, how long will it be before there is another internal or external challenge to their authority? And surely no banker would want to lend beyond their estimation of that date. There is, I know, some concern also about where KIO funds might go if one ever got into the situation of having two governments of Kuwait - the Al-Sabahs in exile and a Kuwaiti populist regime in the country itself.

Pricing too could be a problem, and mainly for technical reasons. Kuwait unlike Saudi Arabia is not regarded as prime risk under the new Bank for International Settlement capital adequacy guidelines. Loans to the Kuwaiti government unlike those to the Saudi government will require capital backing, and banks are currently very short of capital. Kuwait must therefore expect to pay more for its loans or get a Saudi guarantee. One thing we probably could all agree on is which option Kuwait would find more palatable.

As far as non-sovereign borrowing is concerned, Kuwaiti banks settled all their interbank interest payment liabilities as soon as they were allowed, but their

7

0194

creditworthiness will not have been enhanced by the decision not to publish balance sheets until end-1991 or by rumours of imminent mergers. In any case, Kuwaiti commercial banks' borrowings were always basically a function of short-term trade credit rather than any vehicle of medium-term balance of payments borrowing, and as such do not provide an alternative to state borrowing.

Private sector creditors in Kuwait have seen their businesses totally disrupted and have not unnaturally stalled on foreign loan payments, even though certain trading families undoubtedly had enough foreign assets to meet obligations. They will now have to rectify past positions before they can expect further credit, and quite possibly deal on a fully collateralised basis until a track record is reestablished.

There are four other means by which Kuwait could be expected to finance its current account deficits: by re-dressing direct Kuwaiti sovereign risk as exporting countries' risk by use of official export credit; by stalling on foreign payments to contractors, and so effectively gaining short-term unnegotiated credit; by forcing the private sector to repatriate its foreign assets; or by attracting foreign investment. The first two means are more or less contiguous paths along the same route, as if the Kuwaitis start delaying on payments, it seems certain that companies will only agree to work in Kuwait under official cover - which would apparently be available, more readily from some quarters than others.

Despite much talk of private domestic capital playing a more prominent role in post-crisis Kuwait, it would hardly be the case that we are looking at incremental funds if the private capital deployed in Kuwait represented the compensation payments made by government to businesses destroyed by the war. And yet is perhaps only under some kind of government guarantee that private money will return to Kuwait in significant quantities.

Prospects for foreign investment are more intriguing with certain government spokesmen apparently advocating an end to the domestic monopoly in both the oil and financial sectors. If part of the new economic order in the Gulf and the Arab world can realistically entail greater foreign penetration and still maintain popular support, then foreign investment presents a valid option.

IRAQ:
Turning to the subject of Iraq's international financial resources and obligations, I would have to say that Iraq has made such a right fool of much of the international financial community over the last few years, that I would not blame bankers for trying to get their own back now. But spite will not be the only response to Iraq's requests for financial assistance, and banks will have to work out where their interests lie in terms of doing new business.

Circumstances make an assessment of Iraq's foreign debt and assets position more difficult. On the debt front, a starting point seems to be the $14.7 billion of claims identified as of mid-1990 by banks and export credit agencies. To which can be added a further $6.5 billion of Eastern European claims and about $500 million of claims from

8

0195

multilateral organisations. On top of this there is estimated to have been about $4 billion of arrears awaiting capitalisation at the time of the invasion, and I am certainly not convinced that the $1.5 billion aunauthorised Banca Nazionale del Lavoro loan had yet been acknowledged. So in August 1990 Iraq probably owed as much as $27 billion before loans to Saudi Arabia and Kuwait were counted in.

Since the invasion, Iraq's debt could well have jumped quite considerably. In the first place it can be assumed that unpaid interest has been capitalised. But more significantly large volumes of banks' contingent exposures to Iraq, such as confirmations of letters of credit, will have crystallised into direct claims. These factors together will probably have added another $4 billion to Iraq's debt figures. As far as foreign assets are concerned, unpaid interest on Iraqi deposits can be expected to have boosted Iraqi balances abroad, and a few more secret accounts appear to have been found. At the end of September 1990 Iraq had a traceable $3 billion worth of deposits with BIS banks. This month they put in a claim to release $i billion of these funds for essential imports. What Iraq has gained since the invasion is the possibility of making claims under performance bonds on contracts which foreign firms left unfinished. This could represent quite a large amount, and one which European banks have expressed due concern about.

The UN position on Iraq's foreign debt obligations is clear. Paragraph 17 of resolution 687 decided that all Iraqi statements made since 2 August 1990 repudiating its foreign debt were null and void, and demanded that Iraq adhere scrupulously to all its obligations concerning servicing and repayment of its foreign debt. Would that it was so easy to achieve this objective! The UN has also made it clear that the compensation fund being set up to cover invasion-related damage will not deals with defaulted loans unless it can be proved than losses on the loans were a direct result of the Iraqi invasion of Kuwait. On the other hand it is also made clear that none of the existing 'frozen funds' of Iraq will be diverted into the Fund.

So essentially commercial bankers and official creditors seem to be faced with a situation where they have a maximum offset capacity of 10 per cent. In addition, many banks will be well provided against their Iraqi exposure, perhaps even fully, and they could therefore consider a write-off. The legal position on offsetting loans against deposits is complex and varies from country to country. Banks with non-syndicated exposure to a particular Iraqi borrower who is also a depositor might have the option of netting out their position, but banks involved in syndicated loans to Iraq would be in a much more invidious position vis a vis the rest of the banking community. The room for individual initiatives will narrow if banks or official creditors opt for a London or Paris Club approach to Iraq's debt problems.

With provisioning levels against Iraq already very high, there remain the financial options of a significant write-off of debt or the encouragement of an active debt for equity programme. Bankers hate finally writing off debt, and fears of moral hazard will certainly be very much to the fore given Iraq's past record. A debt for equity programme could gain appeal if Iraq is truly to move towards a more private sector oriented and less centrally controlled economy, but the funds generated would effectively come from industrial investors buying out the banks.

In pondering on the willingness of bankers to resume lending to Iraq or governments to begin aid donations we inevitably stumble upon the question of the fate of Saddam

9

0196

Hussein. One only has to compare the haste with which an aid programme has been put together for Bangladesh and the dithering surrounding humanitarian aid to Iraqis to realise how great a stumbling block Saddam is. But aid has always been more about politics than business, and I'm by no means as sanguine that commercial finance will not find a way to work with Saddam Hussain if he survives.

'SOVEREIGN' RISK
For bankers the equation in deciding whether to lend to either Kuwait or Iraq may unfortunately reduce to the question of who controls the economic centre of the country in questions - and by economic centre I essentially mean the oil industry.

As I come to the end of my presentation, I would like to indulge in an exercise of lateral thinking and quote a few sentences from a recent speech given by Viktor Gerashchenko, head of the Soviet Union's Central Bank or Gosbank. In arguing strongly for the need to keep a centralised banking system - and therefore for his job - Gerashchenko made the following points, and I quote: "The 'multiplication' of a single Soviet sovereign borrower will magnify credit risk for the country as a whole due to the republics having an unrecognised credit standing and because of political unrest in some of them. The complexity of the problem of distribution of Soviet sovereign liabilities between the republics and lapsing control over their foreign borrowings will build up uncertainty towards the main Soviet borrower as well. The multiplicity of republican monetary regimes will create extreme complications for foreign investment in the USSR. The uncontrolled process of trade liberalisation and the mounting of trade arrears provides an example of the problems in store"

It seems to me that Gerashchenko makes a good point about the innate conservatism of international bankers and their policies towards sovereign risk. What he fails to show even the slightest concern for is the desperation of many citizens in the Soviet Union for a new decentralised and more accountable form of government.

I trust that many of you will see where my lateral thinking leads. In a world where market forces are increasingly accepted and lauded, international finance seems to be lagging in its penchant for strong centres and single risks. It would be indeed sad if the conditions for mobilising finance for the reconstruction of either Kuwait or Iraq included the imposition of strong and essentially undemocratic central government. It would also be a short-term solution and one that would probably lead to another huge reconstruction bill being faced in the early years of the next century.

Thank you for your attention.

KUWAIT:

" ....a deliberate attempt was made to extinguish Kuwait, its national identity, the pride of its people in their history and achievement. The manner of destruction, with its coordinated vandalism and looting, leaves an indelibe image. "

IRAQ:

"Iraq has, for some time to come, been relegated to a pre-industrial age, but with all the disabilities of a post-industrial dependency on an intensive use of energy and technology....near-apocalyptic results upon the economic infrastructure... "

Source: UN report on humanitarian needs in Kuwait and Iraq, end-March 1991

IRAQI DAMAGE TO KUWAIT DURING PERIOD OF
OCCUPATION

	US$ BN
LOSS OF OIL EXPORT EARNINGS	8.5
POWER NETWORK	1.0
PORTS, AIRPORTS, KUWAIT AIRWAYS	2.0
VEHICLE FLEET	5.0
TELEPHONE AND COMMUNICATIONS	1.0
RESIDENTIAL HOUSING	2.5
HOTELS	0.5
URBAN INFRASTRUCTURE	0.5
MEDIA FACILTIIES	0.5
NON-VEHICLE RETAIL AND WHOLESALE GOODS	1.0
GOLD	0.5
	=====
	23.0

Source: UN report on damage assessment
in Kuwait, April 1991

0199

The War Balance – Current Earnings, 1990–91

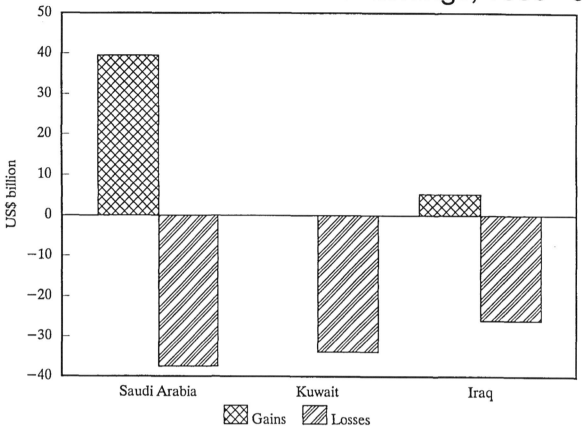

Kuwait Current Account Estimates, 1990–92

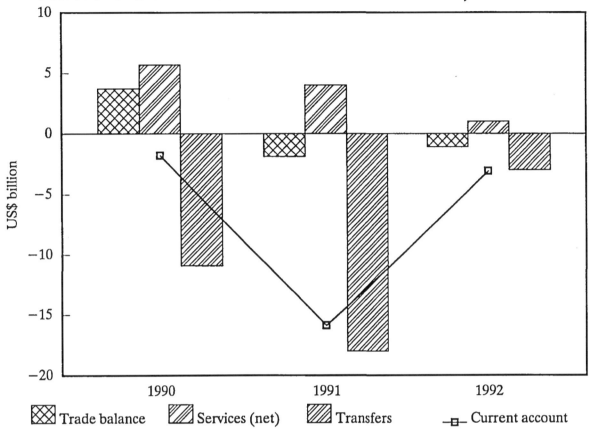

0201

KUWAIT FOREIGN ASSETS ESTIMATES

METHOD 1: CUMULATIVE CURRENT ACCOUNT SURPLUS
(US$ BILLION)

1987	113
1988	117
1989	126
1990	124
1991	110

METHOD 2: EXTRAPOLATION FROM RFFG FIGURES
(US$ BILLION)

		OIL REVENUE ALLOCATION	INTEREST INCOME
JUNE 1988	58	7.5	6.0
JUNE 1989	71.5	11.0	7.0
JUNE 1990	89.5	0.0	7.5
JUNE 1991	77.0 (INCL. US$20 BILLION WITHDRAWAL)		

METHOD 3: EXTRAPOLATION FROM KIO'S UK-QUOTED EQUITY
PORTFOLIO

	(a) UK-QUOTED	(b) UK OTHER (a) X 3	(c) GLOBAL (b) X 6.7
JAN. 1991			
UK£ BILLION	2.3	6.9	46.2
US$ BILLION	4.4	13.3	89.3
APRIL 1991			
UK£ BILLION	2.9	8.7	58.3
US$ BILLION	4.9	14.8	99.1

0202

걸프사태 : 자료 및 언론보도, 1990-91. 전3권 (V.2 자료, 1991.4-5월)

KIO's UK Quoted Equity Portfolio

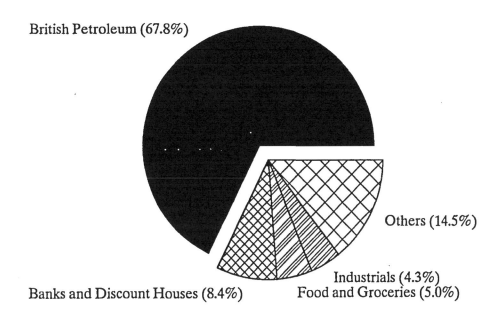

British Petroleum (67.8%)

Others (14.5%)

Industrials (4.3%)
Food and Groceries (5.0%)

Banks and Discount Houses (8.4%)

Source: Paul Barker Associates, London

0203

KIO's UK quoted equity portfolio by sectors
(including BP stake)

% of KIO Portfolio

15 April 1991

	Mkt Cap Pounds mn	KIO Share %	KIO Share no.mn	KIO Por %
Banks and Discount Houses				
Barclays	7490.600	0.160	11.985	0.420
Cater Allen	107.600	3.880	4.175	0.146
Gerrard and National	131.900	3.330	4.392	0.154
King and Shaxson	23.700	6.330	1.500	0.053
Midland Bank PLC	1748.300	10.600	185.320	6.490
Royal Bank of Scotland	1445.800	2.340	33.832	1.185
				=====
				8.447
Building, Timber, Roads				
Baldwin	14.000	3.050	0.427	0.015
Barratt Developments	207.400	0.810	1.680	0.059
Heywood Williams	177.400	4.600	8.160	0.286
NSM	67.600	19.970	13.500	0.473
Taylor Woodrow	844.300	4.000	38.268	1.340
				=====
				2.172
Drapery and Stores				
Hogg Robinson	91.800	11.200	10.282	0.360
				=====
				0.360
Electricals				
Cable and Wireless	5745.900	0.610	35.050	1.227
				=====
				1.227
Engineering				
TI Group	849.200	0.970	8.237	0.288
Triplex Lloyd	57.300	8.430	4.830	0.169
VSEL Consortium	145.800	0.220	0.321	0.011
				=====
				0.469
Food, Groceries etc				
Argyll Group	2998.800	2.210	66.273	2.321
Hillsdown Holdings	1401.600	5.490	76.948	2.695
				=====
				5.016

0204

Hotels and Caterers

Trusthouse Forte	2145.800	3.200	68.666	2.405
				======
				2.405

Industrials (Misc.)

Barry Wehmiller	87.900	15.000	13.185	0.462
Boots	3743.000	0.400	14.972	0.524
BTR	7037.700	0.600	42.226	1.479
Fisons	3305.100	0.950	31.398	1.100
Unilever	6150.600	0.320	19.682	0.689
				=====
				4.254

Insurances

Bradstock Group	79.000	11.200	8.848	0.310
Hogg Group	118.400	5.630	6.666	0.233
London and Manchester	412.600	1.160	4.786	0.168
Royal Insurance	2274.800	1.330	30.255	1.060
Saltire Insurance	7.350	14.330	1.053	0.037
Sedgwick Group	1002.100	0.580	5.812	0.204
				=====
				2.011

Property

Hammerson	830.400	0.920	7.640	0.268
Mountleigh	170.600	0.740	1.262	0.044
Rosehaugh	91.900	5.000	4.595	0.161
Trencherwood	17.500	4.000	0.700	0.025
				=====
				0.497

Transport

Hays	524.000	10.000	52.400	1.835
Lep Group	208.600	14.560	30.372	1.064
				=====
				2.899

Investment Trusts

Scottish Amer. Inv. Trust	254.900	11.080	28.243	0.989
Second Market Inv. Co.	225.300	10.560	23.792	0.833
				=====
				1.822

Finance and Land Trusts

Newmarket	9.970	20.190	2.013	0.070
				=====
				0.070

0205

Oil and Gas

Aviva Petroleum	30.700	4.900	1.504	0.053
British Petroleum	********	9.800	1936.382	67.812
Expl. Comp. of Louisiana	32.600	14.900	4.857	0.170
Great Western Res	99.600	8.100	8.068	0.283
New London Oil	16.900	5.660	0.957	0.033
			=======	
			68.351	
Total			2855.514	100.000

0206

IRAQI FOREIGN DEBT
(US$ BILLION)

PRE-INVASION

BIS/OECD BANKS AND OFFICIAL CREDITORS	14.7
EAST EUROPEAN CREDITORS	6.5
MULTILATERAL AGENCIES	0.5
INTEREST ARREARS	4.0
BANCA NAZIONALE DEL LAVORO	1.5
	27.2

POST-INVASION

INTEREST ARREARS	2.0
GUARANTEES CALLED	2.0

GRAND TOTAL	31.2

0207

14. REBUILDING KUWAIT & SOCIO-ECONOMIC CHANGE AFTER THE OCCUPATION

By Dr. Mohamad Al-Rumaihi
EDITOR-IN-CHIEF
"Sawt Al-Kuwait"
&
"New Arabia"

10th May, 1991

0208

A new Kuwait is born.   A whole generation has been changed, strengthened and made more aware of their existence,   surroundings and the wider world.   In short, a country and a people have been transformed.

The seven month occupation of Kuwait has indeed brought about severe damage to the infrastructure, which will soon be totally restored   but the socio-economic change caused by the occupation is sure to remain, accompanied by the blessings of the people, the Crown Prince and Prime Minister and other members of the government.

Post-war Kuwait will never be the same as Kuwait before the 2nd of August, 1990.

The cost of reconstructing and rehabilitating Kuwait has been estimated at between $50-100 billion.   Dozens of contracts have already been signed with foreign companies which   are helping in the job of reconstruction.   However, for the process to be carried out on a full and proper scale, it is of the utmost importance that oil production resumes as soon as possible.

Kuwait will require between two and five years to re-establish an economy, similar to what it had before the invasion.

Obviously, priority is being given to restoring the basic necessities of life.   Water supplies, for example, are not only vital for Kuwait's population, but for those companies engaged in reconstruction work as well.   So far, Kuwait has recovered one fifth of its water supplies, after desalination plants were sabotaged by Iraq's invading troops.   It is expected that 50% of Kuwait's water capacity will be recovered by the end of 1991.

0209

Before leaving Kuwait, Iraqis placed demolition charges on power plant and in control rooms at the generating stations.   They drained high purity water from high pressure boiler systems, ignited fuel storage facilities, and destroyed power and water distribution lines.

In Kuwait, power and water plants are combined.   Gas is used as fuel for both electricity generation and water desalination.   As a result, normal resumption of water and electricity is a linked exercise.

The emergency food plan for the coming three months was devised on the assumption that the population would be around 800,000 persons, much lower than the pre-invasion level.   Food is currently being distributed through 40 cooperative outlets.

Before the invasion, there were 3,300 doctors and 9,900 nurses in charge of medical care in Kuwait, most of whom were foreigners who left after the invasion.   The government is now seeking the employment of several hundred foreign nurses.

The renewal of telecommunications is one of the priorities in Kuwait's reconstruction programme.   Rebuilding the network is expected to cost around $800 million.   Both satellite and mobile telecommunications are major constituents of Kuwait's long term reconstruction strategy.   So far,   AT&T from the United States has installed a portable satellite ground station, with a twenty two foot dish and associated electronic gear.

On the business side, Kuwait was undergoing radical plans before the war to privatise its telecommunications.   If these plans are pursued in the future, it could mean further acceleration in the reconstruction programme.   Before the 2nd of August 1990, there were 800,000 cars in Kuwait, 85% of which were private cars.   Two thirds were reported as stolen, looted or damaged.   The government is currently arranging for the purchase of new cars.

0210

- 3 -

On the whole, the priority areas in the reconstruction programme are food, water, energy, medical care, gas, telecommunications, environmental protection, civil engineering, oil and oil production.

The cost of reconstructing Kuwait's oil industry has been estimated at $10-20 billion.   There will also be the question of Kuwait's downstream industries, such as petrochemicals and refining.

Work has already started in dealing with some of the less damaged oil wells, but due to the large number of burning wells (600), at least two years will be needed to deal with all of them, although the government is pressing for this time table to be reduced.

On the brighter side, Kuwait hopes to resume oil exports within a year, and not the two years that was previously forecast.   However, no definitive timescale has been agreed.

In the meantime, black clouds of poisonous fumes are polluting Kuwait and its neighbouring Gulf states.   Health hazards have already been reported. Cases of bronchial asthma, other respiratory problems, skin infections, boils and diarrhoea are on the rise.

However, pollution is not the only source of danger to Kuwaitis.   Mine fields and live ammunition and other ordnance left behind by the fleeing Iraqis pose a great threat to life and limb.   Several cases of death   and injuries have been reported resulting from such explosions.   Efforts of the allied forces are now being exerted to remove these mines, but it is an enormous job and unfortunately, the threat is expected to last for years to come.

Rebuilding Kuwait is a most difficult and painstaking job, but it is not impossible for our people.   The invasion crisis has not only revealed the unique tenacity and patriotism of our people, but has also endowed them with solidarity and unity in the face of difficulties, the first of which is rebuilding our country: economically, politically and most of all socially.

0211

- 4 -

As normal life is slowly and gradually making a return to Kuwait, a new concept of self-reliance and awareness of the outside world with all its harsh realities is becoming deeply embedded in our souls.

The population estimate on 1st August 1990 was 2,200,000 persons, 70% of whom were non-Kuwaitis, who either worked for the government or in the public sector.   Some of them had their own businesses.   Nonetheless, the government was supplying all of them with the same services offered to ordinary Kuwaiti citizens.   There were only three exceptions: land, estate and stocks and shares.

The Iraqi invasion made us ask ourselves this question?   To whom should the Kuwaiti government supply its services?   As an initial step, we believe that it is absolutely essential that the government rely on its own nationals, i.e: local manpower rather than expatriates.   Marginal employment will be reconsidered, and priority, in all cases, given to Kuwaitis.   What is certain is that the previous population, estimated at 2.2 million, will not be restored.

On the other hand, the reconstruction plan will be linked to the estimate of population.   In saying so, I would like to identify an issue of extreme importance, i.e. the situation of other nationals living in Kuwait, and more specifically the Palestinians. The Amir of Kuwait H. H. Sheikh Jaber Al Ahmad Al Jaber Al Sabah has promised that no reprisals would be taken against Kuwait's Palestinian community.   The actual number of those arrested or detained are very few. Those who have been held were proved to have committed crimes against Kuwaitis during the occupation.

Among the outcomes of the Iraqi invasion on Kuwait is some new thinking on education and young people.

The Kuwaiti National Curriculum was in the past laid down by other Arab nationals who installed their own viewpoints of history, as well as alien concepts and ideas, all of which became important elements in shaping the minds of young Kuwaitis.   Moreover, most of our teachers were expatriates.   We intend, through a new amended curriculum to re-examine

0212

- 5 -

Arab strategies concerning culture and education and re-install concepts of national statehood, emphasising the Kuwaiti identity and Arab nationalism.

On the technical side, Kuwait University, which used to cater for 12,000 students with a total of 3 million books, was robbed of its contents.   It needs total rehabilitation and re-equipment.

On an emotional level, which is no less important than other levels, our children were exposed to what can only be described as an overdose of fear, death and psychological damage.   They need special care and attention to compensate them for what they have already lost, and to prepare them to confront the difficulties that lie ahead.

The task of reconstructing Kuwait will never be comprehensively addressed, unless the issue of women is seriously tackled.   Kuwaiti women proved their steadfastness and inner strength during the crisis, whether they were living inside or outside Kuwait.   Previous allegations of extravagance were definitely proved wrong.   Kuwaiti women who remained in Kuwait throughout the crisis offered a most wonderful example of self sacrifice and challenge in the face of danger and death.

H. H. Sheikh Jaber's recent promise that consideration would be given to enfranchising Kuwaiti women to take part in elections, thus comes as a small token of gratitude to them.   It is definitely in the best interests of our country that women get the vote and play an active part in political life.   This would enable them further to strengthen their role in building and working for their country.

The participation of women in elections comes in the context of a more comprehensive move toward democracy that will be highlighted in the Parliamentary elections for a new National Assembly to be held by the end of 1992.

0213

- 6 -

The road to new Kuwait is long, harsh and full of obstacles.　But with our faith in God,　our trust in the leadership of the Amir H.　H.　Sheikh Jaber Al Ahmad Al Sabah and the Crown Prince & Prime Minister H.　H.　Sheikh Saad Al- Abdullah Al Salem Al Sabah, and　fortified by the re-moulding of our people during the occupation, our task will surely, with God's will, be fulfilled.

Beyond the crisis: the Gulf in the 1990s

15. IRAQ: Priorities and plans for reconstruction.
Economic reconstruction issues.

Jonathan Crusoe, Middle East Economic Digest(MEED)
8 May 1991

0215

The situation deteriorated considerably following

several weeks of allied bombing following the outbreak of

fighting on 17 January. Apart from military targets and

nuclear, chemical and biological facilities, targets listed

by the Pentagon included lines of communications and anything

that supported the war effort. As a result, the country's

economic infrastructure suffered heavy damage, in particular

oil, power generation and industrial installations, telephone

exchanges and other communications facilities, and roads and

bridges. The cutting of power supplies to hospitals--already

affected by the depleted supply of imported drugs and medicines

--water and sewage treatment plants has increased the possibility

of epedemics. The general . situation was further exacerbated

by the outbreak of fighting in the south and north following

the Gulf war ceasefire, as predominantly Shia and Kurdish forces

sought to subvert government control.

0216

Efforts to repair the damage and restore essential

services have been underway since the ceasefire, although

hampered in the north and south by the continuing fighting.

However, it was not until 2 May, that the government announced

that it had initiated a six-month crash rebuilding

programme, running from 27 April to 31 December. Priority

objectives are: food and medicine imports; essential reconstruction;

restoring oil products and exports; and restoring industrial

production.

No cost estimates have been given, but the government

has made it clear that the various ministries involved had the

necessary resources. Nevertheless, they are also asked to

exert themselves to augment existing resources, as well as

generate fresh resources to meet the government's objectives.

Import programme:

This is to be financed under the current state budget. No

figures were released for the budget--which was announced in

January this year--but it did take into account the UN trade

embargo. The main aim of the programme is to meet current

rationing requirements and the basic needs for intermediate

and capital goods. To this end, the government has asked

the UN either to allow Baghdad to export $ 1,000 million worth

of oil to pay for the required imports, or to unfreeze

$ 1,000 million worth of assets held in foreign banks.

0218

The Oil sector:

As early as 21 March, the cabinet approved a plan giving

priority to repairing crude oil pumping stations in the

south, and resuming drilling and exploration programmes.

About 6,000 local technicians have been involved in restoring

production at refineries at Baiji and Daura, to the extent

that petrol and kerosene rationing was lifted by early May.

Under the crash programme, repairs will also be carried out

to other refineries, pumping stations, gas processing plants,

and export installations, particularly the Mina al-Bakr

crude oil offshore export terminal in the Gulf.

0219

Industry:

The Industry & Military Industrialisation Ministry has

named several sectors where production must be restored:

or work resumed: drug manufacturing, geological surveys and

mining, and phosphate, fertiliser and sulphur production, and

electricity generation and transmission. Repairs will also

be carried out in factories making electrical equipment, light

fittings, bricks, cigarettes and textiles.

0220

Essential reconstruction:

Apart from restoring power supplies, teams are also working

to start-up water and sewage treatment plants. However, the

greatest effort   - is being made to restore communications.

A higher state engineering effort committee was set up on

the orders of the president; chaired by Defence--and former

Industry & Military Industrialisation Minister--Hussain Kamel,

the committee has been charged with rebuilding bridges

and damaged stretches of major roads. Hussain Kamel has also been

instructed to head the effort to restore communications.

0221

These are main priorities listed under the government's

crash programme. However, there is at least one other sector

where the government is also making strenuous efforts to

work at maximum capacity.

Agriculture:

On 12 April, a national agricultural campaign was launched

with the slogan: "Agriculture . . . a weapon in the hands of

the leader for thwarting the economic embargo." To some extent,

this continues a similar programme launched after the

imposition of sanctions in 1990 to boost local agricultural

production to help offset the effects of the embargo. The

government has again increased the purchase price for staple

crops, now paying over $ 2,500 a tonne for first grade wheat.

Farmers have been given priority in using machinery and equipment,

petrol and electricity supplies. Dams are being rebuilt and

irrigation networks restored.

0222

At the same time, the cabinet confirmed at the end of April

a Revolution Command Council decision in September 1990 that

uncultivated agricultural land would be confiscated.

Resuming economic activity is also a key factor in perhaps

the most important priority for Saddam Hussain--staying in

power. The loyalty of the Republican Guard and a number of

army   units enabled the president to crush revolts in the

north and south, and cabinet changes have served to

strengthen his control over government. There is more urgency

attached to the liberalisation programme--the new constitution

allowing for democratic elections, the introduction of a stock

exchange, and changing the law to allow private banks.

However, Saddam Hussain must not only feed his people,

he must also employ them--military conscripts and the popular
and
army are now being demobilised--he must also persuade them

that he can lead them in rebuilding the country.

0224

FUTURE PLANS

Some indication of Iraq's spending plans can be gained from

a letter sent to the UN on 3 May seeking a five-year moratorium

on reparation payments to help revitalise the economy. Over

the next five years, the letter said, the government plans

to spend about ID 66,000 million ($ 212,900 million). Reports

suggest that during this period, Iraq anticipates exporting

2 million barrels a day (b/d) of oil in 1992, rising to

3 million b/d between 1993-95. Total income is estimated by

Baghdad, during this period, at ID 20,000 million ($ 64,516

million). What is not clear, is what oil price Baghdad is

reckoning on, or whether the calculations take into account

a percentage of oil revenues removed by the UN for reparations.

0225

According to Iraq's letter, spending will break down

approximately into $ 42,600 million a year; this compares

with spending of $ 70,000 million and $ 77,000 million

budgeted for in 1989 and 1990. With Iraqi imports in the

region. of between $ 8,000 million-10,000 million annually in

recent years, and anticipating continuing demands from Baghdad

for debt rescheduling, the government clearly anticipates

heavy spending on development, perhaps in the region of

$ 18,000 million-20,000 million a year. This is in line with

investment spending planned for 1990. The letter also indicates

a deficit running at about ID 9,000 million ($ 29,000 million)

a year, considerably more than the budget deficits of

ID 6,000 million ($ 19,354 million) in 1990 and ID 7,000 million

($ 22,580 million) in 1989.

0226

The overall message is that Baghdad intends spending
heavily on development in the next five years. Much of the
money will obviously be used to rebuild key economic installations,
but allocations may be destined for major projects that were
were underway when Iraq invaded Kuwait. These include: a
second petrochemical complex (PC 2); a new refinery; expansion
of fertiliser plants; an aluminium smelter; iron and steel
factories; truck, car and other   industrial manufacturing
plants. Two new power stations were under construction, and
a new railway line and dams were planned.

0227

Logically, Baghdad should concentrate on building

up industries which can make use of local resources, which

will meet local demands, and generate hard currency from exports.

It would make sense to invest in a new refinery and expand

the fertiliser and sulphur industries. However, Saddam Hussain's

determination to press ahead with development both during the

Gulf war with Iran and the period following the August 1988

ceasefire resulted in massive financial commitments to some

very grandiose schemes when logic perhaps suggested that he

should conserve his financial resources, pay off his debts

and concentrate on building up the oil and agricultural

sectors.

0228

Had more resources been invested in the oil sector,

then Saddam Hussain might not have felt so threatened by

Kuwait boosting its oil exports in 1990. Instead, a programme

to upgrade facilities in existing oil fields and bring new

fields into production fell further and further behind schedule

particularly as Hussain Kamel, the Industry & Military

Industrialisation Minister, demanded a greater share of

foreign currency allocations for his own projects. As a result,

Iraq was still involved in negotiations with international

contracts^{ORS} in July 1990 for oil field projects that had been

tendered in 1988.

Recent cabinet changes promise little for the oil sector.

Following former oil minister Issam Abdel-Rahim al-Chalabi's

replacement by Hussain Kamel in late-1990, Amer al-Saadi, a former

senior undersecretary in the industry ministry has taken over

as acting oil minister.

0229

The new post of minister of state for oil affairs has been given to Usama Hammoudi, a former director of the industry ministry's Technical Corps for Special Projects (Techcorp).

Another loser in the battle for scarce foreign currency allocations was the agricultural sector. Here, logic suggests that the government must attach new priority to this sector, especially following the implementation of Turkey's dam and irrigation programme on the upper reaches of the river Euphrates. This promises a much reduced flow downstream for Iraqi irrigation projects, and increases the importance of dam and barrage construction plans for the river Tigris. Funds will have to be found to complete construction of the Bekme and Badush dams, and continue with design work on at least three more dam and irrigation projects.

0230

A decision will also have to be made about allocating

funds for the $ 2,500 million Jazira plain irrigation scheme

as well as other expensive land reclamation projects in the

north and south

On a smaller scale, it is essential that the government

invest in equipment and facilities--tractors, harvesters, pumps

and cold stores--technical assistance and advice needed to

exploit more fully the country's agricultural potential.

Between 1983-89, Baghdad has been forced to spend an average

$ 2,500 million a year on food imports. Only under the recent

urgings of the government has wheat production began to creep

back up towards the 2.6 million tonnes produced in 1972.

Since that year, it has been declining, reaching only 490,000

tonnes in 1989/90.

0231

The government has also signalled its intentions to

continue with its economic liberalisation programme. It will

continue to seek to engage private sector resources to boost

economic development. However, the government must also

come to terms with inflation, which was especially rampant

after the introduction of a free market system in 1988, and

introducing a stock exchange and allowing private banks may

not be the answer if the private sector refuses to buy into

unprofitable state industries, and if the government continues

to maintain a traditionally heavy hand of control over

all aspects of the economy, particularly foreign currency

allocations.

0232

ECONOMIC RECONSTRUCTION ISSUES

The government has reported early success in restoring

limited power and telephone services. The restoration of

refining capacity has enabled the government to not only

resume   petrol and kerosene supplies, but to cut the price

of petrol as well. However, it is clear that Saddam Hussain

needs the financial and technical assistance from the outside

world to revitalise his economy. There are a number of

obstacles in the way of this challenge.

0233

iraq20

1) the UN embargo

The UN Security Council's sanctions committee has authorised

the release of frozen Iraqi assets to enable Baghdad to

pay for essential imports. Deals have already been struck

with New Zealand, Australia and Thailand to buy milk powder,

wheat and rice, Baghdad says. But, the ban on importing

raw materials, spare parts and machinery and equipment, and

on exporting crude oil, still applies and will continue to

do so until the UN is satisfied that Iraq has satisfied the

terms of resolution 687. Clearly Iraq's State Company for Oil

Marketing (SOMO) is confident of this happening; it has already

telexed its former customers advising them that exports will

be resumed--probably through Turkey--in the third quarter of

1991.

0234

The main obstacle to the embargo being lifted is probably Saddam Hussain himself, although there have been some suggestions that some foreign governments might prefer to see a weakened Saddam Hussain in control, than see Iraq riven by civil war. Some countries, Turkey and Brazil for example, may be prepared to resume trade links with Baghdad on a normal basis once sanctions are lifted. Others however, like the US and possibly the UK, are likely to introduce strict export controls which could include banning trade with Iraq completely.

16. The Prospects of Political Change in Kuwait.

Dr Ahmed Al-Khateeb

I   Historical background.

- The election of Sabah I.

- Murbarak's coup against his brothers.

- The 1921 and 1938 democratic movement.

- The struggle for democracy until the declaration of the 1962 constitution by Abdullah - Alsalem Al-Sabah which was followed by the first parliament.

II   The struggle for democracy until the dissolution of the 1985 parliament.

- 1962 parliament was dissolved and replaced in 1967 by a Pro-government one.

- the election of 1975

- 1976 the parliament was dissolved.

- 1981 the election of the parliament, which was also dissolved in 1986.

III   The constitutional movement

- An election was demanded in 1986 within two months, which is a constitutional right (Article 107).

- The peak of this movement lead to a confrontation with the government which lasted from December, 1989 - May, 1990.

- The formation of the National Assembly.

IV   From the time of the invasion until the present.

The internal changes are:

- The total rejection of the invasion.

- The unity of the Kuwaities with the government.

- The failure of the government to protect the people and the country.

1

0236

- The continuation of the government's failure in exile, to deal with the crisis.

- The promise of the government in Jaddeh to go back to the 1962 constitution.

- The government's refusal to resign and form a new national government better able to deal with the new situation.

- The increased desire of the people for a new government to be formed, which would be different to the existing government.

- The people's determination for a stronger parliament and the formation of the constitutional front.

- The failure of the government to restore the basic needs.

The External Changes are:

- The G.C.C. Leadership Meeting in Doha.

- The Saudi influence in Kuwait which has been experienced through out the history of democracy in Kuwait.

- The external focus on the country, and the threat to democracy, by the Saudi and Syrian army.

- The continued objection will lead to a confrontation with the government and the external forces.

- The American and European role in this situation must be stronger.

- The need of official policy to promote democracy in Kuwait, and hence deterring the regional forces from taking any action.

- The continued absence of the western government will lead to the continued instability of Kuwait and the Gulf states.

- The restoration of democracy in Kuwait will annul the incorrect interpretation of the United Nation resolution (the restoration of the legitimate government), the Royal family.

- The legitimate government is the government which comes through and under the constitution of 1962.

2

0237

Given the current obsession in certain US quarters

with uncovering suppliers of dual-use technology to Iraq, and

the ongoing BNL banking scandal, Baghdad has hardly sought

to give the impression that its military manufacturing

ambitions are a thing of the past. Industry officials,

especially Amer al-Saadi who was responsible for the missile

development programme, were promoted in the recent cabinet

changes, and despite stating that the rebuilding of civilian

industries will take priority over weapons' manufacturing

factories, the government recently announced that four

state enterprises formerly involved in military projects

--including Nasr, Qaqa and Huteen--will be retooled. Although

these factories will now be involved in civilian industry,

their continuing existence--and the continuing existence of

the Industry & Military Industrialisation Ministry--is hardly

likely to endear Baghdad to Washington.

0238

2) Reparations

Analysts estimate that potential claims against Iraq under

paragraph 19 of resolution 687 will easily reach $ 50,000

million. The US and the UK are pressing for up to 40 per cent

of the value of annual oil exports; others advocate Baghdad

being required to pay no more than 10 per cent. Whatever is

decided, it is   apparent that Iraq will be paying reparations

for at least five years and possibly more than 10.

3) Debt

Iraq's total debts are estimated at about $ 80,000 million.

Apart from Kuwait and Saudi Arabia, its   . chief creditors

are the countries that Iraq will look to to provide the

equipment and technology it needs to develop--Japan, the US,

Frande, Italy, Germany and the UK. Previously, Baghdad has

followed a policy of linking debt rescheduling with the

provision of. fresh credits. To date there has been no

indication of how Baghdad will tackle its debt problem, and

nor it seems, has there been any coordinated response to

the problem from Baghdad's creditors. This despite the fact

that some observers considered the time was right to force

Iraq to accept multi-lateral rescheduling rather than the

bilateral approach followed so far.

0240

4) Financing

With Baghdad's revenues under pressure to meet reparation

payments, debt repayments and urgent import payments, there

will be little left to fund major development work. Iraq will

once again have to seek credits from its main creditors. In its

favour is the interest that companies all over the world are

expressing in Iraqi reconstruction. The Times on Tuesday

reported the arrival of foreign businessmen in Baghdad. "The

war   occurred and an instant market opened," the paper

quoted one businessman as saying. Eventually commercial pressure

may force reluctant governments to once again extend financing

to a regime facing a long struggle to get to its feet   again.

정 리 보 존 문 서 목 록

기록물종류	일반공문서철	등록번호	2021010223	등록일자	2021-01-28
분류번호	721.1	국가코드	XF	보존기간	영구
명 칭	걸프사태 : 자료 및 언론보도, 1990-91. 전3권				
생 산 과	북미1과/중동1과	생산년도	1990~1991	담당그룹	
권 차 명	V.3 해외주요언론보도 분석, 1991				
내용목차					

0001

걸프 事態 關聯 世界 主要 言論 報道 分析

1991, 1, 19,

美　　洲　　局

0002

1. 사 설

※ 참 고 :

NYT (New York Times)   WP (Washington Post)

WSJ (Wall Street Journal) CSM (Christian Science Monitor)

언론매체명	주 요 내 용
NYT	o 부쉬 대통령의 대 이라크 개전은 정당한 것으로서 아래 목표 하에 실행 되었음. - 쿠웨이트 해방 - 걸프 지역에서의 안정 확보 - 후세인 대통령에 의한 세계 에너지 공급 지역 장악 가능성 방지 - 냉전이후 집단 안보 체제 유지를 위한 확고한 선례 구축 o 상기 목표 달성 여부는 전쟁의 수행 방법에 달림 - 지나치게 과도한 무력 사용 자제 - 중동 지역에서의 미국의 장기적 이해 관계를 감안, 신중한 목표 설정과 계산된 공격 (careful targeting and measured strikes)이 요구됨
WP	o 부쉬 대통령의 전쟁 결단 지지 - 평화적 해결위한 모든 노력을 경주하였으나 전쟁외에는 대안이 없었음. o 후세인 이라크 대통령은 질서있는 세계에 있어서의 미국의 이해 관계에 심각한 위협 초래 - 주권 국가 침략 - 세계 세력 균형에 중요한 중동 지역 지배 시도

0003

2. 분석 기사

언론매체명	주　　요　　내　　용
NYT, WSJ	o 전쟁 발발에 따른 심리적 영향으로 일시적인 유가 상승 추세이나, 비축량 충분으로 큰 변동 없을 것임. (현재 운송중인 원유 포합하여 OPEC의 170일분 생산량에 해당되는 40억 배럴 비축) 　　- 전쟁 발발로 $3-4 상승 　　- 최초 수주간은 $35-$40까지 상승 (사우디 유전에 큰 피해 발생시는 $50까지), 이후에는 점차 하락 예상 o 부쉬대통령, 세계 원유가 안정을 위해 미국의 전략 예비 유전 개발 지시 　　- 30일동안 일 112.5만 배럴 생산
NYT	o 석유가는 전쟁후에도 $30 수준이상으로 유지될 것임. o 걸프 사태로 미국 경기 침체 유발, 전후에는 3/4분기 부터 경기 회복 전망

0004

[1.18(금)]

1. 사 설

언론매체명	주 요 내 용
CSM	○ 다국적군의 공격을 지지하며, 유엔 결의 실행과 이라크를 쿠웨이트로 부터 격퇴 시키려는 목표는 정당 ○ 전후 중동에서 정치, 안보 구조의 조정 노력 배가와 이를 위한 모든 가능성 검토 필요 ○ 미국은 이라크-팔레스타인 문제의 상호 연계를 거부해 왔지만, 이 문제는 사실상 존재하고 있으며, 계속 현안이 될 것임 - 이스라엘의 최대 라이벌인 이라크의 패배는 이스라엘의 안보에 대한 우려를 감소시키고, 팔레스타인 문제 해결을 위한 협상 여건을 성숙시킬 것이나, 미국의 주도적 역할이 요구됨
WSJ	○ 이라크의 패배는 중동에서의 안보 불안 감소, 안정된 유가, 전세계적으로 잠재적 침략 행위 억제 효과를 가져올 것으로 전망 ○ 그러나, 가장 중요한 소득은 미국인의 자신감, 자부심 회복일 것임. - 개전초 다국적군의 성공은 부쉬대통령의 정치적 리더쉽에 대한 국민 신뢰를 회복시킴 ○ 또한 금번 전쟁에서 나타난 자신감, 결단력, 지도력이 과거의 퇴보적 분위기를 일신하여, 미국이 국내문제에 적절히 대처해 나갈수 있도록 새로운 분위기를 조성하는 계기가 되기를 바람.

0005

2. 분석기사

언론매체명	주 요 내 용
WSJ	o 이라크 패전과 후세인 제거시 전후 정세 전망 - 아랍 민족주의 강화와 회교 근본주의(Islamic Fundamentalism) 득세로 중동 각국의 국내 정세 불안 조성 - 이라크내 집권 수니파와 시아파간 갈등 심화로 정치적 혼란 가중 - 쿠르드족 자치 독립운동 확산시 터어키, 이란, 시리아등 인접국의 개입 및 충돌 가능성 - PLO의 세력 약화와 시리아의 역내 주도권 장악 시도 가시화
NYT	o 미군의 성공적인 공습에도 불구, Cheney 국방장관의 발언대로 전쟁이 그렇게 쉽게 끝날것 같지 않으며 상당기간(for a significant period) 지속 예상 o 다국적군은 쿠웨이트로 부터 이라크군 격퇴와 향후 역내 안정 확보라는 군사 목적을 달성하는 범위내에서 전쟁을 제한함이 필요
WP	o 걸프 전쟁 발발 이후 미국에서의 신 에너지 전략 필요 - 국내 생산량 증가, 대체 연료 개발, 석유가 인상 및 에너지 사용 억제 등
NYT	o 부쉬 대통령의 대 이라크 공격 개시 결단은 베이커-아지즈간 제네바 회담이 결정적 계기가 된 것으로 알려짐. - 동 회의 전까지, 전쟁 불가피론이 주류를 이루었음에도 불구, 일부는 마지막 순간, 이라크의 태도 변경 기대 - 6시간 27분의 회담에도 불구, 이라크측은 한치의 양보 의사를 보이지 않음. - 아지즈 이라크 외무장관의 부쉬 대통령 친서 접수 거절

0006

3. 논 평

언론매체명	주 요 내 용

WP
(David S.
Broder)
	o 후세인 이라크 대통령의 거취 문제 관심 - 유엔 결의는 동 문제를 언급한 바 없고, 또한 동 대통령 제거를 위해서는 많은 희생이 따를 것임.
	
	o 금번 전쟁의 결과가 "새로운 세계질서"에 끼칠 영향 불명확
	
	o 하기 3가지 문제에 대한 부쉬 행정부의 대처 방법에 따라 금번 전쟁에 대한 평가 결정
	
	  - 전후 중동에서 안정된 세력 균형과 이스라엘 안보-팔레스타인 권리의 상호 조화
	
	  - 전후 "신세계 질서" 형성시 금번 전쟁에 소극적인 경제대국 독일.일본의 향후 역할, 언제까지 미국이 세계 경찰국으로서의 역할을 계속할 것인지 여부, 언제까지 소련 내부의 탄압 행위를 방관할 것인지에 대한 결정
	
	  - 미국내 우선 과제인 기아와 무주택 문제에 관심을 신속히 돌려야 함.

4. 기고문 (Steinbruner 브루킹스 연구소 대외정책 연구실장)

언론매체명	주 요 내 용

NYT	o 미국 군사 행동의 목적은 이라크 군이 최소한의 병력을 유지한 채 항복하도록 유도하는 것임.
	
	   - 완벽한 승리를 위한 과도한 군사 행동 자제와 강화 조건에 관대할 필요성 강조
	
	o 보급선이 차단된 쿠웨이트내 이라크군의 투항 유도 필요
	
	o 전쟁 종결후, 동 지역내 미군 주둔은 국제 안보 협정 체제로 전환되어야 함.
	
	   - 유엔 후원하 수개국 군대로 구성되는 연합군 주둔
	
	   - 이라크의 쿠웨이트 재 침공 가능성 방지

0008

1991. 1. 21.

外　　　務　　　部

美　　　洲　　　局

0009

[1.20(일)]

1. 해설기사

※ 참 고 :

NYT (New York Times)   WP (Washington Post)
WSJ (Wall Street Journal) CSM (Christian Science Monitor)
LAT (Los Angeles Times)

언론매체명	주　　　요　　　내　　　용
WP (Don Oberdorfer)	**걸프 전쟁은 국제 정치 질서 변동을 반영** ㅇ 정치적 측면 - 아랍 세계의 주도권을 장악하려는 이라크 대 이를 저지 하려는 여타 아랍제국과 중동에서의 절대적 영향력을 유지 하려는 미국등 서구 연합군의 일대 결전 - 냉전 체제의 붕괴로, 중동지역에서 미국의 헤게모니에 대항 하는 소련 세력이 없어진 상태에서 다국적군 연합이 가능 ㅇ 전략적 측면 - 걸프 전쟁에서의 첨단 미사일 체계의 등장은, 고대 페르시아 전쟁에서 알렉산더 대왕의 투석기 사용과 같은 획기적인 군사 전략의 변화를 의미 ㅇ 정보적 측면 - 위성 통신 체계의 발달로 CNN에 의한 전세계 동시 다발적, 지속적 중계방송 가능 - 미국의 시각과 주장이 강조됨으로써 향후 정보 체계 장악의 정치적, 전략적 중요성 일깨움

- 1 -

0010

언론매체명	주　　　요　　　내　　　용

	o 경제적 측면
	
	   - 금번 전쟁을 통해 이윤 동기에 의해 움직이는 석유, 무기
	     시장의 본질이 드러남.
	
	   - 전쟁의 진행에 따라 미국 및 세계 경제에 많은 어려움이
	     예상되는 바, 동 경제문제 해결이 향후 미국의 군사적
	     우위 유지를 위한 기초가 될 것임.
	
	         Bush Book ...

2. 기고문 (Jeane Kirkpatrick 전 유엔 미국 대사)

언론매체명	주　　　요　　　내　　　용

LAT
(Syndicate)
	o 금번 걸프전쟁은 아래와 같은 후세인 대통령의 상황에 대한
	오판에서 비롯됨.
	
	   - 전쟁의 목표를 단순한 쿠웨이트 점령이 아닌 팔레스타인
	     해방으로 미화시킴으로써 아랍제국의 지지를 얻을 수
	     있다고 생각
	
	   - 금번 전쟁으로 이스라엘 점령 지역에서 자행되는 모든
	     부정을 제거하고, 가난과 외세 지배를 종식시킬 수 있을
	     것으로 생각
	
	   - 미국이 주장하는 쿠웨이트 해방이란 명분에 불과하며,
	     진정한 목표는 걸프지역과 동 지역의 석유 자원에 대한
	     패권을 확립함으로써, 전 세계를 지배키 위한 것이라고
	     생각
	
	   - 이라크인들은 금번 전쟁이 서방측의 걸프지역에 대한
	     석유자원 지배 의도에 대항하여 부정, 가난과 외세 지배
	     종식 욕구의 싸움이라고 주장하고, 따라서 결코 국지전
	     (a local or regional war)으로 끝나지 않을 것으로 기대한
	     점.
	
	     · 인도네시아에서 서 아프리카에 이르기까지 10억의
	       회교인들이 식민주의에 대항하여 투쟁할 것으로 생각

- 2 -

0011

3. 분석기사

　　가.　미국의 군사 전략 (WP. 1. 20자)

　　　　o　국제적, 국내적 지지를 기반으로 조기에 전쟁을 종결 함으로써,
　　　　　　전쟁 장기화로 말미암은 확전 위험 가능성 방지에 주력

　　　　o　공군력 우위를 최대한 활용, 이라크를 가능한한 약화 시킨후
　　　　　　지상전에 돌입함으로써 인명 피해를 가급적 줄이려는 계산

　　　　o　미국의 목표는, 후세인 대통령이 제거된 이후의 중동 질서 재편에
　　　　　　있으므로 이라크에 대한 직접 공격은 당분간 계속될 것으로 예측

　　나.　미국의 전후 중동 질서 구상 (WP. 1. 20자)

　　　　o　이라크의 전체주의 체제 와해

　　　　o　이라크의 후세인 대통령이 제거된 후, 쿠웨이트와 이라크에
　　　　　　다국적군이 잠정 주둔, 동국의 복구 계획에 주도적 역할을
　　　　　　하게될 것으로 예상

　　　　o　미국은 전후 중동 질서 형성에 주도적 역할을 기피하고
　　　　　　있으며, 사우디 아라비아가 미국을 대신하여 어느정도 주도적
　　　　　　역할을 할 것으로 예상

- 3 -

0012

4. 주요 사실 보도 내용

가. 이라크에 대한 3가지 평화안 제의 (WP. 1. 28자)

　　o 유엔 안보리 의장(자이르)은, 걸프 전쟁 발발이후 평화를 위한
　　　첫번째 외교 노력의 일환으로, 소련, 인도, 알제리가 제안한
　　　평화안의 내용을 유엔 주재 이라크 대사에게 전달

　　　- 인도 제의　：　쿠웨이트로 부터의 이라크군 철수를 요청
　　　　　　　　　　　하고 이라크에 대한 무력 사용을 허가한
　　　　　　　　　　　유엔 결의의 이행 방법에 관한 인식의
　　　　　　　　　　　전환(new thinking) 가능성을 타진

　　　- 알제리 제의　：　쌍방간 정전 촉구

　　　- 소련측 제의　：　유엔 안보리 결의를 이행하도록 후세인
　　　　　　　　　　　대통령을 설득, 이라크 군대를 쿠웨이트로
　　　　　　　　　　　부터 철수 촉구

　　o 주 유엔 이라크 대사는 본국과의 통신 두절로 상기 3가지
　　　제의를 직접 전달하기 어렵다고 밝힘.

　　o 유엔주재 외교 소식통은 상기 평화안 제의가 전쟁을 중지
　　　시킬수는 없으나 향후 협상의 기반을 조성하는데 기여할 것
　　　으로 평가

　　　- 미국을 포함한 다국적군 구성 국가와 이라크는 현재로서는
　　　　외교적 해결 방안을 선호하고 있지 않은 것으로 예측

- 4 -

나. 이라크, 이스라엘에 대한 공격으로 요르단에서 신뢰 회복(NYT. 1. 28자)

ㅇ 개전초 미국의 성공적 공격에 분노하고, 이라크에 배신감을
느꼈던 요르단인들은, 이스라엘에 대한 이라크의 공격이 개시
되자 환호

ㅇ 요르단의 후세인 국왕은 팔레스타인과 이라크의 감정을 자극
하지 않기 위해 서방의 대이라크 공격을 '아랍-이슬람 국가와
국민에 대한 잔인한 공격'으로 비난 하였으나, 이라크의 대
이스라엘 미사일 공격에는 언급 회피 : 요르단에게는 이라크
지지외에는 대안이 없음을 나타내는 것

ㅇ 요르단은 이스라엘을 공격하지 않음으로써 이라크를 자극
시키느냐 또는 공격합으로써 이스라엘을 자극하느냐는 선택의
기로에 있음

- 5 -

걸프 事態 關聯 世界 主要 言論 報道 分析

1991, 1, 22,

外 務 部

(美 洲 局)

0015

1. 기고문

※ 참 고 :

NYT (New York Times)   WP (Washington Post)

가. Rowland Evans와 Robert Novak (WP. 1. 21자)

　o 전후 미국의 신 중동 정책 수립 시급

　　- 미 행정부는 그간 전쟁 수행 전략 수립에만 몰두하고,
　　　전후 중동의 신질서 수립을 위한 정책 대안 준비에는
　　　소홀

　　- 최근에야 부쉬 대통령은, 국가안전보장회의(NSC)의
　　　Robert Gates 부보좌관에게 전후 전략 수립을 지시

　　- 중동에서 반미 감정의 확산 방지가 가장 난제가 될
　　　것임.

　　　· 후세인 대통령의 패퇴후, 미국이 중동에서 철수
　　　　하기를 원하는 반미 민족주의자 및 이슬람 근본
　　　　주의자(Moslem fundamentalists)들의 득세 예상

　　　· 아랍인들의 반미 감정 비등에 효과적으로 대응치
　　　　못할 경우, 미국이 금번 전쟁으로 얻은 이익을
　　　　모두 잃게 될 것임.

　o 전후 중동에서의 국제 정치질서 변화 예상

　　- 이집트와 사우디 아라비아 : 이라크 패배후 영향력
　　　　　　　　　　　　　　　　　　　증대 예상

　　- 이 란 ; 걸프지역의 강자로 영향력 계속 유지

- 1 -

0016

- 시리아 : · 전통적으로 소원했던 미국과의 관계가
금번 전쟁을 계기로 급속히 호전되고
있으나 터키와는 분쟁 가능성 존재
· 시리아는, 터키가 전후 이라크, 터키
및 이란내에 거주하는 쿠르드족을 선동
할 것이며, 이는 시리아의 안보에 큰
위협이 될 것으로 생각

- 미국은, 전후의 정치적 현실이 허용하는 한, 이스라엘이
팔레스타인 문제를 해결하도록 영향력을 행사할 것임.

나. James Reston (NYT. 1.21자)

o 이라크의 통신시설이 더욱 파괴되고 이라크 군대의 보급로가
완전 차단될때 까지 지상전 개시가 연기되어야 함.

- 중동에서 후세인 대통령의 영향력을 감소시키는 가장
좋은 방법은 지상전에 의해 이라크군을 궤멸시키는 것이
아니라 항복으로 유도하는 것임.

- 현 수준의 공습을 계속함으로써, 미국은 이라크의 통신
체계를 대부분 파괴하고 후세인 대통령의 지휘 체계를
마비 시킬수 있을 것임.

- 성급한 지상전으로 다국적군에 많은 인명 피해가 발생할
경우, 부쉬 대통령의 정치적 입지와 그가 구상하는 전후
신 세계 질서 형성에 큰 부담이 될 것임.

- 이라크를 완전 무력화 하여, 이란과 시리아가 중동의
강국으로 부상하는 것은 미국의 이해에 부합되지 아니함.

- 2 -

0017

2. 해설기사 (이태리 La Republica, 1. 21자)

   o 이스라엘은 대 이라크 보복 공격을 자제함으로써 걸프
     전쟁의 확전을 방지

      - 금번 자제로 이스라엘은 역사상 처음으로 자위권을 포기

      - 이스라엘은 금번 대 이라크 보복 자제로, 미국이 전후
        팔레스타인 평화회담 개최에 계속 반대해 줄 것으로
        기대

   o 미국은 걸프 전쟁에 대한 지지를 조건으로, 관련국에
     다음의 내용을 사실상 보장

      - 이집트의 모든 외채 탕감과 새로운 차관 제공

      - 소련이 발트해 3국 분리 독립 문제를 무력으로 해결
        하는 것을 허용

      - 1989. 6월 중국의 천안문 사태에 대한 묵인

- 끝 -

- 3 -

0018

걸프 事態 關聯 世界 主要 言論 報道 分析

1991. 1. 23.

外 務 部

(美 洲 局)

0019

1. 기 고 문

```
┌─── 참    고 ──────────────────────────────────┐
│                                               │
│  NYT (New York Times)        WP  (Washington Post) │
│                                               │
│  CSM (Christian Science Monitor)              │
│                                               │
└───────────────────────────────────────────────┘
```

가. <u>Flora Lewis</u> (NYT, 1.22자)

<u>후세인 대통령의 제거가 중동의 장기적 평화를 위한 최선의 방책</u>

o 다국적군의 전쟁 목표 변화

  - 대외적으로 표명한 공격목표는 쿠웨이트의 해방 이었으나
     실제 목표는 이라크의 군사능력을 철저히 파괴함으로써
     이라크를 충분히 무력화 시키는 것임.

  - Cheney 미 국방장관도 이러한 미국 정부의 결의를 명백히 함.

  - Hurd 영국 외무장관은, 쿠웨이트가 해방이 되더라도 쿠웨이트에
     대한 이라크의 위협이 잔존할 경우 이라크내에서의 지상전
     수행 가능성도 시사

o 다국적군의 입장 표명 자제에도 불구, 금번 전쟁의 진정한 목표는
   후세인 대통령의 축출임

  - 중동 지역에서의 장기적인 세력 균형을 이루는데 필수조건

  - 세계에서 가장 잔혹한 후세인 독재정권 축출로 이라크가 민주
     국가로 발전할 수 있는 기회 부여

- 1 -

0020

o 상기 목표에 대해 사우디등 아랍제국은 시각 차이 노정

  - 그동안 대부분의 아랍 제국은 후세인 정권 지지

    · 다양한 종교적 분파로 구성된 이라크가, 역내 불안 요소가
       되는 것을 막고, 시아파가 인구의 약 52%를 차지하는
       이라크에 이란이 영향력을 행사하는 것을 방지하기 위한
       최선의 방법으로 강력한 후세인 정권 지지

  - 아랍의 왕조국들은, 이라크내 민주 정부 수립을 불원

  - 터키는, 쿠르드족의 독립운동이 자국내로 확산될 것을 우려
     하여, 동 쿠르드족의 독립운동을 억제할 수 있는 강력한
     이라크 정부의 등장 선호

나. <u>Andrew Rosenthal</u> (NYT, 1. 22자)

<u>미국의 정치적, 군사적 목표 : regional power로서의 이라크 무력화</u>

o 미국의 금번 걸프전쟁의 목표는 유엔 결의 내용보다 훨씬 광범위

  - 유엔은, 쿠웨이트로 부터 이라크 군의 철수만을 요구

  - 미국은, 역내 안전 보장을 위한 항구적 대책 마련 노력

o 부쉬 행정부는, 쿠웨이트로 부터 이라크군 격퇴 이외에도, 이라크가
   향후 중동 지역 강국 역할을 포기 하도록 이라크 군사력을 충분히
   파괴하려는 전략 구사

- 2 -

0021

- 개전초 부터, 이라크 원자력 발전소 및 화학무기 생산 공장은
  다국적군 공습의 일차적 목표

- Cheney 미 국방장관은, 이라크 군대가 향후 타국에 대한 공격적
  도발을 행할 수 없도록 철저히 무력화 시킬 것임을 공언

다. <u>Turgut Ozal 터어키 대통령</u> (WP. 1. 22자)

o 세계는 이라크의 쿠웨이트 접령을 신 세계 평화 질서에 대한
  심각한 도전으로 간주, UN의 이름으로 이라크를 응징하게 됨

o 터어키는 쿠웨이트의 주권회복과 이라크의 철군을 요구하고,
  유엔의 대 이라크 경제 제재에 적극 참여하였음.

  - 미국을 비롯한 많은 국가의 평화적, 외교적 해결 노력에
    대한 이라크의 거부 자세로 평화 회복을 위한 전쟁이
    불가피

o 터어키는 다국적군의 군사행동 지지

  - 터어키 의회는 외국군 주둔 및 터어키군 해외 파견 승인

o 터어키는 이라크에 선제공격을 않을 것이며, 전후 중동지역
  안정에 대한 국제사회의 관심을 촉구함.

  - 전후 아랍, 이스라엘 분쟁의 근본적인 해결 노력이 요구됨

o 중동 제국간의 경제적 상호 의존 관계 증대가 향후 중동 평화
  정착의 관건임.

- 3 -

0022

- 터어키는 아랍제국에 수자원 공급에 관한 회의를 제의한
바 있음.

- 석유자금을 활용한 경제 협력 증대는 역내 제국간 우호증진과
주민 복지문제 해결에 기여할 것임.

- 또한, 중동 각국의 정치적 민주화 필요

라. Jim Hoagland (WP, 1.22자)

중동문제에 대한 미국의 접근

o 걸프 전쟁의 의미 : 미국이 사상 초유로 중동문제에 직접 개입
하는 계기

- 제반 평화 제의를 거부하고 주변국을 무력 제압하려는 후세인의
기도에 대한 미국 및 연합국의 군사적 대응은 불가피한 것으로
평가

o 후세인의 전략 : 이스라엘을 개입시켜 확전 유도

- 부쉬 대통령의 조기 개전 및 이라크 화생방 전력 조기 제압
결정은 적절했음.

o 걸프 전쟁의 이익 : 지역 안정 유지를 위한 미국의 개입은 역내
국들에 신뢰감 조성. 이를 바탕으로 전후
평화 구도 설정시 부쉬 행정부의 적극적
역할 기대

- 4 -

0023

- 미국이 직접 개입함으로써, 이스라엘과 아랍 민족주의와의 직접
  충돌이 가져올지도 모르는 더 심각한 위험이 미리 제거됨

- 이스라엘도, 아랍제국과의 직접 대결을 피하고 후세인 제거후
  미국이 주도할 중동평화 노력에 참여하는 방향으로 정책 선회

2. 사 설 (오스트리아 DIE PRESSE, 1.21자)

이스라엘의 대 이라크 보복

o 이성이 지배하는 한, 이라크의 대 이스라엘 미사일 공격에 의한
  다국적군의 분열 가능성은 희박

- 이집트와 시리아는, 쿠웨이트 해방전쟁을 이슬람 세계의 성전
  (holy war)으로 전환시키려는 후세인 대통령의 술책을 충분히
  인식

o 이스라엘은 대 이라크 반격을 자제하여야 함

- 이스라엘이 참전할 경우, 전후 건설적인 중동 질서 재편 가능성
  전무

- 이스라엘이 반격하는 경우에도 다국적군에서 이탈하지 않겠다는
  시리아와 이집트 정부의 성명에도 불구, 동국의 회교 근본주의자
  들의 정치적 입지 강화

- 국민 여론이 반유태 전선을 형성할 경우, 무바라크 이집트 대통령과
  아사드 시리아 대통령에게는 선택의 폭이 극히 제한될 것임.

- 5 -

0024

3. 해설기사

    가. CSM (1. 22자)

걸프전쟁 관련 유엔의 역할

o 걸프 전쟁시, 유엔은 대 이라크 결의 채택으로 분쟁의 중재자로서의
   중립적 역할 상실

   - 유엔은 전쟁의 승인자와 중재자로서의 기능을 동시에 수행할 수
      없음.

o 그러나, 향후 동 전쟁의 막바지 해결에 유엔의 적극적 역할 기대

   - 정전과 군대 철수 감시를 위한 평화 유지군 파견

   - 쿠웨이트에서의 전후 복구 사업 참여

   - 향후 중동 지역에서의 군비통제 움직임 주도등

o 또한, 미국과 이라크의 정전 조건 절충등 유엔 사무총장의 적극적인
   외교적 역할 기대

   - 이라크의 후세인 대통령은 80년대 이란-이라크전의 정전협상 관련,
      유엔 안보리를 적극 활용한 전력

- 6 -

0025

나. WP (1.22자)

시리아, 이집트의 다국적군 잔류

o 시리아, 이집트는 이스라엘이 대 이라크 보복 공격시에도 다국적
  군 잔류의사를 표명

  - 국내의 반 이스라엘 여론에도 불구하고 이라크 편에서 미국에
    대항했을 때의 손실을 감안한 불가피한 선택

o 시리아는 다국적군에 대한 협조의 댓가로 쿠웨이트에 적용한 UN
  원칙을 팔레스타인에도 동일하게 적용할 것을 요구

o 이스라엘은 대 이라크 보복 공격을 자제함으로써, 팔레스타인
  문제와 아랍.이스라엘간 분쟁 해결을 위한 국제적 논의에서
  발언권 강화를 위한 포석

4. 분석기사 (NYT, 1.22자)

걸프전쟁 관련 뉴욕타임스-CBS News 공동여론 조사 결과 분석

o 부쉬 대통령에 대한 지지율의 기록적 수준 유지

  - 1.17. 여론 조사시 지지율은 86%, 1.20. 조사시 84%선으로 유지
    (진주만 공격후, 루즈벨트 대통령에 대한 지지에 상응하는 비율)

- 7 -

0026

o 전쟁 조기 종결 여부에 대한 낙관적 견해는 다소 감소

- 1.17. 여론 조사시 40%가 수주내 종결 예상, 1.20. 조사시에는 20%로 감소

o 전쟁이 장기화 될 경우, 부쉬 대통령에 대한 상기 지지율의 계속 유지 여부 불명확

5. 사실보도 (이태리 La Republica, 1.22자)

<u>이태리회사, 모형무기 생산 판매</u>

o 이태리 토리노 소재 MVM 회사는 지난 8년간 플라스틱 모형 탱크 항공기 및 미사일 발사대를 제작, 전세계에 판매 (단, 동 회사는 모형 스쿠드 미사일 발사대는 제작치 않았다고 밝힘)

- 판매제품
  · 탱크 : 미제 M60, M107, 영국제 Chieftain, 소련제 T55
  · 항공기 : Panthom, F-15, F-16 등

- 가 격
  · 탱크 1대 : 2.5만불
  · 항공기, 미사일 발사대 : 3만불

o 동 모형 무기는 실형과 같아 위성이나 정찰기도 식별 불가능

o 이라크 군의 동 모형무기 보유여부는 불확실하나, 이라크측은 동 제품에 대한 관심을 수차 표명

o MVM 회사는 고객 명단을 밝히기를 거부   - 끝 -

- 8 -

0027

걸프 事態 關聯 世界 主要 言論 報道 分析

1991. 1. 24.

外 務 部

(美 洲 局)

0028

1. 기 고 문

```
┌── 참  고 ────────────────────────────────┐
│  NYT (New York Times)        WP (Washington Post)  │
└────────────────────────────────────────┘
```

가. <u>Leslie H. Gelb (NYT, 1.23자)</u>

중동 평화 구도

o 부쉬 행정부가 모색중인 전후 평화구상은 중동 평화 회의가
   아니며, PLO(아라파트)에 대한 정치적 타격을 주는데 있음

   - 역내 경제협력과 군축을 통해 이스라엘과 시리아간의
     협상을 유도함으로써 중동평화회의를 대체

   - 이스라엘이 강경입장을 완화하여 접령지역(요르단강 서안과
     가자지구) 팔레스타인들과 직접 대화를 하도록 함으로써
     이들을 PLO 수뇌부와 분리

   - 영국, 불란서 및 아랍제국의 중동평화회의 개최 요구에 대해
     미국은 회의 개최를 가능한 지연시키도록 설득 예상

o PLO는 걸프전쟁에서 이라크측을 지지함으로써 전후 팔레스타인
   문제 해결을 위한 국제적 논의에 참여를 보장받기 어렵게 됨

o 팔레스타인 문제 해결에 시리아와 이스라엘의 태도변화가
   필수적

- 1 -

0029

- 소련의 후원을 상실한 시리아는 경제 재건을 위해 사우디에
  의존해야 하므로 사우디는 시리아에 이스라엘과의 관계개선을
  종용할 수 있음

- 시리아는 중동전쟁에서 빼앗긴 골란 고원의 회복을 위해서
  이스라엘과 협상 필요

- 이스라엘도 팔레스타인 자치 문제에 유연한 자세를 취하는
  것이 아랍 제국과의 평화협상에 도움이 됨을 인식

o 아랍.이스라엘의 오랜 적대관계에도 불구하고, 미국은 걸프전쟁을
  계기로 기존 중동 질서의 재편을 위해 대담한 구상을 모색중임

나. Charles Krauthammer (WP, 1.23자)

걸프전쟁의 목적

o 포로 학대와 생화학무기 사용은 전쟁 법죄에 속하며 전범자들은
  종전후 처형될 것임을 이라크에 명백히 전달해야 함

- 전쟁은 쿠웨이트 해방이라는 목적으로 시작 되었으나,
  지금은 전범 처벌이라는 다른 목적도 대두됨

o 다국적군의 기본 목표는 쿠웨이트 해방을 위해 이라크를 괴멸
  시키는 것이 아니라 약화시키는 것임

- 쿠데타, 후세인 암살등으로 휴전이나 쿠웨이트로 부터의
  이라크 철수 가능성이 있지만, 목표는 철군만이 아닌
  이라크의 무조건 항복을 받아내는데 있음

- 2 -

0030

o 전후 이라크에 대한 군정통치 보다 다음 조치 필요

　- 이라크의 모든 군사시설에 대한 현장 감시

　- 이라크의 모든 생화학 무기 및 핵무기 생산능력 제거

　- 이라크 군사력 감축 (주변국 수준 또는 이하)

o 주변국으로부터 이라크 보호를 위한 미군의 이라크 점령 필요

다. Tom Wicker (NYT, 1.23자)

TV에 비친 걸프전쟁

o 방송매체와 첨단 무기의 위력으로 개전 초기 승전 분위기가
조성 됐으나, 이라크 TV에 방영된 포로들의 모습이 준 충격은
새로운 변수로 등장

　- 지상전 개시로 사상자가 속출하게 되면 여론의 향방이
　　달라질 수 있음.

　- 국방부는 개전 초기의 압도적 승리 주장에서 다소 후퇴

o 방송 보도의 낙관적 분위기에도 불구, 향후 고려되어야 할 문제

　- 후세인이 이스라엘을 공격하여 아랍세계의 대변자 역할을
　　함으로써 전쟁 목적이 흐려질 가능성

　- 중동 석유에 가장 많이 의존하고 있는 일본, 독일의 걸프
　　전쟁에서 수동적 태도

　- 걸프 전쟁에 투입되는 막대한 예산에 대한 여론의 동향

- 3 -

0031

- 당초 미군 파병 목적은 이라크로 부터의 사우디 방어였으나
  상황이 이라크의 무조건 항복을 요구하는 전쟁으로 변했다는
  점

2. 사설

가. NYT (1.23자)

<u>공습의 성과</u>

o 미국민은 정부의 전황 설명에 대해 회의를 품기 시작

o 개전 초기 이라크 상공에서 제공권 완전 장악과 스커드 미사일
  대부분 파괴 발표는 오판으로 판명

o 국방부는 전쟁 초기 단계부터 지나친 보안으로 미국민을 실망
  시키고 있음. 회의와 불신은 정보 부재 속에서 커가는 것임

나. WP (1.23자)

<u>전자오락게임</u>

o 전쟁은 전자 오락게임과는 달리 양측의 실제 희생없이 수행될수
  없음.

o 전쟁을 쉽고, 안전하게 수행하고 있다고 알림으로써 지지자들을
  더욱 고무시킬 수 있다는 사고는 잘못

- 4 -

0032

- 텔 아비브 참상과 B-52 폭격이 어느정도의 이라크측 사상자를
  초래하느냐와 같은 전쟁의 현실을 최대한 알려야 함.

3. 해설기사 (WP, 1.23자)

<u>고르바쵸프, 걸프 전쟁의 확전 방지 호소</u>

o 후세인 대통령을 무책임하다고 비난하고, 걸프사태를 정치적
  방법으로 해결할 것을 촉구

  - 소련 군부는 미국이 현재 악천후를 이유로 전투기 출격을
    자제하면서 전술 변화를 모색중이라고 관측

  - 소련 최고회의는 전쟁 종결과 평화회복 촉구 결의 채택

- 끝 -

걸프 事態 關聯 世界 主要 言論 報道 分析

1991. 1. 25.

外　　務　　部

(美　洲　局)

0034

1. 기 고 문

가. <u>Paul Kennedy (WSJ, 1.24자)</u>

<u>쇠락하는 제국의 전쟁</u>

o 1.18자 WSJ 사설은, 걸프전쟁의 성공적 수행으로 미국이 쇠락
   하는 강대국이 아님을 증명했고, 미국민의 자존심과 자신감을
   회복 시켰다고 주장

o 역사적으로 강대국이 제국주의적 팽창 정책을 추구하는 과정에서
   자신의 능력 이상으로 세계 도처에 군사력을 유지함으로써 쇠락의
   길로 접어들게 됨

   - 미국도 세계 도처에서 도전을 받고 있으며 걸프전쟁도 그 한
      예임

o 미국이 강대국으로 남기 위해서는 군사력 유지의 기본이 되는
   경제. 사회적 국내 기반을 강화해야 함

   - 걸프전쟁을 계기로 미국은 군사적 승리를 통한 자존심
      고취보다 내실있는 국력 배양을 우선적 목표로 삼아야
      할 것임

- 1 -

0035

나. Joshua Muravchik (NYT, 1.24자)

걸프전쟁의 영향

(미국내)

o 베트남 전쟁이후, 이념적으로 평화주의자들에 의해 지배되어온
민주당에 심각한 영향 예상

- 미국 유권자의 대다수가, 금번 걸프전쟁이 정당하고 성공적
이었던 것으로 평가한다면, 동 전쟁에 반대해 온 민주당은
비싼 대가를 치루게 될 것임

o 그러나, 민주당내에서도 금번 걸프전쟁과 관련하여 부쉬대통령을
지지한 의원들의 정치적 입지 강화 예상

- 상원 : Joseph Lieberman, Albert Gore등

- 하원 : Stephen Solarz, Les Aspin, Dave McCurdy, Dante
Fascell등

(아랍세계)

o 후세인의 패배로 아랍 과격주의자 대신, 현실주의자 및 온건론자
들의 득세 예상

- 과거 아랍정치의 문제는, 현실 무시에서 비롯
· 이스라엘과 서구제국의 존재 무시
· 범아랍주의, 종교적 광신주의 및 이념적 급진주의가 지배

o 금번 걸프전쟁은 아랍인들이 범아랍주의의 허상 인식의 계기

- 2 -

0036

(Pax Americana의 성립)

o 금번 전쟁의 승리로, 진정한 의미에서의 Pax Americana 성립

- Pax Americana라는 용어는 제2차 세계대전 직후 사용

- 그러나, 당시에는 소련이라는 초강대국의 존재로 인해 진정한 의미의 Pax는 부존재, 냉전의 도래 및 양극 체제 성립

- 지난 2년간, 소련의 쇠퇴로 양극 체제가 일극(unipolar) 체제로 전환

- 세계적으로 민주주의와 자유시장 경제 체제 부활로 미국의 이념적 승리

- 금번 전쟁의 승리로, 이념적 측면뿐 아니라 군사적 측면 에서도 진정한 Pax Americana 성립

o Pax Americana 는 타국 지배가 아닌 새로운 세계 질서(new world order) 확립을 지향하여야 함

다. Helen Cobben (CSM, 1.24자)

걸프전쟁 이후의 중동문제

o 전쟁이 장기화되면 정치적 해결책을 고려할 필요가 있음

o 단기전으로 끝날 경우에도, 군사적 승리를 전후 중동질서의 성공적 재편으로 연결시킬 치밀한 구상이 요구됨

- 3 -

0037

- 1982년 이스라엘은, 팔레스타인 문제에 캠프 데이비드
  협정에 의한 평화적 해결 대신 무력해결을 선택함으로써,
  군사적 승리에도 불구하고 이후, 시리아의 군사력 강화와
  팔레스타인 주민 반발 심화에 따른 중동정세 악화를 초래한
  선례

o 미국은 걸프전쟁의 군사적 승리에도 불구하고, 전후 중동
  지역에서 더 중대한 도전에 직면할 것으로 예상

- 중동에서의 평화질서 구축 문제

- 각국의 화해 유도 문제

- 군축 및 경제개발 문제

o 현재 미 행정부에는 중동지역 문제에 정통한 전문가가 부재하며,
  이는 전후 중동 정치 질서 재편에 장애 요인이 될 것임

2. 사설

가. The Times (1. 24자)

o 걸프사태에 대한 EC 12개국의 입장 균열은, 영국 Hurd 외무장관이
  경고한 바와 같이 장래 중대한 결과를 초래할 것으로 우려

- 미국은 다국적군 군사작전에 대한 독일, 벨기에등 EC 제국의
  소극적인 지원에 분개

- 특히, 독일의 태도에 대한 불만 접증으로 미국에서 고립주의
  주장 대두

- 유럽 집단안보에 위기 예상

- 4 -

0038

o   EC 국가들의 걸프전쟁 참여 현황

    - 영, 불, 이태리 : 다국적군 참여

    - 화란, 덴마아크 : 호의적인 전비 부담

    - 독일, 스페인, 벨지움 : 초연한 자세 ✓

o   '초국가주의' 정신없이 EC의 정치 통합 논의는 무의미하며, 장기적
    으로 유럽 안보에도 위협

나. 일본 경제신문 (1. 24자)

    o 걸프전쟁은 후세인의 전략대로 장기화 조짐

    o 다국적군의 목표는 쿠웨이트에서의 이라크군 축출에서 후세인
       체제의 타도로 확대

    o 일본은 다국적군에 대한 자금 지원과 유엔 결의를 충실히 이행
       하는데 노력해야 함

- 5 -

0039

3. 분석기사

가. WP (1. 24자)

걸프전쟁에 있어 다국적군의 목표 변화

o 개전초기 다국적군의 전쟁 목표

- 쿠웨이트로 부터 이라크군의 격퇴, 합법정부 회복

- 역내 평화 및 안정 확보

o 전쟁 수행과 함께 상기 목표의 확대

- 이라크 군사력의 충분한 약화

- 대량 파괴무기(생화학 및 핵무기) 생산 능력 파괴

- 후세인 대통령의 축출 여부에 관계없이, 온건한 이라크
  정부 수립

- 걸프 지역으로 부터의 석유의 안정 공급 확보

o 걸프 전쟁의 재정적 부담 증가, 감정의 증폭에 따라 상기
  목표는 더욱 확대될 것이나, 아래 사항 고려 필요

- 이라크 및 경쟁국(시리아, 이란등)간 세력 균형 유지

- 6 -

0040

- 이라크가 철저히 무력화 됨으로써 야기될 수 있는 역내 힘의 공백 상태를 방지하기 위해 이라크의 군사시설은 파괴시키되, 정치,경제 및 사회적 기초는 유지

나. NYT (1, 24자)

이라크의 숨은 의도(Hidden Cards)

o 미국은 걸프전쟁이 3개월이상 지속될 것으로 보며, 일부 관리들은, 최소 2주일후 지상공격 개시를 예상

o 미국으로 망명한 전이라크 주재 소련무관 Sakharov는, 이라크는 우세한 적으로 부터 공격을 받으면 초기에 은폐하고, 기회가 오면 대규모 반격을 가하는 전통적인 소련 전술에 익숙하다고 밝힘

o 이라크는 지상전이 개시되기 전에는 은폐한 전력을 사용하지 않을 것임

o 이라크의 의도는 전쟁에서의 승리가 아니라, 이스라엘의 개입을 유도해 다국적군을 와해하고, 전쟁 지연을 통해 미국 여론을 악화시킴으로써 심리적 타격을 주는 것임

- 끝 -

- 7 -

0041

걸프 事態 關聯 世界 主要 言論 報道 分析

1991. 1. 29.

外　務　部

(美　洲　局)

0042

1. 사설

```
┌─ 참 고 ──────────────────────────────┐
│                                                      │
│  NYT (New York Times)        WP  (Washington Post)   │
│                                                      │
│  CSM(Christian Science Moniter)  WSJ(Wall Street Journal) │
│                                                      │
└──────────────────────────────────────┘
```

가. WP (1.28자)

국내 정치와 걸프전쟁

o 신임 공화당 전국위원회 위원장인 Clayton Yeutter의 걸프전
  관련 최근 발언이 새로운 정치 쟁점으로 부상

  - 금번 걸프전쟁은 1992년 대통령 선거의 주요한 정치적
    이슈가 될 것이며, 대통령의 대이라크 무력사용 승인
    결의 채택에 반대한 대다수의 민주당 의원들은 내년
    선거에서 불리한 입장에 처할 것으로 언급

o 특히 공화당원들은, 민주당의 유력한 대통령 후보인 조지아
  주의 Sam Nunn 상원의원과 뉴 저어지 주의 Bill Bradley
  상원의원이 금번 걸프전쟁을 반대함으로써 1992년 선거에서
  타격을 받을 것으로 예상

- 1 -

0043

o Yeutter 위원장의 발언에 대해 다수 민주당원들은 반발

  - 특히 Nebraska 주의 Bob Kerrey 상원의원은, 월남전에서의
     개인적 경험과 정치적 소신으로 걸프전쟁에 반대한 것이며,
     만일 공화당원들이 정치적 계산에 의해 대 이라크 전쟁
     개시 결정을 하였다면 분명히 잘못된 것이라고 응수

o 걸프전 관련 결의안 채택시 각의원들이 취한 찬.반 입장에
   따라 후일 정치적 책임을 지는 것은 당연하며, 내년 선거시
   유권자들의 판단에 좋은 근거가 될 것임.

나. Die Presse (오스트리아 1.28자)

원유 유출 전략

o 후세인의 원유 유출 전략에 대해 지구의 환경보존에 관심있는
   세계 각국이 분개

  - 다국적군의 쿠웨이트 상륙 저지와 함께 모든 수단을 동원해
     전쟁을 계속할 것이라는 심리적 압박을 가하려는 목적임.

  - 후세인이 이라크인을 포함한 인류의 운명을 고려하지 않고,
     환경 훼손등의 전략도 주저없이 이용할 것임이 명백해짐.

  - 전세계의 환경 보존 단체들이 후세인에 대항해 단결하고 있음.

- 2 -

0044

2. 분석기사

가. David Wessell (WSJ, 1.28자)

o Ricard Darman 예산국장, 91년 회계년도 재정적자가 3,180억불
  로 급증 예상

  - 걸프 전쟁 비용을 제외하고도 금년도 재정적자가 기록적인
    3,180억불에 달할 것으로 평가.   그러나 우방국이 상당
    규모의 전비를 분담함으로써 걸프전쟁에 따른 세금 증가는
    필요 없음.

  - 걸프전쟁이 3개월간 지속된다면, 약 600억불의 전비 소요가
    예상되며, 사우디와 쿠웨이트가 각각 135억불씩 추가 분담금
    제공을 약속함으로써 우방국이 부담할 총액은 약 450억불로
    예상됨.

  - 부쉬 대통령이 2.4(월) 제안할 예산안에는 91년중 걸프전쟁
    수행을 위한 300억불의 수권 예산액과 150억불의 현금 지출분이
    계상됨.   그러나, 전쟁비용과 우방국 분담금은 더 늘어날
    것임.

나. David Rogers (WSJ, 1.28자)

친 이스라엘 단체 로비 활동

o 미 의회의 대 이라크 전쟁 승인 결의에 친 이스라엘 단체들의
  의회 막후 로비가 치열 했던 것으로 판명

- 3 -

0045

- 미국내 친 이스라엘 로비 단체(PAC)가 각종 조직, 인원을 동원, 행정부와 함께 민주당 의원에 대한 로비를 전개했음을 인정함.

- 그러나, 민주당 의원들의 진보성향, 유대계의 직접적 활동이 가져올 국내외 반감 우려에 따른 내부 이견도 많았던 것으로 보임.

o 현재 친 이스라엘계 의원을 중심으로 대 이스라엘 원조 증액 논의가 대두되고 있음.

- Stephen Solarz 의원등은 친 이스라엘 분위기를 유도, 개전 승인 결의 채택에 기여

3. 기고문

가. Anthony Lewis(NYT, 1.28자)

대통령의 균형 감각

o 부쉬 대통령은 걸프전쟁 수행 노력으로 새로운 세계 질서 확립 필요성을 말하고 있으나, 쏘련의 발트해 3국에 대한 무력 탄압 문제에 대해서는 소극적임.

- 발트해 사태로 고르바쵸프 체제가 보수화, 독재화 경향을 보임.

- 쏘련의 보수 세력은 걸프 사태 이후 미국의 패권에 우려, 고르바쵸프의 걸프전쟁 지지를 비난함.

- 4 -

0046

o 걸프 전쟁에 대한 소련의 지지가 필요한 미국은 발트해 사태에
   있어 대쏘 비난과 응징을 자제함.

o 소련의 구시대 회귀는 부쉬 행정부가 구상하는 새로운 세계
   질서 확립에 장애가 될 것으로 보임. 걸프문제 해결을 위해
   쏘련 문제를 희생 시키지 않는 균형있는 대외 정책이 요구됨.

나. <u>William Safire (NYT, 1.28자)</u>

o 터어키가 다국적군에 협조적인 자세를 보이고 있는 것은
   걸프전쟁후 전후 처리 과정에서 원유와 영토 할당을 받고,
   EC와의 관계를 강화키 위한 것임.

o 쿠르드(Kurd) 족도 이라크에 대해 깊은 원한을 갖고 있으므로
   미국은 대이라크 지상전을 전개하는데 터어키와 Kurd족을 활용
   해야함.

다. <u>William Respberry (WP, 1.28자)</u>

o 미국인은 장기전쟁을 거부하는 것이 아니라 목적이 불분명한
   전쟁을 위한 희생을 거부함.

o 지상전 개시로 인명피해가 늘어나면 반전 데모가 격화되고,
   다국적군의 결속도 와해 될 것임.

o 부쉬 대통령은 몇주간 공중폭격을 한후 전쟁을 일단 종식하고,
   대 이라크 경제제재로 복귀 해야 함.

- 끝 -

- 5 -

걸프 事態 關聯 世界 主要 言論 報道 分析

1991. 2. 1.

外 務 部

(美 洲 局)

0048

1. 사 설

┌─── 참 고 ───────────────────────────────┐
NYT (New York Times)   WP (Washington Post)

CSM(Christian Science Monitor) WSJ(Wall Street Journal)
└──┘

가. WSJ (1. 31자)

연두교서에 나타난 지도력

o 금년 연두교서에서 걸프사태와 관련, 부쉬대통령은 강력한
   지도력을 보여줌.

   - 전쟁목표에 대한 명료한 설명
   - 미국민의 단결강화
   - 걸프전쟁 종료후 국내문제 해결을 위한 기반 조성

o 부쉬대통령은 우방국과 후세인에 대항하는 연대 구축에 있어
   지도력을 보여 왔는 바, 걸프전 이후에도 이러한 지도력을
   더욱 강화할 수 있을 것으로 봄.

o 부쉬 대통령이 어려운 시기에 강력한 지도력을 발휘할 수 있다는
   것이 금년 연두교서에서 가장 중요한 점임.

- 1 -

0049

나. <u>NYT (1. 31자)</u>

부쉬 대통령의 집권 3년

o 부쉬 행정부 전반기는 동구권 자유화, 중남미 민주화, 남아공
   인권 상황 개선 및 국내 경제성장등을 달성함.

o 그러나, 집권 후반은 경제 침체와 함께 걸프사태로 인한
   국론 분열을 겪고 있음.

   - 부쉬 대통령이 지난주 이라크 파괴와 후세인 제거로 전쟁
      목적 확대의사를 비친데 대해 미국민 사이에 제한전쟁을
      요구하는 여론 비등

o 부쉬 대통령의 연두교서, 미. 소 외무장관 공동선언에서 전쟁
   목적을 제한할 것임을 보여줌으로써 미국민의 여론을 진정시킴.

2. 분석기사

가. <u>Andrew Rosenthal (NYT, 1. 31자)</u>

미국의 걸프전쟁에 대한 입장 불변

o 1. 29 (화) 발표된 미. 소 외무장관간의 성명이 걸프사태에 대한
   미국의 입장 변화로 해석된다는 논란이 있었음.

   - 성명내용 : 이라크가 쿠웨이트로 부터 철수한다는 명료한
                 약속을 한다면 적대행위 종식이 가능하다고
                 양 장관은 계속 믿고 있음.

- 2 -

0050

o 미정부는 상기 성명의 해석이 잘못된 것으로 걸프사태에 대한
   미국의 입장은 불변임을 이스라엘과 다국적군 참가국에 설명
   하는데 부심하고 있음.

o 상기 성명의 의도는 소련을 계속 반이라크 대열에 묶어두고, 전후
   중동질서 재편 과정에서 소련의 참여와 역할을 보장해주기 위한
   것임.

   - 이라크의 완전한 파괴를 원치 않는다는 보장을 소련측에
     줌으로서 걸프사태에 대한 미.소간 협조 인상을 부각키
     위한 의도

나. Michael Dobbs (WP, 1.31자)

o 소련은 미.소 외무장관 성명이 걸프사태에 대한 미국의 중대한
   입장변화를 보여준 것으로 이를 환영

   - '베스메르트니크' 소련 외무장관은 동 성명이 1976년 밴스-
     그로미코 성명이후 중동문제에 관한 최초의 의견일치라고
     의미 부여

   - 소련측 분석가들은 동 성명에서 미국이 금번 걸프전쟁을 여타
     아랍 분쟁(팔레스타인 문제)과 간접적으로 연계시킨 것으로
     평가

다. S. Armstrong (CSM, 1.31자)

이라크의 전략은 장기 소모전

o 후세인은 은폐전략으로 군사력을 보전, 전쟁을 장기화시켜,
   다국적군의 결속이 와해되도록 유도하고 있음.

0051

- 3 -

- 장기 지상전이 유리하다고 판단, 대규모 선제 공격은
  없을 것임.

o 후세인은 전쟁을 통한 승리는 기대할 수 없으므로, 자신의
  생존과 계속적인 집권으로 아랍 세계내에서 입지를 강화, 정치적
  승리를 목표로 하고 있음.

라. James H. Webb 전 해군성 장관 (WSJ, 1. 31자)

전투에서 성공하더라도 승리 보장은 불확실

o 전쟁에서의 승리를 정치적 승리로 연결시키기 위해서는 다음
  요소를 고려해야 함.

- 인적, 재정적 손실
  · 예상밖으로 손실이 클 경우 반전 여론 비등

- 향후 2-3년간 걸프지역에 미칠 영향
  · 중동지역 세력균형을 통한 안정 유지
  · 시리아등 강경세력 등장
  · 터어키, 이집트등 내부의 반전 분위기
  · 미국 비호하의 사우디, 쿠웨이트 지도층에 대한 여론
    악화

- 국내정치에 미칠 영향
  · 탈냉전으로 둔화된 보수.자유 진영의 대립 개념 재등장
  · 분쟁 개입에 대한 판단 기준 변동 가능성

- 4 -

0052

o 미국이 세계에서 남은 유일한 초강대국이라는 생각은 자기 기만
   으로서 미국 사회내에 해결해야 할 문제가 산적해 있고, 앞으로
   경제 정책의 방향도 확고하지 못함.

o 전후 새로운 세계질서 확립도 중요하지만 국내문제 해결을 위한
   명확한 정책의 재정립이 필요함.

                                        - 끝 -

걸프사태 : 자료 및 언론보도, 1990-91. 전3권 (V.3 해외주요언론보도 분석, 1991) 499

걸프 事態 關聯 世界 主要 言論 報道 分析

1991. 2. 5,

外 務 部

(美 洲 局)

0054

1. 기고문

┌─── 참 고 ──────────────────────────────────┐
│   │
│ NYT (New York Times)   WP (Washington Post)   │
│   │
│ WSJ (Wall Street Journal)   │
│   │
└──┘

Zbignew Brzezinski (NYT, 2.4자)

제한전쟁과 국익 극대화

o 걸프전쟁의 결과가 부쉬대통령이 공언해온 냉전이후의 새로운
  세계 질서 형성에 시금석이 될 것임.

  - 후세인이 국제사회의 압력에 굴복해서 타협안을 받아들이고
    철군을 실행했더라면, 새로운 세계 질서 수립에 획기적
    전기가 되었을 것임.

  - 미국이 걸프사태의 외교적 해결에 적극성을 보이지 않았다는
    인상을 남긴데 아쉬움이 있으며, 군사적 해결은 새로운 세계
    질서 형성을 위한 기회 제공과 함께 새로운 문제점도
    수반할 것임.

o 미국은 전쟁에 의한 손실을 최소화하고 정치적 이익을 극대화
  하는 전략을 선택해야 함.

  - 후세인의 장기 지상전화 및 이스라엘 유인 전략에 대응해,
    전쟁목적을 쿠웨이트 해방으로 제한하여 이라크와의 지상전
    을 피하고 현재와 같은 집중적 공습으로 쿠웨이트내 이라크
    군을 고립, 무력화 시킴으로써 궁극적으로 철군 또는 투항을
    유도하는 방식을 고려해야 함.

- 1 -

0055

- 이와함께 이라크 내의 잔류 군사력에 대한 공습을 계속하여, 이를 약화시킴으로써 후세인의 정치적, 군사적 패배를 안겨 준다면 그의 정치적 입지가 크게 흔들릴 것임.

o 미국이 향후 대외정책을 원활히 수행하기 위해서는 중동문제에 지나치게 깊이 개입해서는 안되며, 걸프전쟁의 장기 지상전화는 상당한 정치적 손실을 초래할 것임.

- 지역정세 불안 가증 및 역내 반미 감정 고조

- 이라크 및 인근국의 사회 혼란 야기

- 미국의 걸프 개입 장기화로 여타 주요 문제 도외시 우려

- 미국내 전쟁 지지 여론 약화 및 국론 분열

o 부쉬대통령은 냉전이후의 새로운 세계 질서에 대한 전반적인 비전을 제시해야 함.

- 지역 안보 구상을 위한 지속적이고 적극적인 노력이 필요 하며, 여기에는 이스라엘, 아랍 평화 정착 문제와 이라크, 레바논 재건 및 역내 부의 재분배등 경제회복 계획이 포함 되어야 함.

- 소련 및 동구의 민주화와 경제개혁에 좀더 관심을 갖고, 직접적인 지원과 자극을 가하는 것이 장기적으로 보아 걸프 문제 해결 보다 새로운 세계 질서 형성에 더 중요한 요소임.

- 미국내 사회, 경제 구조의 개선을 위한 포괄적 계획 수립이 필요하며, 이는 냉전이후의 여유 자금을 지역 분쟁에 투입 하는 대신 국내 문제에 전환시킴으로써 가능할 것임.

- 2 -

2. 사 설

The Times (2.4자)

무기 판매 억제

o Hurd 영국 외무장관은, 중동의 향후 치열한 군비 경쟁 위험성에
   대해 우려를 표명하고, 이를 방지하기 위해 적절한 대책을 취할
   것임을 약속

o 이와같은 무기 판매 억제에 관한 전향적 자세는 국제정세의
   주요한 변화를 반영

   - 소련으로 부터의 위협감소로, 제3세계 국가에 대한 무기
     지원을 않을 경우, 공산화 될 것이라던 종래의 우려 감소

   - 금번 걸프전에서, 서방세계가 이라크에 판매한 군사장비로
     다국적군이 희생되는 모습에 세계 여론이 경악

o 그러나, 효과적인 무기 판매 통제 체제 확립에는 많은 곤란 예상

   - 서방 방위 산업은, 연구 개발 자금을 대의 무기 판매에 의존

   - 이란-이라크 전쟁시 교전 당사자에 대한 무기판매 금지에
     관한 원칙적 합의를 53개국 이상이 무시

   - 아랍제국에 대한 미국의 무기 판매 통제는 미국이 이스라엘에
     대한 무기 공급을 계속하는 한 논란 상존

   - 특히, 경화 부족으로 어려움을 겪고 있는 동구제국이 잉여
     무기를 판매할 가능성 농후

- 3 -

0057

o 무기 판매 통제 방안

  - 종래의 COCOM(Coordinating Committee for Multilateral Export Controls)이 모델 방안으로 활용 가능

  - G7과 스페인, 베네룩스 3국이 참여하고 있는 미사일 기술 통제 체제(Missile Technology Control Regime)의 확대

3. 분석기사

가. R.W. Apple(NYT, 2.4자)

언론과 군부간의 불신

o 걸프전쟁이 채 한달도 안되서 이미 미군당국과 특파원간에 군부가 제공하는 전황 자료의 불확실성과 보도통제를 둘러싸고 불신이 심화되고 있음.

  - 월남전 당시 '5시의 우둔한 행사'라고 조소적으로 표현되던 일일 브리핑 보다 걸프전쟁 브리핑은 유용하고 쓸만한 것이 없음. 어떤 경우는 현장에서 특파원이 취재해서 보도한 내용까지 브리핑에 나타나지 않고, 때로는 브리핑 내용 자체도 틀리는 경우가 있음.

o 월남전에서 불리한 보도가 전쟁에 대한 여론 악화를 유도했다고 믿고 있는 다수의 군장교들은 불리한 기사가 나가는 것을 최대로 억제하기 위해 몰두하고 있음.

- 4 -

0058

- 군 당국은 전황 취재에 '풀(POOL)'시스템을 채택하고, 전투
  지역 부근에 파견되는 특파원 수를 소수로 제한

- 풀 시스템에서 소외된 언론사들은 법무성에 불법성을 제소
  하여, '풀 시스템은 걸프전 취재를 위한 항시적(Permanent)
  인 제도가 아니다'라는 일견 양보성 발언을 얻어내긴
  했으나, 걸프현장에서는 조금도 변화의 조짐이 없음.

나. <u>Gerald F. Seir (WSJ, 2.4자)</u>

전쟁종식 시나리오

o 후세인이 굴복할 가능성이 전무하며 미국도 바그다드까지 진격
  할 의도가 없음을 천명한 가운데 몇가지의 전쟁종식 시나리오를
  상정할 수 있음.

o 쿠웨이트내 이라크군의 궤멸

- 쿠웨이트내의 이라크 군에 대한 집중적 공중폭격으로 보급로
  및 통신을 차단하고 지상군 공격으로 방어선을 돌파하여
  이라크군의 철수 또는 투항을 유도함.

o 이라크 내부에서의 와해

- 이라크 군부에 의해 후세인이 암살되거나 쿠데타로 축출되는
  경우와 미국의 공격 또는 이스라엘의 후세인 제거 작전이
  성공을 거두는 경우임.

- 5 -

0059

o 이라크군의 철수

 - 이라크가 쿠웨이트에서의 철수를 확고히 약속하면 전쟁이
   종결될 수 있다는 지난주 미.소 공동성명에 입각한 시나리오
   임.

o 미국의 후퇴

 - 전쟁의장기화, 이라크의 화학무기 사용, 이에대한 이스라엘의
   보복공격 및 이란의 참전으로 이어지는 일련의 사태로 부쉬
   대통령이 더 이상의 확전을 막기 휘해 휴전을 모색해야만
   하는 최악의 시나리오임.

- 끝 -

- 6 -

0060

걸프 事態 關聯 世界 主要 言論 報道 分析

1991. 2. 4.

外 務 部

(美 洲 局)

0061

1. 사 설

```
┌─ 참  고 ──────────────────────────────────┐
│ NYT (New York Times)        WP  (Washington Post) │
└──────────────────────────────────────────┘
```

가. <u>WP (2. 3일자)</u>

카프지 전투

o 이라크는 사우디 영토내의 카프지에 지상공격을 개시하여 승리를
   주장하고 있으며, 이는 이라크의 전략적 의도를 드러내는 것임.

   - 많은 인명손실로 다국적군을 지상전으로 유도

   - 미국과의 전쟁에서의 승리를 대대적으로 홍보

   - 후세인이 계속 권좌에 남아, 걸프전 종식을 추구

o 이에 대응, 미국등 다국적군은 이라크 남부와 쿠웨이트의 이라크
   지상군에 집중적으로 공중폭격을 가하는 등 현재까지 미국의 의도
   대로 전쟁을 수행하고 있음.

   - 지상전 개전시기를 지연시켜 인명손실을 최소화 하고, 이라크의
     화학무기 사용을 억제하면서 지상군에 큰 타격을 주고 있음.

o 현재 다수국가의 외교가에서 걸프전 종식에 대해 거론하고 있으나,
   카프지 전투에서 나타난 이라크의 전략 의도를 볼때 진정한 전쟁
   종식은 후세인이 UN 결의안을 수락하고, 쿠웨이트로 부터 이라크
   군의 완전 (Closely Monitored) 철수가 이루어질때 가능함.

- 1 -

0062

나. NYT(2, 2자)

걸프전쟁과 월남전

o 부쉬대통령등 미국내 보수주의 세력은 과거 월남전에서 패배의
  영향으로 많은 지역 분쟁 해결에 있어 미국의 정책이 실패
  했다고 판단, 금번 걸프전쟁에서는 대 이라크 경제 제재를
  포기하고 군사적 해결을 추구하고 있음.

o 미국은 더이상 전세계에 걸쳐 공산주의와 대립관계에 있지 않으며,
  또한, 케네디 대통령 스타일의 Pax Americana정책을 수행할 여유도
  없으므로, 또다른 '월남전'을 피하기 위해서는 과거와 같은 헤게모니
  추구의 환상을 벗어나 집단안보 체제 구성을 위해 노력 해야 할
  것 임.

다. Le Figaro(2, 2자)

o 걸프전 결과로 소련의 영향력 쇠퇴, 미국의 세력 강화, 유엔의
  활성화 및 서방과 아랍간 갈등 표출등 국제정세 변화가 예상됨.

o 걸프사태 초반에는 정치통합 원칙에 대한 EC 12개국의 합의가
  있었으나, 걸프전에 대한 EC의 확고한 공동정책은 수립치
  못하고 각 회원국이 개별적 정책으로 대처함.

  - 영.불은 걸프전에 참여한 반면, EC는 내부적으로 분열됨.

  - 걸프전 종식후의 유럽 장래 전망은 불투명하며, 일부 영.미
    언론은 걸프전으로 인해 향후 EC 정치 통합은 불가능할
    것이라고 보도함.

- 2 -

0063

- 12개 회원국의 다양성은 각국내 전쟁 찬반론의 대립과
  비교할때 사소한 문제인 바, EC에 필요한 것은 외교, 국방
  분야의 공동정책 결정 및 시행을 위한 정치 통합이 급선무임.

o 정치통합을 추진하지 않을 경우, EC는 국제사회에서 약소 세력권
  으로 남아, 동구 및 제3세계등의 요구에도 적극 대응치 못하게
  될 것이므로, 향후 유럽의 안전과 이익보장을 위해 정치 군사
  통합이 필요함.

2. 분석기사

가. <u>Robert E. Hunter (WP 2.3자)</u>

<u>걸프전쟁의 조속한 종결 방안</u>

o 미국은 이라크의 군사력을 최대한 약화시키고 후세인을 제거하여,
  중동 질서를 재편하려 하고 있으며 이제까지의 대규모 공습으로
  이라크의 군사시설 및 무기를 대량 파괴하고 후세인의 위치를
  위협하고 있음.

o 미국이 전쟁 목적을 어느정도 달성함에 따라 외교적 방법과
  이라크의 쿠웨이트 철군으로 전쟁을 종결하는 방안을 고려할
  필요성이 대두됨.

  - 후세인의 이성적 판단을 유도하는데 전범처리, 핵무기 사용
    위협등은 도움이 되지 않을 것임.

- 3 -

0064

o 후세인의 전략적 의도를 재고해 볼때, 부쉬 행정부가 이라크의
　완전한 패망이 아닌 군사적 약화로 걸프전쟁을 종식시킬 수
　있음.

－ 후세인이 생화학 무기의 사용과 전세계적인 테러공격 감행
　능력이 있음에도 자제하고 있다는 것은 아직 협상의 여지가
　있음을 암시

－ 후세인은 이스라엘, 사우디 및 미국과 직접 대결한 최초의
　아랍 지도자라는 명망 획득

o 미국은 전쟁 종결단계에서 후세인이 최악의 선택을 피하고,
　소규모 전과로 체면을 살린뒤 쿠웨이트로부터 철군토록 유도하여
　전쟁을 조기 종식시키는 차선책을 강구할 필요가 있을 것임.

나. Yousset M. Ibrahim(NYT, 2.3자)

걸프전쟁에 대한 아랍제국의 우려

o 걸프전쟁으로 아랍의 상처가 심화되고, 큰 혼란이 초래되어 아랍
　제국들이 정치 체제에 위협을 받고 있음.

－ 알제리아에서 사우디 아라비아에 이르기까지 다국적군에
　대한 반대 여론이 점차 비등

∴ 알제리, 요르단, 예멘, 수단, 말레이지아, 파키스탄등 회교
　국가에서 친이라크 시위 발생

－ 모로코의 하산왕은 모로코 군대를 사우디로 부터 철수
　시키라는 야당의 거센 압력에 경고

- 4 -

0065

- 이집트 45,000명의 군대를 사우디에 주둔시키고 있으나,
  친이라크 시위에 대비하여 대학에 휴교령

o 많은 아랍제국은 팔레스타인 문제와 쿠웨이트 해방을 연계
  시킬 것을 주장하고 있으며, 금번 걸프전에서 미국이 생각하는
  승리와 아랍제국이 생각하는 승리에 대한 인식의 차이를 보임.

o 또한 걸프전쟁은 아랍제국간 해묵은 영토분쟁을 다시 야기 시킬
  소지가 있으며, 전후 처리 과정에서 역내 아랍국간의 콘센서스
  형성이 이루어지지 않는다면 새로운 혼란이 초래될 수도 있음.

3. 기고문(Martin Walker 영국 Guardian지 워싱톤 지국장, NYT, 2.2자)

The Wrong Cause at the Worst Time

o 걸프위기가 빚은 비극은 부쉬 대통령이 소련의 민주개혁 지원을
  희생해가면서 이라크라는 작은 목표물에 대한 외교, 정치, 경제적인
  노력을 편중하고 있다는 사실임.

- 지금까지 서방의 대소 지원은 미미한 것이며, 소련이 유엔
  안보리에서 미국의 걸프정책을 지지해준 댓가로 약속한
  10억불의 긴급식량 차관 제공과 미국의 대소무역 규제법안
  폐기가 실행되지 않았음.

o 냉전을 궁극적으로 종식하려면 소련의 자유화와 무역 확대가 필요
  하나, 부쉬 행정부는 아랍 봉건 왕조 유지와 제국주의적 이해관계가
  달린 원유를 위해서 전쟁을 수행함으로써 냉전종식의 중요한 기회를
  상실하고 있음.

- 끝 -

걸프 事態 關係 世界 主要 言論 報道 分析

1991. 2. 5.

外 務 部

(美 洲 局)

0067

1. 기고문

```
┌── 참 고 ──────────────────────────────────────────┐
│  NYT (New York Times)          WP  (Washington Post)  │
│  WSJ (Wall Street Journal)                            │
└───────────────────────────────────────────────────┘
```

Zbignew Brzezinski (NYT, 2,4자)

제한전쟁과 국익 극대화

o 걸프전쟁의 결과가 부쉬대통령이 공언해온 냉전이후의 새로운
  세계 질서 형성에 시금석이 될 것임.

  - 후세인이 국제사회의 압력에 굴복해서 타협안을 받아들이고
    철군을 실행했더라면, 새로운 세계 질서 수립에 획기적
    전기가 되었을 것임.

  - 미국이 걸프사태의 외교적 해결에 적극성을 보이지 않았다는
    인상을 남긴데 아쉬움이 있으며, 군사적 해결은 새로운 세계
    질서 형성을 위한 기회 제공과 함께 새로운 문제점도
    수반할 것임.

o 미국은 전쟁에 의한 손실을 최소화하고 정치적 이익을 극대화
  하는 전략을 선택해야 함.

  - 후세인의 장기 지상전화 및 이스라엘 유인 전략에 대응해,
    전쟁목적을 쿠웨이트 해방으로 제한하여 이라크와의 지상전
    을 피하고 현재와 같은 집중적 공습으로 쿠웨이트내 이라크
    군을 고립, 무력화 시킴으로써 궁극적으로 철군 또는 투항을
    유도하는 방식을 고려해야 함.

- 1 -

0068

- 이와함께 이라크 내의 잔류 군사력에 대한 공습을 계속하여, 이를 약화시킴으로써 후세인의 정치적. 군사적 패배를 안겨 준다면 그의 정치적 입지가 크게 흔들릴 것임.

o 미국이 향후 대외정책을 원활히 수행하기 위해서는 중동문제에 지나치게 깊이 개입해서는 안되며, 걸프전쟁의 장기 지상전화는 상당한 정치적 손실을 초래할 것임.

- 지역정세 불안 가증 및 역내 반미 감정 고조

- 이라크 및 인근국의 사희 혼란 야기

- 미국의 걸프 개입 장기화로 여타 주요 문제 도의시 우려

- 미국내 전쟁 지지 여른 약화 및 국른 분열

o 부쉬대통령은 냉전이후의 새로운 세계 질서에 대한 전반적인 비전을 제시해야 함.

- 지역 안보 구상을 위한 지속적이고 적극적인 노력이 필요 하며, 여기에는 이스라엘. 아랍 평화 정착 문제와 이라크, 레바논 재건 및 역내 부의 재분배등 경제회복 계획이 포함 되어야 함.

- 소련 및 동구의 민주화와 경제개혁에 좀더 관심을 갖고, 직접적인 지원과 자극을 가하는 것이 장기적으로 보아 걸프 문제 해결 보다 새로운 세계 질서 형성에 더 중요한 요소임.

- 미국내 사희. 경제 구조의 개선을 위한 포괄적 계획 수립이 필요하며, 이는 냉전이후의 여유 자금을 지역 분쟁에 투입 하는 대신 국내 문제에 전환시킴으로써 가능할 것임.

- 2 -

0069

2. 사 설

The Times (2.4자)

무기 판매 억제

o Hurd 영국 외무장관은, 증동의 향후 치열한 군비 경쟁 위험성에 대해 우려를 표명하고, 이를 방지하기 위해 적절한 대책을 취할 것임을 약속

o 이와같은 무기 판매 억제에 관한 전향적 자세는 국제정세의 주요한 변화를 반영

  - 소련으로 부터의 위협감소로, 제3세계 국가에 대한 무기 지원을 않을 경우, 공산화 될 것이라던 종래의 우려 감소

  - 금번 걸프전에서, 서방세계가 이라크에 판매한 군사장비로 다국적군이 희생되는 모습에 세계 여론이 경악

o 그러나, 효과적인 무기 판매 통제 체제 확립에는 많은 곤란 예상

  - 서방 방위 산업은, 연구 개발 자금을 대의 무기 판매에 의존

  - 이란-이라크 전쟁시 교전 당사자에 대한 무기판매 금지에 관한 원칙적 합의를 53개국 이상이 무시

  - 아랍제국에 대한 미국의 무기 판매 통제는 미국이 이스라엘에 대한 무기 공급을 계속하는 한 논란 상존

  - 특히, 경화 부족으로 어려움을 겪고 있는 동구제국이 잉여 무기를 판매할 가능성 농후

- 3 -

0070

o 무기 판매 통제 방안

   - 종래의 COCOM(Coordinating Committee for Multilateral
     Export Controls)이 모델 방안으로 활용 가능

   - G7과 스페인, 베네룩스 3국이 참여하고 있는 미사일 기술
     통제 체제(Missile Technology Control Regime)의 확대

3. 분석기사

   가. R.W. Apple(NYT, 2.4자)

언론과 군부간의 불신

o 걸프전쟁이 채 한달도 안되서 이미 미군당국과 특파원간에
  군부가 제공하는 전황 자료의 불확실성과 보도통제를 둘러싸고
  불신이 심화되고 있음.

   - 월남전 당시 '5시의 우둔한 행사'라고 조소적으로 표현되던
     일일 브리핑 보다 걸프전쟁 브리핑은 유용하고 쓸만한 것이
     없음.   어떤 경우는 현장에서 특파원이 취재해서 보도한
     내용까지 브리핑에 나타나지 않고, 때로는 브리핑 내용
     자체도 틀리는 경우가 있음.

o 월남전에서 불리한 보도가 전쟁에 대한 여론 악화를 유도했다고
  믿고 있는 다수의 군장교들은 불리한 기사가 나가는 것을 최대로
  억제하기 위해 몰두하고 있음.

- 4 -

0071

- 군 당국은 전황 취재에 '풀(POOL)' 시스템을 채택하고, 전투 지역 부근에 파견되는 특파원 수를 소수로 제한

- 풀 시스템에서 소외된 언론사들은 법무성에 불법성을 제소하여, '풀 시스템은 걸프전 취재를 위한 항시적(Permanent)인 제도가 아니다'라는 일견 양보성 발언을 얻어내긴 했으나, 걸프현장에서는 조금도 변화의 조짐이 없음.

나. Gerald F. Seir (WSJ, 2.4자)

<u>전쟁종식 시나리오</u>

o 후세인이 굴복할 가능성이 전무하며 미국도 바그다드까지 진격할 의도가 없음을 천명한 가운데 몇가지의 전쟁종식 시나리오를 상정할 수 있음.

o 쿠웨이트내 이라크군의 궤멸

- 쿠웨이트내의 이라크 군에 대한 집중적 공중폭격으로 보급로 및 통신을 차단하고 지상군 공격으로 방어선을 돌파하여 이라크군의 철수 또는 투항을 유도함.

o 이라크 내부에서의 와해

- 이라크 군부에 의해 후세인이 암살되거나 쿠데타로 축출되는 경우와 미국의 공격 또는 이스라엘의 후세인 제거 작전이 성공을 거두는 경우임.

- 5 -

0072

o 이라크군의 철수

  - 이라크가 쿠웨이트에서의 철수를 확고히 약속하면 전쟁이
    종결될 수 있다는 지난주 미. 소 공동성명에 입각한 시나리오
    임.

o 미국의 후퇴

  - 전쟁의장기화, 이라크의 화학무기 사용, 이에대한 이스라엘의
    보복공격 및 이란의 참전으로 이어지는 일련의 사태로 부쉬
    대통령이 더 이상의 확전을 막기 휘해 휴전을 모색해야만
    하는 최악의 시나리오입.

                                    - 끝 -

0073

김수현

```
┌─────────────────────────────────────────┐
│  걸프 事態 關聯  世界 主要 言論 報道 分析  │
└─────────────────────────────────────────┘
```

1991. 2. 6.

外　　務　　部

(美　洲　局)

0074

1. 사설

┌─ 참 고 ─────────────────────────────────┐
│ NYT (New York Times)   CSM (Christian Science Monitor) │
└───────────────────────────────────────┘

가. The Times (2.5자)

대 이라크 공습

o 공습에 의한 작전의 성공여부는 폭격의 정확도에 달려 있음.
  다국적군 폭격의 정확성은 단기적으로나 정치적으로 완벽한
  전쟁을 보장해 줄것이나, 공습 목표 지역을 확대해서는 안됨.

o 아랍국가들 뿐만 아니라 다국적군에 소속한 여타국가들도 이라크
  민간인 사상자가 많이 발생하는 것을 원치 않음.

  - 후세인은 민간인 피해 발생을 최대한 선전, 정치적 목적에
    이용하려 함.

나. CSM (2.5자)

다국적군의 결속

o 부쉬행정부는 대 이라크 UN 결의, 전쟁비용 분담등 외교적 수단을
  동원, 걸프사태를 이라크에 대한 국제사회 전체의 응징으로
  성립시키는데 주력해 왔음.

- 1 -

0075

o 전쟁이 장기화되고, 지상전 가능성이 높아진 가운데 각국은
  종전의 미국 지지 태도를 재고하고, 자국의 여론이나 이익을
  염두에 두고 걸프전을 국내 정치에 이용하기 위해 독자적
  행동을 할 움직임을 보이고 있으므로, 미국은 이러한 움직임이
  다국적군의 결속을 약화시키기 전에 전쟁을 조기 종결해야
  함.

   - 소련은 걸프사태를 발트해 국가에 대한 무력 탄압에 이용

   - 유럽은 다국적군에 의한 군사적 해결에 이견

   - 중동지역에서는 미국의 대이라크 집중 공습으로 반미
     무드가 고조

   - 중국은 유엔 제재를 무시하고 대이라크 무기 판매에 따른
     이익을 추구하고 걸프전을 국내 인권 탄압에 이용

o 미국은 쿠웨이트 해방 이후에는 다국적군의 결속이 흔들릴 수
  있다는 인식을 갖고 걸프전을 수행하고, 새로운 질서 구상을
  해야 함.

2. 분석기사

 가. <u>Mansour Farhang (NYT, 2.5자)</u>

                        <u>이란의 전략</u>

o 미국은 과거 이란-이라크 전쟁기간중 현실주의 정책에 따라
  양국에 공히 무기를 판매함으로써 전쟁 장기화 및 이라크의
  군사적 팽창을 초래하였음.

                    - 2 -

                                        0076

o 현재 이란은 걸프전쟁에서 군사적 개입을 피하고 중립을 유지
하면서 미국과 이라크의 장기 소모전이 가져올 중동에서의
자국 입지 강화 전략을 추구함.

- 이란은 이라크의 약화를 내심 기대하고 있으나 이라크에서
친미 정권이 들어서는 것은 불원

- 외견상 적극적인 중재노력을 통해 전후 처리 문제에 발언권
강화 기도

- 이라크 전투기의 도피를 허용함으로써 미국과 이라크에 대해
향후 활용할 정치적 수단 마련

o 미국은 걸프전쟁을 이란과의 관계개선의 기회로 진지하게 활용
해야 하며, 과거 레이건 시절의 정책이 오늘날 이라크의 팽창
주의를 불러왔다는 사실을 이란에게 인식시켜야 함.

나. *Thomas Friedman (NYT 2.5자)*

이란의 평화 제의

o 이란의 중재 제의는 1979년 이후 최초의 대미 접촉 공식 제의
로써 미국은 이를 대 이란 관계개선과 동시에 대 이라크 연합
유지에 활용 가능할 것임.

o 이란의 중재제의 의도는 다음과 같이 분석됨.

- 전후 걸프지역에서의 입지 강화

- 이라크가 어느정도 약화되면 미국이 걸프지역에 더이상
개입하는 것을 방지하려는 의도

- 이라크에 동정적인 국내 강경 회교세력에 대한 무마 수단

- 3 -

0077

다. Marshall Ingwerson (CSM 2.5자)

전쟁 장기화 반대 압력

o 미국은 사상자수를 최소화 하기 위해 집중공습을 통한 쿠웨이트
  내 이라크 군사력 약화를 추구하고 있으나, 다음과 같은 정치적
  변수를 고려, 걸프전쟁을 조기 종식시켜야 함.

  - 전쟁이 장기화 될수록 아랍 세계에서 후세인의 위상이 제고
    될 우려

  - 미국 국내 경제 침체 가능성

  - 미국내 전쟁 지지 여론 악화

  - 사막 기후 변화로 인한 전쟁 수행의 애로 발생

o 걸프전쟁이 장기화 되면 후세인에 대한 지지가 반미 감정으로
  전환될 가능성이 있으며, 또한 전쟁기간보다 사상자 수가 전쟁
  지지 여론에 더 큰 영향을 줄 것이므로 이라크 민간인의 대량
  살상이나 이라크의 완전 파괴는 다국적군 참여 아랍국에 정치적
  위험 부담을 주어 다국적군 결속에 와해가 우려됨.

- 끝 -

1991. 2. 7.

外 務 部

(美 洲 局)

0079

1. 사설

```
┌─ 참  고 ──────────────────────────────────┐
│  NYT (New York Times)      CSM (Christian Science Monitor) │
│  WSJ (Wall Street Journal)  WP (Washington Post)           │
└────────────────────────────────────────────┘
```

WSJ (2.6자)

제2의 월남전

o 걸프사태 관련 최근에 일고 있는 논란은 후세인을 굴복시키기
   위한 지상전의 필요성과 개전시기의 문제임.

o William Cohen 공화당 상원의원 등은 공습을 수개월 계속해야
   한다는 여론을 대표하는 바, 이러한 지상전 연기 여론은
   사상자 발생 가능성을 우려한 것이나, 걸프전이 장기화되면
   또다른 월남전으로 여론에 비춰질 수 있음.

   - 월남전에서 공중공격이후 지상전 전개라는 소위 '점진적
     대응'(graduated response) 방식은 완전히 실패했음.

   - 후세인이 많은 희생자를 발생시켜 비등하는 반전여론을
     이용, 전쟁에 승리하려는 전략을 구사하고 있어 전쟁의
     조기종식으로 희생자를 최소화 해야 함.

o 월남전 당시 반전여론은 높은 사상율 때문이 아니라, 명확한
   전쟁목표와 승산이 없었기 때문에 발생한 바, 걸프전을 종결
   시키기 위해 지상공격의 필요성과 개시시기를 결정해야 됨.

- 1 -

0080

2. 기고문

가. <u>R. Evans & R. Novak (WP, 2.6자)</u>

<u>소련의 걸프 게임</u>

o INF 조약 체결이후 폐기 대상이며, 스커드 보다 파괴력, 정확도가
  뛰어난 소련제 SS-12 중거리 미사일로 후세인이 이스라엘과 사우디
  를 공격할 가능성이 있다고 백악관이 공표함.

  - 이와함께 스커드와 SS-12 미사일에 생화학 탄두가 정착되어
    있고, 이를 예멘에서 사우디로 발사할 가능성이 있다는 정보도
    포함됨.

o 한편, 통일 독일정부는 소련이 INF 조약을 위반하여, 1984년이후
  24기의 SS-23 미사일을 동독에 계속 배치하여 왔음을 미국측에
  확인함.

o 이같은 소련의 군축 조약 위반은 군부에 의해 계획적으로 자행
  되었고 세바르드나제 외상의 사임이 이러한 군부의 음모와도
  관련이 있을 것이라는 추측이 나돌고 있으며, 소련 군부가 걸프
  전에서 이라크를 비밀리에 지원하고 있다는 의심도 있으나 확인
  되지 않음.

o 미 행정부는 소련측의 군축 조약 이행 여부에 대한 의회 보고서
  에서 실상을 밝히는 것을 꺼리고 있으며, 이는 보수,강경화가
  현저해진 소련이 유엔의 대이라크 결의를 위반한 사실을 호도
  하는 결과가 될 것임.

  - 미국은 정치적 곤경에 빠져 있는 고르바쵸프의 입지를 약화
    시키지 않기 위해 비난을 자제하고 있음.

- 2 -

0081

나. <u>NYT (Leslie H, Gelb)</u>

걸프전의 군사적 의문점

o 월남전 당시 '존슨' 대통령의 공격 목표 선정등 작전 내용에
  일일이 간섭했던 것과는 달리 금번 걸프전에서는 부쉬대통령이
  정책 결정만 하고 군장성들에게 많은 재량권을 주고 있음.

o 따라서, 부쉬 대통령이 군지휘부의 의견에만 의존, 중요한 군사적
  문제를 확인하지 않고 지상공격 결정을 내릴 우려가 있음.

  - 쿠웨이트내 이라크군 보급로 차단을 위한 다국적군 공습의 효과

  - 쿠웨이트내 이라크군이 보유한 보급품 규모

  - 화학전에 대한 다국적군의 충분한 대비 여부

  - 다국적군의 지상 공격 방향을 이라크군이 상세히 파악하고
    역공을 가할 위험성

o Schwarzkopf 중동 주둔군 사령관과 Powell 합참의장이 걸프전을
  지휘하지만, 월남전시 '존슨' 대통령의 경우와 같이 최종 책임은
  부쉬대통령이 지게됨.

- 3 -

0082

3. 분석기사

가. <u>Martin Fletcher (The Times 2.6자)</u>

<u>백악관, 후세인 존속 고려</u>

o 부쉬 행정부는 후세인이 쿠웨이트에서 철수하고, 이라크와 아랍
  세계에서 정치적, 군사적 세력을 유지, 미국으로 하여금 이라크를
  계속 공격할 명분을 상실케 하거나, 중동지역에 군사력을 장기적
  으로 주둔시켜야 하는 상황 발생을 전후 질서 형성에 고려해야 됨.

  - 이라크 항공기의 이란 도피, 생화학 무기 사용 자제, 테러
    공격 자제등은 후세인이 이러한 상황을 고려하고 있음을
    시사함.

  - 백악관과 국무부간에 후세인 존속과 전후 걸프정세에 대한
    논쟁이 있음.

o 부쉬 대통령의 강경 입장 고수에도 불구하고, 후세인에 대해서는
  전범처리 이외 다른 방안이 가능하며, 미국은 인명손실 최소화를
  위해서 외교적 해결방법을 포기하지는 않은 것으로 보임.

나. <u>요미우리 신문(2.7자)</u>

<u>핵사용 찬성 여론 증가</u>

o 미국장병의 인명손실을 줄이기 위한 전술핵 병기 사용 여부에
  대한 갤럽 여론조사에서 찬성 45%, 반대 45%의 결과를 나타내,
  핵전문가들을 놀라게 하였음.

- 4 -

0083

- 이는 개전전 1개월초에 같은 질문에 대한 조사에서 찬성 24%, 반대 75%였던 것과는 대조를 보임.

o 다국적군이 지상전을 개시하여 미군 사상자수가 급증하거나 이라크가 화학병기를 대량으로 사용할 경우, 핵 사용론은 더욱 강화되어 부쉬행정부에 압력으로 작용할 것으로 예상됨.

- 미군 당국은 핵무기 존재여부에 긍정도 부정도 않은 방침을 취하고 있으나 Green Peace등의 추계에 따르면, 현재 미군 함정에 약 500발의 핵탄두가 탑재되어 있고, 터키영내에 약 300발의 핵폭탄이 있는 것으로 알려짐.

다. Alfred Rubin (CSM, 2.6자)

중동회의 개최의 난점

o 중동문제 해결을 위해 모든 관계 당사국이 참여하는 회의 개최에 많은 어려움이 있음.

o 팔레스타인 참여 문제

- PLO 의 팔레스타인 대표성

o 이라크의 역할 문제

- 금번 걸프전쟁을 계기로 한 팔레스타인 문제에 대한 연고권 주장

- 5 -

0084

o 골란고원에 대한 시리아와 이스라엘의 입장

   - 시리아의 골란 고원 장악 의도와 골란 고원을 군사적으로
      중립화 하려는 이스라엘 이해의 조정 문제

o 레바논 내부 사정

   - Druze, Maronite Christian, Amal, Shiite등 사분오열된
      레바논의 대표권 문제

o 이집트의 입장

   - 이스라엘이 통치하고 있는 West Bank와 Gaza 지구에 대한
      책임을 떠맡게 되는 것을 불원

o 전체관련 아랍국이 참가하는 회의에 의한 중동문제의 원만한
   해결은 불가능한 바, 우선 가능한 분야부터 부분적인 해결이
   바람직함.

                                        - 끝 -

걸프 事態 關聯 世界 主要 言論 報道 分析

1991. 2. 9.

外 務 部

(美 洲 局)

0086

1. 사설 (WP, 2.8자)

```
┌─── 참 고 ──────────────────────────────────────┐
│  NYT (New York Times)        WP (Washington Post) │
└─────────────────────────────────────────────────┘
```

<u>전쟁 목적</u>

o 이라크 본토에 대한 집중 공습은 다국적군을 보호하기 위한 작전
  으로 정당화 될수 있으나, 전후 처리를 고려, 이라크가 국가로서의
  영토 및 문화기반은 유지하도록 공습을 제한하여야 함.

o 현재 다발적으로 거론되고 있는 정전 논의는 쿠웨이트에서의
  이라크군 철수를 위한 실질적인 조치가 수반되지 않는다면
  단지, 후세인에게 UN 결의 이행을 회피하는 시간적 여유를
  주는 것에 불과함.

o 후세인이 쿠웨이트 철군 이후 권력을 유지한다 하더라도,
  대이라크 경제.군사적 제재를 계속함으로써, 이라크의 잠재적
  위협을 제거하고, 후세인이 자체 붕괴되도록 유도할 수 있을
  것임.

o 다만, 이라크가 먼저 대규모 지상공격을 개시하거나 화학
  무기 사용으로 전쟁을 확대할 우려가 있으므로 미국은 전쟁
  목적에 확신을 갖고 이를 주도해야 함.

- 1 -

0087

2. 기고문

가. <u>Walid Khalidi (NYT, 2.7자)</u>

<u>후세인의 계략</u>

o 다국적군의 지상전 가능성이 짙어진 가운데, 후세인은 쿠웨이트
   를 고수하면서 다국적군의 공격을 유도, 전쟁을 장기화 시키고
   아랍세계에서 자신의 위상을 제고함으로써 정치적 승리를 추구
   하고 있음.

o 다국적군이 쿠웨이트 해방작전에서 인명손실을 많이 입을 경우,
   이라크 진격에의 유혹을 받기 쉬우나, 전쟁을 쿠웨이트 해방
   으로 한정하는 것이 다국적군에 참가한 아랍국가들에 명분을
   줄 것임.

   - 미국의 이라크 진격시 아랍국가들이 동참할 가능성이 없으며,
     주변 회교 세력들의 개입을 초래해 이라크가 레바논화 할
     우려가 있음.

o 현재까지 이라크 영토가 입은 피해를 감안할때 전쟁을 UN이
   정한 한도에서 끝내는 것이 전후 중동 신질서 수립에 도움이
   될 것임.

나. <u>William Safire (NYT, 2.7자)</u>

o 걸프전에서 세계각국이 보인 실리추구 태도는 미국의 우방국에
   대한 평가를 재고 하게 하고, 전후 미국의 대외 관계에 지대한
   영향을 줄 것임.

   - 영국의 일관된 태도는 높이 평가

- 2 -

0088

- 다국적군에 참가하고 있는 불란서는 이라크에 대한 유화 정책 추구

- 독일은 전비 분담에 수동적

- 일본은 분담전비를 비군사적 목적에 사용할 것을 고집

- 아랍제국은 다국적군에 대한 경제적, 군사적 참가에 적극적

- 이스라엘은 대 이라크 보복 자제로 미국의 전쟁 수행에 기여

- 소련과 중국은 걸프사태를 국내 문제 해결에 이용

- 터어키의 향후 지상전에 참가 여부 주목

다. <u>John Mcarsheimer (NYT, 2, 8자)</u>

<u>쿠웨이트에서의 지상전</u>

o 쿠웨이트에서 지상전이 벌어지면 수개월동안 지속되고, 수천명의 미군 사상자가 발생할 것이라고 하나, 실제로는 일주일 이내에 쿠웨이트를 해방하고, 사상자수도 1,000명 이내로 줄일 수 있음.

- 우세한 전력으로 쿠웨이트-사우디 국경 한지역을 집중 돌파

- 이라크군이 이동하는 것을 공군력으로 분쇄

- 쿠웨이트 영내 진입후 직접 교전을 피하면서, 이라크 군을 고립시키고 보급로를 차단

- 3 -

0089

o 이라크 남부에 주둔하고 있는 공화국 수비대나 쿠웨이트내
  이라크 군은 다국적군의 공군력으로 인해 상호 이동이나 지원이
  불가할 것인 바, 특정지역 돌파작전이 최대 규모의 직접 교전이
  될 것이며, 사상자 수도 작아질 것임.

라. <u>A. M. Rosenthal (NYT, 2. 8자)</u>

후세인의 방송매체 활용 전략

o 후세인은 걸프전에서 바그다드 주재 서방기자들을 이용해 세계를
  상대로 여론을 조작하는 교묘한 대언론 전략을 구사함.

o 걸프전 보도에서 결정적 역할을 해온 CNN이 중립적 보도를 위해
  노력한 점은 평가하지만, 후세인의 주장을 일방적으로 전달하는
  역할을 하기도 했음.

  - CNN의 Peter Arnett 기자도 다른 취재진들과 마찬가지로
    이라크 당국의 검열에 따라, 민간인 피해 상황등 이라크
    측에 유리한 사실만 보도하게 되고, 군사시설 피해 상황등
    불리한 사실 보도는 금지당함.

  - 방송 매체는 활자 매체와 달리 반복 보도를 통해 특정 주장의
    선전 수단으로 악용될 수 있으므로 편집자나 앵커는 뉴스의
    보도 가치를 판단하여 취사 선택하여야 함.

o 부쉬 대통령은 이라크의 군사 시설 피해 상황을 밝힘으로써
  이러한 후세인의 전략에 대응해야 함.

- 4 -

0090

3. 분석기사

가. <u>Thomas L. Friedman (NYT, 2.7자)</u>

<u>베이커 국무장관이 밝힌 전후 걸프 구상</u>

o 베이커 미 국무장관이 하원 외교분과 위원회에서 전후 걸프지역
  에서의 미군사력 주둔과 이라크 복구사업을 골자로 한 미행정부의
  전후정세 구상을 걸프사태 발발후 최초로 발표

  - 이는 어떤 형태이든 후세인의 제거를 전제로 한 구상으로
    보임.

o 전후 구상은 기본적으로 5가지 주요 사안을 근간으로 함.

  - 걸프지역 세력균형과 상호 침략 방지를 위한 안전 보장
    장치 마련

  - 화생방 무기의 공급 차단을 포함한 군축 협상

  - 역내국간의 빈부격차 해소를 위한 경제 재건 계획

  - 팔레스타인 문제 및 아랍-이스라엘 분쟁 해결 노력

  - 미국의 중동 석유 의존도를 낮추는 정책 추구

o 상기의 구상은 미의회, 이라크 국민과 아랍 세계를 겨냥한
  포석으로 보임.

  - 미 행정부가 군사적 성공을 정치적 승리로 이끌 준비가 미진
    하다는 의회의 우려 불식

- 5 -

0091

- 미국 및 다국적군의 공격 목표는 후세인이며 이라크 국민이
  아님을 현시

- 아랍, 이스라엘 분쟁 문제등을 아랍세계 국가들과 협의해 풀어
  갈 의사가 있음을 시사

o 베이커 국무장관은 걸프지역의 안전보장 장치는 걸프협력 회의
  등과 같이 역내 국가전체의 참여를 기반으로 해야 하며, 전후
  걸프협력 회의나 UN 산하의 지상군 유지 가능성을 밝히고,
  국경 보장을 위해서 미국이 걸프지역에 해, 공군력을 주둔시킬
  수 있음을 암시함.

나. Opinion (모로코 일간지 2, 8자)

미국의 신 국제질서

o 베이커 미국무장관이 밝힌 전후 처리 구상은 과거 미국 주도하의
  중동방위조약기구인 '바그다드 협정'의 새로운 개정판으로 다음과
  같은 문제점이 있음.

- 팔레스타인 문제에 관한 해결책을 구체적으로 언급하지 않고
  다만 이스라엘과 인접 아랍국간의 화해만 강구하고 있음.

- 지역 안보를 위한 유엔 감독하의 지상군 주둔 제의는 유엔을
  통한 미국의 중동 지배, 이란의 역할 강화, 아랍국의 독립
  제한 및 이스라엘의 안전보장을 목적으로 함.

- 이집트나 시리아에 대한 언급이 없어, 정세 변화에 따라
  군사 강국인 이들이 제2의 이라크가 될 수도 있다는 것을
  간과함.

- 이스라엘의 군비나 핵무기 보유에 관해 침묵함으로써 이스라엘에
  미국의 신 국제질서를 방어하는 역할을 부여하려함.   - 끝 -

73

걸프 事態 關聯 世界 主要 言論 報道 分析

1991. 2. 12.

外 務 部

(美 洲 局)

0093

1. 사설

┌─ 참 고 ──────────────────────────────────────┐
│ CSM (Christian Science Monitor) WSJ (Wall Street Journal) │
└──┘

WSJ (2. 11자)

애 국 심

o 걸프전을 기화로 노란 리본과 성조기로 상징되는 미국의 애국심을
  강조하는 분위기가 팽배함.

o 미국 문화는 비판적인 지식인 엘리트 계층이 대중 여론을 주도
  하는 전통을 유지하였으나, 월납전이후 지식인 계층의 시각이
  부정적으로 변함.

  - 애국심, 성조기는 제국주의적 팽창을 상징하는 우익 보수
    주의자들에게 해당되는 말로써 지지할 수 없다고 인식.

  - 미국의 지식인들은 미국이 국내외적으로 많은 문제점을 안고
    침몰해 가고 있다고 보고, 미국이 보유한 잠재력과 우수한
    자원에 대한 평가를 거부.

  - 그레나다 침공에 대해 지식인층은 자조적, 비판적 자세.

o 걸프전을 계기로 이러한 편향적인 시각에서 벗어나, 지난
  25년간 무시되었던 미국인의 자신감과 애국심을 회복해야 함.

- 1 -

0094

2. 본석기사

가. <u>John Dillin (CSM 2.11자)</u>

공화당, 92년 선거에서 우세 기대

o 공화당 중진들은 걸프전쟁이 내년 선거에서 공화당에 상당한
   정치적 이익을 가져다 줄 것으로 기대

   - 민주당이 반대했던 걸프전쟁에 대한 광범위한 국민적 지지

   - 부쉬 대통령의 탁월한 전쟁 수행 능력

   - 공화당이 주도한 80년대 국방력 증강 계획(패트리어트 미사일,
     스텔스 전폭기 등)이 금번 전쟁의 성공적 수행에 결정적 기여

o 공화당 의원들은 부쉬대통령의 걸프전 수행 자세를 지지하나,
   세금증액등 국내문제에서 민주당에 보인 타협적 태도에는 불만
   을 표시

   - 냉전 체제 붕괴등으로 보수주의 정책 기반을 상실함으로써
     내년 선거에서는 마약문제, 국방력 강화등을 핵심 이슈로
     부각시켜야 한다는 주장 대두

o 공화당의 Phil Gramm 상원의원은 내년 선거에서 공화당이 부각
   시켜야 할 이슈를 다음과 같이 제시

   - 걸프전쟁과 국방력 강화에 대한 민주당의 소극적 자세 비난

   - 중동평화 정착에 미국이 주도적 역할 담당

   - 제3세계에 개혁 자본주의 수출

- 2 -

0095

- 멕시코를 포함한 세계 최대의 북미 자유무역권 형성

- 남미를 포함하는 전체 미주대륙 자유무역협정 추진

나. C.Walker, M. Dejevsky (The Times 2.11자)

지상전 연기론 대두와 소련의 평화 중재 움직임

o 고르바쵸프 소련 대통령 특사 '프리마쾨프'가 유엔 안보리
  개최(2.13)를 앞두고 2.9일 저녁, 후세인의 쿠웨이트 철수를
  설득키 위한 새로운 외교적 노력의 일환으로 바그다드로 향발함.

o 반면, 부쉬대통령은 최근 걸프지역을 방문하고 돌아온 체니
  국방장관과 파웰 합참의장으로 부터 전면적인 지상전 개시
  시기를 연기하도록 건의 받은 것으로 보임.

o 사상자수 극소화, 악전후에 따른 보급품의 해상 수송상의 애로,
  선원들의 사우디 항해 거부 움직임으로 현지 지휘관들은
  지상전 연기를 건의하고 있으며, 또한 시리아, 사우디, 이집트도
  준비가 완료되기 이전에 지상전 개시를 원치 않고 있음.

o 이와같이, 지상전 연기 압력이 있으나, 체니 국방장관은 공중
  폭격에만 장기적으로 의존하는 것도 반대하고 있는 바, 부쉬
  대통령에게 브리핑시 2월말경 지상전 개시를 건의할 것으로
  예상됨.

- 끝 -

- 3 -

0096

걸프 事態 關聯 世界 主要 言論 報道 分析

1991. 2. 13.

外　　務　　部

(美　洲　局)

0097

1. 사 설

WSJ (2. 12자)

동구와 걸프 전쟁

o 걸프전쟁에서 동구 국가들은 일관된 다국적군 지지 입장을 보입
   으로써 향후 동구 국가들의 대외 정책 기조를 제시함.

   - 동구의 압도적인 걸프전 지지 여론은 서구의 이중적 태도와는
      대조적

   - 체코는 사우디에 화학전 전문 요원 파견

   - 헝가리와 폴란드는 의료요원 파견

   - 루마니아, 불가리아는 걸프전 지지 표명

o 걸프사태로 인한 초기의 유가상승과 대 이라크 무역손실에 따른
   경제적 어려움을 감안한다면, 동구의 걸프전 지지 여론은 특기
   할만함.

   - 이는 독재와 억압에 민감한 동구의 정치적 현실 반영한
      것으로 역사적 체험을 바탕으로한 동구의 대외 정책은 향후
      국제정치에 크게 기여할 것으로 기대

- 1 -

0098

2. 기고문

<u>A.M. Rosenthal (NYT 2.12자)</u>

<u>모스크바와 바그다드</u>

o 걸프전쟁이 아직 종결되지 않았음에도 전후 평화 구상을 위요한
  미.소의 경쟁이 시작됨. 고르바쵸프가 이러한 신호를 보내고
  있음.

  - 후세인을 정치적으로 지원, 실제 비용의 지불없이 걸프
    지역에서의 영향력 유지

  - 다국적군의 대 이라크 공중폭격은 유엔이 승인한 쿠웨이트
    해방 범주를 벗어난 것이라고 미국에 경고

o 고르바쵸프는 유엔 결의를 벗어난 후세인 제거 시도에 반대할
  것이라는 또다른 신호를 보내고 있으며, 부쉬 대통령은 후세인
  제거후의 중동평화를 구상하고 있음.

3. 분석기사

가. <u>Edward Cody (WP 2.12자)</u>

<u>망명정부, 전후 쿠웨이트 재건 논의 시작</u>

o 쿠웨이트 망명 정부는 전후 쿠웨이트 사회의 재건 방향에 관해
  논의

  - 쿠웨이트 고위 관리들은 걸프사태가 쿠웨이트 정치 구조를
    근본적으로 흔들어 놓았으나, 전후의 민주화 및 개혁에 관해
    아직 구체적으로 결정된 바는 없음을 시인

- 2 -

0099

o 부쉬 행정부와 UN 결의는 알사바 왕가의 복귀를 걸프 전쟁의
  주목적으로 천명한 바 있으나, 이라크 점령기간중 쿠웨이트
  에서 새로운 정치 세력이 부각 되었으며, 왕가는 이들 세력과
  협상해야 할 것이라는 의견이 상당수 존재함.

  - 이와함께 '86년 해산된 의회에 더 많은 권력이양을 요구해온
    쿠웨이트 야당 지도자들의 정치적 입지 강화 예상

o 쿠웨이트의 Mutawa 기획장관은 이라크의 쿠웨이트 침공 및 PLO의
  이라크 지지로 인해 전후 전통적인 아랍 형제국가 개념은 재고될
  것이라고 주장

  - 망명정부는 걸프사태 이전에 국가기관.산업시설등에 고용되었던
    팔레스타인인들과 여타 외국인들을 대체하는 방안 검토

나. Marshall Ingwerson (CSM 2. 12자)

지상전 전개의 한계

o 지상전 개시가 임박한 가운데 부쉬 대통령은 지상전을 쿠웨이트
  해방에 한정시킬 것인지, 이라크 본토까지 진격할 것인지를
  결정할 문제에 직면함

  - 쿠웨이트 해방으로 제한할 경우, 후세인의 잔류 군사력이
    여전히 위협으로 작용

  - 이라크 본토 진격은 전쟁 목적 확대 비난과 사상자수 증가로
    걸프전에 대한 지지 상실 우려

- 3 -

0100

o 미국은 이라크 군의 쿠웨이트 철수를 위한 실질적 조치가 선행
  되지 않는다면, 현재 소련, 이란 및 회교국간에 다각적으로 논의
  되고 있는 중재안들을 거부할 것으로 예상

  - 전문가들은 후세인이 자진 철수를 거부하고 다국적군에 최대한의
    피해를 줌으로써 정치적 승리를 시도하고 있다고 관측

o 후세인이 생화학 무기를 사용하거나 쿠웨이트 철수후에도 주변
  국에 공격을 계속한다면 다국적군이 이라크 본토로 진격할
  명분을 얻게 될 것이나 이의 실행은 상당한 정치적 모험이 될
  것임.

  - 전쟁을 쿠웨이트 해방에 한정한다면, 전후 미군이 주변 아랍국에
    계속 주둔해야 하며, 이라크를 점령한다면 미군이 이라크 보호
    를 위해 주둔해야 하는 상황 발생

o 지난주 발표된 베이커 구상은 전후 후세인이 권력을 유지하는 경우
  에도 대 이라크 경제 제재를 계속함으로써 그의 정치적 생명을
  단축시킬 수 있음을 시사

                              - 끝 -

                    - 4 -

                   0101

걸프 事態 關聯 世界 主要 言論 報道 分析

1991. 2. 18.

外 務 部

(美 洲 局)

0102

1. 사 설

가. WP (2. 16자)

대 이라크 군사 압력 계속 필요

o 이라크가 내세운 쿠웨이트 철군 조건은 이라크가 전쟁에서 승리할
   경우에나 가능한 것들임.

o 아지즈 이라크 외상의 모스크바 방문은 이라크의 의도를 파악하는
   기회는 될수 있으나, 이는 단지 다국적군의 결속을 와해하고
   시간적 여유를 벌기 위한 것임.

o 미국 주도하의 다국적군은 후세인이 전략을 바꾸도록 계속 군사적
   압력을 행사해야 함.

나. NYT (2. 16자)

이라크가 평화를 원한다면

o 이라크의 조건부 쿠웨이트 철군 제의는 다국적군의 분열을
   조장하려는 것으로 진정한 협상 의도가 없음.

- 1 -

0103

o 후세인이 평화를 원한다면, 무조건 철수 의사를 명백히 하고, 철수를 즉시 실행해야 함.

다. NYT (2.17자)

후세인의 생존 전략

o 후세인의 쿠웨이트 철수 제의는 다국적군의 결속을 와해시키기 위한 것임.

  - 다국적군의 지상전 개시 연기 의도
  - 장기적으로는 협상 시도
  - 도덕적 승리와 군사력 보유로 계속 집권

o 군사적으로 불리한 것을 알고 있는 후세인이 이러한 제의를 한 배경을 살펴보면, 그동안 왜 생화학 무기를 사용치 못하고, 테러리스트 동원이 미비 했는지를 알수 있음.

o 철군 제의 이후 이스라엘 및 사우디에 계속된 스커드 미사일 공격은 이스라엘의 참전 유도와 여타 제3세계 아랍국가의 여론을 겨냥한 것이나, 후세인의 전략에 피할수 없는 결함이 있음.

  - 전투기의 대 이란 대피로 과거 이.이전 승리 주장 기반 상실

  - 쿠웨이트를 포기한다면, 국내 지지 기반 상실

o 후세인은 생존을 위해 계속 교활한 수단을 사용할 것임.

- 2 -

0104

2. 기고문

가. Jeffrey Smith 및 Barton Gellman (WP 2.16자)

미국, 이라크 신속한 철수 요구

o 미국 관리들은 쿠웨이트내 이라크군이 군장비와 보급품을 현위치
  에서 포기하고, 신속하고 확실하게(Speedy and unequivocal)
  철수할 것을 요구

  - 국무부 대변인 : 가시적, 전면적이며 확실한 철군
                      (Visible, Massive and Unequivocal)

  - 국방성 대변인 : 이라크의 안전한 철수 보장을 위한 교섭은
                      이라크가 미국의 요구를 무조건 승락할때
                      가능

o 미국과 연합국측 외교 소식통은 철수 절차 문제와 관련, 이라크와의
  교섭 및 유엔 옵서버에 의한 감시가 있어야 한다고 말하고 있어
  궁극적으로 유엔 평화 유지군의 휴전 감시를 시사함.

나. Tom Wicker (NYT 2.16자)

아랍인이 본 걸프 전쟁

o 후세인은 군사적으로 심각한 타격을 입었으나, 정치적으로는 아랍
  세계와 유럽, 소련의 지지를 획득해 감으로써 미국 및 다국적군의
  구상대로 장래 평화를 구축하는 것을 어렵게 하고 있음.

- 3 -

o 민간 시설물에 대한 공습 선전과 조건부 철군 제의는 미국내
　여론이 아니라 시리아, 이집트, 사우디등 다국적군 참가국 및
　여타 아랍국의 대중 여론을 겨냥한 것임.

- 사우디, 민간인 희생자 보도를 제한

- 미국의 공습에 대한 시리아, 이집트내의 여론 악화

o 아랍인들의 여론을 감안한다면, 후세인의 철군 제의를 진지하게
　검토할 필요가 있었음.

- 이라크의 제의를 일축하고 공습을 계속하는 미국의 행동은 아랍인
　들에게 후세인과 이라크를 파괴하려는 의도로 비추어짐으로써,
　반미 감정을 증폭시키고 다국적군의 결속을 동요시킬 우려

다. Jim Hoagland(WP 2,17자)

후세인 대통령의 무력화

o 이라크의 휴전 제의는 후세인 대통령의 무력화를 입증

- 쿠웨이트에서의 전쟁은 미국 공군력에 의해 이미 판가름

- 다국적군의 폭격으로 이라크의 통신 체계 및 특히 후세인
　대통령의 비밀 경찰 조직인 정보부(Directorate of General
　Intelligence)의 기동력이 마비

- 휴전제의 소식에 기뻐하는 이라크인들은 후세인 대통령을
　지지, 찬양만 하는 존재가 아님을 나타냄.

o 이라크의 휴전 제의에 대한 부쉬 대통령의 대응은, 다국적군의
　목표가 후세인 제거에 있음을 암시

- 4 -

0106

- 후세인은 쿠웨이트에서 철수하더라도 이라크내에서 권력 유지를 희망

- 쿠웨이트에서 뿐 아니라 이라크에서도 후세인은 제거되어야 함.

3. 분석기사

가. <u>Richard Morin (WP 2.16자)</u>

<u>민간인 희생자 발생에 대한 여론 조사 결과</u>

ㅇ 최근 Washington Post와 ABC 방송이 공동실시한 여론조사에서 절대다수가 미국의 공습으로 인한 이라크 민간인 희생자 발생의 책임은 이라크에 있다고 믿고 있으며, 걸프전쟁을 지지하는 것으로 나타남.

- 미국의 공습으로 다수 민간인 사상자를 낸 건물은 군사시설물

- 민간인 희생자 발생 가능성에도 불구하고 공습은 계속 필요

- 미국 기자들의 이라크내 활동에 대해 43%가 찬성, 48%가 반대 의사를 표시

ㅇ 이는 현재 걸프전을 수행에 있어 미국내의 분위기를 반영하는 것으로, 2차대전 당시와 유사한 현상이라고 전문가들이 분석

- 월남전, 한국전과는 달리 전쟁의 목적이 분명

- 전쟁 지지자의 다수 의견은 지상전이 불가피하다고 봄.

- 5 -

0107

나. <u>Glenn Frankel (WP 2.17자)</u>

아랍 동맹국들의 전후 중동 안보 구상

o 반 이라크 전선에 가담중인 아랍 8개국 외무장관 회담에서 전후 중동 안보를 위한 정치. 경제 구상 제시

   - 동 제안들은 전후의 안보 구상을 최초로 구체화 시켰다는 의미 내포

o 아랍 소식통은 회담후 발표된 성명를 토대로 8개국 외무장관들이 몇가지 기본 사항에 합의한 것으로 분석

   - 이라크의 무조건적인 쿠웨이트 철수, 전후 걸프 평화유지군 운영, 전후 150억불 상당의 걸프 개발 기금 설치 등

   - 평화유지군은 1만명 이상의 이집트, 시리아, 사우디군으로 구성

   - 걸프전 참가 서방제국의 지상군은 철수하되 해. 공군은 계속 주둔 가능

   - 걸프개발 기금은 역내 국가간의 경제적 불균등을 해소하기 위한 것이나 대부분의 자금이 이집트, 시리아등에 할당될 가능성이 높음.

o 걸프전에서 PLO의 대이라크 지지 때문에 금번 외상회담 성명에서 PLO에 대한 언급이 누락되었고, 이스라엘이 반대해온 국제 평화 회의에 대한 언급이 없다는 점이 특징임.

- 6 -

0108

- 아랍 외무장관들은 PLO가 팔레스타인 자치 운동의 명분에
  손상을 입힌 것으로 지적

- 중동지역의 군축과 이의 아랍.이스라엘 분쟁 해결 연계를
  제안

다. Hoffman & D. Balz (Wp 2.17자)

미국, 이라크 제의에 대한 소련의 거부 기대

o 부쉬 대통령은 고르바쵸프-아지즈간 회담에서 소련이 이라크와
  타협하지 않고, 이라크군의 무조건 철수라는 UN 결의를 요구할
  것으로 확신하며, 고르바쵸프로 부터 이를 보장 받았음을 표명

o 고르바쵸프는 걸프사태를 정치적.외교적 방법으로 해결할 여지가
  남아 있음을 강조

- 미국 전략가들은 동 회담이 이라크의 성실성에 대한 시험대인
  동시에, 국내 보수파와 다국적군측으로 부터의 압력에 직면한
  고르바쵸프에 대한 도전이 될 것으로 평가

라. Thomas L. Friedman (NYT 2.17자)

후세인, 최초의 양보 암시

o 후세인은 자신의 약점을 은폐하고, 현재의 입장에서 후퇴함으로써
  얻어낼수 있는 댓가를 타진해 보기 위해 여러가지 조건을 내걸은
  평화협상을 제안하였으나, 그 자체가 하나의 양보인 것을 부인할
  수 없음.

- 7 -

0109

o 중동전문가들은 후세인이 비록 지상전에서 패배하더라도, 서방
   세계에 도전하여 수천명의 사상자를 주게되면 아랍세계에서 영웅
   으로 찬양 받을 것으로 믿고 있다고 말해 왔으나, 금번 전쟁에서
   어떤 것을 얻어 냈다고 국민들에게 보여 주지 못하면, 정치적
   위기에 직면 예상

o 이러한 사실이 후세인이 평화제안에서 이라크의 철수를 이스라엘의
   점령지역에서 철수와 연계시키고, 걸프전 참전국들이 이라크에 가한
   피해를 복구해야 한다고 요구한 배경임.

o 프리마코프 소련특사의 방문을 통해 금번 이라크의 제의를 유도한
   소련조차도, 최초에는 환영하였으나 제의내용에 대해 냉담한 자세를
   보임.

   - 소련은 어느정도 독자적 행동을 보여 주려 하고 있으나, 후세인이
      자기 자신을 구할 준비가 안되어 있으면 소련은 서방국가와
      소원해 지는 것을 원치 않을 것임.

                                            - 끝 -

                        - 8 -

                                        0110

걸프 事態 關聯 世界 主要 言論 報道 分析

1991. 2. 19.

外　　務　　部

(美　洲　局)

0111

1. 사설 (WP 2.18자)

```
  참    고

NYT (New York Times)          WP (Washington Post)
```

전후 미국과 이스라엘 관계

o 팔레스타인 문제를 위요한 미.이스라엘간의 갈등이 걸프전에서 양국간
   고도의 전략적 협력으로 극복됨

   - 이스라엘 : 이라크의 스커드 미사일 공격에 대해 보복 자제

   - 미   국 : 이스라엘에 페이트리어트 요격 미사일 제공

o 미국과 이스라엘은 전후 전개될 아랍-이스라엘 분쟁의 새로운 국면에
   예의 주시 하고 있음.

   - 미국은 아랍측 요구의 수용 필요성 인정

   - 이스라엘은 자신의 의사에 반하는 미측 요구에 강경 입장

o 이스라엘이 미국의 동맹국이며, 이라크에 안보 위협을 받고 있으나,
   전후 어떤 형태이든 팔레스타인 문제가 다루어져야 함.

   - 이스라엘-팔레스타인간의 공존을 위한 시도가 필요하며, 미국은
     이를위해 적극적인 역할을 해야 함.

- 1 -

0112

2. 기고문

가. William Safire (WP 2.18자)

고르바쵸프의 지상전 재촉

o 최근 소련이 걸프전 중재에 적극 개입하는 이유는 후세인에 명분
   을 주고, 다국적군의 완전한 승리를 저지하는데 있으며, 이는
   지상전 개시를 앞당기게 할 것임.

   - 소련은 중동에서의 서방 세력 확장에 반대, 향후 무기 판매를
     위해 후세인의 권력 유지 희망

o 미국은 소련의 중재역할로 이라크를 외교적으로 보호하게 될
   가능성을 우려, 지상전을 조기에 개시해야 할 입장에 처함.

   - 미국은 공습을 계속함으로써, 이라크 군사력을 무력화 하고,
     인명피해를 최소화 할수 있으나 소련의 개입으로 조기 지상전
     유혹을 받음.

   - 고르바쵸프의 의도대로 걸프전이 전개될 우려가 있음.

나. Anthony Lewis (NYT 2.18자)

종전 게임의 시작

o 후세인이 최초로 철군 가능성을 언급한 사실은 걸프전 종식을
   위한 게임이 개시 되었음을 의미하며, 가능한 조속한 전쟁
   종결은 미국의 이익을 극대화하는 것임.

   - 현재 다국적군의 결속, 소련의 협조와 이란의중립 유지

- 2 -

0113

- 아랍세계의 여론 악화에도 불구, 반 이라크 아랍국들의 결속
  건재

- 전쟁이 금후 1개월 이상 장기화되면 사상자 증가와 아랍세계의
  반서방 감정 심화로 미국 이익의 손상 우려

o 걸프전을 장기화 시키지 않고, 이라크군의 쿠웨이트 철수라는 목적
  을 달성하기 위해서는 이라크에게 선택의 여지를 남겨두어야 함.

o 전쟁목적을 쿠웨이트 해방 이상으로 확대하자는 여론이 있으나,
  이는 걸프지역에 반미 분위기를 고착시키는 정치적 손실을 초래
  할 것임.

o 미국은 바그다드 공습을 중단하고 쿠웨이트내 이라크군에 대해서만
  공습을 집중함으로써 정치적, 도덕적 부담을 최소화해야 함.

다. <u>Jeane Kirkpatrick (WP 2, 18자)</u>

<u>후세인의 사기극</u>

o 후세인은 적의 의지력 약화가 중요하다는 것을 알고, 2, 15, 평화
  제의를 통해 적을 분열시키며, 이라크를 희생자로 부각시키려고
  시도함.

- 쿠웨이트 철수 조건으로 제시한 사항들의 비현실성

- 걸프위기는 이라크의 쿠웨이트 점령이 아니라, 미제국주의와
  시오니즘의 패권주의 시도가 원인이라고 주장

- 소련의 중재 노력 평가, 골란고원 반환을 요구함으로써 시리아의
  환심 유도등으로 다국적군 분열시도

- 3 -

0114

- 이라크를 아랍세계의 '역사적 권리' 회복만을 원하는 침략의
  희생자로 부각

o 후세인은 대서방 비난이 담긴 금번 평화제의를 통해 미국의 목표와
  안목을 시험하고 있으며, 걸프전이 의지력의 싸움인 것을 재확인
  시켰음.

- 끝 -

- 4 -

걸프 事態 關聯 世界 主要 言論 報道 分析

1991. 2. 28.

外　　務　　部

(美　洲　局)

0116

1. 사설 (WP 2. 19자)

┌─ 참 고 ───┐
│ NYT (New York Times)   WP (Washington Post) │
└──┘

고르바쵸프의 제안

o 고르바쵸프의 제안은 걸프지역에서 미국의 계속되는 영향력
  확대를 방지하고, 전후 걸프재건에 있어 소련의 역활과 이익을
  강화코저 하는데 목적이 있음.

  - 철군 촉진을 위해 후세인의 체면을 살려 주어야 한다고 하나,
    이는 다국적군의 목적과 다름.

  - 미국은 일방적으로 제시된 소련의 제안에 구속될 수 없음.

o 소련은 정치, 군사적 능력을 활용, 이라크로 하여금 철군하도록
  압력을 가해야 하며, 이라크가 외교 선전을 통해 시간여유를 갖고
  전열을 재정비토록 허용해서는 안됨.

  - 걸프전을 위요한 미. 소간의 경쟁이 심화되고 있으나 아직은
    서로 협조할 여지가 있음.

- 1 -

0117

2. 기고문

A.M. Rosenthal(NYT 2.19)

소련-이라크 동맹(Soviet-Irak Axis)

o 고르바쵸프와 사담 후세인은 중동에서 잃었던 세력을 만회하고
  국내적으로 생존하려는 공동 목표를 가지고 모스크바-바그다드
  동맹(Moscow-Baghdad Axis)을 형성하고 있음.

- 양국의 동맹관계는 전부터 유지되어왔고, 이라크의 쿠웨이트
  점령 이후에도 변합이 없으며, 고르바쵸프의 특사는 정치적
  으로 이라크을 위해 활동했음.

- 고르바쵸프와 후세인이 추구하는 것은 중동 평화가 아니라
  그들 자신의 생존과 권력 유지임.

o 금번 전쟁에서 후세인은 패배할 것이나, 군사력을 유지, 계속
  위험스런 인물이 될것이며, 소련은 이라크에 대한 군사지원
  기회를 노릴것임. 그러나 미국은 쿠웨이트 해방을 위한 원래
  군사작전 계획대로 전쟁을 수행해야 함.

- 2 -

0118

3. 분석기사

<u>William Drozdiak (WP 2, 19자)</u>

<u>걸프전에서 유럽의 분열</u>

o 걸프전에서 구주 각국의 정책상 균열은 향후 구주 공동안보 체제 형성에 문제를 제기

o 유럽은 걸프전에서 소극적이며, 이기적 행동으로 향후 유럽 안보를 미국에 의지하기 어렵게 됨.

  - 중동 석유에 대한 의존도가 높은 유럽이 걸프 사태 해결에 적극적 역할을 기피

  - 영.불의 참전도 실제로는 걸프지역에서의 자국 영향력 확보 목적

- 끝 -

- 3 -

걸프 事態 關聯 世界 主要 言論 報道 分析

1991. 2. 25.

外　　務　　部

(美　洲　局)

0120

1. 사설 (NYT, 2.24자)

┌─── 참 고 ──────────────────────────────────────┐
│ NYT (New York Times)   WP (Washington Post) │
└───┘

지상전의 범위 제한

o 미국은 지상전을 신속히 완료해야 하며 지상전의 목표를 제한 하는
  것이 미국의 장기적 이익에 부합

  - 이라크의 완전 파괴는 전후 이란.시리아등 주변국에 대한 이라크
    의 위치를 과도하게 약화시켜 지역 안정에 역행

  - 이라크 완전 점령은 전후 이라크 재건에 대한 미국의 개입을
    불가피하게 장기화할 가능성

  - 미국의 이라크 점령시, 소련내 보수파를 자극하여 미.소간의
    새로운 긴장 조성 우려

o 따라서, 미국은 당초의 전쟁 목표를 고수 해야 합.

- 1 -

0121

2. 기고문

가. <u>Thomas Friedman (NYT, 2.24자)</u>

<u>불확실한 장래</u>

o 미국은 외교정책에서의 도덕적 선명성을 내세워 쿠웨이트 해방을
  위해 후세인과 전쟁을 하고 있으나, 중동지역은 다양한 역사적
  내부갈등이 내재된 곳으로 도덕적 선명성 보다는 전후 중동
  질서에 관한 확고한 정책 수립에 더 관심을 기울여야 함.

  - 전후 질서와 관련, 미국의 아랍 동맹국들은 신질서 수립
    보다는 전쟁이전 상태로의 현상유지를 희망함.

  - 미국은 전후 중동지역의 경제적 불평등 해소를 원하나
    전후 복구와 아랍 내부 분열로 인해 역내 부국들의 협조
    난망

  - 미국 주도하 아랍제국의 반 이라크 전선 형성은 자국의
    생존과 이익을 위한 것으로, 전후 아랍-이스라엘 문제
    해결에서의 동일한 협조 가능성은 희박

  - PLO의 팔레스타인 대표권에 관한 미국 및 아랍제국의
    회의적 시각이 걸프전을 계기로 더욱 심화됨.

  - 냉전 종식에도 불구, 걸프전 협상 과정에서 미.소의 경쟁
    관계가 상존함이 입증됨.

- 2 -

0122

나. <u>Richard Cohen (WP 2. 24자)</u>

지연 전술

o 과거 월남전과 한국전에서 평화협상 지연으로 많은 희생자가
   발생했던 경험을 잘 기억하고 있는 다국적군은 단지 시간을
   벌기 위한 이라크측의 평화협상에는 응하지 않겠다는 입장임.

   - 이라크는 자신의 휴전안을 제시하고, 소련의 중재안에 동의
     하는등 평화적 해결을 제안하였으나, '쿠웨이트로 부터 신속한
     철수'라는 유엔의 기본 요구사항에 부합되지 않기 때문에
     어느것도 받아들일수 없는 것임.

o 후세인은 어떠한 단계에서 철수를 한다해도 쿠웨이트 영토 점령
   을 위해 전쟁을 다시 시도 할 것이므로 이라크의 평화제의를
   단지 지연 전술로 간주하는 것은 당연함.

다. <u>Peter Tarnoff (NYT 2. 24자)</u>

현 상태에서 전쟁 종결 필요

o 부쉬 대통령은 다국적군이 이미 승리하였음을 인정하고 전쟁을
   조기 종결 해야함.

   - 후세인은 쿠웨이트를 사실상 포기
   - 이라크의 경제. 군사 시설 상당 부분 파괴
   - 다국적군과 미국민은 부쉬대통령 강력 지지
   - 소련은 서방세계와의 경제협력이 필요함으로 인해 후세인을
     최후까지 지원하기는 곤란

o 단지 휴전 조건을 유리하게 이끌기 위한 지상전의 연장은 인명
   손실만 크게 초래할 것임.   - 끝 -

- 3 -

0123

건우

걸프 事態 關聯 世界 主要 言論 報道 分析

1991. 2. 26.

外 務 部

(美 洲 局)

0124

1. 사설

```
┌─ 참  고 ──────────────────────────────────────┐
│                                               │
│  NYT (New York Times)          WP (Washington Post)  │
│                                               │
└───────────────────────────────────────────────┘
```

가. NYT (2.25자)

전쟁에 따른 외교적 손실

o 순조로운 지상전 전개에도 불구, 미국은 걸프전에서 소련과의
   마찰로 인해 외교적 손실을 감수하게 됨.

   - 미국은 후세인을 생존시키려는 소련의 중재 태도에 불만

o 고르바쵸프는 중동지역에서 미국의 주도권 저지를 바라는 강경
   세력과 대서방 협력 필요성 사이에서 균형을 유지하는데 부심
   하고 있으나, 결과적으로 유엔 안보리 결의 채택과 대 이라크
   압력 행사등에서 미국을 지원함.

o 후세인의 재무장 방지와 중동 정세 안정을 위해서는 소련의
   협조가 필수적이므로 미국은 고르바쵸프에 대한 비난을 자제하고,
   소련의 이익을 고려해 줌으로써 걸프전으로 인한 외교적 손실을
   최소화 해야 함.

- 1 -

0125

나. **WP (2, 25자)**

지상전

o 반 이라크 다국적군의 형성 및 지상전 참가를 가능케 한 미국의
   외교 노력을 높이 평가되며, 부쉬 대통령은 유엔 결의 채택과 다국적군
   결성 과정에서 미국의 주도권을 균형있게 행사하고 있음.

   - 중립적인 프랑스가 공습 개시후, 적극적인 미국 지지로 선회

   - 무력 사용에 대한 소련측의 지지를 확보

o 미국은 후세인을 존속시키려는 소련의 중재안을 거부하면서도
   소련과의 충돌을 피하기 위해 노력

   - 이라크의 현실 인정과 유엔 결의 준수를 촉구하는 국제사회의
     노력이 실패했음이 입증된 시점에서 지상전 개시

2. 기고문

가. **William Safire (NYT, 2, 25자)**

4가지 선의의 거짓말

o 이라크의 소련 제안 수락 에도 불구하고, 미국이 지상전을
   시도할 경우 다국적군의 분열과 세계여론의 비난을 초래할
   것이라고 한 세계 언론의 관측은 오산이었으며, 여론은
   '부쉬'를 지지하고 있음.

- 2 -

0126

o 이와관련 진실을 가리고 있는 다음의 악의없는 거짓말을 분석해볼
  필요가 있음.

  - 후세인을 구하려는 고르바쵸프의 시도는 '유용' 했다는 표현

  - 전쟁 목표는 쿠웨이트 해방이지 후세인의 제거가 아니라는 주장

  - 유엔 안보리가 다국적군을 통제한다는 주장

  - 지상전이 개시되면 이라크군의 치열한 저항이 예상된다는 주장

o 이와같은 선의의 거짓말은 외교적 또는 전술적 목표가 있는
  것이나, 패배의 목전에서 국민에게 승리를 장담하는 후세인의
  말은 악의의 거짓말인 바, 전후에 전법재판 대신 후세인의
  운명을 이라크 국민의 손에 맡길수 있을 것임.

나. <u>Anthony Lewis (NYT 2, 25자)</u>

<u>전후 평화에 대한 기원</u>

                                              2

o 걸프전 이후 중동이 정치적으로 더욱 안정되고, <u>진보된 지역이</u>
  될 것인지에 대하여 긍정적인 답변을 하기 어려움.

  - 전후 이라크에 합리적인 정권이 수립되어 인근국가와 선린
    관계를 유지할 것으로 기대하는 것은 환상임.

- 3 -

0127

- 국민의 동의 없이 통치하여온 쿠웨이트 왕족에 대한 향후
  태도가 불투명

- 미군의 철수가 정치적으로 바람직하고 시급한 문제이나,
  이는 전후 중동의 안보 체제와 관련되는 문제로 미군의
  개입보다 더 미묘한 사항임.

- PLO의 대이라크 지지, 이스라엘 정부의 극우성향 강화등
  제반 환경을 고려할때 금번 전쟁으로 인해 중동문제 해결이
  어려워 질 것으로 우려됨.

o 미국민들이 군사력으로 세계문제를 해결할 수 있다고 생각하여,
  군수 산업발전을 위해 민간부문의 연구발전을 소홀히 한다면
  이는 큰 재난이 될 것임.

다. Stanley Hoffmann (NYT 2.25자)

무질서의 방지

o 지상전의 압승 전망에 따라 전후 질서에 대한 미국민의 자신감이
  증대되고 있으나, 냉전시대보다 더 혼란스러울 것으로 예상됨.

o 후세인의 쿠웨이트 점령과 같이 국내 정치의 갈등을 대외적으로
  해소하려는 시도를 예방하기 위해서는 그동안 도외시된 집단
  안보 형성 노력이 필요함.

- 역내의 세력 균형 달성과 전반적인 군축이 우선 요구됨.

- 4 -

0128

o 냉전종식이후 국제사회에서는 자국 이익 추구와 현상타파를
   목표로 국내의 정치적 갈등을 대외 진출로 연결시키려는
   행위가 증가할 것으로 보이나, 유엔이 항상 집단 행동을 주도해
   주기를 기대하기는 곤란함.

o 그러나, 신국제 질서의 수립을 위해서는 집단행동을 위한 구조
   마련이 필수적으로 요망됨.

                                        - 끝 -

                        - 5 -

                      0129

1991. 2. 27.

外　　務　　部

(美　　洲　　局)

0130

1. 기고문

┌─── 참 고 ──────────────────────────────────┐
│   │
│ WSJ (Wall Street Journal)   WP (Washington Post) │
│   │
└──┘

가. Henry Kissinger (WP 2. 26자)

세력균형을 통한 신국제 질서

o 미국은 제한적인 목적보다는 영구 평화의 이상실현을 위해 전쟁을
  수행해온 전통이 있으며, 금번 걸프전에서도 이를 기대하고 있으나
  이러한 이상 실현 여부는 의심스러움.

o 금번 걸프전에서 미국 주도하 다국적군의 결속과 유엔결의는
  각국의 이해관계에 따라 성립된 특수한 상황으로 다시 재현될 수
  없는 경우임.

  - 소련 : 국내문제 및 경제원조 획득 필요로 미국과 마찰 불원

  - 중국 : 동북아에서 일본, 소련의 견제 세력인 미국과의 관계
           고려

  - 시리아 및 이집트의 반후세인 전열은 중동내의 역사적 갈등과
    경쟁관계에 기인

- 1 -

0131

o 미국은 세계를 지배할 자원도 없고, 이는 미국의 가치에 부합되지
   않으므로 신국제 질서 형성에 있어 세력균형 정책으로 복귀해야
   합.

   - 걸프문제도 중동지역 국가간 세력 균형으로 해결

   - 동북아 역시 일. 중. 소의 세력 균형으로 안정 유지

o 미국은 국내 응집력, 경제적 자생력, 우월한 군사력을 바탕으로
   이러한 세력균형 추의 역할 답당할 수 있을 것임.

나. **Neg Greenfield (WP 2. 25자)**

          <u>고르바쵸프의 양면적인 면모</u>

o 걸프전을 계기로 고르바쵸프에 대한 미국민의 인식은 혼란을
   갖게 되었으나, 언론 매체는 그의 양면성을 단순한 기사거리로만
   보도할 뿐 현실을 반영하지 못함.

   - 고르바쵸프는 변화하고 분열하는 사회를 운영하는 현실
      정치가임.

o 미. 소의 이해관계가 일부 일치하고, 부쉬. 고르바쵸프 양인의
   교묘한 수단으로 걸프전 초기의 협력이 가능했으나, 종전
   단계에서는 고르바쵸프가 전후처리에 소련의 이익을 계산하여
   미. 소간의 갈등이 노정됨.

o 사실상 중동에서의 소련과 미국의 이익은 상호 부합될 수
   없으므로, 고르바쵸프를 단순한 흑백논리로 인식할 필요는 없음.

                    - 2 -

                              0132

다. <u>Mark Helprin (WSJ 2. 26자)</u>

걸프전의 교훈

o 걸프전에서 미국의 전략이 성공적이었다는 교훈을 얻었으나,
  향후 보다 어려운 상황에 적용될 중요한 교훈도 간과해서는
  안됨.

o 걸프전쟁으로 재래식 무기에만 의존한 유럽 방위가 어려워지고,
  핵무기 사용의 개연성이 높아짐.

  - 유럽 주둔 미군의 철수로 유사시 미군의 유럽 전개에 장기간이
    소요됨이 입증

  - 소련은 미군의 전개를 저지할 군사력 및 원거리 공격 수단
    보유

  - 소련의 공군력은 미군의 군사작전에 결정적 위협 요소

  - 미국의 사상자 발생을 최소화 하려는 전략 노출

o 지식인들은 무기의 호전성을 비난하면서도, 적국의 무기에
  대해서는 무감각 하므로, 금번 걸프전의 교훈을 냉정히 검토
  해야 함.

  - 이라크의 소련제 무기에 곤욕을 겪었음에도, 소련의 군축
    조약의 범주를 벗어난 소련의 보유 무기에 대해서는 무감각

- 3 -

0133

라. <u>Rowland Evans and Robert Novak(WP 2, 25자)</u>

<u>월남 후유증 탈피</u>

o 백악관이 소련의 평화중재에 우려했던 것도 석유나 이스라엘
  또는 이라크의 팽창주의 보다는 과거의 쓰라린 경험과 관련됨.
  즉 걸프전을 통해 월남 후유증에서 벗어나 미국이 전쟁에서
  승리할 수 있다는 것을 과시할 수 있는 기회임.

o 그러나, 부쉬 대통령은 고르바쵸프의 평화중재 노력에는
  '사의를 표명'하는 부드러움을 보였는 바, 이는 소련 내부에서
  강경파들의 재부상을 우려했기 때문임. 소련의 중립적 입장
  확보가 반 후세인 연합전선 형성에 불가피한 것임.

o 후세인은 여러가지 철수 조건을 내세움으로써 지상전 개시를
  보다 용이하게 하였으며 한편, 소련이 아랍 세계와 서방간의
  대립을 야기 시키기 위해 후세인을 유도했다는 의심도 있음.

o 만일 이라크가 무조건 철수에 동의했다면 미국은 월남전의
  중압감에서 벗어나 세계 지도자적 위치를 회복하기 위한 의지력을
  과시 할 기회가 없었을 것임.

                                        - 끝 -

걸프 事態 關聯 世界 主要 言論 報道 分析

1991. 2. 28.

外 務 部

(美 洲 局)

0135

1. 사설

┌─ 참　고 ──────────────────────────────────────┐
│ WP (Washington Post)　　　　　　　 NYT (New York Times) │
│ CSM (Christian Science Monitor)   │
└──┘

가. WP (2. 27자)

철　군

o 후세인의 철군 조건은 자신의 군사력과 정치적 입지를 보존
　하여 종전 협상에서 미국과 유엔으로 부터의 압력을 최소화
　하려는데 목적이 있음.

o 그러나, 다국적군측이 철군조건을 검토하는 동안에도 후세인은
　쿠웨이트 파괴, 민간인 납치 살해, 스커드 미사일 공격등을
　계속함.

o 따라서, 다국적군은 후세인이 12개 UN결의를 준수하고 그 조건에
　따라 철수할 것을 계속 요구해야 함.

나. NYT (2. 27자)

종전에 대한 신중한 고려

o 걸프전에서 미국의 목적은 후세인 개인의 제거보다는 이라크가
　장차 중동지역의 위협요소가 되지 않도록 만드는데 있으며, 이는
　UN의 요구와도 부합됨.

- 1 -

0136

o 이라크의 완전 파괴는 주변국에 대해 상대적으로 이라크를 지나치게
   약화시키고, 소련등에 대 이라크 무기 공급 구실을 줄 우려가
   있음

o 이라크의 무제한적 파괴는 향후 이라크에 대한 무기 공급의
   여지를 남기는 것이므로, 이라크의 UN 결의 수락 및 휴전제의를
   받아들이고 철군을 허용할 필요가 있음.

다. CSM (2, 27자)

                         소련과 걸프

o 소련은 접경국인 이라크에 이해관계를 가질 수 밖에 없으므로
   미국으로서는 걸프지역 안정 회복을 위한 유력한 동반자인 소련
   과의 관계 유지가 필요함.

   - 고르바쵸프의 중재노력은 실패했으나, 전후에도 그의 역할은
      여전히 중요함.

o 소련이 아랍세계의 반미감정에 따른 반사적 이익을 추구할 것
   이라는 우려가 있으나, 그러한 시도는 전후의 아랍세계에서는
   성공하지 못할 것임.

o 신국제 질서 논의에 소련이 포함되어야 하며, 부쉬 대통령은 정상
   회담을 재개해야 함.

2. 기고문

가. <u>Alon Ben Meir (CSM 2.27자)</u>

평화를 위한 준비

o 부쉬 대통령은 걸프전에서 이스라엘과 아랍을 동시에 보호
  하는 의지와 노력을 보임으로써 전후 중동지역의 새로운 세력
  균형과 동맹체제 탄생의 발판을 마련함.

  - 걸프전으로 중동 안보 체제에 이스라엘의 참여가 유도되고
    팔레스타인 문제가 선결과제로 부상

  - 아랍세계의 이스라엘 생존권 인정이 팔레스타인 자치 문제
    해결의 전제임

o 미국은 이스라엘의 생존권을 인정하는 아랍제국과의 상호 방위
  조약 체결을 통해 중동 안보 체제를 형성할 수 있을 것임

나. <u>Robert C. Noel (CSM 2.27자)</u>

이스라엘과 중동 안보

o 베이커 국무장관의 전후 중동 군축 방안은 무기 공급 통제만
  강조하고, 이스라엘이 기 보유한 핵무기는 용인하는 것으로
  보임.

o 아랍제국은 이스라엘의 군사적 우위를 거부할 것이나, 이스라엘
  도 자국의 군사적 우위를 포기하지 않을 것임.

- 3 -

0138

o 미국은 중동지역에 군축 조약 체결을 강요하는 대신 역내 정치적 갈등 해소와 군축 협상을 병행함으로써 중동안보 문제를 해결해야 함.

  - 유럽 안보 협력 회의(CSCE)의 방식을 따르는 것이 적합하나, 미행정부는 단편적인 해결 방안 마련에 안주하려 하고 있음.

다. Leslie H. Gelb (NYT 2.27자)

군사적 승리후의 걸프 정책

o 미국의 전후 정책에 대한 의견은 다음과 같이 요약 가능함

  - 이라크의 민주화
    · 제2차 세계대전후의 독일, 일본에서와 같이 점령국 정부 수립
    · 그러나, 국제사회의 지지 획득 곤란

  - 후세인의 제거
    · 후세인 제거시 여타 문제 해결이 순조로울 것임
    · 그러나, 후세인은 아직도 수십만의 추종자에 의해 보호받고 있음.
    · 후세인 제거를 위해서는 다국적군의 바그다드 진주를 상정 할수 있으나 이는 상당한 정치적 부담이 우려됨.

  - 신 국제질서 구축
    · 군비 통제, 경제발전, 아랍-이스라엘간 평화 회담 개최등을 주요내용으로 하는 집단 안보 체제 지향
    · 그러나, 구체적인 대안 제시가 미흡함.

- 4 -

0139

- 세력 균형
  · 키신저의 주장대로 이라크, 이란, 시리아와 기타 지역강국간 균형 유지
  · 그러나, 미국의 상기 3개국에 대한 영향력 행사에는 한계가 있음.

o 미 행정부의 전후 정책에 포함되어야 할 사항

- 이라크에 대한 계속적인 경제 제재 조치로 후세인 제거 노력 지속

- 이라크의 공화국 수비대에 대한 공격은 계속하되 이라크로 부터는 조속 철수하여야 함.

- 소규모의 해공군력을 제외하고 미국 및 서구제국 군대를 걸프 지역으로 부터 철수하여 아랍인들의 자체적 해결 유도

- 시리아-사우디-이스라엘간 회담과 이스라엘-팔레스타인 회담의 조속 개시

- 끝 -

- 5 -

0140

걸프 事態 關聯 世界 主要 言論 報道 分析

1991. 3. 2

外 務 部

(美 洲 局)

0141

1. 기고문

```
┌─ 참 고 ─────────────────────────────────┐
│ WP (Washington Post)        NYT (New York Times) │
└──────────────────────────────────────────┘
```

가. Jim Hoagland(WP 2.28자)

걸프지역에서의 새로운 지도국 : 사우디

o 이라크군의 패퇴로 걸프지역에는 약화된 세력 균형(a healthy balance of weakness)이 새로이 형성될 전망

 - 미국의 군사력과 정치적 의지에 따라 신국제 질서 형성 예정

 - 과거 급진적인 아랍 민족주의 퇴조

o 걸프지역에 있어 사우디의 지도력 부상

 - 이란, 이라크의 군사력 약화

 - 석유자원을 무기로 하는 사우디가 향후 동 걸프지역에서 중요 역할 수행 예상

 - 그러나, 인구 700만에 불과한 사우디의 지도력에는 한계가 있으므로 사우디와 미국간의 전략적 동맹관계에 의존해야 함.

- 1 -

0142

나. Doug Bandow (WP 2.28자)

최악의 구상 : 중동판 NATO

o 중동지역 안보체제 구축에 미국의 역할을 강조하는 사람들은
   대체로 중동판 NATO 구성에 집착하는 것으로 보임

   - 정치. 경제. 종교적 대립의 역사로 점철된 중동지역에 유럽
     식의 NATO 유지는 부정적 효과 초래 예상

   - 미국이 지역분쟁에 불가피하게 개입될 우려

o 미군의 중동지역 주둔은 아랍제국의 기존 정권에 대한 정치적
   인기 하락 및 이에따른 국내 정세불안 조성 가능

   - 요르단 후세인 왕의 입지 약화
   - 중동 이외 회교 지역에 반미 감정 확산
   - 소련의 보수파 자극
   - 사우디. 쿠웨이트등 역내 국가들의 민주화 저해

o 유럽의 NATO는 미국과 유럽제국에 민주주의. 자유라는 공동
   가치와 소련이라는 공동의 적이 존재했으므로 가능 했으나
   이라크가 충분히 약화된 지금 중동안보는 아랍 제국 스스로에
   맡겨야 함.

- 2 -

0143

2. 분석기사

가. Gerald F, Sieb (NYT 2, 28자)

<u>전후 구상에 관한 고찰</u>

o 미 행정부는 이라크의 군사적 패배로 중동지역 안보의 기틀이
   마련됐으며 향후 이 지역에서의 외국군 철수가 역내 안정
   유지에 관건이라고 판단, 다음과 같이 전후 구상중인 것으로
   보임.

   - 쿠웨이트, 이라크 국경에 비무장 지대 설치
   - 걸프국가들과 이집트 군대로 구성된 평화 유지군 운영
   - 걸프지역의 새로운 안보 체제 성립후 미군 철수
   - 아랍, 이스라엘 문제 논의

o 그러나 전후 구상에 있어 걸프전으로 비롯될 후유증을 고려해야
   함.

   - 이라크에 대한 파괴가 역내 반서방 감정을 악화시켜, 시리아,
     이집트, 사우디등의 회교 원리주의 활동을 자극시킬 우려

   - 팔레스타인의 이라크 지지로 팔레스타인 국가 성립에 대한
     이스라엘의 반발 격화 예상

o 또한, 이라크의 패배에 따른 세력 공백에 이란이 침투하여 역내
   서방세력의 축출을 선도할 것으로 전망

- 3 -

0144

- 석유가격과 생산량에 대해 이란-사우디간 의견 대립 가능성

- 이란이 이라크내 시아파를 자극하여 사우디등을 위협하게 될 우려

- 이란내 이라크 공군기를 영향력 행사의 도구로 활용 가능

나. <u>Steve Lohr (NYT, 2.28자)</u>

<u>미국기업의 전후 복구사업 독점</u>

o 쿠웨이트 재건은 정치, 경제, 사회등 광범한 영역에 걸쳐 이루어 질 것임.

- 향후 5년간 500-5,000억불의 복구비 소요 추정

- 전쟁 기여도에 따라 복구사업에의 참여 지분을 결정한다는 쿠웨이트 망명정부의 정책에 따라, 세계유수의 미국기업들이 복구 사업계약을 거의 독점.

- 쿠웨이트 망명정부는 민간기업 역합 확대에 의한 자유시장 경제강화, 산업 및 행정의 효율성 증대, 외국인 근로자 고용 축소등 사회 전반적 정책 변화를 구상.

o 미국기업들은 지금까지 체결된 약200건의 복구사업 계약중 약70% 를 독점한 것으로 알려짐.

- 쿠웨이트의 미국기업 선호 경향에 대한 여타국의 반발이 증대되고 있으며, 영국은 Hurd 외무장관의 경제사절단 파견등 조치를 통해 복구사업 지분 확보를 위해 노력

- 4 -

0145

o 일부 분석가들은 복구사업 참여 경쟁이 증가하면, 쿠웨이트 정부
  가 비용, 신뢰도, 기술 수준등을 고려하여 참여 업체를 선택하게
  될 것으로 전망.

  - 과거 쿠웨이트의 주된 수입대상은 일본, 독일등이었으며 미국은
    10%이하에 불과 하였음.

                                                    - 끝 -

                            - 5 -

                            0146

걸프 事態 關聯 世界 主要 言論 報道 分析

1991. 3. 4

外 務 部

(美 洲 局)

0147

1. 사설 (NYT 3. 3자)

```
┌─── 참  고 ──────────────────────────────────┐
│ WP (Washington Post)          NYT (New York Times) │
└──────────────────────────────────────────────┘
```

전쟁에서 평화로
(중동 평화 질서 구축에서 고려해야 할 사항)

o 중동지역에서의 군비 통제

- 이라크의 재무장 억제를 위해 엄격하고 검증 가능한 군비 제한
  조치 수락 요구 필요

- 미국, 소련, 프랑스, 중국, 브라질등의 대 이라크 무기 판매
  자제

- 군비 제한은 이스라엘도 대상이 되어야 하며, 이는 아랍제국의
  대 이스라엘 승인 촉진 가능

o 상호 안전보장 협정 체결

- 이스라엘이 포함되고, 역외 강대국이 보장해야 함.

- 이스라엘측은 팔레스타인의 정치적 권리 행사와 유엔 결의
  이행을 위한 대안을 제시할 필요가 있음.

o 집단 안보 체제 강화

- 금번 걸프사태는, 유엔 안보리가 40년간의 침체기 이후 중요성
  을 인정 받게 되는 계기

- 1 -

0148

- 그러나 전비 분담등에 있어서는 이견 노출

- 단점을 보강하여 확고한 집단 안보 체제가 구축되어야 함.

o 중동지역 정치세력과 경제 세력의 접촉 확대

- 사우디, 쿠웨이트등 부유한 산유국가와 요르단, 예멘, 튜니지아
  등 빈곤국간의 균형적인 관계 유지 필요

2. 기고문

가. Craig R. Whitney (NYT 3. 3자)

다음 과제는 불안정한 사막위에 안정된 미래 건설

o 후세인의 위협이 제거되고, 동서대결에 따른 위협이 없어진
  지금이 중동문제를 해결할 수 있는 적기로 기대되고 있으나,
  군사력의 우세가 정치적인 면에서는 때때로 환상에 지나지
  않은 경우가 있음.

  - 소련의 아프가니스탄과 동구에서의 경험

  - 미국의 월남전 실패

o 외부로 부터 강요된 정치적 해결은 거의 성공할 가능성이 없는
  바, 연합국 지도자들은 걸프 협력 위원회(GCC)와 이집트등
  주요 아랍국들의 입장을 우선적으로 고려할 것임.

- 2 -

0149

o 베이커 국무장관은 영.불.독일의 압력으로 이번주에 걸프지역
  에서의 전후 안보와 아랍-이스라엘 문제를 협의 하기 위해
  사우디, 이집트, 시리아, 이스라엘, 터어키 및 소련을 순방
  예정임.

o 고르바쵸프는 최근 소련 내부 분열 방지를 위해 군부의 정치적
  지원에 기대하고 있고, 이것이 소련 보수 세력의 입장 강화를
  의미한다면, 중동 평화 구축은 더욱 어려울 것임.

  - 누가 지도자가 되든 소련은 걸프지역에 중요한 정치적
    이해를 갖고 있음.

나. <u>Jim Hoagland (WP 3. 3자)</u>

<u>걸프전후 세계에서의 미국</u>

o 걸프전은 세계 에너지 시장, 아랍-이스라엘 분쟁, 제3세계에
  대한 무기 판매 및 소련내 권력 투쟁등에 중대한 변화를 주는
  계기가 될 것임.

  - 중동지역에서 사우디의 역할 강화 및 소련 세력의 퇴조가
    이번 전쟁이 초래한 두드러진 정세 변화임.

o 부쉬 대통령은 신국제 질서를 구축함에 있어 미국의 막강한
  힘과 함께 그 능력의 한계를 고려해야 함.

  - 미국은 걸프전을 통해 국제 정치를 좌우할 수 있는 실력을
    과시했으나, 이로 인해 Pax Americana를 강요해서는 안됨.

o 사우디 관리들은 전후 아랍 국제정치가 사우디, 이집트, 시리아
  3국에 의해 좌우될 것으로 관측

- 3 -

0150

o 이라크의 쿠웨이트 침공 당시 이를 억지할 걸프지역의 미 군사력이
  불충분 하였으므로, 향후 이를 보완할 새로운 안보 협력 체제 구축
  필요성 강조

  - 역내 아랍국가들과의 정기적인 합동 군사 훈련 실시

  - 중동지역에 미 공군 계속 주둔

  - 걸프지역 미 해군력의 증강 배치

나. Thomas Friedman & Patrick E. Tyler (NYT 3.3자)

  미국, 걸프사태 발생 초기부터 전쟁 수행 결정

o 부쉬 행정부는 작년 가을 미군의 중동 파병 목적이 사우디 방위와
  UN의 대 이라크 경제 제재 수행에 있음을 표면적으로 주장하면서,
  한편으로 쿠웨이트로 부터 이라크군 축출을 계획

o 부쉬 대통령은 대 이라크 군사행동 계획의 일환으로 1월의 공중
  공격 및 2월의 지상공격 계획 수립에 착수하여, 다국적군의 이라크
  영내 진격에 의한 이라크군 포위, 고립 작전을 구상

o 상기의 전쟁 계획은 이라크의 철군을 유도하기 위한 미국의
  외교적 노력과 병행됨.

  - 걸프사태 초기에 후세인의 의도 및 대응 수단에 대하여 미
    행정부내 논쟁이 있었던 것으로 보임.

  - 이스라엘의 대 이라크 보복 공격 허용 여부가 가장 논란의
    대상이었음.

                                              - 끝 -

외교문서 비밀해제: 걸프 사태 5

걸프 사태 언론 보도 및 분석

초판인쇄 2024년 03월 15일
초판발행 2024년 03월 15일

지은이 한국학술정보(주)
펴낸이 채종준
펴낸곳 한국학술정보(주)
주 소 경기도 파주시 회동길 230(문발동)
전 화 031-908-3181(대표)
팩 스 031-908-3189
홈페이지 http://ebook.kstudy.com
E-mail 출판사업부 publish@kstudy.com
등 록 제일산-115호(2000. 6. 19)

ISBN 979-11-6983-965-5 94340
      979-11-6983-960-0 94340 (set)